CLUES AND CORPSES

Todd Downing (c. 1950)

Courtesy Confederate Memorial Museum & Cemetery, Atoka, OK

CLUES AND CORPSES

The Detective Fiction and Mystery Criticism of Todd Downing

CURTIS EVANS

COACHWHIP PUBLICATIONS
Greenville, Ohio

This book is dedicated to
Geoff Bradley and Steve Lewis
Preservers of Mystery History

Clues and Corpses: The Detective Fiction and Mystery Criticism of Todd Downing, by Curtis Evans

Coachwhip Publications, Greenville, OH
CoachwhipBooks.com

ISBN 1-61646-145-4
ISBN-13 978-1-61646-145-4
LCCN: 2012952605

Front cover: Todd Downing, courtesy Confederate Memorial Museum & Cemetery, Atoka, OK
Back cover: Covers of mystery novels by Todd Downing, courtesy Bill Pronzini.

TABLE OF CONTENTS

AUTHOR'S NOTE

In a 1934 review of an omnibus collection of Dorothy L. Sayers novels, Todd Downing speculated that "when and if detective fiction establishes its right to the dignity of critical studies, some bespectacled student will find material for a thesis in the subject of femininity in the genre." Although Todd observed that the most devoted "readers of mystery yarns are predominantly masculine," he reflected that women authors consistently produced "some of the best work in the field." With impressive prescience Todd Downing thus foresaw the major focus of much of twenty-first century mystery genre scholarship—whether or not he realized that his imagined "bespectacled student" was quite as likely to be female as male.

Although feminist mystery scholarship laudably has done much to redress critical neglect of and/or disdain for the British Crime Queens Agatha Christie, Dorothy L. Sayers, Margery Allingham and Ngaio Marsh, unfortunately it also has fostered a tendency to bifurcate the mystery fiction of the Golden Age (c. 1920-1939) into two hostile camps, parted by the Atlantic Ocean: the feminine British cozy, associated with the aforementioned Crime Queens; and the masculine American hard-boiled private eye tale, associated with Dashiell Hammett, Raymond Chandler and other writers for pulp fiction magazines. Both male writers and female writers not fortunate enough to be crowned "Queens of Crime" tend to receive comparatively little attention from mystery genre scholars. Even writers as prominent in their day as, from the United States, S. S. Van Dine, John Dickson Carr, Ellery Queen, Rufus King and Rex Stout, and, from Great Britain, Freeman Wills Crofts, John Street, H. C. Bailey, Nicholas Blake and Michael Innes receive only the barest fraction of the attention lavished on the American hard-boiled boys and the British Crime Queens.[1]

This critical neglect of so many Golden Age mystery writers has gravely hampered understanding of the Golden Age of detective fiction. Fair play, puzzle-oriented (or classical) detective fiction was the exclusive province of neither a single country nor a single sex. It was published on both sides of the Atlantic, by both men and women. (Indeed, it seems certain that a majority of classical detective fiction writers throughout the 1920s and into the 1930s were men.)

Todd Downing's reviews of mystery fiction in the *Daily Oklahoman*, which span the years from 1930 to 1937, reveal to us the neglected riches of the Golden Age. Yes, there are books by

1 An exception to this generalization is Catherine Ross Nickerson, *The Web of Iniquity: Early Detective Fiction by American Women* (Chapel Hill, NC: Duke University Press, 1998), which includes analysis of Golden Age mystery fiction by Mary Roberts Rinehart. See also Jeffrey Marks' *Who Was That Lady? Craig Rice: The Queen of Screwball Mystery* (Lee's Summit, MO: Delphi Books, 2001) for an informative study of a slightly post-Golden Age American writer. For more on the problems with the conventional approach of modern mystery genre studies, see the analysis in my book *Masters of the Humdrum Mystery: Cecil John Charles Street, Freeman Wills Crofts, Alfred Walter Stewart and the British Detective Novel, 1920-1961* (Jefferson, NC and London: McFarland, 2012) and a couple articles by critic Jon L. Breen, "Cherchez les Femmes: The American Tradition of Mystery Novels by Women," *American Spectator* 9 (July 2004) and "The Ellery Queen Mystery: Why is the Corpus No Longer Alive?," *American Spectator* 10 (October 2005) at http://www.weeklystandard.com/Content/Public/Articles/000/000/004/272hwrue.asp and http://www.weeklystandard.com/Content/Public/Articles/000/000/006/140ioyto.asp, reprinted in the author's *A Shot Rang Out: Selected Mystery Criticism by Jon L. Breen* (Vancleave, MS: Ramble House, 2008). In "The Ellery Queen Mystery" Breen precisely states the "over-simplified conventional wisdom" (before debunking it): "Classic detective fiction . . . is British and feminine. . . . Tough fiction noir . . . is American and masculine. . . ."

Agatha Christie and Dorothy L. Sayers, by Dashiell Hammett and James M. Cain, but there is much more as well. There is, for example, classical detective fiction by authors who now are out of print, yet who were once highly esteemed. To be sure, Todd praised Christie's *The A.B.C. Murders* (1935) and Sayers' *Gaudy Night* (1935), Hammett's *The Thin Man* (1934) and Cain's *The Postman Always Rings Twice* (1934), yet he similarly lauded, for example, Anthony Abbot's *About the Murder of Geraldine Foster* (1931), George Birmingham's *The Hymn Tune Mystery* (1931) and Anthony Wynne's *The Silver Scale Mystery* (1931) (*Murder of a Lady* in England). Indeed, in 1934 Todd listed the Wynne title as one of his six favorite detective novels (of the Crime Queens/hard-boiled boys only Agatha Christie made the list—see appendix two).

But there is more. Surprisingly, given the rise of feminist mystery genre criticism in the last several decades, the extent of psychological crime fiction produced by women writers in the Golden Age, especially during the 1930s, is much under-appreciated today. Todd Downing's praise of such American and British writers as Marie Belloc Lowndes, Ethel Lina White, Elisabeth Sanxay Holding and Mary Roberts Rinehart (the latter once derided by some critics as a so-called "HIBK," or Had I But Known, "feminine anxiety" writer) should guide modern scholars and fans to fallow fields that may yet yield abundant harvests. Additionally, Todd Downing's reviews highlight the comparative decline in the 1930s of the traditional thriller associated with Edgar Wallace in the face of the popularity of hard-boiled (or, as Todd Downing sometimes called it, "side-of-the-mouth") fiction.

Todd Downing's crime fiction reviews in the *Daily Oklahoman* are engagingly written and evince a coherent aesthetic sense of mystery genre writing. Between November 1932 and May 1934 Todd had a column entitled "Clues and Corpses," wherein he reviewed two or three books, typically at 150 to 250 words to a book (though some of the earlier columns in this period have shorter pieces and some of the longer pieces run as high as about 350 words). Before and after these dates, single mystery reviews by Todd, of similar length, appeared individually on the *Daily Oklahoman*'s literary page, beginning in 1930 and ending in 1937. The length of most of the Downing reviews contrasts with the roughly forty-words-a-title capsule mystery reviews by "Judge Lynch" (William C. Weber) found at this time in the *Saturday Review*, for example, or Anthony Boucher's 1940s reviews in the *San Francisco Chronicle*, which devoted about fifty words to each title. Todd's book reviews benefit considerably from the extra space he was allowed and they make exceptionally entertaining and informative reading.

Like such other mystery reviewers in his day as Anthony Boucher, Dashiell Hammett and Dorothy L. Sayers, Todd Downing did not merely read detective fiction, he also wrote it. Between 1933 and 1941, Todd Downing published nine detective novels, eight of which partly or entirely take place in Mexico. Todd's Mexican settings were his signature contribution to Golden Age mystery fiction, yet his best detective novels—the seven with his primary series detective, intrepid United States customs agent Hugh Rennert—also are models of mystery genre writing, well-plotted and stylishly written; and they received much praise in their day. The great English detective fiction critic Edward Powys Mathers ("Torquemada") once declared that Todd Downing was "a born detective story writer." Happily, eight of Todd Downing's detective novels were reprinted in 2012. *Clues and Corpses* highlights for modern readers key elements in Todd's genre writing.

Clues and Corpses also provides the greatest biographical account yet given of Todd Downing, a middle class, small-town Oklahoman who also happened to be one-eighth Choctaw. Todd was extremely proud of his Choctaw heritage, which influenced both his choice of specialization as a student and later instructor at the University of Oklahoma (he taught Spanish) and his fiction and non-fiction writing. Additionally, in the last couple of decades Todd has gained notice in academic circles as a significant indigenous American writer. Most notably, James H. Cox in *The Red Land to the South: American Indian Writers and Indigenous Mexico* (University of Minnesota Press, 2012) devotes two chapters to two of Todd Downing's books: his detective novel *The Cat Screams*

(1934), set in Taxco, Mexico, and his non-fictional study of Mexico, *The Mexican Earth* (1940). *Clues and Corpses* looks at Todd's Choctaw heritage, as well as additional influences on him, such as his non-indigenous ancestry and his family's religious and political affiliations. Such sources as contemporary newspapers and family letters allow rare glimpses into the life and times of a 1930s mystery writer. Especially interesting is Todd's struggle to balance his love for Oklahoma and the small-town environment he knew from his birth in Atoka in 1902 with his desire to experience the more cosmopolitan world of a writer and intellectual in the metropolises of the northeastern United States.

My own paternal grandparents, contemporaries of Todd Downing, had extensive Oklahoma connections. Ada Smith was one of three daughters of Isaiah Smith, a politically aware farmer who named his only son after the Populist politician and writer Ignatius Loyola Donnelly. (Perhaps not altogether unexpectedly the son modestly chose to go by the name Don.) Ada lived some thirty years in Oklahoma. She and John Evans were married in Oklahoma City in 1920, the year Todd started college at Norman, and the couple spent most of the rest of the decade teaching at schools in Kellyville, Wewoka and Sayre. A cousin of my Grandfather Evans, Otis Sullivant, joined the staff of the *Daily Oklahoman* in the 1920s, about the same time Todd Downing began reviewing books there; eventually Otis Sullivant became the dean of political reporters in the state. Ada's and John's son, my father, was born in Amarillo, Texas, graduated from the University of Texas at Austin and, like Todd, became professionally interested in Mexico. Between the ages of three and sixteen I was taken along on five trips to Mexico. (For one full year, as well as another summer, I lived there.) The combination of family background with my love of mystery fiction made this particular writing project seem inevitable to me. But it would not have been possible to do it all alone. I want to thank the staff of the Confederate Memorial Museum and Cemetery Information Center in Atoka, Linda Lynn of the *Daily Oklahoman* and, finally, Bill Pronzini for his advice and input and for first kindling my interest in Todd Downing with one of his tales of *1001 Midnights*.

Todd Downing (c. 1930)

Courtesy *Sooner Magazine*

PREFACE
BILL PRONZINI

THE first Todd Downing novel I read was *Vultures in the Sky*, some thirty years ago. At that time, even though I had four of his books on my shelves, I hadn't read one and had no clear idea of who Downing was or what kind of mysteries he wrote (other than the fact that most were set in Mexico). I was then and still am an avid collector of vintage mystery and detective fiction, with emphasis on titles published prior to 1960. I bought those four Downings because they bore the Doubleday Crime Club imprint. Crime Club titles were and still are a collecting passion of mine, in large part because their long list of authors were among the upper echelon of purveyors of fictional murder and mayhem—Anthony Berkeley, Margery Allingham, Leslie Charteris, Miles Burton, Jonathan Latimer, Georgette Heyer, Rufus King, Stuart Palmer, and Arthur Upfield, to name just a few—and because of their superior period dust jacket art.

What prompted me in 1983 to finally read one of the Downings was the fact that my wife, Marcia Muller, and I were then engaged in compiling *1001 Midnights: The Aficionado's Guide to Mystery and Detective Fiction*—a massive 870-page project that required us, over a period of several months, to read or reread and write a review of an average of one book per day in order to meet the publisher's deadline. This schedule allowed little time to savor individual works unless we found them to be something special. For me, *Vultures in the Sky* fell into that rarefied category.

I picked it from among the other Downing titles I owned because of its train setting, another of my passions as a reader and collector. A realistically depicted background is one of the qualities I look for in a mystery novel; others include interesting and believable characters, especially the protagonist(s), an evocative prose style, and a cleverly constructed plot with no loose ends. *Vultures* has all of these to recommend it, and more as Curt Evans notes in his discussion of the novel later in these pages. U.S. Customs agent Hugh Rennert, hero of this and six other titles, I found to be an appealing and memorable creation. In my *1001 Midnights* review, I wrote that *Vultures* is "an expertly crafted whodunit, well-written . . . and offering a vivid, detailed portrait of Mexico in the mid-1930s," and further stated that "anyone who likes his mystery plot enlivened by frequent glimpses of another culture both old and new is certain to find Downing's work enjoyable."

I enjoyed the novel so much that when I'd finished all the required reading for *1001 Midnights*, I read the other Downings I owned and then sought out copies of the remaining titles until I had a complete set. All of the Rennerts proved to be as entertaining and informative as *Vultures in the Sky*, especially the other four that Curt Evans lauds as the author's strongest works: *The Cat Screams*, *Night Over Mexico*, *Murder on the Tropic* and *The Last Trumpet*.

Downing's mystery fiction seems to have been under-appreciated during his lifetime; despite several positive media notices, only one of his books, *The Cat Screams*, was reprinted as a mass market paperback (by Popular Library in 1945, with very modest sales). My *1001 Midnights* review, unfortunately, did little to stimulate interest except among a handful of other aficionados. If his name was known at all, it was for *The Mexican Earth*, his highly regarded nonfiction book about Mexico and Mexican history and culture. Even today, few readers of Golden Age mystery and detective fiction are familiar with Downing's detective stories.

Even more deeply obscured by the mists of time are the mystery reviews he wrote for the Oklahoma City *Daily Oklahoman* in the 1930s. Over the course of the genre's history, a large number of crime fiction writers have doubled as reviewers and critics of the work of their peers, both in England and in this country. Primary among the American contingent are Anthony Boucher, justifiably considered the field's premier critic, and Jon Breen, who in my opinion is unparalleled among present-day analysts. Other prominent mystery writers whose reviews were often quoted in publishers' ads and on book covers: Dashiell Hammett and Kathleen Sproul in *The Saturday Review of Literature*, Dorothy B. Hughes, Craig Rice, Frances Crane, and Helen McCloy and Davis Dresser in various newspapers, and John Dickson Carr in *Ellery Queen's Mystery Magazine*.

Downing's reviews seem to have been almost completely ignored by publishers and to have found little audience outside his native Oklahoma. Yet few of his peers wrote more incisive notices of then-current crime fiction. He had, as Curt Evans has said, "a coherent aesthetic sense of the mystery novel," and was adept at conveying a book's essential strengths and weaknesses in very few words. His reviews may be read and enjoyed from both a historical perspective and for their insightful capsule commentary on individual books and authors.

Now, finally, thanks to the sterling efforts of Curt Evans and Chad Arment of Coachwhip Publications, Todd Downing's detective novels will no longer languish in obscurity. Though written and published in the 1930s, the best of them are sure to give modern readers a fresh and flavorful taste of American Golden Age detective fiction at its most adroit. Their settings, characters, and classically constructed plots have stood the test of time remarkably well, and their striking impressions of life and death South of the Border are unequaled anywhere in the genre.

Reading the present volume was a pleasure. Until this impeccably researched and richly detailed account of Todd Downing's life and work, I was not aware of his book reviews, all of which are collected here, or of the particulars of his Choctaw heritage and the other personal and professional factors that shaped him as a man, a writer, and a champion of the country he knew so well. The wealth of background information and the in-depth commentary on the Rennert canon is not only fascinating in its own right, but provided a fresh perspective on and increased my admiration for the best of the novels upon a recent rereading.

Hearty congratulations to Curt Evans. Like *Masters of the "Humdrum" Mystery,* his recent book about the British Golden Age detective novel and a trio of its notable practitioners, *Clues and Corpses* is a fine piece of popular culture scholarship.

PETALUMA, CA.
OCTOBER 2012

INTRODUCTION
Todd Downing (1902-1974)
Crime Writer and Critic

Crime writers can be far from easy to kill. For over half a century Agatha Christie—the most enduringly famous and popular of the classical mystery novelists who began writing in the period between World War One and World War Two known as the Golden Age of the detective novel—published scores of mystery tales. More than thirty-five years after her death in 1976 Christie very much remains with us still, in the form of seemingly endless successions of paperback reprints and British television film adaptations starring either a series of Miss Marple incarnations or, in the role of Hercule Poirot, the imperishable David Suchet. To cite some additional examples, locked room master John Dickson Carr's mystery writing career lasted from 1930 to 1972, New Zealand Crime Queen's Ngaio Marsh's from 1934 to 1982, Nero Wolfe creator Rex Stout's from 1934 to 1975 and that of Ellery Queen (actually two American cousins) from 1929 to 1971. All these authors have titles in print even today and they continue to claim many devoted fans.

Admittedly by the above standards the crime writing career of Todd Downing (1902-1974) was but a briefly flaming candle, one snuffed out before the author had reached even the age of forty. Downing published nine mystery novels between 1933 and 1941, an average rate of one a year, unexceptional by genre standards (also, a novella appeared in 1945). After the 1940s the publishing world and the reading public alike for decades forgot Todd Downing's existence as a mystery genre writer, despite the acclaim once afforded his tales. While a vastly different Oklahoma crime writer contemporary of Downing's, noir novelist Jim Thompson (1906-1977), achieved greater renown posthumously, Downing's literary reputation dwindled after his death.

In 1986, Bill Pronzini—like Todd Downing both a writer and a scholar of crime fiction—lauded Downing's crime novels in his and Marcia Muller's *1001 Midnights: The Aficionado's Guide to Mystery and Detective Fiction*, avowing that the Oklahoman's nine mystery novels "all are well worth investigating."[1] It has taken the rest of the world yet more years to catch up with Pronzini's perception, however. Over the last two decades Todd Downing has been the subject of increasing academic interest, on account of what he has to say in his work about Mexico and indigenous culture. In 2012 the University of Minnesota Press published Professor James H. Cox's *The Red Land to the South: American Indian Writers and Indigenous Mexico*, two chapters of which are devoted to two of Todd Downing's books. Moreover, eight of Todd Downing's mysteries were reprinted in 2012 as well. Todd Downing may have been down in the ring, but he was not out for the count. Now is the time for a serious appraisal of his genre work as a mystery fiction writer and reviewer.

Part One: The Author from Atoka

In the 1980s crime writer and critic Bill Pronzini took admiring notice of Todd Downing as a mystery writer, while in the last twenty years both Wolfgang Hochbruck and James H. Cox have perceptively discoursed on Todd Downing as a notable Native American author. (Professor Cox deems Downing "one of the most prolific and most neglected American Indian writers of the twentieth century.")[2] Yet about the man himself, divorced from the

1 Bill Pronzini and Marcia Muller, eds., *1001 Midnights: The Aficionado's Guide to Mystery and Detective Fiction* (New York: Arbor House, 1986), 216-217.

2 James H. Cox, *The Red Land to the South: American Indian Writers and Indigenous Mexico* (Minneapolis, MN, and London: University of Minnesota Press, 2012), 27.

mystery writing and Native American contexts, comparatively little has been written. The first section of this introduction paints a fuller picture of Todd Downing's still relatively unknown life.

Bare bones biography is easily given. George Todd Downing was born in the town of Atoka, Choctaw Nation, Indian Territory (later Oklahoma), on March 19, 1902. He was the son of Samuel (Sam) and Maud Miller Downing (1872-1954/1872-1965) and grandson of Awilda Shields Miller (1849-1939), all hugely important influences in his life. An older brother, Gordon (1900-1902), died in infancy and a sister, Ruth, was born in 1904. After graduating from Atoka High School in 1920, Todd attended the University of Oklahoma, receiving his B.A. in 1924 and his M.A. in 1928. During the summers Todd took classes in Spanish, French and anthropology at the National University of Mexico. When in Mexico he earned money by acting as a guide for American tour groups. Fluent in five languages (Choctaw, English, French, Italian and Spanish), Todd served as an instructor in Spanish at OU for ten years, from 1925 to 1935. In the latter year he resigned his instructorship in order to pursue a fulltime career as a novelist. After a brief stay in New York City—where his sister Ruth, who got her B.A. from OU and her M.A. from Columbia University, had found employment as a psychiatric social worker—Todd returned to Atoka to live with his parents and grandmother. Todd's first detective novel was published in 1933 and from that year to 1941, he produced a total of nine such works, as well as a non-fiction book on Mexico, *The Mexican Earth*, which saw print in 1940. A planned historical novel about Mexico, *Under the Rose*, never appeared, nor did any other Todd Downing fiction after 1941, aside from a novella originally written in the early 1930s. In the 1940s Todd worked in Philadelphia as a copy writer with several advertising agencies, but in the 1950s he went back to teaching, first for a one-year stint at Washington College in Chestertown, Maryland, and then for several years at Massanutten Academy in Woodstock, Virginia. After Todd's father died in 1954, Todd returned to the family home in Atoka to live with his elderly mother, until her death in 1965. Todd continued to live in the Downing family home until his own death in Atoka in 1974, when he was seventy-one years old. During his last twenty years in Atoka, Todd taught Spanish and French at the same high school from which he had graduated in 1920. In the 1970s, near the end of his life, he became Emeritus Professor of Choctaw Language and Choctaw Heritage at Southeastern Oklahoma State University (then Southeastern State College) in nearby Durant—a fitting, though unfortunately short-lived, close to his career as an educator.[3]

From Todd Downing's father came the Choctaw heritage that Todd so cherished. Todd's paternal grandfather, George Thornton Downing (1814-1880), whose family went back into Northumberland County, Virginia, for six generations, was born in Kentucky and raised in Indiana. In 1834, the year of the death of his father John from cholera (contracted by him while working on a Mississippi river boat around New Orleans), George Downing married Sophia Wales (1816-1897), with whom he had thirteen children. Around 1845, the Downing family moved to the vicinity of Bonham, county seat of Fannin County, Texas. There George Downing farmed and speculated in land, supporting a seemingly endlessly expanding family. (The last child of George and Sophia was born in 1858.)[4]

3 For general information on Todd Downing's life, see Cox, *Red Land*, Chapter One passim; Wolfgang H. Hochbruck, "Mystery Novels to Choctaw Pageant: Todd Downing and Native American Literature(s)," in Arnold Krupat., ed. *New Voices in Native American Literary Criticism* (Washington. D. C.: Smithsonian Institution Press, 1993), 205-221 passim; Ruth Downing, "The Downing Family" and Charlene W. Smith, "Todd Downing" in *Tales of Atoka County Heritage* (Atoka, OK: Atoka County Historical Society, 1983), 246-247 and 247-248; Frank Parman, "George Todd Downing (1902-1974)," *Encyclopedia of Oklahoma History and Culture* (Oklahoma Historical Society), at http://digital.library.okstate.edu/encyclopedia/entries/D/DO013.html.

4 On Downing family genealogy, see: "Lora B. Tindall, "The Families of George T. Downing," *Fannin County—Family Pages*, http://www.txfannin.org/familypages.php?fam_ID=11; Mrs. O. A. Keach, "John Downing of Fairfields, Northumberland County, Virginia, and His Descendants," *William and Mary Quarterly* 25 (July 1916): 41-51, 96-106.

During the Civil War George Downing apparently was involved in providing supplies to Boggy Depot, a Confederate outpost that was located in Indian Territory, about sixty miles north from Bonham. In his capacity as a Confederate supplier George Downing made the acquaintance of Boggy Depot resident Melissa (or Millissa) Armstrong, who was one-half Choctaw (and apparently some Chickasaw) and came to Indian Territory with her parents on the Trail of Tears in 1832. Melissa Armstrong evidently made a great impression on the father of thirteen, now about fifty years old. In 1866, Downing left his Texas wife and family, first turning over to them his farm and all other property, and moved to Boggy Depot, where he married Melissa Armstrong.[5]

The new couple together had four children (making George the father of a grand total of seventeen children): Moses, Mary, Samuel and Martha. After being bypassed by the Missouri–Kansas–Texas Railroad in 1872 (the year Sam Downing, future father of Todd, was born), Boggy Depot fell into decline. George Downing moved with his new family to the burgeoning nearby town of Atoka, named for a Choctaw Nation leader and signer of the Treaty of Dancing Rabbit Creek, which exchanged Choctaw land in Mississippi for acreage in Indian Territory. Melissa Armstrong died in Atoka sometime before 1878. That year George Downing married yet again, though his first wife still lived. George died two years later, however, in 1880; and his children by Melissa, all minors, were parceled out to be raised in the homes of neighbors. Martha and Moses (Mose) were educated at Atoka

5 Tindal, "George T. Downing." Most of the children from George Downing's first marriage "kept in touch with him and loved him despite his shortcomings," writes Lora Tindall. George's son Hiram (1853-1924) moved, at the age of fourteen, to Indian Territory shortly after his father, working there as a cowboy. He claimed land located in modern-day Norman, Oklahoma, during the Land Rush. Hiram's son William Bryan Downing (1880-1966) may have been the Bill Downing who with his wife visited with Todd Downing and Todd's parents at the funeral of Todd's grandmother Awilda Shields Miller in 1939. Maud Miller Downing to Ruth Shields Downing, [9] February 1939.

Baptist Academy, a boarding school for Choctaw children. Martha, who throughout her life maintained a relationship with her brother Sam, became a schoolteacher and married future University of Oklahoma medical school dean Dr. Leroy Long, then a promising young doctor. Mose moved twenty miles away from Atoka to Caddo, where he farmed, but he was not personally close to his brother. Mary made what seems to have been an unfortunate marriage and became a source of anxiety for Sam in later years.[6]

After the death of his father, Sam Downing was ultimately taken in by David Crocker Blossom (1850-1913) and his wife Emma Charles Blossom (1858-1915), a pivotal development in Sam's life. Though by origin a rock-ribbed Yankee if ever there were one (Blossom's family came from Wells, Vermont, and his line of descent included a grandmother named Thankful Bodfish and a great-grandmother named Mehitable Goodspeed), David Blossom evidently possessed an ample adventurous streak. At the age of eighteen or nineteen he migrated to Indian Territory, where he first worked as a freighter for the Missouri–Kansas–Texas Railroad before becoming a licensed government trader to the Shawnee and Kickapoo Indians at Shawnee Mission. In 1879, he married Emma Charles, the daughter of Joel Charles, Superintendent of the Mission's Quaker school for Indian children. Three years later the couple settled in Atoka, where David Blossom purchased a half-interest in the mercantile business of

6 Tindal, "George T. Downing"; Downing, "Downing Family," 246-247. On Mary and Mose Downing, see E. H. Rishel interview, 22 June 1937, Indian Pioneer Papers, Indian Pioneer History Project for Oklahoma, at http://www.okgenweb.org/pioneer/ohs/risheleh.htm; On Leroy Long, husband of Martha Downing, see Basil A. Hayes, *Leroy Long: Teacher of Medicine* (Oklahoma City: by the author, 1943). Perhaps one source of division between brothers Sam and Mose was Mose's apparent embrace in the 1920s of the Ku Klux Klan. In 1924 a Caddo Klan meeting—supposedly attended by the largest crowd ever gathered in the county—was held in Mose Downing's pasture. *Caddo Herald*, 1 August 1924, quoted at *Caddo—My Home Town*, at http://mem55.typepad.com/caddo_my_home_town/2010/10/kkk-1924.html. "Samuel" was a common Downing family name in Virginia, dating back to the seventeenth century.

David N. Robb, one of Atoka's most important citizens and a man with fingers in many local pies. A Republican, Blossom was appointed Atoka postmaster during the administrations of Benjamin Harrison and Theodore Roosevelt. With evident justification, *Leaders and Leading Men of the Indian Territory* (1891) deemed Blossom "a superior businessman" who was "very popular throughout the county."[7]

David Crocker Blossom and his wife Emma Charles already had two small sons, Charles (1880) and Eugene (1881), when they took guardianship over young Sam Downing. The couple would go on to have two additional children of their own, another son and a daughter; but distinctions were not made among their brood of dependents. (In 1939 the Blossoms' two surviving sons, Eugene/Gene and Charles/Charley, would serve as pallbearers at the funeral of Sam Downing's mother-in-law.) Like the Blossoms' other children, Sam Downing was raised in the Presbyterian faith, Blossom being an elder in the church as well as Superintendent of the Sunday school; and for his advanced education Sam was sent for two years, 1889-1891, to Earlham College, Indiana. A progressive Quaker school, Earlham College had accepted its first African and Native American students a decade earlier, in 1880. At Earlham, Sam became friends with Luther H. Ratliff and Joseph F. Ratliff, members of a well-known Indiana Quaker family.[8] No doubt Emma Blossom's own Quaker missionary background played an important role in shaping the course of Sam Downing's education.

7 *Daily Oklahoman*, 22 February 1907, 6, 24 May 1913, 5; H. F. O'Beirne, *Leaders and Leading Men of the Indian Territory, with Interesting Biographical Sketches*. Volume I. *Choctaws and Chickasaws: With a Brief History of Each Tribe: Its Laws, Customs, Superstitions and Religious Beliefs* (Chicago, IL: American Publishers' Association, 1891), 81; Joseph B. Thoburn and Muriel Wright, *Oklahoma: A History of the State and Its People*, Volume III (New York: Lewis Historical Publishing Company, 1929), 222.

8 O'Beirne, *Leaders and Leading Men*, 81. Thoburn and Wright, *Oklahoma*, 222, Thomas D. Hamm, *Earlham College: A History*, 1847-1997 (Bloomington and Indianapolis: Indiana University Press, 1997), 46-48; "Directory Earlham College," *The Earlham College Bulletin* 13 (August 1916): 50.

Returning to Atoka in 1891, Sam Downing became Atoka County Clerk before establishing a "bustling drayage business." When the Spanish-American War broke out in 1898, Sam joined the Indian Territory Cavalry, serving as a Choctaw and Chickasaw interpreter with Theodore Roosevelt's Rough Riders. This experience gave Sam a lifelong devotion not only to Theodore Roosevelt but to the Republican Party (most likely his guardian David Blossom was important in this respect also). Admittedly, Sam's devotion to the Grand Old Party was tested when Roosevelt, out of office for one term, sought the Republican nomination in 1912, pitting Roosevelt's wartime comrade loyalists against supporters of President William Howard Taft. At a district GOP convention in 1912, partisan emotions ran high. A fervent Roosevelt supporter, Sam made national news by getting into a fistfight with another Choctaw GOP delegate, Taft supporter Victor M. Locke, Jr. In the story "Dynamite Fails in Roosevelt Boom" the *New York Times* made an amused note of "a fistic encounter between Gov. Victor M. Locke, a chieftain of the Choctaw Nation, and Sam Downing, a Rough Rider and Roosevelt shouter." Whether or not Sam brought himself to vote for Taft in the general election (Roosevelt, the candidate of the Progressive Party, was not even on the ballot in Oklahoma), for the rest of his life he deemed himself not only an American Indian but a Republican and a Presbyterian; and his children were raised accordingly. Sam's life largely illustrates the sort of "mixed-blood" acculturation process described by Choctaw scholar Devon Abbott Mihesuah: "[W]hite men married Choctaw women and produced mixed-bloods who eventually became prominent community leaders. These mixed-bloods were often educated in white schools and exposed to Christianity, learned patriarchal thought subsuming females, and became impressed with the American system of governance."[9]

9 Thomas Hamm to Curtis Evans, 28 September 2012; Downing, "Downing Family," 246-247; "Dynamite Fails in Roosevelt Boom," *New York Times*, 24 January 1912, 1; Devon Abbott Mihesuah, *Choctaw Crime and Punishment, 1884-1907* (Norman, OK: University of Oklahoma Press, 2009), 84-85. I would qualify Mihesuah's statement, however, with the observation

Downing House, Atoka, Oklahoma
Photo by Author

Atoka, Court Street, 1910s

Courtesy Confederate Memorial Museum & Cemetery, Atoka, OK

Atoka Presbyterian Church

Courtesy Confederate Memorial Museum & Cemetery, Atoka, OK

To be sure, there is no question but that Todd Downing's contemporaries and Todd Downing himself placed great importance on his indigenous heritage. Like his father, Todd was an enrolled member of the Choctaw nation. Book reviews and publicity pieces alike stressed Todd's Choctaw ancestry. "Gruesome Mexico Book Penned by Atoka Indian" boasted the headline to the review of Downing's mystery *Night over Mexico* (1937) in the *Daily Oklahoman*. Similarly, in its "Meet the Author" blurb (possibly written by the author himself) the 1945 Popular Library reprint edition of Todd's praised detective novel *The Cat Screams* declared Todd "especially qualified to write about Mexico, as an Indian country, since he is one quarter Choctaw, his paternal grandmother having been one of the survivors of the Trail of Tears, when the Choctaws were forced to migrate from Mississippi to Indian Territory in 1832."[10]

Todd's most important statement concerning his indigenous heritage is found in "A Choctaw's Autobiography," a short essay published in 1926 in the Tulsa, Oklahoma journal *The American Indian*. As James Cox has noted, this essay functioned as Todd's ethnic manifesto, in which before a Native American reading audience he staked his claim to Choctaw heritage and political consciousness. "Though only a quarter-blood Indian," Todd declares, "that much gives [the writer] the proudest distinction he can ever gain—that of being a real American." (In point of fact Todd was an eighth-blood Indian.) Todd avows that "the American Indian" is the "noblest product that the human race has produced."[11]

In "A Choctaw's Autobiography" Todd characterizes his father Sam Downing as someone who "has always been a power among the Choctaws." He amplifies thusly:

that within the Downing household, anyway, the women—Awilda Miller, Maud and Ruth—were outspoken and independent-minded and exercised a good deal of influence.

10 *Daily Oklahoman*, 31 October 1937, 71.

11 Todd Downing, "A Choctaw's Autobiography" [1926], in J. M. Carroll and Lee F. Hawkins, eds., *The American Indian, 1926-1931* (New York: Liveright, 1970), 49.

> During the Spanish-American war he was a member of Theodore Roosevelt's Rough Riders serving the incomparable "Teddy" as interpreter with the Choctaw and Chickasaw members of this organization. He was a member of the statehood delegation at Washington that secured statehood for Oklahoma. At present he is a member of the Choctaw Tribal Council and is taking a leading part in the efforts to wrest from the United States government the fulfillment of promises which have never been fulfilled and to prevent further encroachment upon the rights of the Indians.[12]

Consistently in his 1926 manifesto Todd takes a condemnatory stance toward the matter of the United States government's treatment of the Choctaw Nation. When he observes that the government of the United States is "dedicated to liberty and the proposition that all men are created equal," his observation clearly is deliberately tinged with irony.[13] Throughout his life Todd's great pride in his Choctaw heritage and his conviction of the wrongs done those whom he viewed as his people never faltered.

Todd's father Sam remained quite involved in Choctaw affairs into the 1930s. From correspondence of Todd's maternal grandmother, Awilda Shields Miller (known to Todd simply as "Nanna"), we learn that Sam Downing often had political talks with other prominent Choctaws at the family home in Atoka. In a March 1933 letter to her granddaughter (and Todd's sister) Ruth Downing, for example, Awilda reported that "we had just settled ourselves for the evening, Dad, Mamma & I, when Henry Bond came in. I suppose he has important business to talk about, pertaining to their Indian Affairs." Henry Jesse Bond, a full-blood of Choctaw and Chickasaw descent, was a Presbyterian minister, former county judge and three-term Atoka county treasurer who

12 Downing, "Autobiography," 49. See *Daily Oklahoman*, 2 July 1926, 7.
13 Ibid.

had testified to the United States Congress a few years earlier on the condition of Native Americans in Oklahoma (Sam Downing's literal sparring partner from the 1912 GOP political convention, Victor Locke, also testified at the same Congressional hearing). In 1939 Henry Bond would number as another member in the company of distinguished pallbearers at Awilda Miller's funeral.[14]

An earlier, 1930 letter by Awilda Miller gives us another glimpse into Sam Downing's responsibilities in local Indian affairs. To her granddaughter, Awilda related a tale of Sam Downing's strained relationship with a much different sort of man, a murderous character named J. J. McIntosh. Sam was guardian of McIntosh's daughters, the man having beaten, according to Awilda, his "two wives to death, and made so much trouble." When Awilda wrote her letter, McIntosh had just died from wounds suffered in a fight with another Indian during a Democratic political rally at the Atoka county courthouse. According to Awilda, McIntosh had been "too attentive" to the wife of this other man, who stood "well in their [i.e., Indian] community." "There is no one willing or able to pay [the dead man's burial] expenses," Awilda reported, so the responsibility for the matter had fallen on Sam, as so often happened in Atoka. "Dad has been annoyed all day with phone calls," Awilda complained. "I heard him say a while ago, 'Pretty soon I'll go out and bury that man myself—just as he deserves to be buried.'"[15]

Sam Downing was again involved in Choctaw affairs in January 1931, when Red Cross relief was being administered to families ravaged by the Depression. "Our relief work began yesterday," Awilda wrote Ruth. "Mamma was down all afternoon. . . . Mamma said there's some of the most wretched looking people

14 Awilda Shields Miller [ASM] to Ruth Shields Downing [RSD], 9 March 1933; Thoburn and Wright, *Oklahoma*, Volume III, 217-218; *Survey of the Conditions of the Indians of the United States: Hearing before a Subcommittee of the Committee on Indian Affairs*, U. S. Senate, 71st Congress, Second Session (1929), 5317-5321.

15 ASM to RSD, 19 October 1930.

here yesterday [that] she ever saw. Dad is going to see that some of these poor Indians get a share. The country people have had nothing to sell but wood. The warm weather has hindered that. Dad says he has seen loads of wood that would ordinarily bring $1.68 or $2.00 sell for .60 cents. Hogs and chickens are about all eaten. There was no food for them."[16]

Given Sam Downing's obvious significance within the Atoka County Choctaw community and Todd Downing's own pronounced interest in his indigenous heritage, one can understand and appreciate the emphasis that has been laid upon it, both by Todd's contemporaries and by modern scholars. Yet just as there were, as we have seen, non-indigenous influences in the life of Sam Downing, so were there in Todd's. And, as in the case with Sam, so in Todd's case have these influences received little notice, an omission I seek to correct here.

Both Todd Downing's paternal grandparents had been deceased for over two decades when Todd was born. Todd was but ten when his maternal grandfather, Daniel M. Miller (1841-1912) died, but his maternal grandmother Awilda Shields Miller (1849-1939) for nearly three decades after her husband's demise resided in the home of her daughter Maud Miller Downing and her son-in-law Sam Downing, playing an important role in the lives of her grandchildren Todd and Ruth (the latter of whom was given the surname Shields as her middle name, in honor of her grandmother's family).

In the previous century Awilda Shields Miller had lived a life out of a crime novel. This was through no culpability of her own, except indirectly through her choice of a marriage partner, made when she was but eighteen or nineteen years old. Although Daniel M. Miller at the time seemed one of the most promising young fellows in Monroe County, Iowa—a true up-and-comer—Awilda's marriage to this man produced for her, as will shortly be seen, what surely must have seemed an inordinate share of trouble and heartache.

16 ASM to RSD, 21 January 1931.

Through his grandfather Daniel M. Miller, Todd Downing gained not just a memorable ancestor but a striking thread of Germanic heritage in his ancestral coat of many colors. Daniel M. Miller's great-grandfather, Elder Jacob Miller (1735-1816), was an important Church of the Brethren, or Dunker, minister, who in 1801 carried his gospel to Ohio (specifically near Dayton, in Montgomery County). His son Daniel (1780-1858), also a Dunker minister, migrated to Parke County, Indiana, later moving with much of his family to Monroe County, Iowa, in 1853. The Dunker faith appears to have attenuated in Daniel's son Lewis (1817-1888), father of Daniel M. Miller and nine other children. Daniel M. Miller, it seems, was of no particular religious persuasion until he married Awilda Shields and adopted her Presbyterian faith as his own.[17]

Daniel M. Miller was an ambitious man on the move. He became a schoolteacher in 1857, at the age of sixteen. By 1863, when he was twenty-two, he had moved to Albia, seat of Monroe County, and found employment as a store clerk. The next year Daniel joined Company C of the 46th Regiment, Iowa volunteers, serving as sergeant. His company was stationed in Memphis and Collierville, Tennessee, guarding the Memphis and Charleston Railroad, and it was involved in repulsing the Confederate attack on Memphis on August 21, 1864. After returning from the war, Daniel became Deputy District Court Clerk for three-and-a-half years before purchasing a partnership in a dry goods business. Apparently having an interest in culture (or perhaps the ladies), Daniel in 1868 was appointed Secretary of the newly-formed Albia Lyceum. That same year he married Awilda Shields, daughter of James D. Shields (1816-1887), a doctor originally from Pittsburgh, Pennsylvania. A daughter, Maud, was born to the couple in 1872, followed by a son, Max, ten years later in

17 Rev. Merle C. Rummel, *The Virginia Settlement or the Four Mile Church of the Brethren*, at http://www.union-county.lib.in.us/GenwebVA4mile/Table%20of%20Contents%204M.htm; Charles R. Tuttle and Daniel Durrie: *An Illustrated History of the State of Iowa* (Chicago, IL: Richard S. Peale, 1876), 721.

1882, a year before the Miller family fortunes collapsed, in an explosion of infamy.[18]

In 1875 Daniel M. Miller became the cashier for Albia's newly formed Monroe County Bank. Among the bank's directors were Daniel's father Lewis and his father-in-law James Shields. (Lewis Miller later became the bank president.) In 1876, *An Illustrated History of the State of Iowa* reported that Daniel and Awilda Miller had "a convenient and pleasant residence [in Albia], and a little daughter to cheer their home." By this time Daniel Miller was, recalled Frank Hickenlooper (son of one of the bank stockholders) in the 1896 *History of Monroe County, Iowa*, "one of the most popular men of Monroe County." In 1882 came the great crash, however. An audit of the Monroe County Bank conducted that year showed liabilities greatly exceeded assets. Culpability was found to rest with the bank cashier. In 1883 Daniel Miller "was arrested, convicted of embezzlement, forgery, and fraud, and sentenced to seven years at hard labor in the penitentiary at Fort Madison, Iowa." For good measure, Daniel also was expelled from the Albia First Presbyterian Church, its having been discovered that as the institution's bookkeeper and collector Daniel had made off with church funds as well. The contagion from Daniel Miller's shocking misdoings also struck Daniel's (presumably innocent) brother Samuel, the Monroe County sheriff. His family in disgrace because of Daniel's criminal conduct, Samuel Miller hastily resigned from his law enforcement office.[19]

18 Tuttle and Durrie, *Iowa*, 721; *The History of Monroe County, Iowa* (Chicago: Western Historical Company, 1878), 454, 466, 469. National Park Service, The Civil War, Regiment Details, Union Iowa Volunteers, 46th Regiment, Iowa Infantry, http://www.nps.gov/civilwar/search-regiments-detail.htm?regiment_id=UIA0046RI. One man in Miller's regiment was killed in action, while thirty-one died from disease. According to the U. S. census, Max Miller was living with his sister and brother-in-law, Maud and Sam Downing, in Atoka in 1910. Family correspondence refers to him as late as 1939.

19 Tuttle and Durrie, *Iowa*, 721; Frank Hickenlooper, *An Illustrated History of Monroe County, Iowa* (Albia, IA: by the author, 1896), 158, 167-169, 249.

After his release from prison (with time off for good behavior), Daniel Miller left Iowa with his family. The Millers settled in Indian Territory at Atoka in 1891, the year Sam returned home from Earlham College. Apparently the Miller family established and operated an Atoka restaurant. Awilda Miller had family connections in Indian Territory, which likely influenced the couple's decision to relocate there. Through her mother, Eliza (Robb) Shields, Awilda probably was a first cousin of Atoka merchant David N. Robb, a business partner of Sam Downing's guardian David C. Blossom. Both David N. Robb and his brother Andrew W. Robb of Muscogee (Creek Nation) were prominent Indian Territory citizens. Additionally there was a sister, Magaretta (Retta) Robb, who taught school in Muscogee in the 1870s. Before moving to Indian Territory, the Robb siblings had, like the Millers, lived in Monroe County, Iowa. Like Awilda Miller, the Blossoms and the Downings, the Robbs were the staunchest of Republicans and Presbyterians. In 1882, at the Atoka home of her brother David, Retta Robb married William P. Paxson, a Presbyterian minister and Superintendent of the southwestern division of the American Sunday School Union. After her husband's death in 1896 Retta Robb Paxson settled in Atoka, residing with her widowed niece Nettie Robb McLaughlin. The two women were known as Aunt Retta and Aunt (sometimes Cousin) Nettie to the Downings, with whom they had a close relationship for decades.[20]

With their connection to the respected Robb siblings, the newly-arrived Millers happily found themselves embraced by Atoka society. In the 1890s Atoka's newspaper, the *Indian Citizen*, lauded daughter Maud Miller as "talented, capable and accomplished," both "as a business woman and a society girl

20 *The record in the matter of the application for enrollment as a citizen by intermarriage of the Choctaw Nation of Maud Downing*, Department of the Interior, Commission of the Five Civilized Tribes, *Fold3—Historical Military Records*, www.fold3.com; *Indian Citizen*, 18 May 1899; Wally Waits, "Andrew W. Robb and Family," 13 February 2008, *Muskogee History and Genealogy*, at http://www.muskogeehistorian.com/2008/02/andrew-w-robb-and-family.html; *The Sunday-School World* 22 (1882): 371.

too." Like her mother, Maud was a member of the Presbyterian Church, where no doubt she was brought into close proximity with that young up-and-coming mixed blood Atokan, Sam Downing. Maud married Sam at her parents' home in 1899.[21] Evidently the taint of Daniel Miller's crimes and imprisonment had been left behind the Millers in another state, just as had been the bigamy of Sam Downing's father.

A product of the great American melting pot at its most highly spiced, Todd Downing himself grew up in placid and comfortable middle class surroundings, in a big foursquare house with his parents Sam and Maud, his sister Ruth and, after his grandfather's death in 1912, his Nanna Miller. (Uncle Max Miller seems to have been a presence for some time as well.) Like many future fiction writers, Todd as a boy was intensely interested in the world of imagination, whether as depicted on the printed page or on celluloid film. Todd's library of nearly 2000 books, bequeathed by him to Southeastern Oklahoma State University, includes a goodly number of volumes published in the late nineteenth and early twentieth centuries that likely constituted the great bulk of his adolescent reading. Among these volumes are works by Edward Bulwer-Lytton, Wilkie Collins and Charles Dickens (both in collected works series, dates unknown), H. Rider Haggard, Rudyard Kipling, Arthur B. Reeve, Sax Rohmer, William Shakespeare (in a 1912 collected works edition), Sir Walter Scott, Robert Louis Stevenson and Alfred, Lord Tennyson. Taken together, the books by these authors that Todd Downing owned indicate that as a youth the Oklahoman had a heavy exposure to the romantic literature of adventure. (In his 1934 review of Valentine Williams' Scotland-set mystery thriller, *The Portcullis Room*, Todd tellingly refers to his "early initiation into Walter Scott.")

Most striking—at least in terms of sheer volume—are fifty-six books by H. Rider Haggard (1856-1925), the once hugely popular English writer of adventure novels set in exotic locations around the globe. Haggard is best remembered today for

21 Downing, "Downing Family," 246-247.

King Solomon's Mines (originally published 1885), *Allan Quartermain* (o.p. 1887) and *She* (o.p. 1887). Of these three novels Todd owned an original edition only of *She*. (He owned no copy of *King Solomon's Mines* and his copy of *Allen Quartermain* is from 1949.) Todd did, however, own an original edition of Haggard's *Montezuma's Daughter* (1893), a tale set in Mexico during the era of the Spanish conquest.[22]

Dating mostly from 1883 (suggesting more books from a collected works edition), Todd's fourteen Walter Scott works include the Waverley novels *Kenilworth* (o.p. 1821) and *The Fortunes of Nigel* (o.p. 1822), the poetry collection *The Lady of the Lake* (o.p. 1810) and, more unusually, *Demonology and Witchcraft: Letters Addressed to J. G. Lockhart Esq.* Although this latter volume was originally published in 1830, Todd's copy was one of his newest books, dating from 1970, less than four years before his death—confirming that this particular work, at least, was not among Todd's childhood reading! Additionally we find, among earlier works in Todd's library, a 1909 edition of Robert Louis Stevenson's *Treasure Island* and an undated edition of Stevenson's *The Master of Ballantrae*, 1890s short story collections by Rudyard Kipling, *The Complete Works of Alfred Tennyson* (1878 ed.) and Tennyson's *Idylls of the King* (1912 ed.).[23]

Notable in terms of Todd's development as a mystery writer and critic are the books by Arthur B. Reeve and Sax Rohmer that he owned. In some of his 1930s crime fiction reviews Todd comments nostalgically on these two authors. Arthur B. Reeve (1880-1936) was an American mystery writer best known for creating the scientific detective Dr. Craig Kennedy. Reeve's Great Detective appeared in eighty-two stories between 1910 and 1918 (first

22 On H. Rider Haggard and his works, see D. S. Higgins, *Rider Haggard: A Biography* (New York: Stein & Day, 1983).

23 Possibly the 1878 Tennyson edition belonged to Todd's grandmother, who may have named her daughter, Maud, after the title character of the 1855 Tennyson poem. Nanna Miller referenced Dickens once in a 1930 letter to Ruth, when she told Ruth she had named her new, extremely cheerful, songbird (a gift from Todd) "Tiny Tim." ASM to RSD, 30 (?) December 1930.

in newspapers and magazines, then later in book form), when Todd was between the ages of eight and sixteen. In one April 1936 review in the *Daily Oklahoman*, Todd referred to Reeve's fiction "as we knew [it] twenty years ago," while in a May 1934 review he reminisced about the

> days when we used to wait each Saturday night for the 6 o'clock train to bring a big-town newspaper containing the latest installment of a yarn by Mr. Reeve [*The Exploits of Elaine*]. Later, it ran for endless weeks as a movie serial, starring, if memory serves, Pearl White. . . . More or less consciously ever since we have been comparing our thrillers with these chapters read between the railway station and home. We followed Mr. Reeve and his sleuth, Craig Kennedy, through magazine after magazine, until the formula wore thin.

Todd owned two books by Arthur B. Reeve: the 1915 book edition of *The Exploits of Elaine* (appropriately enough) and the 1917 story collection *The Treasure Train*.[24]

Sax Rohmer (1883-1959) was an English thriller writer best known for his diabolical "Oriental" criminal mastermind Dr. Fu Manchu, who starred in a long series of "Yellow Peril" novels published between 1913 and 1959. Reviewing a non-series Rohmer thriller, *The Bat Flies Low*, in December 1935, Todd deemed it "the best of the Rohmer yarns since the early days of Fu Manchu." Todd's collection of Sax Rohmer novels included not only *The Bat Flies Low* (1935) and *The Shadow of Fu Manchu* (1948), but first editions of seven novels published between 1913 and 1921, including the first three Fu Manchu novels (*The Insidious Dr. Fu-Manchu*, 1913; *The Return of Dr. Fu-Manchu*, 1916; and *The Hand of Fu Manchu*, 1917) and *The Quest of the Sacred*

24 *Daily Oklahoman*, 20 May 1934, 49; On Arthur B. Reeve see John Locke, ed., *From Ghouls to Gangsters: The Career of Arthur B. Reeve*, Vols. I and II (Castroville, CA: Off-Trail Publications, 2007).

Slipper (1914), in which the Muslim Hassan of Aleppo temporarily replaces Dr. Fu Manchu as the villainous Eastern fiend.[25]

Todd Downing's boyhood reading seems typical fare for a bookish middle-class American lad growing up in the middle of what Michael Dirda calls the Golden Age of storytelling. Although the adventures-in-exotic-lands element in Todd's youthful fiction reading is suggestive of the authors' future interest—both in his mysteries and his non-fiction writing—in Mexico, it certainly would not seem, at first blush, to have fostered Todd's strong anti-colonialist and pro-indigenous mindset in the 1930s and 1940s. Indeed, it must be admitted that much of Todd's adolescent reading material in fact has been denounced for promoting Euro-American imperialism and racism. In *Rider Haggard and the Fiction of Empire: A Critical Study of British Imperial Fiction*, for example, Wendy Roberta Katz insists that "Haggard's romances . . . illustrate a total mentality, a philosophy of life, an idea of humankind completely in harmony with the imperial ideology."[26]

Sax Rohmer's Fu Manchu novels today are especially controversial and deeply divisive. On the one hand, the reader "Francesca H." on the website Amazon.com, for example, denounced *The Insidious Dr. Fu-Manchu* (in a January 26, 2012 one-star review tellingly titled "It's difficult to enjoy a story when I keep getting offended") as a "ridiculously racist novel," while blogger Anna Chen ("Madame Miaow") launched a blistering jeremiad against Sax Rohmer in 2010, when BBC 4 had the temerity to air a mock documentary on Dr. Fu Manchu. "This invention [Dr. Fu Manchu] by a lower-middle-class writer for his similarly conservative-minded brethren diverted class anxieties and fears about an emerging working-class empowered by the unions onto an exotic Other," pronounced Chen. On the other

25 *Daily Oklahoman*, 8 December 1935, 59. On Sax Rohmer, see Van Ash, Cay and Elizabeth Rohmer, *Master of Villainy: A Biography of Sax Rohmer* (Bowling Green, OH: Popular Press, 1972).

26 Wendy Roberta Katz, *Rider Haggard and the Fiction of Empire: A Critical Study of British Imperial Fiction* (Cambridge and New York: Cambridge University Press, 1987), 4.

hand, William Patrick Maynard, the licensed continuer of Fu Manchu thrillers, passionately defended the same novel "Francesca H." criticized, arguing that it infuses Rohmer's "Asian villain with an integrity and dignity that inspires sympathy in the reader" and creates "a complex portrayal of the West's political enemies as people worthy of respect and capable of open dialogue." Perhaps Todd Downing glimpsed something of the same quality in his adolescent reading of Sax Rohmer almost a century ago that Maynard has found more recently. Certainly Todd cannot be categorized as that which Anna Chen conceives to have been the typical Sax Rohmer reader: a lower-middle-class conservative Englishman fearful of an emergent working class.[27]

Admittedly, Todd Downing came from a small-town, Middle American, middle class, politically conservative and traditionalist Christian background. Those individuals who were the most important adult influences in Todd's youth—his father, mother and grandmother—all were staunch Republicans and Presbyterians. Nanna Miller's letters to Ruth Downing open a window on the social and political attitudes of the Downing elders.

When in October 1932 Ruth, who was living in New York City and working on her master's degree at the New York School of Social Work (affiliated with Columbia University), wrote her

27 William Patrick Maynard, "Blogging *The Insidious Dr. Fu-Manchu* by Sax Rohmer, Part Five—'The Green Mist,'" 25 April 2010, *Seti Says*, http://setisays.blogspot.com/2010/04/blogging-insidious-dr-fu-manchu-by-sax_25.html; Anna Chen, "BBC jumps the Orientalist shark: Fu Manchu in Edinburgh," 8 August 2010, *Madame Miaow Says*, http://madammiaow.blogspot.com/2010/08/bbc-jumps-racist-shark-fu-manchu-in.html. Also see the two one-star reviews of *The Insidious Dr. Fu Manchu* at Amazon.com. Note also this expression of dismay with the Sax Rohmer novel *The Quest of the Sacred Slipper*, by a Connecticut bookseller in his AbeBooks ad offering the book for sale: "Rohmer was a great story teller. . . . This tale, however, for pure unadulterated bigotry and Euro-centrism takes the cake. I hate to come across as a knee-jerk 'new Leftist,' but its endorsement of Anglo-Saxon thievery and supremacism is out of control." For a recent, more sympathetic consideration of Sax Rohmer, see Gary Lachman, "The Yellow Peril of Fu Manchu," 6 July 2012, *Gary Lachman*, at http://garylachman.co.uk/2012/07/06/the-yellow-peril-of-dr-fu-manchu.

grandmother (possibly in jest) that she was planning to vote for Norman Thomas, the Socialist candidate for President, an agitated Awilda fired off a rapid response on November 2, just six days before Election Day. "You certainly were joking when you wrote [that] you had about decided to vote for Norman Thomas for President," Awilda hopefully began, before pleading:

> Anyway let me implore you to pause and reconsider that decision—so much is involved in a vote at this election [that] one needs to pray as well as *think*. You said Thomas has been a Presbyterian preacher. Admitting that fact nowadays does not mean that he is a safe man to entrust with the guidance of affairs in our country. While [Thomas was] in Oklahoma he was [a] guest of, and orated from, the pulpit of the Unitarian preacher, who denies the Divinity of Christ. Let us not put a man at the head of our country who is not a Christian. This year's vote is almost a solemn Privilege. Keep yourself on the safe side. Your Great Grandfather went into the Republican Party when [it was] first organized. You are the youngest in the line. Do not let anyone persuade you to desert us.[28]

Other letters from Awilda Miller are peppered with criticisms of the Democrats and the godless and praiseful of Republicans and the God-fearing. The Republican Party and the Presbyterian Church were the institutional cornerstones of Awilda's life. Whatever her husband may have been in his heart, Awilda Miller remained a devoutly faithful member of the Presbyterian Church her whole life; and the subject of religious faith entered her letters to her granddaughter with some frequency. In 1930,

28 ASM to RSD, 2 November 1932. Presumably the great grandfather of Ruth Downing's to whom Awilda Miler is referring is Awilda's father James D. Shields, who would have been about thirty-eight years old when the Republican Party was formed in 1854.

for example, after Ruth wrote Awilda asking her for advice to give a New York friend who was a self-admitted religious skeptic, Awilda gave the matter grave consideration:

> I can scarcely write you how much I appreciated your writing as you did, but am wondering if I shall be able to help your friend, as I so wish to do. In the first place, his great mistake no doubt is the same as countless persons are making—not accepting the fact that the Bible is a *supernatural* book. [It] cannot be put [on the] same plane as Ancient History. . . . I do not wonder that there is so much unbelief and skepticism abounding today, because there are so many preachers and teachers wise in their own conceit who are leading people away from the truth. Blind leaders of the blind.[29]

In matters of national and state politics as well, Awilda Miller often felt that it was the blind who were leading the blind. Yet Awilda was not one to yield her principles. Although amidst a calamitous economic depression much of the country deserted Republican President Herbert Hoover in the 1932 election, Awilda steadfastly stood by her party's man, even after he went down to a dismal defeat. In March 1933, Awilda wrote Ruth urging her not to "fail to read" journalist Mark Sullivan's *Saturday Evening Post* article, "President Hoover and the World Depression." (Sullivan is said in the 1920s to have "enjoyed as close a personal relationship with Hoover as any journalist of his time.") According to Awilda, Sullivan's article gave "one a view of the tremendous obstacles Hoover met, with no help from a Democratic Congress." The next year, in September 1934, Awilda, now 85, wrote disparagingly to Ruth of Franklin Roosevelt and his administration. "Presume you are sharing the 'New Deal's' high

29 ASM to RSD, 7 December 1930.

cost of living. Am glad you have at least *one* friend [in New York City] who shares our feelings for Roosevelt and his 'Brain Trust' cabinet. We heard a splendid Talk over Radio by Jim Reed, a prominent Democrat [a retired three-term Missouri senator]. He did overlook the *charming smile* of the president. I do not know what we would do without the Radio."[30]

The elder Downings were just as much in opposition to Oklahoma Democrats as they were to national New Dealers. While Todd may well have been much more sympathetic than his forebears to the New Deal president (see note 31), he nevertheless surely shared his family's disdain for William Henry Davis Murray (1869-1956), governor of Oklahoma from 1931 to 1935. "Alfalfa Bill," as he was known, was a Democrat from the populist wing of the party, the hero of country people and the bane of city slickers. Originally from the memorably named town of Toadsuck, Texas, Murray became a Farmers' Alliance activist in that state before moving to Tishomingo, Chickasaw Nation, Indian Territory, where, like George Downing, he married a mixed-blood Native American. Although he served as President of the Oklahoma State Constitutional Convention in 1907, the first Speaker

30 ASM to RSD, 9 March 1933, 20 September 1934; Louis W. Liebovich, *Bylines in Despair: Herbert Hoover, the Great Depression and the U. S. News Media* (Westport, CT: Prager, 1994), 34. James A. Reed (1861-1944) retired from the United States senate in 1929 and returned home to Missouri, though he reappeared on the political circuit in the 1930s and 1940s to speak out against the economic policies of Franklin Roosevelt. In one of his public talks, "Common Sense in Government," he declared that "Common sense in government does not undertake to create impossible Utopias or waste its energies in vain attempts to remake the world, or to alter the course of human nature. It deals with conditions as they exist; it seeks in a practical way to produce the best possible result with the materials at hand." See Daniel McCarthy, "Show Me a Statesman," review of Lee Meriwether, *Jim Reed, Senatorial Immortal: A Biography* (1948; rept., Whitefish, MT: Kessinger, 2007), 20 November 2008, *The University Bookman*, http://www.kirkcenter.org/index.php/bookman. Such rhetoric not unnaturally made Reed "a pariah to the national Democratic Party." Gary M. Pomerantz, *The Devil's Ticket: A Vengeful Wife, A Fatal Hand and a New American Age* (New York: Crown, 2009), 204.

of the Oklahoma House of Representatives and a two-term member of the United States House of Representatives from Oklahoma, Murray's political career stalled in the 1920s; and with various family members he abandoned the United States to start an agricultural colony in the South American country of Bolivia, only returning to his native land in 1929, after he had lost most of his money in the quixotic venture. With the onset of the Depression Murray thought that his political wheel of fortune might well turn. In this case his perception was acute. Entering the race for the Oklahoma governorship in 1930, as state unemployment was rapidly rising (the unemployment rate would reach 29% by 1933), Murray not only easily captured the Democratic nomination but overwhelmed the Republican candidate, getting 59% of the vote, in spite of the intense opposition he faced from the hostile metropolitan press.[31]

Part of the intense urban opposition in Oklahoma to Bill Murray stemmed from the marked animus that he displayed toward the state's colleges. During his campaign Murray flayed advanced education for making "high-toned bums" of college students and vowed to "throw a bomb into the state's education

31 Arrell Morgan Gibson, *Oklahoma: A History of Five Centuries* (Norman, OK: University of Oklahoma Press, 1981), 221; James N. Gregory, *American Exodus: The Dust Bowl Migration and Okie Culture in California* (Oxford and New York: Oxford University Press, 1989), 13. Both Todd's fictional and nonfictional work makes clear his strong opposition to colonialist policies of the United States and European countries in regard to Latin America, particularly Mexico. His detective fiction reviews also reveal the occasional stray liberal sentiment. For example, in his review of Willoughby Sharp's *Murder of the Honest Broker* (1934), Todd makes the following sarcastic comment (startlingly apropos in 2012): "It's axiomatic with mystery writers that readers like to vent their spleen vicariously upon the corpse, so what's more welcome these days than a nice, well-fed financier?" Similarly, in 1935, in a review of Francis Beeding's spy thriller *Death in Four Letters* Todd makes a hostile reference to Adolf Hitler's "brazen challenge to the world and his piffle anent racial solidarity." Finally, in a review of Ward Greene's anti-lynching crime novel, *Death in the Deep South* (1936), Todd praises the book for its powerful indictment of American racism and violence.

system." The new governor proved especially hostile to the University of Oklahoma, his main Democratic opponent, millionaire oilman Frank Buttram, just happening to be head of the university's board of regents. (Not only had Buttram graduated with a B.S. in chemistry from the University of Oklahoma in 1910, but his wife, Merle Edelweiss Newby, taught in the university's music department.) Murray vowed to slash what he saw as the unconscionably high level of university appropriations, noting scornfully, for example, that OU wanted $150,000 to build a campus swimming pool. "Well as far as I'm concerned they can go to the creek to swim," Murray scornfully declared of OU students. "You can't get through life by graduating from football, baseball or highballs."[32]

In her letters to Ruth Downing, Awilda Miller kept up a steady refrain of criticism of Alfalfa Bill. In August 1930, for example, with the Oklahoma gubernatorial campaign in full stride, Awilda wrote Ruth that the "piteously hot" weather of the last two months had finally been interrupted by rain ("we had about given up hope of ever breathing damp air again"). She then expressed her wish, in reference to the big election, that "since it is cooler, people may be saner." "If Bill Murray is Gov[ernor] of Okla[homa] and Ma Ferguson of Tex[as]," she asked rhetorically, in a jab at

32 Gibson, *Oklahoma*, 223. Richard A. Luthin, *American Demagogues: Twentieth Century* (Boston: Beacon Press, 1954), 112; Keith L. Bryant, Jr., *Alfalfa Bill Murray* (Norman, OK: University of Oklahoma Press, 1968), 187. On George Franklin (Frank) Buttram, see his obituary in the *Daily Oklahoman*, 19 December 1966, 37. Professor Luthin devoted a chapter to Bill Murray in his *American Demagogues*, placing Alfalfa Bill alongside such notables as Theodore Bilbo, Ma and Pa Ferguson, Eugene Talmadge, Huey Long and Joe McCarthy. In his memoir *Seldom Disappointed*, Oklahoma mystery writer Tony Hillerman (1925-2008)—who, like Todd Downing, made use of Native American material in his genre novels—recalled interviewing an octogenarian Murray in 1951, after his son Johnston was elected governor of Oklahoma. At "the second floor room of a down and outer hotel" that the elder Murray now called home, Hillerman wanted to talk about Johnston Murray, but Alfalfa Bill "didn't. He wanted to talk about Alfalfa Bill." Tony Hillerman, *Seldom Disappointed: A Memoir* (New York: HarperCollins, 2001), 255.

populist politicians, "who would choose to locate in either state?"[33]

By October, Awilda had despaired of any hope that Murray might be defeated in his quest for the governorship. The economic devastation in her state, she realized, made Murray's appeals irresistible to multitudes of desperate people. Referring to her granddaughter's job as a social worker in New York City, Awilda wrote Ruth that her "work must be interesting," but then asked her whether it was "not hard to witness so much trouble. I mean the kind [of trouble] not even charity can relieve." That was what too many Oklahomans were experiencing. "The unemployment situation is widespread," conceded Awilda, and that harbored ill for Murray's opponents:

> I was downtown one day last week for the first time since we came [back] from Norman [Oklahoma, home of the University of Oklahoma]. Everybody looks so old and careworn. In fact I saw very few familiar faces. Most of the people looked as if they had come in from the country and were not sure what they had come for. I am sure they will vote for "Bill" Murray believing he will help them, just as they thought Walton would give every family their own home. [The latter reference is to Jack C. Walton, a 1920s Progressive governor.]

33 ASM to RSD, 24 August 1930. Awilda's ominous references to prolonged droughty weather signal the beginning of the meteorological conditions that would foster the massive Great Plains dust storms of the 1930s and the creation of the Dust Bowl. Ma Ferguson was the nickname of Miriam Amanda Wallace Ferguson (1875-1961), Governor of Texas in from 1925 to 1927 and later from 1933 to 1935. Ma Ferguson's husband, Governor James Ferguson ("Pa"), was impeached, convicted and removed from office in 1917. During her first term, Ma Ferguson gave an average of over one hundred pardons a month, resulting in accusations of bribe-taking on her part. Attempts, unsuccessful, were made to impeach her as well.

Awilda noted that a highway bill had been introduced in the Oklahoma legislature to "give work this winter to the farmers if it carries," but she was sure "the Murray crowd" would block it, as it was "being pushed by the Republican nominee for gov[ernor]."[34]

After "Alfalfa Bill" won the gubernatorial election and assumed office in 1931, the agitation about him in the Downing household moved from the higher ideological plane to that of the purely practical. Governor Murray was launching a major offensive against all that he deemed laxity, luxury and licentiousness in Oklahoma higher education:

> [Murray] attacked university professors who failed to teach eight hours a day, six days a week, twelve months a year. In his opinion, attendance at professional meetings was a waste of time, and the new student union building was a "country club" for students. . . . There were, he declared, too many college graduates in the state. Professor William Bennett Bizzell of the University of Oklahoma was accused of being a poor educational leader, of allowing drunkenness among the faculty, and of mismanaging funds. Murray sent Alva McDonald, a former United States marshal, to Norman to investigate "flagrant immorality and corruption."[35]

34 ASM to RSD, 19 October 1930; Gibson, *Oklahoma*, 215. A 1932 *Daily Oklahoman* article on Ruth Downing described Ruth's work as "mending broken homes, setting things right for deserted wives and children, assisting bewildered foreigners to find a place in this strange new world, saving people from starvation, helping them to find employment." See "Making People Happy Is Interesting Job Held by Young City Woman in New York," *Daily Oklahoman*, 3 October 1932, 2.

35 Bryant, *Alfalfa Bill*, 203; Todd Downing's uncle-in-law, Leroy Long, retired as the dean of OU's medical school the year Murray took office, but the University Hospital that Dean Long had guided into being in 1919 attracted the ornery eye of Alfalfa Bill, who sacked the head of the hospital. Murray also "issued an executive order allowing chiropractors to practice there." Ibid., 204.

Legislatively, Murray threatened state colleges with slashed appropriations, the elimination of intercollegiate athletics and a fraternity tax. While some of Murray's proposals could be dismissed as, from the collegiate perspective, mere irritants and indignities, the threat of severe cutbacks in university appropriations meant that there was a real danger that in the not-so-distant future Todd might be joining the great ranks of Oklahoma's unemployed. Awilda wrote Ruth on January 21, 1931, nine days after Alfalfa Bill had taken his oath of office, informing her granddaughter that the family had just received a letter from Todd, in which he expressed his concerns over the possible actions the Governor might take against the University. "They are all so worked up over Murray's attitude toward the University," Nanna Miller wrote. "They were all so strong for Buttram. He [Murray] is going to hurt and hamper all he dares."[36]

Once in office, Governor Murray sought retribution against no less a personage than Frank Buttram himself, attempting to oust his former Democratic primary opponent from the board of regents. Though Murray was stymied in his attempt, Buttram eventually offered the Governor his resignation, which was duly accepted. After the Buttram affair and Murray's removal from office of the president of Southwestern Teacher's College (members of the college faculty there had publicly opposed constitutional amendments Murray supported), no less a progressive journalistic entity than the *New Republic* took notice of the goings-on in Oklahoma and editorialized against Alfalfa Bill, denouncing the Governor as "an incorrigible enemy of academic freedom" who had launched "what is little less than a reign of terror among the publicly supported institutions of the state." Chastised the *New Republic*: "As a result of the governor's activities, no member of the faculty of any state educational institution [in Oklahoma] dares to draw a free breath."[37]

36 ASM to RSD, 21 January 1931.

37 "Paper Labels Governor as 'Academic Freedom Enemy'," *Daily Oklahoman*, 19 August 1932, 10.

When Governor Murray spoke in Norman, Awilda wrote Ruth that the family was anxious to know what the local reaction was. "We are rather curious to hear how Murray—I never dignify him by [the title] Gov[ernor]—got along at Norman yesterday, where he was to address the Murray Country Club [apparently a sarcastic reference to the Governor's formation of "Murray Clubs" across the state to drum up support for his policies]. Am sure Dr. Bizzell's admonition to the students would be to act courteously, even if it was not deserved, but as Bizzell was out of town they may have been unruly." According to the *Daily Oklahoman*, a group of students attending the speech indeed had determined to speak out in defense of President Bizzell, were he to be denounced by Alfalfa Bill, but since on this occasion the Governor opted to be non-confrontational, so did the college crowd.[38]

Although acrimony between the two hostile camps was avoided on the occasion of Governor Murray's 1931 Norman speech, the university community remained highly wary of their antagonist over the course of his entire term in office. "Have not heard from Brother [Todd] so far this week," Awilda wrote Ruth in March 1933. "But we know from the [*Daily Oklahoman* that] they are having a nerve wracking time at O. U. these days. And *Books Abroad* [a journal Todd helped manage] comes out next week. We expect any day to hear that Bill Murray has decided that shall cease." In point of fact, however, neither *Books Abroad* nor Todd himself ever became victims of Governor Murray's "reign of terror" against Oklahoma academia. In one of his rare surviving letters, Todd in May of that year was able to express cautious optimism that his job was safe from Murray's guillotine for the time being, though the situation at the university sadly was "more unsettled than ever," in his view. "We had a department meeting Wednesday and Dr. House announced that he had been notified by the president that our force [in the languages department] would be cut from 20 teachers to 18. I don't think

38 "Murray Plans One-Day Move For Petitions," *Daily Oklahoman*, 10 May 1931, 9. ASM to RSD, 10 May 1931.

that there is much danger of my head falling, but you never can tell." Todd had learned that his first detective novel, *Murder on Tour*, had been accepted by a publisher, a particular relief in Oklahoma's current political environment. "I am going to hang on here as long as possible," he explained to Ruth, "but if the book sells well, I can be independent of the state of Oklahoma if I want to be. It's a great feeling."[39]

After the success of his second detective novel, *The Cat Screams* (1934), Todd Downing determined to try to make himself "independent of the state of Oklahoma." Despite the fact that a much less college-averse Democrat, Ernest Marland, was elected governor in 1934 (indeed, an embittered Bill Murray, in an ironic twist, effectively threw his support to Marland's Republican opponent), Todd in 1935 resigned his position as an instructor at the University of Oklahoma, hoping to make his living as a fulltime writer. After a New York City sojourn, Todd returned to Oklahoma in 1936 and took up residence with his family in Atoka. Probably after publishing his last novel in 1941, Todd moved to Philadelphia, where he worked as an advertising copy writer throughout the 1940s.[40] In the 1950s he taught for about five years at schools in Maryland and Virginia, before returning to live in Atoka around 1955.

Todd's family ties clearly were binding. Although as a student and teacher at the University of Oklahoma Todd resided for fifteen years (1920 to 1935) at Norman, some hundred miles distant from Atoka, he wrote and visited his family frequently (like many a college student after him he brought his laundry back with him when he visited). After Sam Downing's death in 1954, Todd, never having married, returned to the family home in Atoka to live with his octogenarian mother. After Maud Downing's death at the age of 93 in 1965, Todd continued to reside at the family home until his own death in 1974. Thus about

39 ASM to RSD, 30 March 1933; Todd Downing to Ruth Shields Downing, [?] March 1933.

40 Gibson, *Oklahoma*, 225.

fifty-five of Todd's seventy-one years on earth were spent in Oklahoma, forty or so of these in the old Downing home at Atoka. Todd lived alone in the house for less than a decade.

Surviving family correspondence makes clear that Todd had close relationships with his father, mother, grandmother and sister. His relations with more distant family members and with the people of Atoka itself seem more ambiguous, however. No doubt like many another creatively gifted individual coming from a small town environment, Todd seems to have had something of a love-hate relationship with his native ground. To be sure, in the scarce surviving correspondence of Todd's that we have, he never refers to Atoka with the corrosiveness that characterizes Willa Cather's embittered, alcoholic Kansas lawyer Jim Laird in her story "The Sculptor's Funeral" (1905), who condemns the place of his nativity, Sand City, as a "hog-wallow" and a "dead little Western town." Yet Todd did complain in 1939 that he had come to be "rather at odds with Atoka and all it represents" (see below).[41]

Acrimony seems not to have characterized Todd's relationship with his own immediate family. Indeed, the Downings by all appearances were an exceptionally tightly-knit family, well aware that they occupied a position of uncommon responsibility and trust in Atoka. We have already seen the pride Todd expressed for his father's standing as a leader within the Choctaw Nation. Certainly the Downings, though not rich, were among the most economically prosperous of Atoka families, whether indigenous American or not. Using home ownership and home value as criteria, in 1930 the Sam and Maud Downing household was in the

41 Willa Cather, "The Sculptor's Funeral," in Robert K. Miller, ed., *Great Short Works of Willa Cather* (New York: HarperCollins, 1993), 46-47. A more recent manifestation of Willa Cather's attitude is found in the Paul Simon song "My Little Town" (1975). "And after it rains there's a rainbow/But all of the colors are black/It's not that the colors aren't there/It's just imagination they lack/Everything's the same back . . . in my little town," runs part of the first verse. "Nothing but the dead and dying back in my little town," runs the chorus.

top 10% of Atoka's nearly 500 households in terms of wealth. Among 1930 Atoka households with Native American members, which accounted for about 12% of Atoka households that year, the Downing house was surpassed in value only by those of Keturah Leflore, mixed-blood widow of the late mixed-blood merchant Louis Campbell LeFlore (a great nephew of the famed antebellum Mississippi Choctaw principal chief Greenwood LeFlore), and wealthy attorney Joseph G. Ralls, whose wife Eva Standley was a daughter of the prominent mixed-blood Confederate veteran Captain James Stirman Standley. Even among the total population of Atoka, there were only some two dozen households with homes that surpassed the Downing house in monetary value.[42]

One of the families the Downings regularly socialized with in the 1930s was the Memmingers, consisting of mother Margaret Burrows Memminger and her adult children Charles and Martha. The Memmingers shared the Downing's religious faith, Presbyterianism, if not their political persuasion, the Memmingers being Democrats. Margaret Memminger was the widow of Thomas F. Memminger, president of the Atoka State Bank for over twenty years and a three-term Oklahoma state senator. Like Awilda Miller's husband, Daniel, Thomas Memminger was of German heritage and as a younger man had been a bank cashier in another state (Nebraska rather than Iowa). However, Thomas Memminger's path to success had never been obstructed by the dual pitfalls of criminality and penal servitude. The younger male Memminger, Charles, was, like Todd, a University of Oklahoma graduate (class of 1914). Like his father, Charles Memminger was elected to the Oklahoma state senate, serving one term from 1931 to 1935.[43]

42 Joseph B. Thoburn, *A Standard History of Oklahoma*, Vol. 6 (Chicago and New York: The American Historical Society, 1916), 1503; "Necrology," *Chronicles of Oklahoma*, Vol. 10, No. 4 (December 1932): 615-617; 1930 United States Census, Oklahoma, Atoka County.

43 "Necrology," *Chronicles of Oklahoma* 5 (Sept. 1927): 359-360, Oklahoma Historical Society's Chronicles of Oklahoma, at http://digital.library.okstate.edu/Chronicles/v005/v005p348.html.

Despite the fact that the Downing and the Memminger families regularly socialized with each other, there seems to have been something of a feeling on the part of the Downings that the wealthier Memmingers put on airs. In her letters Awilda always refers to Charles Memminger as "Senator," seemingly somewhat satirically. On two occasions in 1931 Awilda wrote about having escaped attendance at functions held at Mrs. Memminger's house. "[Cousin] Nettie and Mamma are going to [the] Memmingers this afternoon to an old-fashioned Rook Party," Awilda wrote Ruth in January, "So thankful I do not have to go." In October she informed Ruth with relief that a ladies club meeting at the home of Mrs. Memminger (president of the ladies club) had been postponed. "Mamma & I dreaded it as [the Memmingers] have been in California all summer, and we would have had to listen to [daughter] Martha's recital of where they had been and what they had seen, with *views* to 'ooh & ah' over. She is worse & more of it, since Charles is Senator Memminger."[44]

Though they may not have quite kept up with the Memmingers, the Downings unquestionably played important parts in Atoka affairs, on both institutional and purely personal levels. Like Mrs. Memminger, Maud Downing was quite active in the Presbyterian Church. On one occasion when Maud taught a Sunday school class the chosen lesson was Christ healing the centurion's servant (one of two miracles Christ performed for a Gentile). "A Gentile showing such great faith," approvingly noted Awilda in a letter to Ruth, where she discussed Maud's lesson. "Being fair to other races was one point strongly stressed." Whether or not such a precept sank in with Maud's Sunday school students, inclusive messages of racial and ethnic tolerance were never wasted on Todd and Ruth.[45]

When at the height of the Great Depression in January 1931 the American Red Cross organized a massive relief effort to help the multitudes across the country in desperate need of

44 ASM to RSD, [?] January, 21 October 1931.
45 ASM to RSD, 16 November 1930.

assistance, both Sam and Maud Downing threw themselves into the local effort in Atoka. "Our relief work began yesterday," Awilda wrote Ruth on January 21. "First Aid from Red Cross. . . . Mamma was down all afternoon. It is so stupendous they work in relays. She has to go again next Tuesday, for all day. They could not care for half the people." Three weeks later, Awilda expressed concern to Ruth that "Dad will be sick with this rush and turmoil, distributing the Red Cross relief. It is now four o'clock. Mamma has just returned from town. As Dad did not come home at noon, she went up there where they are dispensing the goods, to tell him of some phone messages. They were so crowded with applicants she could scarcely push her way through the crowd."[46]

The Downings became personally involved with people in need of help. Awilda related to Ruth the case of the family of Jesse James Russell and his wife Lillie, who the previous year had lived down the street from the Downings. Hearing that Russell, a house carpenter, was sick and knowing that there were eight children in the family to support, Awilda went through all the storage boxes in the house until she "found quite a bundle of material I knew [the Russells] could use for the children's clothes." She asked Maud to take them downtown to the family's new house. When Maud arrived she found that the father was very sick indeed and that the Downing family physician, Dr. Fulton, had only just rushed the eldest son to the larger town of McAlester for an appendectomy. Discovering that the parents "had made no application at [Red Cross] headquarters for aid" and feeling certain the family badly needed it, Awilda and Maud persuaded Sam to personally visit the Russells and size up the situation. When Sam talked with Mrs. Russell, the distraught woman "broke down and cried," Awilda reported. "She said they had never had to ask for help, 'But oh! Mr. Downing we have absolutely nothing in the house but a little flour.' So Dad took her up to the [Red Cross] rooms and had her make out a list. In the

46 ASM to RSD, 21 January, 14 February 1931.

meantime I had made a large kettle of soup with plenty of everything in it, and sent it over." Added the obviously fretted Awilda: "You never saw these things in Atoka."[47]

The Downing family itself claimed one member who during the Depression went on Red Cross Relief, Sam's older sister Mary. While Sam's younger sister Martha had made a good marriage when, as a young and attractive schoolteacher, she wed Leroy Long, an up-and-coming young doctor appointed Dean of the University of Oklahoma Medical School in 1916, Mary had not done nearly so well. Born in 1870, Mary in 1892 married Charles Robert Anglin, nearly twenty years her senior. Lengthy correspondence from 1901 to 1904 between Charles Anglin and the Department of Interior over his rights as a member by marriage of the Choctaw Nation (or perhaps the Chickasaw Nation) suggests a certain economic anxiety on his part. By 1930, Mary, now a widow, lived alone in a poorer section of Atoka. The Downings worried about Mary, but felt the responsibility of aiding her financially properly rested with Sam's wealthy sister Martha. Mentioning in a letter to Ruth that Martha had shown up for a visit at the Downing house bedecked in a fur coat, Awilda added:

47 ASM to RSD, 2 February 1931. Lisa Hatchell, a granddaughter of Lillie Russell, explains that her grandmother was twice married. Jesse James Russell was her second husband. Her first husband, who was twenty years older than she and died in 1915 at the age of forty-nine, had children from a prior marriage, so that in 1931 there were offspring from three different marriages in the Russell household. As Lisa Hatchell relates, it was her father Garland Russell (b. 1915) who had to have the appendectomy. After Garland's appendix burst "it was so bad that they put him in a ward with all the dying people including TB patients and left him there to die. He stayed there several months and finally did recover." Compounding the family's problems, Garland's stepfather Jesse James Russell was, according to Garland, an abusive drunkard. Recalls Lisa Hatchell: "Dad said Mr. Russell would come home drunk and beat him up. Nobody else, just him for some reason. [Dad] said he would hide away in the outhouse or wherever he could until Mr. Russell passed out. Dad said they had to hunt around if they wanted any meat to eat and they ate all kinds, squirrel, etc., whatever they could catch." Lisa Hatchell to Curtis Evans, 23 July 2012.

"I do wonder if she ever sends Mary any money." Mary's name, Awilda pointedly noted, had appeared "on the list for Red Cross aid."[48]

The problem of Mary's need and Martha's inaction finally came to a head in 1934. In September of that year, Awilda reported to Ruth, Sam went to see Martha and "gave her a needed talking to" about Mary's plight. Martha had promised Sam the previous year that "she would see that Mary had what she needed," reported Awilda, but "had done absolutely nothing" for her older sister. "We know Mary is a trial," allowed Awilda, "but just now Martha is the one to look after her. [I] am sure her Leroy would if he knew [about] it." Noting that Martha had announced she was contemplating a trip to New York City, Awilda admonished: "I thought [she might] take the money for the [New York City] trip and send [it] to Mary *as she needed it*, not all in a lump [sum], as it would soon be gone." Mary lived on for ten more years, so presumably received some help from some Downing family quarter.[49]

To be sure, Todd, enmeshed during these years in the fabric of university life, often was absent from Atoka on the occasions discussed above, yet he did try to write once a week when school was in session and he returned home frequently. There seems no question but that the fundamental empathy and decency that characterized the Downing family left its mark on Todd and his writing. For Todd the family home was a welcoming and nurturing environment, where he could work hard on a mystery novel or relax by sitting down at the bridge table to play anagrams (his parents' favorite game) or to help piece together one of the jigsaw puzzles regularly sent to the family as gifts from Todd's Aunt Martha. On cold Sunday evenings at the Downing house

48 ASM to RSD, 14 February 1931. Concerning Martha Downing Long and her fur coat, Awilda wrote in full: "Poor Aunt Martha. She long talked of the fur coat you may have heard about, [and it] has been a 'White Elephant.' We have not had any weather where one needs such a garment. She wore it to Denison, stopping here for a few moments. [W]e saw it and of course it is a beautiful garment—more becoming than I expected it to be." Ibid.

49 ASM to RSD, 20 September 1934.

Todd enjoyed dinners of hot tamales—his favorite dish, Awilda reported, all through the winter of 1929.[50]

The family worried about Todd when he traveled far from hearth and home. When Todd took one of his tour parties down to Mexico in 1930, there was concern in Atoka, given Mexico's instability and the recent horrific Cristero War (1926-1929). "We have not heard a word from Brother since he left, except a few words on a card mailed at San Antonio," Awilda wrote Ruth. "[W]e hoped for another card before this. . . . Of course Mamma will worry and Dad is sure the Bandits have them all captive somewhere." Eventually word from Todd came, causing much relief for Maud, "who was sure he was sick," and for Sam, "who was sure the Bandits had the whole party captive." (Awilda insisted that she contrastingly had maintained her equanimity about the whole situation, remembering that Todd had told them not to worry and that correspondence would be slow in coming.)[51]

Todd and Ruth in turn seem to have been solicitous about their family elders. Awilda, for example, was personally touched by both Ruth and Todd when she received from Ruth a Christmas gift of a robe, over which Todd made a great fuss. "I have just come downstairs, where I have been admiring the beautiful robe which came last evening. I never had a more lovely or appropriate gift. Too lovely for an old lady to be wearing. Todd voiced his admiration, you know how he loves warm, bright colors. . . . I can hardly wait till I can get over to show it to Aunt Retta and Cousin Nettie." Several weeks later a gratified Awilda wrote that not only had Aunt Retta seen and commended the robe, but that Todd had continued to praise it. "I had to wear it every evening while Todd was at home. He is an unusual boy to care what Grandmother wears."[52]

Awilda lauded her grandchildren's career accomplishments, though there may been have some disappointment on the part of the family with Ruth's and Todd's social lives. "We are proud of you

50 ASM to RSD, 7 July 1930, 9 March, 1 November 1933.

51 ASM to RSD, 7 July 1930, [?] July 1930.

52 ASM to RSD, 30 (?) December 1930, 21 January 1931.

and what you are doing," Awilda wrote Ruth concerning Ruth's graduate work at Columbia University, "but [I] am afraid Mamma has never quite gotten over her disappointment that you and Mr. Ash agreed to disagree, or whatever it was that went wrong. She has always said she was afraid Todd had something to do with it. But that is all past long ago, and you are no doubt happier in the work you are doing." Mention occasionally is made in Awilda's letters of Todd "escorting" a young woman somewhere in Norman, but nothing ever seemed to come of it. Todd was "invited to a supper at the Pages," Awilda wrote Ruth in 1931. "From the name of the guests we are sure he had to take Grace Ray [an assistant journalism professor at OU who also reviewed western novels for the *Daily Oklahoman*]. And he is so tired of escorting her anywhere, poor boy." When the family learned that OU's new anthropology professor, Forrest E. Clements (1900-1970), was about Todd's age, they were pleased, thinking he might provide Todd fellowship. "Todd has had to be associated so long with men old enough to be his father," Awilda complained.[53]

Whatever disappointment was felt in the family over Todd's not developing a serious romantic relationship with some nice Norman girl, pride was taken in Todd's writing, as it was taken in Ruth's Colombia University graduate education and metropolitan social work. Both Todd and Ruth were proving not only exceptional Atokans, but exceptional Oklahomans. In the 1930s, Todd with his mystery novels became one of Oklahoma's most prominent writers, receiving much favorable attention from the *Daily Oklahoman*, the state's leading newspaper, not to mention praise in major American papers like the *New York Times*.

53 ASM to RD, 28 September 1930, 14 February 1931. Todd in fact become friends with Clements. He lent Clements a Harry Stephen Keeler detective novel he reviewed (see p. 175) and Clements' cat inspired Todd's 1934 detective novel *The Cat Screams* (see p. 93). Ruth Downing had been a member at OU of Delta Delta Delta sorority and "one of the most popular girls in school," reported the *Daily Oklahoman*. Asked by the newspaper interviewer, "What about a home, and all that sort of thing?" Ruth replied: "I might think about that later, but just now my interest is almost wholly centered in my job." *Daily Oklahoman*, 3 October 1932, 2.

Todd's rise to prominence as a mystery writer owed much, of course, to his own talent and drive, but it also owed something to one of his older colleagues in the University of Oklahoma modern languages department, Kenneth Carlisle Kaufman (1887-1945). Born in Leon, Kansas, Kenneth C. Kaufman moved with his family to Oklahoma in 1898. After graduating from Southwestern State Teachers College, Kaufman earned B.A. and M.A. degrees from the University of Oklahoma in 1916 and 1919, respectively. He headed the foreign languages department at Central High School, Oklahoma City, for a decade before joining the University of Oklahoma modern languages faculty in 1929. Although Kenneth Kaufman only became a full professor at OU in 1937 and the chairman of the modern languages department in 1942, but three years before his death, in the 1930s he rapidly established himself as one of the most popular and well-known OU professors, serving both as the managing editor of the university sponsored *Books Abroad* and, between 1932 and 1945, as literary editor of the *Daily Oklahoman*.[54]

Since 1927 Todd had been writing reviews and serving as advertising editor for *Books Abroad*, a journal devoted to the works of foreign authors, and thus he was a staff member of a few years standing when Kenneth Kaufman became managing editor. From 1928 to 1930, Kaufman had a column of poetry and musings in the *Daily Oklahoman*, "Bittersweet and Sandburs"; and beginning in 1930 both he and Todd began reviewing books, including mysteries, for the newspaper. In the 1930/31 school year, Todd, tired of boarding houses, took up residence with Kenneth C. Kaufman and his family ("Todd is looking forward with great pleasure to his home with the Kaufmans," Awilda wrote Ruth on August 24, 1930), and it seems to have been at this time that his thoughts first turned toward writing mystery fiction. Although in addition to books on Latin America Todd reviewed over two dozen mysteries in 1931, it was not until 1932, when Professor Kaufman became the *Daily Oklahoman* literary editor, that

54 *Daily Oklahoman*, 30 April 1945, 1, 28 December 1947, 58.

Todd's "Clues and Corpses" column was started. Further, it was in the summer of 1931—when his Mexican tour was abruptly canceled due to the fatal shooting of two Mexican college students at Ardmore, Oklahoma, by a local deputy sheriff—that Todd, with time on his hands and the active encouragement of Professor Kaufman, began writing a mystery novel. Speaking of Todd in 1935, after the novelist had resigned his instructorship and temporarily moved to New York City, Professor Kaufman later recalled: "Somewhat to his regret he cannot claim to have had the irresistible urge to write which is supposed to spur on embryo authors. On the contrary, it took the disruption of a tourist party with consequent enforced stay in the proximity of a typewriter, combined with the counsel of the editor of this page, to turn his thoughts in the direction of fiction."[55]

55 ASM to RSD, 24 August 1930; *Daily Oklahoman*, 25 August 1935, 49. James Cox seems to suggest Todd Downing began writing detective novels as a sort of protest over the Ardmore shootings. "Downing chose to respond [to the Ardmore shootings] in a genre that guaranteed . . . the U. S. citizens that perpetrate crimes against Mexican nationals—indigenous and nonindigenous—always face punishment." Cox, *Red Land*, 31, 61-62. I think this interpretation goes beyond the actual evidence we have, though I have little doubt Todd faulted the deputy sheriff for the killings of the Mexican youths. Prosaically, however, it appears that Todd began writing a detective novel the summer of the Ardmore shootings simply because his Mexican trip was canceled and he had time on his hands. Concerning Todd's boarding house life prior to moving in with the Kaufmans, see a May 1930 letter by Awilda, composed during a visit she and Maud made to Norman, where they stayed at Todd's boarding house. "This has been such an unsettled day. We were awakened too early for one thing," Awilda complained. "Last night was the 'Tornado' (whatever that is) and Tom Losey did not get home till after 5 am. Of course he made all the noise imaginable, from the slamming of the front door and all the others leading to his room to dropping one 11 ½ shoe after another on the floor, and so on, till Mamma & I were both wide awake. As the sun was almost up by that time we could not get back to sleep. One by one we found our way to the breakfast table for our coffee and toast. Todd was last . . . [and] while he was eating Mrs. Marriott came downstairs to borrow a few potatoes. When she discovered [Todd] she walked right on in for a visit. Mamma was dressing for church, [and] as I have a blister on one heel she was going alone. When Todd heard that, he jumped up and made for the bathroom, telling her to wait and he would go with her. Mrs. M. went back upstairs, with her potatoes." ASM to RSD, 11 May 1930.

Todd spent his 1931 Christmas break at the family home in Atoka. By this time, he had completed his first novel, submitted it to a publisher and started writing another mystery tale. "Wish you could see us here in the sitting room," Awilda wrote Ruth on December 28, "Dad at [the] library table. Todd stretched out on the couch writing on a book propped up against his knees. Mamma and I on each side [of the] card table . . . writing [letters to you]." The family all hoped that "Todd will soon have his Book accepted," Awilda noted.[56]

That hope had gone unfulfilled by March, causing some concern in the family. By this time Todd apparently had been turned down by at least one publisher. "Sometimes I wish he had never started writing," a concerned Awilda wrote Ruth. "He worked so hard last summer—would look wild-eyed, when he did stop—and after all [that] he may not arrive." Conceding that Todd "seems to enjoy [writing], and it is his affair," Awilda nevertheless disliked that when working on a book Todd ate little, seemingly subsisting on coffee and cigarettes. When Todd's Cousin Leroy Long II—like his distinguished father a doctor—in company with his wife visited the Downing family at Atoka, the family took the opportunity to question him about Todd's physical health. Leroy reported that in his view Todd's family would have no need at all to worry about Todd would Todd but stick to the diet he, Leroy, had prescribed for him, as well as "drink less, or no, coffee and discard to some extent cigarettes." Avowed Awilda about the cigarettes: "Good advice in my opinion. I only wish they would put a large Tax on them."[57]

Reflecting her concern over Todd's overwork and mental stress, Awilda in one letter directed a little acerbic commentary at the people she deemed to be Todd's artistic instigators, the Kaufman family: "I think [the] Kaufmans have started him along this [writing] line. You know they are all so Literary. . . . [W]e will extract a promise from [Todd] to steer clear of Katherine's poetry."

56 ASM to RSD, 28 December 1931.

57 ASM to RSD, 13 March 1932; [?] December 1934. A cigarette tax passed by the Oklahoma legislature and signed by Governor Murray was defeated by referendum in 1933. Bryant, *Alfalfa Bill*, 241.

(Katherine, the would-be poetess sardonically mentioned here, was the Kaufman's daughter; she later married Ralph Hudson, the Oklahoma State Librarian.)[58]

By May 1932, complained Awilda, Todd's book (or "Book" as she always wrote it) still had not been accepted. Todd's proud grandmother defiantly noted that Todd had returned home from OU, bringing with him a bunch of detective novels that he had reviewed for the *Daily Oklahoman*, and those tales were "not half as good as his." Awilda could not say enough about the diligence Todd had exhibited the last year, taking on as he did "classwork, *Books Abroad*, Literary Reviews and Mystery Stories." She was pleased to note too that he seemed to have recovered his equanimity and was no longer looking wild-eyed. In July, Todd conducted another OU tour party in Mexico, this one including President and Mrs. Bizzell, but he probably completed his second mystery manuscript by August.[59]

Finally, in May 1933, word came that Todd's second manuscript, *Murder on Tour*, had been accepted by a publisher, G. P. Putnam's Sons. Like all but one of the Todd Downing detective novels, *Murder on Tour* is set in Mexico. From the title alone, it should be clear that Todd had followed the maxim "write what you know," setting the novel amidst an American tour group seeing the sights in Mexico, like the groups he himself had led for four summers. *Murder on Tour* also introduced Todd's by far most important series detective, customs agent Hugh Rennert, who would appear in seven of Todd's nine novels and his sole novella.

"Don't expect a very coherent letter from me today, but I have some news to tell you," a jubilant Todd wrote Ruth. "A letter from my agent tells me that she has sold one of my books to G. P. Putnam's Sons [*Murder on Tour*]. . . . There's no need to tell you how I am floating around in the clouds." Later that month in the

58 ASM to RSD, 13 March 1932.

59 ASM to RSD, 1 May 1932; In late July the *Daily Oklahoman* reported that Todd had returned home from Mexico (31 July 1932, 45). This was Todd's fourth partial summer spent in Mexico with an OU tour group and his third as tour group director. *Daily Oklahoman*, 8 June 1932, 3.

pages of the *Daily Oklahoman* Kenneth Kaufmann himself made the exciting announcement of Todd's literary breakthrough:

> Add one to the already imposing list of Oklahoma literati who have arrived. Todd Downing, Oklahoma university instructor in modern languages, who is probably Oklahoma's foremost authority on Mexico and things Mexican, and who passes stern if slightly sardonic judgment on current mystery fiction from the Olympian seat of "Clues and Corpses" on this page, has just sold to G. P. Putnam's Sons a detective story of his own, *Murder on Tour.*[60]

In August Professor Kaufman received from Putnam's a review copy of *Murder on Tour* and raved the book. In addition to its ingenious, suspenseful plot, declared Kaufman, *Murder on Tour* was graced by "a wonderfully incisive, economical style and a wonderfully impressive atmosphere of the Mexican setting." In quite an outburst of enthusiasm for his younger colleague's work, Kaufman opined that were Todd Downing to maintain the quality of *Murder on Tour* with his subsequent output "his name will someday rank with that of S. S. Van Dine, Mary Roberts Rinehart and Agatha Christie." To be sure, it was to be expected that a novel by Todd Downing would be well-received in this particular quarter, but *Murder on Tour* also received considerable commendation from the *New York Times Book Review*, which proclaimed the tale a "well fashioned baffler" with "characterization . . . contrived with unusual skill." With such praise as this, Todd Downing was on his way.[61]

In his letter to his sister Todd noted that after publication of *Murder on Tour* in September 1933, Putnam's desired from him "two books a year hereafter." This claim was confirmed in the *Daily Oklahoman* by Kenneth Kaufman, who in his review of *Murder on Tour* noted that "Mr. Downing is under contract to write

60 Todd Downing to Ruth Shields Downing, undated [May 1933?]; "Todd Downing is Latest to Arrive," *Daily Oklahoman*, 28 May 1933, 42.

61 *Daily Oklahoman*, 20 August 1933, 36; *New York Times Book Review*, 20 August 1933.

two detective stories a year for Putnam's." Kaufman added further that in a letter sent to him earlier in the summer, Putnam's president "asserted that he intends to make Todd Downing's name a household word."[62]

Despite Putnam's seeming confidence in Todd and the excellent reviews *Murder on Tour* received, however, Todd's second detective novel, *The Cat Screams*, was published the next year, in September 1934, by another concern, Doubleday, Doran's "Crime Club." For Todd this was a definite step up: Doubleday, Doran and another firm, Dodd, Mead, were the great American war horses of crime fiction publishing, with an array of notable mystery writers in their stables, such as Agatha Christie, Margery Allingham, R. Austin Freeman and Freeman Wills Crofts. The question remains, however, how Todd managed to get out from his contract with Putnam's. In my view there may have been a conflict between the author and his publisher over what was to be Todd's second detective novel for Putnam's. Todd intended his second book to be titled *Murder in Monterrey*.[63] Since *The Cat Screams* takes place not in Monterrey but in Taxco, obviously it cannot be the book titled *Murder in Monterrey*. However, Todd's final published work of mystery fiction, the Hugh Rennert novella *The Shadowless Hour*, takes place in Monterrey and is likely the work that Todd originally intended to publish as *Murder in Monterrey* (see page 121 for further discussion of this matter).

However Todd came to switch publishers, he must have been pleased indeed with the reception the manuscript of *The Cat Screams* received from Doubleday, Doran. According to Todd's new publisher, *The Cat Screams* "was accepted, the contract for it was signed and the book was on the presses twenty-four hours after the manuscript had been read." Additionally, Doubleday,

62 Todd Downing to Ruth Shields Downing, [?] May 1932; *Daily Oklahoman*, 20 August 1933, 36.

63 Todd Downing to Ruth Shields Downing, [May 1933?]; *Daily O'Collegian*, 17 September 1933, 3. On Doubleday, Doran, see See Ellen Nehr, *The Doubleday Crime Club Compendium, 1928-1991* (Martinez, CA: Offspring Press, 1992).

Doran chose *The Cat Screams* as its Crime Club Selection of the Month, an honor only rarely afforded a writer newly acquired by the publisher. In a notably enthusiastic book blurb, Doubleday, Doran praised the author of *The Cat Screams* as a top flight "creator of atmosphere, suspense, and horror" and declared that "stylistically, he is far superior to the average mystery writer."[64] Surely if the reception Todd got from Putnam's for *Murder on Tour* had Todd "floating around in the clouds," Doubleday, Doran's reaction to *The Cat Screams* must have sent him rocketing past the stratosphere. Between 1934 and 1941 Doubleday, Doran would publish eight Todd Downing detective novels, his entire output aside from *Murder on Tour*.

Adapted for stage performance at the Martin Beck Theater in Manhattan in 1942 and reprinted in paperback three years later by Popular Library in 1945, *The Cat Screams* was the best known Todd Downing detective novel; however, Todd's next mystery tale, *Vultures in the Sky*, published by Doubleday, Doran in April 1935, arguably was his best-reviewed work of fiction. Naturally Kenneth Kaufman lavishly praised the tale in the *Daily Oklahoman*: "A highly satisfying maze of clues, each with its logical justification, and all so neatly hidden that it takes a mild form of genius to beat the detective to it. And a plentiful injection of that Mexican atmosphere—sinister, matter-of-fact in the face of death, and yet not melancholy—which is Todd Downing's chief distinction as a mystery writer." Kaufman was again substantially echoed by the *New York Times Book Review*, which praised *Vultures in the Sky* as "tensely dramatic."[65]

In contrast with 1934 Todd actually managed to produce two detective novels in 1935, following *Vultures in the Sky* in April with *Murder on the Tropic* in December. Likely this feat was attainable for Todd because he resigned from the University of Oklahoma faculty at the end of the spring semester, in order to

64 *New York Times Book Review (NYTBR)*, 18 August 1934; Todd Downing, *The Cat Screams* (New York: Doubleday, Doran, 1934).

65 *NYTBR*, 16 June 1942, 7 April 1935; *Daily Oklahoman*, 7 April 1935, 51.

devote himself fulltime to writing. He left Oklahoma in August "for an indefinite stay" in New York City, hoping to establish contacts for his writing career there. He returned to his native state in 1936, but never again would he teach at the University of Oklahoma. Instead, he settled back in at the family home in Atoka. By 1939, Todd's friends back in the OU community were referring to him as "the Hermit of Boggy Creek" (this in reference to Muddy Boggy Creek, which runs by Atoka). "I don't know what Todd does [in Atoka] besides wait for watermelon time to roll around," joked Kenneth Kaufman in the *Daily Oklahoman*. However, Todd did occasionally emerge from his rural redoubt to appear at writers' conferences held at the University of Oklahoma and Oklahoma State University, where he spoke about the art of mystery writing.[66]

Since *Murder on the Tropic* appeared in December 1935, it likely was written by Todd in New York City. With this latest effort Kenneth Kaufman offered his usual praise for a novel by Todd Downing, "Oklahoma Indian and former university teacher." Kaufman was particularly pleased with the high level of suspense maintained by Downing in *Tropic*, noting that the tale was "replete with rattlesnakes, a scion of a Mexican hidalgo family rubbed out by revolution, yellow marigolds, which are, in Mexico, the flower of death, and other horrors too numerous to mention." The *New York Times Book Review* avowed that *Tropic*'s "complications are guaranteed to keep the reader interested and greatly puzzled" and the *Saturday Review* commended the novel's "exotic background, deep-laid and devilish plot, interesting people" and satisfying dénouement, before finally concluding "muy bien!"[67]

In 1936 only one Todd Downing detective novel, *The Case of the Unconquered Sisters*, appeared, in August of that year. "The Mexican atmosphere is played up with a skill which could come only from a long acquaintance with and a true understanding of

66 *Daily Oklahoman*, 25 August 1935, 49; "Downing Likes Oklahoma But Not For Settings," *Daily O'Collegian*, 21 October 1937, 1; "Bullets to Whine on State Literary Fronts," *Daily Oklahoman*, 29 January 1939, 63.

67 *Daily Oklahoman*, 8 December 1935, 59; *NYTBR*, 8 December 1935.

our sister republic below the Rio Grande," pronounced Kenneth Kaufman. For its part the *Saturday Review* praised the novel for its "satisfactorily sinister blend of Mexican lore and scenery, swift action, and . . . class A sleuthing."[68]

Todd in 1937 was once again able to manage two detective novels, *The Last Trumpet* and *Night over Mexico*, published by Doubleday, Doran in June and October, respectively. Kenneth Kaufman deemed the first of the 1937 novels, *The Last Trumpet*, the best of all his former colleague's tales. Kaufman pugnaciously concluded of *Trumpet*: "If you don't like this one, you're pretty hopeless." The *Saturday Review* agreed that the novel was "enjoyable," though it carped that the solution was "slightly dubious" (in this latter assessment the *New York Times Book Review* concurred). As for *Night over Mexico*, this novel, Hugh Rennert's swan song, was the best-reviewed Downing detective novel since *Vultures in the Sky*. Kenneth Kaufman declared of *Night over Mexico* that "as far as atmosphere, tensity, and ingenious solution are concerned, this is one of Todd Downing's best." The *Saturday Review* more than shared Kaufman's enthusiasm for the novel, giving it a superlative capsule review: "Summing Up: Actions and suspense at concert pitch throughout, characterization vivid, background exotic, method and motive of murder unique. Verdict: Excellent." The *New York Times Book Review* expressed similar enthusiasm for the novel, concluding that "Downing has again shown us that Mexico, in the hands of one who knows it, makes an excellent background for a mystery story."[69]

During this period Todd had the gratification as well of seeing his books published in Europe, specifically in England, Italy, Germany and Sweden. English reviewers were as impressed with Todd's crime fiction as Americans. Edward Powys Mathers, who reviewed mysteries (and devised crossword puzzles) under the name "Torquemada" and was one of the most incisive critics of

68 *Daily Oklahoman*, 30 August 1936, 61; *Saturday Review*, 15 August 1936, 18.

69 *Daily Oklahoman*, 6 June 1937, 73, 1 October 1937, 73; *NYTBR*, 30 May 1937, 31 October 1937; *Saturday Review*, 19 June 1937, 16, 23 October 1937, 24.

the genre in the 1930s, greatly admired Todd's work. After reading *Vultures in the Sky*, Mathers pronounced: "It is satisfactory to find our suspicion engendered by *The Cat Screams*, that Mr. Downing is a born detective story writer, amply confirmed by *Vultures in the Sky*." The novel was so perfectly composed Mathers could but conclude that as a detective novelist Todd was "born and not made."[70]

After bidding adios to his series detective Hugh Rennert, Todd produced only two more detective novels, *Death under the Moonflower* (1938) and *The Lazy Lawrence Murders* (1941). Both of these tales, which feature a new series detective, south Texas sheriff Peter Bounty (introduced in *The Last Trumpet*), are disappointing and tended to receive more mediocre reviews (Kenneth Kaufman of course excepted). Todd in the late 1930s seems to have been seized by indecision about where he wanted to go with his mystery fiction. It may be that he was tempted as early as 1938 to drop it altogether, in favor of more "serious" literary endeavors. In 1939 Todd produced no book at all, probably because he was researching and writing the work he would see as his crowning achievement, his non-fiction study of Mexico, *The Mexican Earth*. Published in August 1940, the book was extremely well-received by reviewers. Most impressively, the book received a full-page spread in the *New York Times Book Review*, where the famed Harvard anthropologist Philip Ainsworth Means handsomely praised it:

> If I had been asked a few days ago whether or not it would be possible to put within the covers of a not large volume the essentials of Mexican history from the earliest times to the present, and to add thereto a penetrating, sympathetic and convincing analysis of the problems which have long beset the Mexican people, I would have said "No"

70 *London Observer*, 19 January 1936, 6. One hopes Todd saw this review!

> unhesitatingly. Yet Mr. Downing has done all that, and more."[71]

While researching and writing *The Mexican Earth* Todd in 1939 had to deal with the death, at the age of 89, of his Nanna Miller in February, as well as some of the negative feelings he had about his family relations and his home town that the immediate aftermath of her death brought to surface. Todd was present at the Downing house in Atoka when Awilda had a stroke on Wednesday, February 1. "We found her lying on the floor of her room, unconscious, after lunch," Todd wrote Ruth on Sunday, February 5. Awilda died on Monday, never having regained consciousness.[72]

In the two letters Todd wrote Ruth at this time, he could not contain feelings of exasperation with some of his relations and the town of Atoka in general. His greatest expressed concern was for his mother, who he felt was being more harassed than helped by the invasion of a vanguard of various kinsfolk and a massed phalanx of local Atokans:

> Mamma is taking it better than I would have thought possible. . . . We are trying to keep Aunt Nettie from knowing, because she would be right down and would only be in the way. In fact, we would be better off if so many people weren't offering to help. Mrs. Bond seems to spend most of her time here, asking if there isn't something she can do. And Aunt Martha is in the offing all the time. . . . [I]t wouldn't surprise me to see her driving up any minute.[73]

On Thursday, after the funeral, Todd again wrote Ruth, giving vent to his feelings of frustration with the "well meaning"

71 *Saturday Review*, 17 August 1940, 18; *NYTBR*, 31 March 1940.

72 Todd Downing to Ruth Shields Downing, 5 February 1939.

73 Ibid.

behavior over the last few days of relations and townspeople. He admitted that of late years he "had been rather at odds with Atoka and all it represents," so that "it did me good to see everyone manifesting kindness to us and regard for Nanna. And when I say everyone in town, I mean it almost literally [among Awilda Miller's pallbearers, it should be noted, were the Atoka mayor, the Atoka postmaster, the former Atoka county treasurer and a retired state district court judge]." Yet, Todd bluntly added, "They overdid it." Launched on the wings of recrimination, Todd took full flight:

> I had always known people called but had no idea they made a weekend out of it. They began coming about 8 o'clock Tuesday morning and from that time until last night the house was packed. The Presbyterian women were all here all the time, of course, and sent in all our meals. But they stayed and ate and the house simply rocked with their talk, talk, talk. And people came who had no earthly reason to that I could see. . . . [T]he Fains came about 7 Tuesday night and stayed until almost midnight, talking of nothing but Mrs. Fain's leg. I got complete [sic] disgusted with the whole performance and finally made Mamma stay upstairs and see no one.[74]

Todd then launched into a litany against his two formidable female relatives, "Aunt" Nettie Robb McLaughlin, evidently his mother's second cousin, and Aunt Martha Downing Long, his father's younger sister, reserving a rhetorical shaft for his mother's brother, Max:

> Aunt Nettie came Tuesday morning and is still here, having the time of her life. I don't know

74 Todd Downing to Ruth Shields Downing, 9 February 1939.

> whether I can hold myself in much longer or not and she seems to be going to remain for a long, long time. Aunt Martha arrived about 2:30 Tuesday afternoon, with a carload of food and flowers. That would have been fine if it hadn't been for Aunt Nettie. You can imagine the continual tension with those two contending for first place in the house. Aunt Nettie was always drawing Mamma and Dad and me into dark corners and whispering, "I know Martha means all right, but if she would only quit talking a while." Then Aunt Martha would very pointedly shut doors and say, "Nettie means all right, but why doesn't she quit talking for a while." And Max came yesterday morning—and he hasn't drawn breath yet.
>
> We had the funeral here at the house, with no sermon. We wanted to have it all done quietly and quickly, with only the family present. But I think the whole town was here, most standing in the yard, since they couldn't get in. It was a nightmare experience for me and made things ten times harder for Mamma than there was any necessity for. . . . Poor Mingo [evidently the family dog] has been scared out of a year's growth with so many strange people coming and going. . . . I hear Max down in the kitchen talking to Mamma while she is trying to get dinner. I'd better go down and get him out for a walk or something. I'll write you again when things quiet down a little more.[75]

Todd in 1941 produced a final detective novel, *The Lazy Lawrence Murders* (a stray Hugh Rennert novella, written over a dozen years earlier, appeared in a mystery magazine in 1945).

75 Ibid. In her own letter to Ruth, written the same evening, Todd's mother does not exhibit Todd's high level of agitation over the presence of these various guests.

Yet even though with *Lazy Lawrence* Todd returned to his artistically sustaining Mexican earth, the novel is, like *Death under the Moonflower*, which is set entirely in Texas, over-peopled with characters, difficult to follow and sorely missing the presence of Hugh Rennert. However, Todd was already planning his next big thing: a panoramic historical novel set in Mexico. Titled *Under the Rose*, it was described in *Publishers Weekly* as a "towering, important novel of Mexico in the early 1820s—of gold braid, parades, intrigue, and pageantry seen through the eyes of Jude Donavan, American soldier of fortune." Said to have "sure-fire sales appeal," *Under the Rose* was to be published in March 1942—yet it never appeared.[76]

What withered *Under the Rose*? In the absence of direct evidence one can only speculate, but it seems fair to conclude that Todd hit an artistic impasse and was unable to finish the book. His bid at "serious writing" having failed, why, then, did Todd not go back to authoring detective fiction? Perhaps here too he had hit a creative roadblock. Or perhaps the money was not good enough. At this time when many mystery readers rented mystery novels from libraries, only deigning to even consider buying them in the form of cheap, disposable paperbacks, the average sale of a detective novel in hardback was something like 2000 copies (3000 for the better class one). To make a good living from writing mysteries in the 1940s most genre writers needed either to be big paperback sellers or highly prolific, producing two—or better yet three or even four—books a year.[77] This seems to have been something Todd found difficult to do. In his peak period, 1933 to 1938, he produced two novels in two years only, 1935 and 1937, the other four years managing just one novel annually.

Whatever the reasons, after 1941 Todd's career as a novelist ended. During the 1940s he left Atoka and moved to Philadelphia, where he worked—like an English detective novelist he much

76 *Publishers Weekly* 141 (1942): 325.

77 On detective novel sales in the period when Todd Downing wrote, see Marie F. Rodell, *Mystery Fiction: Theory and Technique* (New York: Duel, Sloan and Pearce, 1943), Chapter 23 ("The Economics of Mystery Fiction").

admired, Dorothy L. Sayers, once had in London in the 1920s—as an advertising copy writer. Todd assured his parents this was the right move for him. "Dear folks—You doubtless think I have forgotten you," he wrote Sam and Maud in one letter from Philadelphia. "But such is *not* the case. I am simply living such a full—and *happy*—life that I never get a chance to write the long letter which I want to write you."[78]

One of the ad firms that employed Todd at this time was the prominent concern of N. W. Ayer & Son; and it is fitting that Todd was involved at Ayer with another man, Ken Slifer, in the creation of the 1944 mystery fiction inspired magazine ad that the agency produced for the Electric Light & Power Association, entitled *The Case of the Crumpled Letter*. "Todd Downing, working with Ken Slifer, over at Ayer, has come up with another good one," approvingly noted the trade journal *Advertising & Selling* that year. This clever and amusing ad, designed around a classic feature of Golden Age detective novels, a keyed house plan—was honored in 1959 with inclusion in Julius Lewis Watkins' *The 100 Greatest Advertisements*.[79]

In a 1945 letter to his parents, written after he had returned to Philadelphia from a trip, Todd assured Sam and Maud that "the copy department had a grand welcome for me, and it's really good to be back." Yet a few years later he left the advertising business altogether, reentering the teaching profession in 1950. Todd briefly occupied a post at Washington College, a private liberal arts college in Chestertown, Maryland, before taking employment for several years at Massannutten Academy, a military school in Woodstock, Virginia.[80]

78 Todd Downing to Sam and Maud Downing, 15 July 1944.

79 *Advertising & Selling* 37 (1944): 56; Julian Lewis Watkins, *The 100 Greatest Advertisements: Who Wrote Them and What They Did* (1949; rev. ed. New York: Dover, 1959), 172-173. Regrettably, Julius Lewis Watkins gives credit for this ad solely to his "old friend" Ken Slifer, in 1959 Vice President and Manager of the Copy Department at Ayer & Son, even though the contemporary 1944 trade journal article clearly co-credits Todd Downing.

80 Todd Downing to Sam and Maud Downing, 11 June 1945; Cox, *Red Land*, 63; *Books Abroad* 26 (1952): 46; *Daily Oklahoman*, 25 July 1960, 37.

After the death of Sam Downing in 1954, Todd returned to Atoka to live with his octogenarian mother, remaining there for the rest of his life, teaching Spanish and French at Atoka High School. This action seems at first blush strange, especially given the criticism of "Atoka and all it represents" that Todd made in his 1939 letter to his sister. One can imagine that for Todd Atoka (Pop. 2548 in 1940) might have come to seem, especially after the book promotion trips to New York City, a backward, even Philistine sort of place. On the other hand, Todd gave a talk at a "Writers' Conclave" at Oklahoma State University in October 1937, where he spoke favorably of his home town and his native state:

> I am often asked why, I, being a native of this state, don't use it as a setting for some of my stories, instead of placing them all in Old Mexico. The reason is not that I do not like Oklahoma, for I do. But for the reading public and the publishers of my books, Oklahoma is still an uncivilized land where the population is composed mostly of rattlesnakes, redskins on the warpath, incorrigible outlaws, and pistol-packing cowhands.

Todd lamented: "Editors refuse to accept [Oklahoma] in fiction as anything else. Consequently, if I should want to write about a small, cultured, ordinary town such as my home place, Atoka, I would move it across the Red River boundary line, to Texas or some other state which is no longer considered a wilderness. Otherwise, no editor would accept the story."[81]

Perhaps Todd's 1937 speech simply was patriotic stuff for home consumption, yet Todd of his own free will returned to Atoka so frequently that it is hard to believe he consistently felt

81 "Downing Likes Oklahoma But Not For Settings," *Daily O'Collegian*, 21 October 1937, 1. Admittedly, the title of this news story does seem somewhat defensive in nature, as if the headline composer sought to assure readers that Todd Downing really did admire his home state, even though he did not write about it.

about the Oklahoma town as Willa Cather and Sinclair Lewis did about their scathingly depicted fictional small towns Sand City, Kansas ("The Sculptor's Funeral") and Gopher Prairie, Minnesota (*Main Street*). Nevertheless, it is possible that Todd may have had a conflicted sexuality that contributed to his sometime sense of frustration with Atoka. In the absence of primary material, this remains a speculative matter, yet the question arises, given suggestive clues from Todd's life, his library and his writing (on the latter see Part Two below).

Awilda Miller's correspondence gives no indication that Todd had any romantic relationships in the period they cover, 1930 to 1934, a time when he was aged about 28 to 32 years. Besides the reference, mentioned above, to Todd, "poor boy," having to escort his OU colleague Grace Ray to a social function yet again, mention also is made of Todd reinstating himself in the favor of a family by making a date with the daughter of the family, Bess. The Downings wanted Bess's mother "to be made perfectly happy," wrote Awilda to Ruth, "and [we were] sure that would do the trick."[82] On neither one of these occasions does Todd sound like anything but a perfunctory partner.

There are references as well to Todd's male friends, such as one Jones (or John?), to whom Todd lent a serape he brought back from Mexico. "Todd will miss him this year," Awilda wrote Ruth, though she grumbled that the young man was a long time in returning the serape. Todd prominently mentions his OU colleague Forrest Clements in his euphoric letter to his sister, in which he tells her of the acceptance by a publisher of his book *Murder on Tour* (this was in 1933, by which time Todd had his own establishment, a studio apartment in Norman):

> I am going through the motions of work but not getting anything done. Forrest was with me when I got the letter and was actually more excited about it than I. The first thing he said was to write you

82 ASM to RSD, 16 November 1930, 14 February 1931.

> immediately. He has always wanted me to break away from this what he calls impasse and now I have an opportunity to do it. I haven't gotten any plans made yet, but it may not be long before I visit New York again.[83]

This is slender enough evidence, to be sure, upon which to conclude that Todd might have had homosexual inclinations. However, another perusal of the books in Todd's library at his death offers support for such a thesis. Among books Todd obtained as an adult are: Pierre Loti's *Aziyade* (1879; rept. 1923) and *Mon Frere Yves/My Brother Yves* (1883; rept. 1947); Walt Whitman's *Leaves of Grass* (1885; rept. 1930); Oscar Wilde's *De Profundis* (1905; rpnt. 1950); two copies of Thomas Mann's *Death in Venice and Other Stories* (1912), the 1925 first English language edition and a later 1954 edition with a newer English translation; André Gide's *Corydon* (1920; rprt. 1947) and *Les Faux-Monnayeurs/The Counterfeiters* (1925; rpnt. 1943); Gore Vidal's *The City and the Pillar* (1948); Nial Kent's *The Divided Path* (1949); James Barr's *Quatrefoil* (1950); Donald Webster Cory's *The Homosexual in America: A Subjective Approach* (1951); and Mary Renault's *Fire from Heaven* (1969) and *The Persian Boy* (1972). Taken together, this seems a suggestive collection of volumes for a twentieth-century American male to have owned.

If Todd purchased his editions of these books in the years when they were published, they fall into three chronological categories:

> 1920 to 1930: *Aziyade*, *Leaves of Grass*, *Death in Venice*
> 1943 to 1954: *Les Faux-Monnayeurs* (*The Counterfeiters*) / *Corydon* / *Mon Frere Yves* (*My Brother Yves*) / *The City and the Pillar* / *The Divided Path* / *Quatrefoil* / *The*

83 ASM to RSD, 7 July 1930; Todd Downing to Ruth Shields Downing, [?] May 1933. Forrest Clements married Sarah White in 1941.

Homosexual in America / De Profundis / Death in Venice (seven of the nine books date from 1947 to 1951)

1969-1972: *Fire from Heaven, The Persian Boy*

These years span Todd's adult life, but the most noteworthy are those middle years, which roughly coincide with the period when Todd left Atoka to live in the northeastern United States.

According to Richard M. Berrong, the series of novels by Pierre Loti, pseudonym of Julien Viaud (1850-1923), "chronicle the struggle of a man to understand his homoerotic feelings and their implications for him." *Mon Frere Yves* Berrong believes to be "the first novel in modern French literature to centre on a positively presented male homosexual love story." Todd actually owned thirty "Pierre Loti" books, most of which he probably purchased when he was in college in the 1920s. No doubt part of the appeal of the Loti works for Todd, a Middle American male with a romantic imagination, was the exotic trans-global settings chosen for them by Viaud, a French naval officer who had traveled round the world. However, today the gay subtext of these works is widely urged, particularly in the case of *Aziyade* and *Mon Frere Yves*. Even in Viaud's own lifetime, notes Berrong, the subtext of these two novels in particular was "obvious enough to foster rumors about Viaud's homosexuality in the popular press of the day."[84]

Walt Whitman's *Leaves of Grass* and Thomas Mann's *Death in Venice* are masterworks that have profoundly influenced gay writing (though of course they have had more universal appeal), as have the works of the French writer André Gide, particularly *Corydon*, his collection of Socratic dialogs defending homosexuality. (Gide's *The Counterfeiters* also is notable for its inclusion

84 Richard M. Berrong, "Pierre Loti (Julien Viaud)," *glbtq : An Encyclopedia of Gay, Lesbian, Bisexual, Transgender, and Queer Culture*, at http://www.glbtq.com/literature/loti_p.html; Richard M. Berrong, *In Love with a Handsome Sailor: The Emergence of Gay Identity and the Novels of Pierre Loti* (Toronto: University of Toronto Press, 2003), 75. Todd also owned Pierre Brodin's 1945 French language biography of Viaud.

of explicitly gay characters.) Oscar Wilde's *De Profundis* is Wilde's famous letter from Reading Gaol ruminating on his relationship with his former lover Lord Alfred Douglas (the first complete edition was published in 1949). Mary Renault's fictionalized tales of the romantic relationships between Alexander the Great and the Macedonian nobleman Hephaestion (*Fire from Heaven*) and the Persian eunuch Bagoas (*The Persian Boy*), were bestselling novels and immediate gay cult classics. Of *The Persian Boy*, a bemused though pleased Gore Vidal in 1973 noted, "the only true love story on the best-seller list is about two homosexualists."[85]

Yet the most suggestive books that Todd owned, in terms of gay content, are the three American novels published between 1948 and 1950—*The City and the Pillar*, *The Divided Path* and *Quatrefoil*—and the 1951 sociological study *The Homosexual in America: A Subjective Approach*. All these works were written by gay men with the conscious intention of portraying homosexuals in a sympathetic light, and they were controversial at the time, incurring the disdain of many heterosexual critics and reviewers. That Todd obtained all four of these books suggests he had something more than an academic interest in the subject of homosexuality in this period.

Among this trio of explicitly gay-themed novels Gore Vidal's book, *The City and the Pillar*, actually was a bestseller in the United States, but the other two works, Nial Kent's *The Divided Path* and James Barr's *Quatrefoil*, were published (along with Donald Cory's *The Homosexual in America*) by Greenberg, a small press that was the major commercial source of gay literature in the United States from the 1930s until the early 1950s, when it was forced to cease publication of gay material by the

85 Gore Vidal, "The Top Ten Best-Sellers According to the *New York Times* as of January 7, 1973," in Jay Parini, ed., *The Selected Essays of Gore Vidal* (New York and London: Doubleday, 2008), 37. In *The Violet Hour: The Violet Quill and the Making of Gay Culture* (New York: Columbia University Press, 2004), David Bergman categorizes Mary Renault as a "homoerotic" writer (p. 45).

threat from the federal government of prosecution on obscenity charges (though in fact Greenberg published nothing that would be characterized as remotely obscene today). Reviews in the mainstream press of all three novels, particularly the latter two, tended to be hostile to their very subject matter. "Their concupiscence is ours greatly magnified, and there is but little more to the fairly lengthy history of Michael than that: his love for Paul, his love for Nikki, his love for John, and so forth, with the parties they go to, the nauseating letters they write, their infidelities and broken hearts," wrote a palpably repulsed Nathan L. Rothman in the *Saturday Review* of the characters in *The Divided Path*. Similarly, the *Kirkus* reviewer complained that Kent's novel was "explicit" in its detail, providing a "sensational, sexological account" of gay life. Being "overt rather than fastidious," *Kirkus* condemningly pronounced, *The Divided Path* was "for the sensation seeker" only. Despite such markedly unsympathetic pronouncements from reviewers, however, many readers of books like *The Divided Path* likely were not so much seeking "sensation" as answers about a central aspect of their being; Todd Downing may have been one such reader.[86]

Arguably *The Divided Path* is of the most interest of these three novels in connection with a study of the life and work of

86 Bergman, *Violet Hour*, 50; Michael Bronski, ed., *Pulp Friction: Uncovering the Golden Age of Gay Male Pulps* (New York: St. Martin's Griffin, 2003), 83. In his *glbtq* entry on Donald Webster Cory (pseudonym of Edward Sagarin, 1913-1986) Claude J. Summers notes that with *The Homosexual in America*, Sagarin provided readers with "a sense of what it meant to be homosexual in 1950s America. Moreover, he argued more boldly than anyone previously for the rights of homosexuals as a group." Sagarin, who spent a year in France in 1931-32 and met André Gide, derived his pseudonym, Don Cory, from Gide's *Corydon*. Claude J. Summers, "Edward Sagarin (Donald Webster Cory)," in *glbtq*, at http://www.glbtq.com/social-sciences/sagarin_e.html. Interestingly, two of the authors of the gay novels published in the period 1948-1951 that Todd owned had Oklahoma connections. Gore Vidal's maternal grandfather, Thomas P. Gore, was a prominent Oklahoma politician who served as a United States senator from the state in 1907-1921/1931-1937, while James Barr, whose real name was James Fugate, was born in Oklahoma in 1922 and apparently

Todd Downing. According to Roger Austen, the novel includes "realistic glimpses" of what a gay man "is forced to endure while growing up in a small town," yet it "focuses more generally on the snug, secure, comforting aspects of small-town life." Austen somewhat patronizingly asserts that while in 1949 *Path* "may well have been pleasant reading for gay men," the modern reader (1977) "is likely to smile at Kent's sentimentalization of small-town life."[87] Yet despite Austen's skepticism on this matter it may well be that for an individual like Todd Downing, a man who had grown up secure and loved (if perhaps not entirely understood) in a small town, the novel's depiction of "small-town life"—pro and con—generally rang true.

It certainly appears that Todd's family ties remained strong in the 1940s and that Todd eventually worked through whatever misgivings he may have had about life in Atoka. Fittingly Todd late in life was honored with an emeritus professorship in the Choctaw language at Southeastern Oklahoma State University in nearby Durant, and he would play a brief though important role in the college's nascent bilingual education program. Todd's final works, both dating from this period, the early 1970s, mark a renewed public embrace of the Choctaw heritage that Todd had so proudly proclaimed nearly a half-century earlier in "A Choctaw's Autobiography." A series of lessons in the Choctaw language Todd designed was published in 1971 as *Chahta Anampa: An Introduction to Choctaw Grammar*. The same year *Journey's*

attended the University of Oklahoma before and after World War Two. Much of Fugate's novel takes place in Oklahoma. In 1955 Fugate also published, in the gay-friendly journal *Mattachine Review*, the essay "Facing Friends in a Small Town," about "his experiences living as a known homosexual in a small Kansas town." On James Barr/James Fugate, see Hubert Kennedy, "A Touch of Royalty: Gay Author James Barr" (San Francisco: Peremptory Publications, 2002). Besides the fact that his real name apparently was William Leroy Thomas, nothing seems to be known about author Nial Kent.

87 For Roger Austen's discussion of *The Divided Path*, see *Playing the Game: The Homosexual Novel in America* (Indianapolis, IN and New York: Bobbs Merrill, 1977), 125-128. He discusses *The City and the Pillar* at 118-125 and *Quatrefoil* at 159-160.

End, a historical pageant play written by Todd, was presented by the Atoka County Historical Society, with Todd as narrator. But Todd had not much longer to write. This accomplished American author, for too many decades now too overlooked, died from a heart attack on January 9, 1974, in Atoka, the town where he had spent most of his life. He was buried beside his parents Sam and Maud, his grandmother Awilda and his older brother Gordon in Atoka's Westview cemetery, under a headstone reading simply Todd Downing March 29, 1902 January 9, 1974. Evidently Todd agreed with the sculptor Harvey Merrick in the Willa Cather story "The Sculptor's Funeral," who, in spite of whatever conflicted feelings he had about his native ground, observed: "[I]t rather seems as though we ought to go back to the place we come from in the end."[88]

Part Two: Murders in Mexico

The Detective Fiction of Todd Downing

As a detective novelist Todd Downing produced a small but impressive body of work, unique within the mystery genre in its Golden Age. Besides being a deft plotter and an exemplary genre stylist, Todd Downing is historically significant among American mystery writers for his use of Mexico as the locus of most of his tales of detection. In the 1930s literary regionalism was on the rise in the works of American mystery authors (for example, Phoebe Atwood Taylor and Cape Cod, Leslie Ford and Maryland) and in the same decade the British writers Elspeth Huxley and Adam Broome set detective novels in Africa; yet Todd Downing stands out for his sustained and deeply informed commitment to the portrayal of local culture in mystery genre fiction. Further, as James Cox has noted in *The Red Land to the South*, Todd Downing deliberately used his Mexican settings

88 Todd's library included two William Cather short story collections, both first editions: *The Old Beauty and Others* (1948) and *Youth and the Bright Medusa* (1920). The latter collection, published when Todd was a college freshman, includes "The Sculptor's Funeral."

(particularly in the novel *The Cat Screams*) to explore an indigenous culture that he, a proud member of the Choctaw nation, greatly valued.

It is Todd Downing's depiction of indigenous society in his books that has fueled modern academic interest in Todd's work, both his detective fiction and his non-fictional book on Mexico, *The Mexican Earth*. But it seems to me that Todd's detective fiction should be assessed as well for its quality *as detective fiction*. In this section, therefore, I analyze the Todd Downing mysteries more broadly, for their plotting and general literary qualities.

Recent analysis of Todd Downing's work tends to look mainly on the Americans who make up the bulk of his characters as an undifferentiated mass of colonialist oppressors. Yet Todd's American characters are much more varied and interesting than that. In truth, Todd's fiction addresses not merely racial relations, but a myriad of human interactions. When Todd's publisher Doubleday, Doran asserted that within the mystery genre the Oklahoman was a leading "creator of atmosphere, suspense, and horror" as well as a top-level "literary stylist," it was not, in my view, exaggerating. With the reprinting of eight Downing novels in 2012 one hopes that Todd's place in the mystery genre will be restored and secured.

Birth of a Mystery Writer

Throughout the 1920s Todd Downing's career preoccupation was that of working toward a master's degree in foreign languages (a goal achieved in 1928). In the process of obtaining his degree the young scholar from Atoka became abidingly absorbed in the history and culture of the people of Mexico, particularly that of the country's indigenous population. Todd's book reviews in *Books Abroad* and the *Daily Oklahoman* and the library of volumes on Spanish and Native American history that he accumulated leave no room for one to doubt the depth of his interest in Mexico. Yet like many another Jazz Age intellectual Todd also became consumed by a craving for—even, dare I say, an addiction to—another source of literary stimulation: mystery fiction. For Todd and other intellectuals of the 1920s, detective fiction and thrillers became the escape reading of choice. In a passage in his first published detective novel, *Murder on Tour*, Todd's major series detective, Hugh Rennert, discusses the peculiar appeal of detective fiction with a young Texas schoolteacher, Gertrude Dean, who avidly devours mysteries:

> "But that's one reason I like murder stories. They're so unreal, not like the kind you read about in the newspapers. Miss Tredkin told me the other day that I shouldn't read so many of them, that they would make me morbid. I didn't try to explain to her the real reason why I read them. I don't think she would have understood."
>
> "No, I don't think that Miss Tredkin understands escape."
>
> "Escape?" she shot him a quick glance. "How did you know?"
>
> "Most people do read them for that reason, Miss Dean. They are just one of the many avenues of escape from the realities of life. They keep one from thinking about—other things."[89]

We have seen above that as an adolescent in the 1910s Todd was a great reader of the escapist crime fiction of Sax Rohmer and Arthur B. Reeve. In the 1920s Todd, along with multitudes of other readers around the globe, discovered a new purveyor of thrilling fictional accounts of crime and mystery: Edgar Wallace (1875-1932). By the late 1920s the incredibly productive English thriller writer was the bestselling novelist in Great Britain, and no slouch in the United States. Todd's 1974 library of books included 1920s editions of two dozen Edgar Wallace novels. During breaks from studying for his master's degree and guiding tourist parties around Mexico, Todd found time to read such nail-biting

89 Todd Downing, *Murder on Tour* (New York: Doubleday, Doran, 1933), 117.

"shockers" as *Terror Keep*, *The Door with Seven Locks*, *The Man from Morocco* and *The Ringer*. In his 1930s book reviews Todd continually used Edgar Wallace as his gold standard among thriller writers ("some of the shivers are worthy of Edgar Wallace," he writes in one 1934 review, for example).

In addition to his two dozen Edgar Wallace thrillers Todd owned 1920s editions of twenty true detective novels and story collections: Anthony Berkeley's *The Wychford Poisoning Case* and *The Silk Stocking Murders*; Earl Derr Biggers' *The Chinese Parrot* (a Charlie Chan tale); Lynn Brock's *The Deductions of Colonel Gore*, *Colonel Gore's Second Case*, *The Slip-Carriage Mystery* and *Murder at the Inn*; G. K. Chesterton's *The Father Brown Omnibus*; S. S. Van Dine's *The Benson Murder Case*, *The Greene Murder Case* and *The Bishop Murder Case*; Mignon Eberhart's *The Patient in Room 18*; Rufus King's *Mystery De Luxe* and *Murder by the Clock*; Marie Belloc Lowndes' *What Really Happened*; Baroness Orczy's *Unraveled Knots* and *Skin O' My Tooth*; *The Mary Roberts Rinehart Crime Book* (an omnibus including two of Todd's favorite mystery novels, *The After House* and *The Red Lamp*); *The Omnibus of Crime*, a short story collection edited by Dorothy L. Sayers; and T. S. Stribling's *Clues of the Caribees*.

In the 1930s Todd continued to read numerous volumes of mystery fiction, many of them review copies for his "Clues and Corpses" column in the *Daily Oklahoman*. Newspaper accounts from this decade assert that Todd downed a detective story daily. Although this claim seems exaggerated, there is no doubt that Todd read dozens of mystery novels annually in the 1930s. For example, his library included the following mystery novels, all published just in 1930: Earl Derr Biggers' *Charlie Chan Carries On*; John Dickson Carr's *It Walks by Night*; Agatha Christie's *The Murder at the Vicarage*; Mignon Eberhart's *The Mystery of Hunting's End*; Rufus King's *Murder by Latitude* and *Somewhere in This House*; Ellery Queen's *The French Powder Mystery*; John Rhode's *Dr. Priestley Investigates*; Anthony Wynne's *The Yellow Crystal*; and no fewer than seventeen Edgar Wallace tales (some of the latter books, it should be noted so as to assure my readers that Edgar Wallace was but a mortal man, are reprints). Moreover, in addition to these twenty-six volumes of fictional crimes, it is highly likely that some of the mysteries that Todd read—as was certainly the case with most American readers of mystery genre fiction at this time—were borrowed from rental libraries.

Thus when Todd Downing began composing his own mystery opus during the summer of 1931, he was well-versed in the genre. Though Todd had the greatest fondness for the works of Edgar Wallace (he obviously concurred with the publisher's mantra that "It is impossible not to be thrilled by Edgar Wallace!"), Todd chose to write not thrillers but more cerebral—and thus more intellectually respectable at the time—fair play detective fiction, where clues are provided so that a sufficiently perspicacious reader can solve the mystery. As detective novelists Todd held especially high opinions, when he himself was writing detective novels, of Agatha Christie, John Dickson Carr, Ellery Queen, S. S. Van Dine, Mary Roberts Rinehart, Mignon Eberhart and the now mostly forgotten authors Rufus King, Anthony Abbot and Anthony Wynne. Like these writers, Todd would produce ingenious and colorful fair play puzzle tales.

Probably the greatest direct early literary influence on Todd's detective fiction was that of Rufus King, one of the most popular American mystery writers of the late 1920s and early 1930s. Nine years older than Todd, King came from a privileged background in New York City and in 1914 graduated from Yale, where he had hobnobbed for four years with Cole Porter while the two young men were members of the Yale Dramatic Association. Todd's library includes all twenty-six novels and short story collections that King published between 1927 and 1958 (including two adventure novels in the style of Jack London and Joseph Conrad). As late as 1936, Todd proclaimed in print that King was "the best living writer of mystery stories." The author from Atoka particularly admired the older writer's three maritime mysteries, *Murder by Latitude* (1930), *Murder on the Yacht* (1932) and *The Lesser Antilles Case* (1934). In 1934 Todd named *Murder by Latitude* as one his six favorite detective novels (he added that either of the other maritime titles could be substituted for *Latitude).*[90] Todd was deeply drawn to the literary sophistication of the Rufus King detective novels in general and the narrative suspense and visceral excitement of the maritime mysteries in particular. Besides generally emulating King's style, Todd clearly modeled one character in his first detective novel, *Murder on Tour* (1933), after a character in King's *Murder by Latitude* and he likely was inspired by King's *Murder on the Yacht* to include a hurricane in his novel *Murder on the Tropic* (1935).

When it came to the setting for his mystery novels, however, Todd decided to do something entirely new. Sensibly drawing on his professional area of expertise as a degreed instructor at the University of Oklahoma and his four summers spent in Mexico, Todd made the land south of the Rio Grande the locus of not only his first published detective novel, but of eight of the nine novels that he would produce between 1933 and 1941. This was Todd's signature contribution to the mystery genre in its Golden Age.

Vacilada and The Glories of Venus

In making his decision to use Mexico as the primary setting for his series of detective novels, Todd Downing was influenced not merely by his own extensive experiences with Mexico but by his reading of a 1931 novel about Mexico, Susan Smith's *The Glories of Venus*. Susan Grant Smith (1882-1934) edited an interior decoration magazine called *Modes and Manners* and worked in the interior decorating department of one of the Wanamaker's stores. Smith published a series of *Made in . . .* books on the arts and crafts of various countries, including Mexico, before she wrote her sole novel, a picaresque tale of literary and artistic expatriates in Mexico.

90 *Daily Oklahoman*, 27 September 1936, 67. For the list of Todd's favorite detective novels, see Appendix Two. On Rufus King, see the series of posts about his work on my blog, *The Passing Tramp*.

Although forgotten today, Susan Smith's *The Glories of Venus* was well-received by an American audience eager to learn more about modern, post-revolutionary Mexico. In November 1931, not long after completing his first detective novel, Todd glowingly praised *The Glories of Venus* in the *Daily Oklahoman*: "Susan Smith knows Mexico and the Mexicans, she knows Americans and how they act in Mexico; last, but not least, she knows how to write."[91]

Todd would refer to *The Glories of Venus* again in a 1937 detective novel, *The Last Trumpet*, and yet again three years later in his non-fictional study of Mexico, *The Mexican Earth*, where he calls *Glories* "to me the finest novel ever written on the Mexican scene." In *The Last Trumpet*, Todd's series detective Hugh Rennert and a friend, Cameron County, Texas sheriff Peter Bounty, discuss the merits of Susan's Smith's novel after Rennert sees Bounty with the book in his hand at the Brownsville Public Library. Rennert avows that the novel is "the one Mexican item . . . on my desert island list" and the two men proceed to discuss it:

> "I understand now," Rennert said, "why you get along with Mexicans so well. Anyone who appreciates *The Glories of Venus* would."
>
> "It expresses things they would if they could. Their attitude toward life and death. *Vacilada*. . . . Bounty turned pages with the true booklover's excitement. "Remember this definition of *vacilada*? 'Life is the greatest insult that can be offered to a human being,' he read, 'and yet if you will only accept that fact, you can manage to enjoy yourself thoroughly a great deal of the time.' Mexico, huh?"
>
> "Um-huh," Rennert agreed. "Mexico."[92]

91 *Daily Oklahoman*, 15 November 1931, 43.

92 Todd Downing, *The Mexican Earth* (1940; rpnt. Norman and London: University of Oklahoma Press, 1996), 177; Todd Downing, *The Last Trumpet* (New York: Doubleday, Doran, 1937), 194-196. In *The Glories of Venus* characters also explain *vacilada* as "the way in which the comic and the tragic are always overlapping in life" and "the defense that a sensitive

Vacilada—a sort of mirthful resignation in the face of death—was hugely important to Todd in his mystery fiction. Significantly, in the final Hugh Rennert mystery, *Night over Mexico*, which Todd also published in 1937, Rennert links *vacilda* to his interest in detection. "I think I know the reason I've continued to poke and pry into cases that others have found gruesome or terrifying," Rennert ruminates. "I'm glad. Because some of my friends have accused me of giving way to a morbid hankering for thrills. That's not it at all. At least I'm satisfied it's not." What it is, it seems, is the allure for Rennert of *vacilada*:

> "It never struck me before last night that what I'm primarily interested in is death itself. . . . Now that's not as morbid as it may sound. And right there's the whole point. Death in Mexico isn't the ugly thing it is in the rest of the world. Instead of dreading it and standing back from it in awe, the Mexican hugs it, sleeps with it, dances with it. Death's a gayer partner for him than life itself. He plays jokes on it just as it plays jokes on him. . . . I think I've been at it more or less consciously for a long time. Getting close to death rather than avoiding it. Trying to make a boon companion out of it as the Mexican does. I believe that's why I've meddled in so many murder cases. Not so much because I've wanted to solve a problem or study people, but because in each instance death has been dramatized. I'd like to keep on until I get rid of more of the fears I absorbed from our own civilization. Until I can be nonchalant rather than tense when death grins at me."[93]

race has built up in order to live under conditions of terror and despair." Susan Smith, *The Glories of Venus* (New York and London: Harpers, 1931), 89-80.

93 Todd Downing, *Night over Mexico* (New York: Doubleday, Doran, 1937), 245-247.

It is unusual in a classical Golden Age mystery to interrupt the narrative for such a philosophical digression as this, but the whole design of *Night over Mexico* is structured around the concept of *vacilada*, which had made such a great impression on Todd in *The Glories of Venus*. In contrast with such Golden Age writers as Raymond Chandler, Dorothy L. Sayers and Anthony Berkeley Cox, Todd, a fundamentally modest person, never made a great noise about attempting to transform the detective novel into "literature" (indeed, he sometimes left the impression that he was conflicted in his mind over whether such a thing was even possible); yet in fact Todd's incorporation of the idea of *vacilada* into his detective fiction gives it a literary quality unusual in its day (and even, one might argue, today). Todd Downing himself was a consummate mystery fan and he believed the first goal of genre writing should be to entertain. Yet he also was a serious scholar and literary stylist who could hardly help but give his own writing within the genre artistic heft. This combination of qualities makes the best of his mysteries—the seven Hugh Rennert novels published from 1933 to 1937—some of the glories of Golden Age detective fiction.

Murder on Tour (1933)

Todd Downing's first published detective novel, *Murder on Tour*, is an assured piece of work by a new author. Although it does not match the level of his five strongest novels—*The Cat Screams*, *Vultures in the Sky*, *Murder on the Tropic*, *The Last Trumpet* and *Night over Mexico*—*Tour* got the Hugh Rennert series off to an enticing start, offering mystery readers clever plotting and polished writing, spiced with the exotic (to North American and European readers) flavor of Mexico. This flavor would intensify as the series progressed.

Following a terse prologue set in a hotel in San Antonio, where a sudden, savage slaying occurs, *Murder on Tour* is divided into three parts: a short opening section also set in San Antonio; a long middle section set in Mexico City; and a lengthy closing section that takes place on a train traveling from Mexico City to

Laredo. The murdered man, a young United States Treasury Department customs agent investigating the looting by Americans of Mexican antiquities, was strangled in his San Antonio hotel room with a black silk stocking (suggested by Anthony Berkeley's *The Silk Stocking Murders*?). With official suspicion centering on the thirteen members of the Intra-America Tour party about to set forth from San Antonio to Mexico City, senior customs agent Hugh Rennert joins the party to catch a killer.

As Todd Downing's by far most important series detective, Hugh Rennert ultimately solves eight murder cases in Mexico and Texas. In his first fictional appearance Rennert is described as "having rather homely but not undistinguished features—thin, dark brown hair brushed back from a high forehead and clear brown eyes, flecked with gray." The set of Rennert's "firm square chin" offsets "a certain almost dreamy look" in his eyes. He is a dreamer then, but also a doer. Elsewhere Todd describes Rennert in decidedly demystified terms simply as a "middle-aged man with gray hair beginning to show at the temples."[94] Todd is careful to present his detective as a regular man, rather than an eccentric, quotation-spouting genius with a collection of esoteric bric-a-brac or a hard-boiled tough guy adept at boozing, bedding and brawling.

Besides sharing with Todd the physical quality of a "firm square chin," Rennert, who also hails from a Midwestern state, has a certain similarity to Todd in his mental makeup:

> Rennert's nature was a sentimental, not to say romantic, one. In his boyhood he had moved on the unstable heights of Scott and Byron; during his university days he had wavered between the magnet of poetry and sophomoric mysticism and that of the stern reality which he saw waiting him at the end of college cloisters. It was at this formative period that he had first seen the sun rise over

94 Downing, *Tour*, 19, 44.

> Popcatepetl and Ixtaccihuatl [famous volcanoes located near Mexico City].[95]

Thus Hugh Rennert, like Todd Downing, possesses a decidedly romantic nature, eagerly devoured romantic literature as a boy and was enraptured and transported by the mystical sight of Popo and Ixi. Further resemblances between the two men suggest themselves over the course of the detective series, although Rennert is some dozen years older than his thirty-one year old creator when he makes his first fictional appearance in *Murder on Tour*.

Characters and setting are more thinly developed in *Murder on Tour* than in the best of the later novels, with pure plot predominating. Local highlights of Mexico City and the surrounding area, such as Chapultepec Castle, Sanborn's department store and the canals of Lake Xochimilco, are touched upon, but they are not integrated into the plot in a significant way. The one notable Mexican element that Todd develops in *Murder on Tour* is the *Dia de los Muertos* (Day of the Dead), which takes place in the novel. This Mexican national holiday in honor of the dead—who, so the belief runs, walk among the living at this time—has indigenous origins. Like his creator, Rennert is fascinated with the Mexican attitude to death. As he grasps a toy skeleton purchased by one of the tour party he ruminates on his longing to share the native temperament:

> Rennert, fingering idly the painted toy, felt stealing over him a curious relaxation of the senses and, at the same time, was vaguely aware of tension. . . . His finger released the spring at the base of the toy. Instantly the little skeleton jumped into life, began his macabre dance. The left hand jerked

95 Ibid., 43. By the time of the last Rennert novel *Night over Mexico* (1937), Rennert's transformative Mexican vista has become the sight of Saddleback Mountain, outside the city of Monterrey.

> the bottle to his lips, the right hand fell to his side. The right hand waggishly thumbed a nose, the left hand fell to his side. The roguish eyes looked into Rennert's.
>
> A boon companion, he mused, with an invitation. *Memento mori*. There flashed across his memory a steel engraving (Was it by Doré?) in an old book which as a boy he had found in the attic. A grim, frightful old man with a long white beard. In one hand he held a scythe, its edge curved like his nose. With the other he beckoned inexorably. Rennert remembered waking in the middle of the night bathed in cold sweat while he stared into darkness at the foot of the bed, where the old man had been standing. Yet the next day, with perverse eagerness, he had stolen up the attic stairs, and gazed again at the picture.[96]

Todd's Day of the Dead theme is linked with the character of the dignified widow Mrs. Priscilla Evans Rankin, a "fragile little woman with pearl gray hair and a quietly beautiful face."[97] Wed after the age of forty to an engineer employed in Mexico who died only three years into the marriage, Mrs. Rankin returns every year to Mexico during the Dia de los Muertos in the hope of seeing her dead husband again. Others versions of this character (likely partly modeled after Todd's grandmother) would appear in *The Cat Screams* and *Vultures in the Sky*.

Although aside from Mrs. Rankin the suspects on the tour bus are not much fleshed out, they are efficiently sketched, easily distinguishable "types," all with something about them to make them suspicious to the reader. Aside from its tinkering with the Day of the Dead idea, *Murder on Tour* cannot be called a deeply thematic novel, but Todd through Rennert does condemn high-

96 Ibid., 81-82.
97 Ibid., 58.

handed acquisitions of Mexican antiquities by officious (sometimes criminal) Americans. Moreover, Todd occasionally satirizes American attitudes toward Mexico, as represented by the various members of the tour party. We are shown, for example, the penny-pinching (or centavo-cornering) American, taking pride at Xochimilco in bargaining a poor Indian flower girl down the equivalent of a couple pennies:

> "How much did you give her?" Miss Tredkin asked, eyeing the bouquet uncertainly.
>
> "Forty centavos," Brody answered. "She wanted fifty."
>
> "How much is that in our money?"
>
> "Oh, about a dime."[98]

Miss Tredkin, a virginal middle-aged temperance crusader from Wichita, Kansas, comes in for a few satirical raps (she also is the woman who deems interest in detective fiction morbid; see page 81):

> "I once read a paper on the evil grip which *pulque* [an alcoholic beverage made from the fermented sap of the maguey plant] has on the Mexican people to our unit of the W.C.T.U. [Woman's

98 Ibid., 57. In *Murder on Tour* Hugh Rennert references the controversial actions of a former U.S. consul in Mexico, Edward Herbert Thompson (1857-1935), who from 1904 to 1910 dredged the sacred well (*cenote*) at the Mayan archeological site of Chichen Itza and sent the relics he discovered to the Peabody Museum of Natural History at Yale University. In the 1920s, the Mexican government claimed that Thompson had done this illegally. However, the Mexican Supreme Court ruled in Thompson's favor in 1944. See Jesse Lerner, "Edward H. Thompson at Chichen Itza's Sacred Cenote," 17 March 2008, *The American Egypt*, at http://theamericanegypt.blogspot.com/2008/03/edward-h-thompson-at-chichen-itzas.html. "Since the Revolution," declares Rennert in *Murder on Tour*, "the Mexican government has awakened to the fact that they are letting foreigners take out of the country most of their great archaeological treasures." Ibid., 223.

> Christian Temperance Union] back in Wichita. I, you know, am from Kansas and our state has always been dry. The liquor interests have done their best to break down our resistance, but in vain. The women of Kansas stand foursquare behind the Volstead Act."
>
> She paused, took a deep breath and continued in a slightly lower voice.
>
> "When I see men, American men, down here in Mexico, reeling in the streets and through hotel lobbies under the influence of drink, forgetful of their manhood and of the ties which bind them to their loved ones at home, I say 'Thank God for Kansas!'"
>
> Her lips closed firmly and she sank back in her seat.[99]

Similarly, Dr. Bymaster, a Colorado professor, is the first in a long line of patronizing American "experts" on Mexico at whom Todd cocks a skeptical eye:

> "Your book, Dr. Bymaster," Rennert grabbed the first thought which came to his mind, "how is it progressing?"
>
> "Excellently. I am anxious to return to the United States and complete my chapter on Mexico."
>
> "What is the scope of your book?"
>
> "It is to be an economic survey of our modern world, with especial emphasis on the undeveloped resources in backward countries, such as Mexico."
>
> He began a summary of the book. When they arrived at the hotel in Mexico City, he had reached chapter four—"The Hinterland of China."[100]

99 Ibid., 93.

100 Ibid., 93-94. Dr. Bymaster strongly resembles an ingenuous Kansas professor in *The Glories of Venus* who is writing about Mexico.

The Cat Screams (1934)

Inspired by the haunting wailing of Mura, a Siamese cat owned by Todd's University of Oklahoma colleague and friend, anthropology professor Forrest Clements, *The Cat Screams* is a detective novel of considerable literary sophistication, combining a deliberate thematic design with a suspenseful narrative and a clever fair play murder puzzle. *The Cat Screams* has been analyzed at length in James Cox's *The Red Land to the South: American Writers and Indigenous Mexico* (2012), and I am in full agreement with Professor Cox's analysis.[101] Of all Todd Downing's detective novels, *The Cat Screams* is the one that clearly deals most intensively with Mexico's indigenous population and its place in the modern world.

In *The Cat Screams*, Hugh Rennert has returned to Mexico, this time as a visitor to the scenic silver mining and tourist city of Taxco. Rennert is staying at the house of Madame Fournier, a French Creole whose "parents had come to Mexico before the Pastry War" and whose father had been a functionary in the court of Emperor Maximilian. Present with Madame Fournier at her house when murder strikes are eight American paying guests, including, besides Rennert, an obnoxious journalist, an arrogant academic, the scion of an Oklahoma oil tycoon, an enigmatic actress, an artist, a highly circumspect gentleman from Dallas, Texas and Mrs. Sarah Giddings of Indianapolis, Indiana, a sympathetic though oddly inscrutable older woman.[102]

Also to be found at Madame Fournier's are three Indian servants and Mura, the titular screaming Siamese cat. "Mura is not happy these days, la *pobrecita*," the fretted Madame Fournier explains, "she is—how do you say it?—in heat. She wants a husband. But these cats in Taxco are not good enough for her, and I do not let her out of the house. I take her to Mexico City soon for

101 *Daily Oklahoman*, 30 September 1934, 47; Cox, *Red Land*, 41-53. At this time Mura was said to be the only Siamese cat in the state of Oklahoma.

102 Probably like Todd's grandmother, Mrs. Giddings is a reader of Tennyson. See Todd Downing, *The Cat Screams* (New York: Doubleday, Doran, 1934), 16-17.

a husband who is of royal blood like she is." The servant Esteban, ill with some unknown malady, fears the screaming cat. "He is an Indian, you know, and superstitious," explains Madame Fournier. "Two nights ago he heard [Mura] screaming. It frightened him. He has been getting worse ever since."[103]

One of the guests soon dies, supposedly of natural causes. Rennert suspects murder, but he is unable to prove his suspicions. Concurrently, quarantine is declared on Madame Fournier's house, because the local authorities fear that Esteban may be infected with smallpox. Thus has the author neatly fashioned the classic closed location situation in his detective novel, in the manner of Agatha Christie's *And Then There Were None*. Soon yet another guest expires—ostensibly a suicide this time—and again in the face of official disbelief Rennert argues that an unknown murderer is at work.

The screaming of Mura becomes a kind of a harbinger of death to the people trapped in the literally isolated house, particularly the Indian servants, who believe in Nagualism, a Mesoamerican folk religion that posits the existence of humans who can transform themselves into animals (the non-indigenous Mexicans in the novel dismiss Nagualism as the backward superstition of "the indios—the ignorant ones"). For purposes of suspense, Todd, like John Dickson Carr, a Golden Age detective novelist he hugely admired, exploits the unnerving idea that there might be an explanation for the plague of deaths at Madame Fournier's that lies beyond the borderland of modern human reason. Note this remarkable passage in *The Cat Screams*, possibly partly drawn from the author's own life (it also fills in a bit of Hugh Rennert biography):

103 Downing, *Cat*, 12, 18-19. The idea of a female cat in heat screaming because her discriminating owner will not let her mate with just any feline riffraff also appears in Susan Smith's *The Glories of Venus*: "I make you a present of Albertine to take home wiz you, Louise," said Morin. "When you get to New York you must find her a nice husband, ozzerwise she will howl *awful*" (195).

Was there some other force at work in the house, some force whose workings were too devious for his straight-thinking mind to follow?

In one of the Psalms there was a phrase that had always stuck in Rennert's mind, it so well epitomized the fears that mankind has always had of the outer darkness, of the unknown things that lurk there—unguessed at by the ordinary individual until he wakes at three in the morning and finds all the world at rest save his mind, superactive. *Negotium perambulans in tenebris.* "The pestilence that walketh in darkness," the psalmist translated. But Rennert had known once an individual in a city near his college town who had other ideas about the psalmist's meaning. He was an old man, an unfrocked minister of the Gospel of whom many things were whispered in the little Midwestern community. He read the Hebrew of the Old Testament and the Arabic of the Koran. By some accident Rennert had become acquainted with him and would occasionally seek him out, fascinated in spite of himself by the old man's vehement discourses on human shortcomings. The "negotium" which walks in darkness, according to him, had been rendered "pestilence" by a translator who feared to put down on paper what was really meant. The "negotium," he would say in a voice that took on the ardor of fanaticism, was the essence of man's fears, the menace which is the more terrifying because sensed rather than seen, and rendered corporeal by devil inventors who realized that a known evil was less to be dreaded than an unknown one. "When you grow older," the old man had told him once, peering into his eyes through thick-lensed glasses, "you will wake sometimes at three in the morning and strain your ears for some sound,

> something to tell you that your fellow beings are about you. There will be no sound, and the darkness will shut you in. Misgivings, denied during the waking hours, will return in increased magnitude. If you are one of those unhappy beings who have imagination you will have a drug handy to bring you oblivion, or else you will turn on the bed light and read your mind into submission. Then, if ever, you will be tempted to commit suicide. For then—and only then—all the flimsy screens which man has built up between himself and the terrors which he denies are down and he can stare beyond. . . ."[104]

This striking discourse on man's eternal fear of the unknown takes *The Cat Screams* beyond a specific critique of colonialism in Mexico. In its invocation of the ninety-first Psalm excerpt translated in the King James Bible as "the pestilence that walketh in darkness," the novel recalls not Native American literature but two masterpieces of twentieth-century horror fiction: E. F. Benson's story "Negotium Perambulans," originally published in the 1923 collection *Visible and Invisible*, and H. P. Lovecraft's tale "The Dunwich Horror," first published in the pulp magazine *Weird Tales* in 1929. Yet, to be sure, the Nagualism theme, along with the presence of the three Native American servants hovering in the background of *The Cat Screams*, also allows Todd, as James Cox puts it, to submerge "a story of indigenous resistance and revolutionary promise within a conventional story of detection."[105] To say more on this matter would be to give away too much of the plot of this fine detective novel, but readers of *The Cat Screams* who are interested in the subject are urged to look up Professor Cox's *The Red Land to the South*. Suffice it to say here that *The Cat Screams* is the first of Todd Downing's mystery

104 Downing, *Cat*, 237-238.

105 Cox, *Red Land*, 43. Todd was a great reader of supernatural horror fiction (see footnote 151).

masterpieces, and a high point of 1930s American crime fiction, fully deserving of the plaudits that have been accorded it.

Vultures in the Sky (1935)

Doubleday, Doran, expected great things from their new author Todd Downing after the publication of *The Cat Screams*. Todd's follow-up novel, the train mystery *Vultures in the Sky*, measured up to the high expectations and was similarly chosen by Doubleday, Doran as a Crime Club Selection. The major literary influence on Todd in the writing of *Vultures in the Sky* appears to have been Agatha Christie's *Murder on the Orient Express* (published in the United States as *Murder in the Calais Coach* in March 1934), which Todd had given a rave review in the *Daily Oklahoman*. Christie's famous train mystery in turn was inspired by the infamous Lindbergh kidnapping case, which journalist H. L. Mencken called "the biggest story since the Resurrection."[106] Like Christie, Todd incorporates both a kidnapping and murder on a train into his novel, though in a much different way.

Most of *Vultures in the Sky* takes place on the Monterrey-San Luis Potosi leg of a long and tense train journey. Nine ill-fated passengers and assorted crew start out on board; a goodly number will not make their destinations. The narrative pace and suspense level maintained by Todd in *Vultures in the Sky* is terrific. Besides the inconvenient fact of a grimly determined, ruthless murderer running amok on the train, there is engine trouble, an impending railway strike (labor in post-revolutionary Mexico is flexing its muscles) and talk of threatened sabotage by militant Catholic rebels, or Cristeros (the so-called Cristero War had only ended in 1929).

The climax of *Vultures in the Sky* occurs after the cars occupied by the main cast of characters have been decoupled from the rest of the train and stranded in the desert north of San Luis Potosi. For good measure the electricity has gone out as well.

106 Michael Newton, *The FBI Encyclopedia* (Jefferson, NC, and London: McFarland, 2012), 197.

Once again Todd conjures modern man's dread of the unknown, of the dark space that lies beyond the flimsy screens erected by civilization, to provoke unease in the reader: "It was a scene which Rennert never was to forget, a taut, fear-clad moment in which eight dissimilar people faced one another, drawn together by the magnet of a common dread of what might lie beyond the light."[107] In Todd's hands *Vultures in the Sky* became one of the most gripping closed setting detective novels in the literature of mystery fiction. Although the solution to the puzzle plot in *Vultures*, while fairly clued, is not on the same exalted level as the virtuoso solution in *Murder on the Orient Express*, for visceral suspense Todd's novel leaves Christie's tale far behind at the station.

In *Vultures*, Todd again graces his detective novel with polished, colorful writing and a memorable gallery of suspicious characters. Of particular interest among the passengers on the death train are the two women, Coralie Van Syle (of the Long Island Van Syles) and Trescinda Trescott, a longtime émigré in Mexico. Both women have poignant back stories, especially Miss Trescott, the latest and most interestingly developed incarnation of the dignified, inscrutable older woman that readers had met before in *Murder on Tour* and *The Cat Screams*. Miss Trescott emerges as almost a co-protagonist with Hugh Rennert and the resolution of her own story is movingly rendered by the author. "When the dust of Mexico has settled upon a human heart, that heart can find rest in no other land," quotes Rennert, in reference to Miss Talcott. He tells another passenger, who deems what he sees as Miss Trescott's ghoulishness in the face of death to be evidence of an unbalanced mind, "I should say rather that [her mind has] adjusted to a nicety with her [Mexican] surroundings."[108]

107 Todd Downing, *Vultures in the Sky* (New York: Doubleday, Doran, 1935), 231.

108 Downing, *Vultures*, 278-279, 288.

By the time of *Vultures in the Sky*, Todd had become a master of suspenseful writing. He effectively uses the omnipresent train-circling vultures—*zopilotes*—as symbols of death:

> Above the flat roofs of the little town the sky was cloudless and blue, bright with a sheen of heat. Two ugly blotches moved in lazy downward spirals, round and round.
>
> Rennert watched them, his eyes narrowed against the glare.
>
> "Something worries you?" he asked quietly.
>
> "It is the *zopilotes*." There was something incongruous about the hollow voice that emerged from the folds of fat about the Mexican's throat. "I do not like them."
>
> "God knows they're common enough in Mexico!"
>
> "But today there are so many. All the morning the sky has not been clear of them. It is," the voice echoed in a shell, "as if they were following this train."
>
> Rennert's laugh sounded harsh in his own ears. "There has been a drought in this section of the country, hasn't there?"
>
> "Yes, señor. For many weeks it does not rain."
>
> "That explains the *zopilotes* then. Livestock and wild animals have died out on the desert, of thirst, and the vultures are waiting for more to die."
>
> The conductor's back was framed by the door. "Of course, señor, that explains them." The door closed behind him with a soft swish.[109]

All through *Vultures* Todd's scenic painting and sense of phrase is impeccable:

109 Ibid., 31-32.

> Outside the window the gathering night was a silence made up of the myriad muted noises of a Mexican countryside. The train had paused momentarily at one of the little groups of adobe huts that huddle about the railway tracks as if for security against the pitiless desert that hems them in. Scarcely worthy of names, they leave the map undotted and the time table uncluttered save for an occasional condescending asterisk.

Through Todd's writing one can taste the dust and feel the heat of that ill-fated train journey, as well as sense the fear and panic of the lost souls trapped in the uncoupled cars, left "staring into the utter blackness of the night which had engulfed the last vestige of man-made light."[110]

The brilliant English crime fiction critic Edward Powys Mathers ("Torquemada") praised *Vultures in the Sky* in the highest terms, in perhaps the most insightful contemporary newspaper review of Downing's mystery fiction. Mathers termed Downing's mystery writing formula the "isolation method," incisively explaining its operation in *Vultures in the Sky* thusly:

> [Mr. Downing] realizes that each man and woman is a mystery turned in on itself and fumbling all the time at its own secrets and hopes and fears. He puts a handful of ordinary people in a train making its slow way, through dust and heat, across the Mexican desert; then he provides murder, and it is at once as if each character had been attached to some psychic battery charging his simplest actions, words, and even thoughts, with dark significance.[111]

110 Ibid., 118, 230.

111 *London Observer*, 19 January 1936, 6. Mathers speculated that the English poet Matthew Arnold "would have used this 'isolation' method if he had written a detective story."

Murder on the Tropic (1935)

In both *The Cat Screams* and *Vultures in the Sky* Todd Downing made effective use of closed settings (a quarantined house in the former, a train in the other). He does so again in his fourth detective novel, *Murder on the Tropic*, which is set in the vicinity of the Tropic of Cancer at an isolated hacienda in southeastern Nuevo Leon, Mexico ("the hacienda lay in a pocket of the mountains, where a precipitous valley debouched onto the desert"). Three Texans—George Stahl, Tilghman Falter and Edward Solier—bought the Hacienda Flores, the latter man, Solier, explains at the beginning of the novel to Hugh Rennert, as a speculative investment, hoping to turn it into "a big hotel a day's drive south of Monterrey on the new Pan-American Highway to Mexico City." The Texas trio formed a company and sold shares in the hotel. Unfortunately, contrary to their information the highway was routed to the east, on the other side of the mountains, from Linares to Ciudad Victoria, leaving the partners with a problematic investment on their hands. George Stahl died of sunstroke on a visit to the hacienda two weeks earlier, leaving his shares in the hotel company to his son-in-law, Mark Arnhardt. Hoping to sell the hacienda to someone who might irrigate it for farming, the partners bought back all the shares, bar those owned by Bertha Fahn, an eccentric spinster residing at the hacienda while she is "making some kind of a study of plants and flowers." Alienated by the partners, Fahn has refused to relinquish her shares. Additionally, someone at the Hacienda Flores—its denizens include, in addition to Falter, Arnhardt and Fahn, Miguel and Maria Montemayor, caretakers; Esteban Flores, a young aviator and grandson of the original owner of the hacienda; Steve and Ann Tolman, the hotel architect and his wife; and Lee, the mercurial Chinese cook—is systematically emptying the hacienda's precious water bottles (transported from Ciudad Victoria).[112]

Solier asks Rennert to go down to Hacienda Flores to obtain Miss Fahn's consent to sell her shares and to investigate the affair

112 Todd Downing, *Murder on the Tropic* (New York: Doubleday, Doran, 1935), 4, 6, 18.

of the water bottles. Solier sold Rennert a citrus farm in Cameron County, Texas, which he is aware lost much of its crop in an early spring freeze; and he offers Rennert a substantial cash payment for undertaking this mission. Rennert has staked most of his means on the citrus farm ("it had been a gamble, of course," reflects Rennert, "but it offered a chance for a steady income, retirement from an arduous occupation, and unhurried indulgence in many long-fondled desires") and he accepts Solier's offer.[113]

Chapter Two finds Rennert at Hacienda Flores, where he soon is once again enmeshed in a mysterious matter of multiple murders. A baffling and insidious "yellow death" that Rennert links to Stahl's earlier demise claims two more victims ("the mention of yellowness was tingeing with bizarre the lives of these commonplace people") and the remnants of a hurricane strike before Rennert finally solves the mystery, in a beautifully designed climax. The use of a hurricane as a screw-tightening device—inspired by one of Todd's favorite detective novels, Rufus King's *Murder on the Yacht* (1932)—works splendidly. Todd again invokes Mexican folklore in an interesting way—this time it is "*los aires*," or the airs, tiny beings, "malignant and mischievous, who dwell about water"—and pays tribute to the cultural endurance of Mexico's indigenous people:

> [Maria] stood, the embodiment of the Mexico that stands self-sufficient by the side of the road while conquering armies march by, to be replaced in days or years or centuries (it doesn't matter) by other armies under other banners. Along the paved highway to the east, Rennert thought, will come another, more dreadful army with billboards and refreshment stands and blatant automobile horns, but Maria and her kind will stand when they pass by.[114]

113 Downing, *Tropic*, 4.
114 Ibid., 65-66.

This attack on the commercial invasion Todd envisioned rolling down the Pan-American Highway perhaps is somewhat ironic when we consider that Todd would spend a decade in the advertising business, but nevertheless it lends an interesting dimension to *Murder on the Tropic*.

Rennert also continues to reflect on his continuing struggle, so important to him, to understand Mexico (the *vacilada* theme):

> He stopped under the archway, staring out over the patio. He was glad that he had no confidant for his thoughts then, for he was fighting off a feeling of uneasiness, of vague, undefined foreboding in the face of some dimly sensed danger. In this damned country (he cursed it often yet knew that this feeling of disquiet which it inspired was, perversely, for him an invariable lodestone) one never felt stability. There was always a faint tremor underneath one's feet, in the air one breathed. As if the volcanoes far to the south were stirring ominously in their sleep.[115]

The Case of the Unconquered Sisters (1936)

Hugh Rennert once again successfully makes his way through a Mexican maze of mystery in *Murder on The Tropic*, solving the case and claiming his monetary reward, which allows him to save his Cameron County citrus farm. This farm will figure largely in the last two novels in the Rennert mystery series, but in the next one, *The Case of the Unconquered Sisters*, Rennert is back to work in the Customs Department, for one last time. When a Texas railway wreck reveals a fresh skeleton (with a bullet hole in the skull) in a shipment of prehistoric ones being sent from Mexico to Southwestern University, Rennert soon is in Mexico City, investigating at the house where the murdered man was staying. The house is the dwelling of the Faudrees, the sisters Lucy and

115 Ibid., 65.

Monica and their niece Cornell. The Faudree sisters are granddaughters of Tindall Faudree, a Confederate veteran who left the United States after the Civil War and established Mexican citizenship (the family motto is *unconquered*, hence the title of the novel). The cash-strapped Faudrees rented rooms in their mansion to the Southwestern University archaeological team conducting a dig in the Pedregal, a great sea of lava bordering the house ("a stormy sea whose black viscous waves had been halted suddenly by putrefaction").[116] Also connected with the household are Marta, the Faudree's mixed race servant (and possible relative), Delaney Roark, a young American embassy official, and John Clay Biggerstaff, an archaeology graduate student. Both of these men exhibit interest in the lovely Cornell Faudree.

Once again, then, Todd presents readers with an interesting Mexican setting centered on a specific building, but the tension present in *The Cat Screams* and *Murder on the Tropic* (on account of the isolation imposed by a quarantine in the one novel and a hurricane in the other) is lacking. The novel also is rather diffuse in interest. While its title suggests that the Faudree sisters themselves are the main focus of the novel, in fact they are not—though the younger sister's repressed sexual interest in her niece's beau, the handsome young Biggerstaff, gets some attention from Todd. Cornell herself is too much the conventional insipid mystery ingénue to be of any real personal interest ("Maybe you'll understand now, Mr. Rennert, why meeting John meant so much to me. He's so clean and healthy—well, I suppose wholesome is the only word").[117] The college professors and students are not memorable; though Todd seems fascinated by Phi Beta Kappa lore (Todd himself was much involved in various fraternity activities at the University of Oklahoma). The

116 Todd Downing, *The Case of the Unconquered Sisters* (New York: Doubleday, Doran, 1936), 46.

117 Downing, *Sisters*, 223. The sex-starved Monica Faudree is constantly invading John Biggerstaff's bedroom, whether or not he is physically present in it. "It was difficult to think of John being Cornell's husband, holding her in his strong arms," Monica reflects as she gazes longingly at John's

Pedregal setting seems promising and Todd makes something out of the folk superstition of owls—*tecolotes*—as harbingers of death, yet local color is painted relatively weakly in this novel. To be sure, in *The Case of the Unconquered Sisters* the mystery plot itself is competently presented, yet *Sisters* is Todd's weakest novel up to this point in his writing career, inferior to even his promising prentice tale, *Murder on Tour*. After three absolutely first-rate mysteries—*The Cat Screams*, *Vultures in the Sky* and *Murder on the Tropic*—Todd's inspiration had for the moment somewhat flagged. Fortunately, 1937 would see a return by the author to the very height of his creative powers, with the final two Hugh Rennert detective novels, *The Last Trumpet* and *Night over Mexico*, tales fully worthy of the earlier trio of genre masterworks.

The Last Trumpet (1937)

In *The Last Trumpet* Hugh Rennert, nearing a half century in age, has retired from the Customs Service to devote himself full time to his beloved Cameron County, Texas citrus farm. The novel takes place in both Mexico and Texas, Todd for this first time developing a non-Mexican setting. Rennert now has a circle of local friends, the most notable member of which is Cameron County sheriff Peter Bounty. In the final two Todd Downing novels, Bounty would fly solo as detective; but in *The Last Trumpet*, he and Rennert, an appealing team, work together.

In addition to incorporating American soil—albeit former Mexican territory—in a novel for the first time, Todd also opened his setting in *The Last Trumpet*. Where in earlier novels, Todd tended to concentrate action in relatively closed locales (houses in *The Cat Screams*, *Murder on the Tropic*, and *The Case of the*

bed. "The bedclothes were rumpled, the way John always disturbed them with those muscular legs of his." At one point, when the injured Biggerstaff is being put to bed by male colleagues, he has to shoo the hovering Monica out of the room with a blunt appeal to her southern genteel sense of sexual decorum: "What I want, Monica, is somebody to help me out of my underwear" (ibid., 91, 167).

Unconquered Sisters; a train in *Vultures in the Sky*; hotels and a train in *Murder on Tour*), in *The Last Trumpet*, action ranges over Cameron County, Texas and across the border to Matamoras, Mexico and its vicinity. Todd would later use a similarly open setting in the first Peter Bounty solo effort, *Death under the Moonflower* (1938), but he is much more successful in *The Last Trumpet*.

The Last Trumpet is a tale of serial killings. Rennert eventually links five deaths—all occurring over Christmas season—to one malign hand. The first murder discovered (though not the first committed) takes place in a bullring in Matamoras, Mexican twin city to Brownsville, the seat of Cameron County. Through use of a hand mirror the murderer while seated in the spectator stands contrives the death by goring of Mexican bullfighter Carlos Campos. The last trumpet of the title refers to the signal for the kill of the bull by the bullfighter, but in the case of Carlos Campos, the opposite result obtains. As the killings continue, Rennert, who is staying outside Brownsville at the country hotel of his friends Rolf and Christine Jester while the brick bungalow on his citrus farm is being completed, comes to suspect that they all are linked to a tragic incident from the past: a railway accident that occurred on the grounds of a hacienda in the Mexican state of Tamaulipas (Carlos Campos was the hacienda owner's son). The precise motive for the crimes long remains elusive, however, even for Hugh Rennert (though fairly clued, it may elude the reader too until Rennert explains all to Peter Bounty in the final chapter).

The action in *The Last Trumpet* ranges over Cameron County and Tamaulipas, but Todd's depiction of Texas is somewhat muted and his Mexican local color is weaker here than in any of his prior detective novels, with two exceptions: the opening bullring section and a single chapter devoted to a visit to a Matamoros nightclub and a flight across the international bridge between Matamoras and Brownsville, where yet another murder takes place. In his depiction of bloody bullfighting and of the tawdry Matamoras nightclub *El Triunfo de las Emociones* (The Triumph of the Emotions), Todd makes manifest his distaste for the touristy border city. "This isn't the real Mexico," the Oklahoma half-blood college student Kent Distant declares derisively of Matamoras to his nightclub date, Janell Lincoln. "Only the dregs. They always come up at the border."[118]

Kent Distant is one of the more interesting characters in *The Last Trumpet*. Given Kent's fictional and Todd's actual background, one assumes Kent is partly autobiographical. By hallowed middlebrow novel tradition Kent and Janell should provide the love interest in *The Last Trumpet*, but it pointedly does not work out that way. As the two young people quickly become bored with each other, Todd Downing's sympathies clearly lie with Kent Distant. From the start, Janell's interest in Kent stands revealed as shallow and patronizing. Initially she avows to her father that "It'd be fun to meet an Oklahoma Indian," yet when she is introduced to Kent she is "a bit disappointed" that he is not "markedly different from the young men she knew in college. Many of them had hair just as black and straight, cheek bones and noses no more prominent than his. He was good-looking, self-confident, that was all."[119]

During their nightclub date any attraction that remains between the two young people dissipates into the stale nightclub air. Kent is disgusted with the scene:

> Although it was early—not much past seven-thirty—this was Saturday night and holiday season, so that most of the tables were occupied by groups of Americans in various states of inebriation. A few enamel-faced women sat alone, smoking and scrutinizing each newcomer with jaded eyes. The odors of cooking and tobacco and perfume were heavy in the air.
>
> "Greenwich Village," was Kent's comment.

118 Todd Downing, *The Last Trumpet* (New York: Doubleday, Doran, 1937), 147.

119 Downing, *Trumpet*, 8.

> He saw that his companion was determined to keep her illusions. "That's probably only the surface, Kent. The guidebooks say that once you cross the Rio Grande you're in another civilization, centuries old. They can't be wrong."

Here Todd, in addition to satirizing Janell's ingenuousness ("I don't even see chili con carne," she naively exclaims when scrutinizing the nightclub's menu), is taking a swipe at shallow guidebooks misinforming Americans about Mexico, one of Todd's most persistent bugbears over the years. In a 1932 *Daily Oklahoman* review of a travel volume on Mexico, for example, Todd had noted critically that "the first chapters are distinctly reminiscent of the guidebook," but then approvingly added that the tome improved after the guidebook gets "tossed into a *barranca*."[120]

Out of the nightclub experience Janell comes away thinking Kent rather a stick in the mud and Kent feeling that Janell is more than a trifle insipid. In addition to their different attitudes toward Mexico, a further wedge that develops between the two college students arises from their differing perceptions of Hugh Rennert. Kent rather idolizes Rennert, quoting the older man's wisdom on numerous subjects during the course of the novel. Janell, on the other hand, has somewhat taken against Rennert, on account of her father having fallen out with the citrus farmer over his murder investigation. (Rennert has been temporarily deputized by Sheriff Peter Bounty.) A definite daddy's girl, Janell quotes her father as dutifully as Kent quotes Rennert:

> "Mr. Rennert's been appointed a deputy sheriff, you know, and—"
>
> "A deputy sheriff? No, I didn't know that. To investigate these—these attacks?"

120 Ibid., 141-142; *Daily Oklahoman*, 31 January 1932, 43 (review of Harry Carr, *Old Mother Mexico*).

> "Yes, and Father says it's gone to his head. He even went so far as to tell Father that he'd been criminally careless because the maid threw away the bullet he got out of Mr. Radisson's hand. Father was angry about it. That's what comes, he said, of giving a man a little bit of authority."
>
> Kent's jaw set. "I don't know anybody," he said stiffly, "who would be better qualified to use authority than Mr. Rennert. Now that he's in charge, the mystery will be solved."[121]

Kent also seems standoffish to Janell when he is reluctant to discuss his Indian father, David Distant, with her. "She would probably think it strange that he didn't go on and talk unreservedly about his feelings, as people she was accustomed to did," Kent reflects to himself at the table. "But it always cost him a wrench to do that, especially where his father was concerned. There was part of one's self that ought never to be exposed. It was—well, sacred, in a way. In a way that white people could never understand."[122]

Three years later in *The Mexican Earth*, Todd wrote in a similarly dismissive fashion of "Miss Blank," an anonymous California coed member of a Mexican tour group whom he met at a dinner at the Hotel Geneve in Mexico City:

> One young lady in particular was ecstatic about Indians: their handicrafts, their babies, their politeness, their musical voices, everything. She was studying indigenous art and folk dances and the Aztec language in the summer school of the National University of Mexico. The highlight of her day seemed to be the time she had joined ("horned in on," I would have said) a family of Indians at their

121 Downing, *Trumpet*, 143-144.
122 Ibid., 142.

> midday meal. She had sat on a hillside with them and eaten their *tortillas*.
>
> "I hate to think of going back home," she told me over her filet mignon. "I'd like to live down here, where I could be with Indians all the time. I think it's wonderful—the way they're coming into their own."
>
> And on and on. I should have held my peace, had she not got me at an inattentive moment with a question like, "What's that word I'm trying to think of?"
>
> I said: "You have Indians out in California, don't you?"
>
> She frowned. "Oh, that's different. They're not—well, yes, I guess they are the same race. But—"
>
> The young man who was my host rattled silverware and introduced a new topic of conversation. I was to sign a contract with him after dinner, giving him authority to handle some transportation arrangements for my own party. Later, in his room, he laughed and said to me:
>
> "Miss Blank is quite a card, isn't she? Uh—you understand she was kidding you, of course? She knew all the time that you're Indian yourself."

Todd was dubious of his friend's attempted exculpation of Miss Blank. In contrast with the objectionable Miss Blank, he avowed, "the person likely to be most free of prejudice is the one who is unconcernedly silent about race and nationality and creed."[123] No doubt the moral of Todd's *Mexican Earth* anecdote applies equally as well to the patronizing and credulous Janell Lincoln of *The Last Trumpet*.

A much more successful relationship takes root in *The Last Trumpet*, however: that between two men, Hugh Rennert and Peter Bounty. The Cameron County sheriff does not appear until

123 Downing, *Mexican Earth*, 9-10.

Chapter Eight of the novel, but Todd then lavishes upon Bounty a page of background detail and description, suggesting that he had major plans in mind for this character. Serving his second term as Cameron County sheriff, Bounty, of "obscure genesis and no political affiliations," has been kept in office "by the devotion of two mutually antagonistic elements": the Mexican-Americans and the "booted, Stetson-hatted gentry of the ranches." To the former Bounty "was Don Pedro, who sat at table with them and acted as godfather to their babies, who was as quick to take their side in matters of racial discrimination as he was to punish their peccadilloes, while to the latter Bounty "was Pete, a rare comrade untouched by affectation or effeteness." The "bustling young businessmen" transforming the Magic Valley, on the other hand, look askance at Bounty, seeing him "as a picturesque but slouchy remnant of a past which had gone the way of the Texas Rangers."[124]

When Rennert meets with Bounty to discuss his suspicion that a serial murderer is active in Cameron County, the sheriff makes a good impression on the amateur detective:

> Bounty was an imperturbable, mildly sensuous man of slight but wiry build. There was something feline about the indolent movements of his body, which always seemed clad in the same blue serge, worn thin and shiny on the seat, the elbows and the shoulder blades. His virile, finely featured face and sleek flaxen hair, too oily, gave him an illusory appearance of youth. His eyes were a baffling blend of blue and hazel. . . . Although heretofore [Rennert] had exchanged less than a dozen words with Bounty his liking for the sheriff had been instantaneous. On the occasion of their first meeting, at the Customs office, he had known that the man was . . . *simpatico*.[125]

124 Downing, *Trumpet*, 116.
125 Ibid., 117.

Bounty is so impressed with Rennert's reasoning about the case that he makes his new friend a special temporary deputy, complete with a shiny badge:

> The deputy sheriff's badge was of nickel. It was large and heavy and, now that the novelty of its possession had passed, Rennert was inclined to think it ostentatious. Since the weather was too warm for a vest, he wore it pinned to the inside of his coat, where it made his lapel sag conspicuously. He had half a mind to take it off and consign it to a pocket. Instead, he buttoned his coat and straightened his shoulders. "Leave it on," Bounty had admonished him. "It will make you feel snug and confident."[126]

Sheriff and deputy work together to solve the case, though it is Deputy Rennert, naturally, who has the great moment of illumination that reveals the truth.

At one point in *The Last Trumpet*, Rennert's friend Rolf Jester urges Rennert to cease trifling with amateur crime detection and take a wife. Similarly, Christine Jester, while talking with Rennert, finds herself wondering, "as she did every time she observed the vitality of his mature yet unlined face, why he had never married. And learned what it was to be happy." Yet in *The Last Trumpet*, the happiness Rennert finds is in the company of his fellow bachelor Peter Bounty (who also, it will be recalled, reads novels and appreciates the fineness of *The Glories of Venus*). Over the course of the book the two men grab a bite at Bounty's favorite place, a "little hamburger joint" down the corner from the library, as well as a more formal Sunday dinner, at Rennert's abashed invitation, at the Hotel Jester. At the latter location an "amused and elated and perhaps envious" Rennert notes that "more than one pair of feminine eyes lingered on the polished

126 Ibid., 125.

and handsome occupant of the chair opposite Rennert's—and returned."[127]

At the end of the novel, the case solved, Rennert returns his deputy sheriff's badge to his superior. Bounty, his voice "low and quick," urges: "Keep it, Hugh. I'll have a vacancy on the regular force the first of the year." Rennert turns Bounty down, not without regret; but Bounty still is able to do one great favor for his *simpatico* friend, as readers of the book will see.[128]

Night over Mexico (1937)

By the end of *The Last Trumpet*, Hugh Rennert seems to have found a place of relative peace and comfort in that brick bungalow nestled among the citrus groves of Cameron County, Texas ("The eyes of Texas are upon you/Till Gabriel blows his horn," writes Todd at one point, quoting the alma mater of the University of Texas). Yet *Night over Mexico* finds Hugh Rennert back in Mexico, in the gravest peril of his life. Rennert's swan song, *Night over Mexico* resolves Rennert's relationship with Mexico in a fitting and moving way.

Concerning what he saw as the increasingly obsolescent mythical quality of the amateur detective after World War Two, the noted crime fiction author and critic Julian Symons in his genre survey *Bloody Murder* related a story of the great American hard-boiled writer Dashiell Hammett allegedly asking, when introducing the classical detective novelist Ellery Queen to a lecture audience, "Mr. Queen, will you be good enough to

127 Ibid., 37, 258.

128 Ibid., 273. The relationship between Hugh Rennert and Peter Bounty may strike a familiar chord with readers familiar with Raymond Chandler's portrayal of a similar relationship between two men, his private detective Philip Marlowe and the serendipitous kindly ex-cop Red Norgaard, in Chandler's classic hard-boiled crime novel *Farewell, My Lovely* (1940). For an interesting take on the male "heroic duo" in the hard-boiled detective novel, see Megan Abbott, "Soft-Voiced Big Men" (review of Robert Crais, *The Sentry: A Joe Pike Novel*), 28 April 2011, *Los Angeles Review of Books*, http://blog.lareviewofbooks.org/post/5011247663/soft-voiced-big-men.

explain your famous character's sex life, if any?" Symons asserts that "such a question could not have been asked before the Second World War," when, he declares, the public supposedly accepted without demur Sherlock Holmes "as a misogynist, [Hercule] Poirot as an ageing bachelor, [and Ellery] Queen as a figure susceptible to feminine beauty but above or outside emotional entanglement."[129]

Symons' confident assertion notwithstanding, however, in truth the detective novel already was changing in significant ways during the 1930s, before the outbreak of World War Two, and many readers were coming to expect more emotional verisimilitude from their detective heroes. Over the course of the 1930s, Dorothy L. Sayers' aristocratic amateur sleuth Lord Peter Wimsey would fall in love and eventually marry (Sayers' sister Crime Queens Margery Allingham and Ngaio Marsh soon followed Sayers' lead with their aristocratic detectives), while across the pond Dashiell Hammett with *The Thin Man* (1934) would introduce to a titillated detective fiction reading world Nick and Nora Charles, the prototype for a band of bibulous and bawdy crime busting couples (in the original Alfred Knopf edition Nora infamously asks Nick, "Tell me the truth: when you were wrestling with Mimi, didn't you have an erection?"). In Todd Downing's case, it appears that by 1937 he himself desired to give his "confirmed bachelor" detective Hugh Rennert—by my estimation age forty-seven in his final novel—some sort of credible interior emotional life; and we see the result in *The Last Trumpet* and *Night over Mexico*.[130]

In *Night over Mexico* Hugh Rennert fatefully returns to Tamaulipas to settle a legal dispute with Mexican owners of a

129 Julian Symons, *Bloody Murder: From the Detective Story to the Crime Novel* (1972; rev. ed., New York and Tokyo: Mysterious Press, 1992), 162.

130 Stephen Altobello, "The Thin Man and the Little Erection, or How to Imagine Myrna Loy Talkin' Dirty," 14 October 2010, *Peel Slowly*, http://peelslowlynsee.wordpress.com/2010/10/14/the-thin-man-and-the-little-erection/. Concerning Hugh Rennert's age, see Todd Downing, *Night over Mexico* (New York: Doubleday, Doran, 1937), 192.

tract of land bordering Rennert's cherished citrus farm. As ever when the retired customs agent visits Mexico, he is plunged into a grim case of murder. Driving through the mountains some sixty miles from his destination, the city of Victoria, Rennert encounters a persistent misting rain, or *chipi chipi*, and a mountain landslide that obstructs the road ahead of him. He is forced to seek shelter—along with ten other people who have preceded him—in a providentially located ranch house. At least the ranch house *seems* providentially located, until people in it start dying. First the Mexican caretaker is found run over by a car, then two more people expire from unknown causes. And an uneasy man with a gun is refusing to allow people to leave the house.

Here we have a highly classic situation, the most famous instance of which is found in the bestselling mystery novel of all time, Agatha Christie's *And Then There Were None* (1939): people trapped in an isolated house being picked off by an unknown murderer. Like the Queen of Crime, Todd manages to wring considerable suspense out of the situation. Everyone in the house seems to have something hide, but whose secrets are relatively innocuous and whose are deadly? And just what is it that is killing people? In attempting to solve this, his last mystery, Rennert is facing no mere academic murder puzzle (though in fact there is a very clever, fairly clued puzzle embedded in the story) but what is for him a literal matter of life and death.

In *Night over Mexico*, Todd presents readers with some of his most atmospheric writing (the omnipresent rain is so oppressive that it begins to feel like the end of the world) and perhaps his most memorable cast of characters. Four individuals stand out particularly. Gulliver Damson, Ph.D., an overbearing chap whose chatty and superficial Mexican travel book, *Heigh-ho, Mexico!* is excerpted at the beginning of each of the three parts of the novel, is Todd's most acidulous portrait of ingenuously arrogant American intellectual "experts" on the land south of the border ("I have done quite a bit of poetry and book reviewing for various magazines. One of my poems was translated into Japanese. But I've always wanted to try my hand at a travel book.").[131] Jesse Elkins, the one-time American oil baron of Tampico who returned with a hard-won fortune to his home town of Acropolis, Kansas, and found life rather intolerably dull ever afterward, is a surprisingly empathetic depiction of an American capitalist "exploiter," given Todd's opposition to American colonialist behavior toward Mexico (which soon found its strongest expression in Todd's *The Mexican Earth*). But the two most fascinating characters of all are Jesse Elkins' much younger wife, Vera, and the mysterious Mr. George Woodmansee.

Although the magnetically attractive Vera Elkins and George Woodmansee appear to be potentially unscrupulous adventurers of some sort or another, Hugh Rennert is powerfully drawn to them both. It is to Vera Elkins that Hugh makes his musings about *vacilada* and the nature of his abiding interest in Mexican murder mysteries. Although Todd's favorite mystery writers tended to come out of the classical tradition, he also admired the work of Dashiell Hammett and James M. Cain; and this admiration is reflected, I think, in the character of Vera Elkins, the closest Todd ever came to portraying an alluring femme fatale:

> Rennert's pause was involuntary, and he wondered, after an instant, how many years it had been since he had gawked in such open tribute at a full-blown feminine form.

> Rennert held her, felt her trembling gradually subside and her warm tears soaking though to his skin. Still the straw man, he reminded himself. Stuffed. If he was ludicrous when he hunted for a pair of pants or was pictured in a bathing suit (why in hell did she keep harping on that?), what would he be if he

131 Downing, *Night*, 127. Dr. Damson hails from Greenwich Village, making *Night over Mexico* the second satirical jab that Todd in 1937 made at this citadel of Bohemia. (Kent Distant disparages the neighborhood in *The Last Trumpet*, it will be recalled.) Here one suspects that Todd was writing from recent personal experience.

> showed how alive he was to the fragrance of the loose hair which tickled his nose and to the odor of clove pinks which he drew in with every breath?

Yet when Rennert passes his hand "over Mrs. Elkins' soft black hair" he does so in a manner "which to an onlooker would have suggested a benediction rather than a caress."[132]

Vera Elkins' masculine equivalent is the sleek, panther-like and devil-may-care George Woodmansee ("a bright hard blade which has flashed across one's vision and vanished"). Emphasis is laid throughout the book on Woodmansee's physical perfection and prowess. After Woodmansee showers outdoors in the rain, he bounds naked back into the room he and Rennert are sharing, "a gleaming statue come to life." Just as he does with Vera Elkins, Rennert feels a connection with Woodmansee:

> Woodmansee had moved with swift lithe steps to Rennert's side, his feet making no noise at all. They stood with elbows touching, and Rennert was surprised at the feeling contact with that hard arm brought: that the two of them were linked by some common quality which was purely impersonal in its nature. He sensed the magnetism, not of congenial flesh and blood, but of tempered steel whose extrinsic worth he respected while knowing that its present immaculateness did not signify that it had never known blood or other fouling.[133]

Despite Rennert's wariness of the potential ruthlessness in Woodmansee's character, a certain rough intimacy develops between the two men over the course of the novel:

> Woodmansee went to the chest in the corner, hauled out two blankets and carried them to the

132 Ibid., 38, 162, 231.
133 Ibid., 91, 211, 238.

> couch upon which Rennert had stretched out. "I promised Miss Pirtle I wouldn't let you take cold. A good kind man, she called you. How does it feel to be one?"
>
> Rennert grunted and pulled the blankets up to his chin. "Sounds like an obituary."

Eventually Rennert invites Woodmansee to return to Cameron County with him:

> "How about Brownsville? Like it?"
>
> "It looks all right. I've only passed through."
>
> "I was thinking you might like to stick around there a bit. I have a house and can put you up with pleasure. I shouldn't be surprised if we located some sort of job that appealed to you. I may possibly be looking for a manager for my farm before long."
>
> Woodmansee's laugh was hard. "Honest work, eh?"
>
> "Um-huh. Oh, if you had to do something devilish once a while you could smuggle a bottle of liquor past the customs officers. What about it? Want to watch grapefruit grow for a spell? You'd look fine in overalls."[134]

What is Rennert's fate in *Night over Mexico*, and that of the other characters? The reader will have to read this ingeniously plotted novel and see.

In addition to chronicling Hugh Rennert's personal fortune, *Night over Mexico* offers some of Todd's most penetrating writing about Mexico and its relationship with the people to the north. For example, there are Rennert's ruminations on Keith Kerwick, the prickly young man holding the gun on his uninvited "guests":

134 Ibid., 220-221, 286-287.

> The more he saw of Kerwick the less impressed he was. Superficially at least there was nothing to distinguish him from many another youngster with whom Rennert had come into contact in Mexico. They compose an undevious, essentially naïve crew who seek adventure and El Dorados south of the Rio Grande and find, in nine cases out of ten, only hard work, dysentery and homesickness. He wasn't altogether tolerant toward their failings; their sublime indifference to the subtleties and complexities of their environment; the gridiron mentality which governs their conduct; their silly Anglo-Saxon racial prejudices. But, he had to admit, they were seldom perverse. More like bulls in china closets. . . .[135]

Then there are Hugh Rennert's thoughts on his first meeting with the great oil man Jesse Elkins, in Monterrey around 1912, when Rennert was a young man "just out of college":

> I didn't take my eyes off him. He had one arm in a sling, I remember. He wore boots and corduroys and a Stetson hat. And a six-shooter. He was slim and hard, somewhat on George Woofmansee's build. . . .[H]e was looking at the sunlight clearing away the mists on old Saddleback [Mountain]. I supposed his mind was on oil wells and a business deal. I wouldn't have believed he was gazing at that mountain exactly as I'd been doing every morning from my window. All the beauty I'd found in Mexico was in Saddleback, but I'd probably have blushed if anyone has caught me admiring a mountain. That simply isn't done by young fellows my age in the United States.

135 Ibid., 31.

It was Jesse Elkins who convinced the young Rennert to stay in Mexico, even though with the exception of Saddleback Mountain, Rennert had been repelled by the strange country, then in the first throes of tumultuous revolution: "I hated—with a very personal hatred—the brutality and the violence and the obscenity. . . . Everywhere I turned I met the scent of blood and death. I was disgusted and, though I wouldn't have admitted it, scared."[136]

Finally, there is Rennert on the matchless blessing of a mixed blood heritage (a point Todd had first made in print over a decade earlier in "A Choctaw's Autobiography"):

> He envied at moments such as this the versatility of Mexicans, who illuminated the drab grayness of *Weltschmerz* [world-weariness] with the skyrockets of *vacilada*. That escape was denied, he firmly believed, to men of a single blood stream. They could appreciate the beauty of the sparks (drink helped here), but when they tried to send up rockets of their own they saw them fizzle out at the damp touch of Anglo-Saxon logic.[137]

Other Works (1938-1945) *(Death under the Moonflower, The Lazy Lawrence Murders, The Shadowless Hour)*

With its appealing combination of Mexican verve and color with the logic and fair play plotting of the classical Anglo-American detective novel, Todd Downing's series of seven Hugh Rennert tales, beginning with the impressive *Murder on Tour* in 1933 and ending with the superb *Night over Mexico* in 1937, has unique merit among the many mysteries produced in the Golden Age of detective fiction. After 1937, Todd produced only two more detective novels, *Death under the Moonflower* (1938) and *The Lazy Lawrence Murders* (1941), in neither of which does

136 Ibid., 194-195.
137 Ibid., 162.

Rennert appear (the sleuth in both is Hugh Rennert's friend Peter Bounty, who is not of especial interest when separated from Rennert's company). Both novels are inferior to those in the Rennert series.

There was, however, one last Hugh Rennert adventure to surface: the novella *The Shadowless Hour.* Published in 1945, in actuality *The Shadowless Hour* must have been written by Todd some dozen years earlier, around the time of *Murder on Tour* (it almost certainly was the work Todd originally hoped to publish as his second novel, *Murder in Monterrey*). In this final published tale Rennert anachronistically is still employed with the U. S. Customs Service, the Cameron County citrus farm, one presumes, just a gleam in his eye. Although the novella is a serviceable tale with characteristic Todd Downing devices—a closed setting (a Monterrey pension, or boarding house), a strongly-conveyed atmosphere (oppressive heat this time), a bit of Native American mysticism (Aztec divination)—it is inferior to the novels *The Cat Screams*, *Vultures in the Sky* and *Murder on the Tropic*, in all of which Todd incorporated elements from *The Shadowless Hour*. The basic plot has considerable resemblance to *The Cat Screams*, while some of the characters reappear, in much better developed forms, in *Cat*, *Vultures in the Sky, and Murder on the Tropic* (one character in *Tropic*, Bertha Fahn, even has the same name as a character in *Hour*, though the two have significant differences).

Of greatest interest are two characters, Jesus Hope, a Mexican college student of Indian and German parentage, and the aforementioned Bertha Fahn, a repressed, intensely religious spinster. In reference to Jesus Hope, Downing writes of the young man's irrevocable link "with the dark people of Mexico, whose blood defies white infiltration by sheer impenetrability," a notable articulation of Todd's belief in the strength of indigenous Mexican resistance to colonialism. As for the Bertha Fahn of *Hour* she, in contrast with the Bertha Fahn of *Tropic*, is latently lesbian, the only explicit instance of a gay character in Todd's fiction. Unconscious of her true motivations, Miss Fahn pursues the lovely Trescinda Cull, trying to get Miss Cull to relinquish her unrequited love for the Texas businessman for whom she works (Todd grafted aspects of Trescinda Cull, including her first name, into no fewer than three female characters in *Cat* and *Vultures*). When Miss Fahn enlists Rennert's aid to "help" Miss Cull, speaking passionately of Miss Cull's great physical beauty, Rennert's eyes narrow slightly, as he discerns

> a facet which he had not suspected glowing now with the reflection of a deep consuming fire within. It wasn't, he thought, a pleasant sight. Neither did he feel that it was the wholly evil thing, which, in the abstract, Miss Fahn would be the first to react against. Did she but know it for what it was—this passion of a chilled repressed woman for beauty and softness and warmth of flesh.

Todd, who at the time he likely wrote *The Shadowless Hour* probably had recently seen the controversial lesbian-themed German film *Mädchen in Uniform* (1931), is somewhat sympathetic, by the standards of his time and place, to Miss Fahn's plight, noting that Rennert does not deem her passion for Miss Cull "the wholly evil thing" that Miss Fahn herself would have deemed it, "in the abstract."[138]

In fewer than forty-five pages Hugh Rennert once again solves a murder in Mexico, but *The Shadowless Hour*, though not completely lacking in interest, is a lesser work, cannibalized by its creator for use in much more substantial Hugh Rennert novels. Nevertheless, it is pleasant to see Rennert in action one last time, providing answers to the puzzling riddles of life and death on the Mexican earth.

138 Todd Downing, *The Shadowless Hour, Mystery Book Magazine* 2 (November 1945): 115, 121. Todd may have seen *Mädchen in Uniform* when visiting his sister Ruth in New York City, where the film received rave reviews after the initial ban on its showing was lifted.

Part Three: Clues and Corpses

The Mystery Criticism of Todd Downing

Todd Downing reviewed crime fiction for the Oklahoma City *Daily Oklahoman* periodically from 1930 to 1937, overlapping the years (1933 to 1935) that Dorothy L. Sayers reviewed crime fiction for the London *Sunday Times*. Granted, the *Daily Oklahoman* is not so prominent a newspaper as the *Sunday Times*, nor is Todd Downing the renowned name in mystery fiction that is Dorothy L. Sayers. Yet while the mystery reviews of Dorothy L. Sayers remain uncollected, Todd Downing's incisive and appealing pieces now have been published. Moreover, Todd Downing donated his library of books to Southeastern Oklahoma State University, where the collection survives today intact. With Todd Downing we thus have an unusually good cache of clues that, when properly deciphered, guides us both to the aesthetic values of a significant Golden Age mystery writer and to the currently much underappreciated richness and variety of 1930s mystery genre writing. Rather than being a time when mystery fiction was dominated on the one side of the Atlantic Ocean by a handful of British "Crime Queens" penning cozy tales of genteel amateur detection and on the other side by American men composing tough, action-oriented stories of the violent clashes of private eyes and professional crooks, the 1930s in both the United States and Great Britain was a period of flux and diversity, when the term "mystery" encompassed an array of different types of tales: traditional thrillers and puzzlers, numerically dominated by male writers; more consciously literary, "manners" detective novels associated with the British Crime Queens Dorothy L. Sayers, Margery Allingham and Ngaio Marsh; and avowedly realistic hard-boiled and psychological crime fiction, the latter of which was often the product of women writers.[139]

139 For two additional published collections of pre-1950 detective fiction reviews see Francis M. Nevins, *The Anthony Boucher Chronicles: Reviews and Commentary, 1942-1947* (Vancleave, MS: Ramble House, 2002) and

At Todd Downing's death his library included nearly 2000 books, more than 500 of which (over 25%) were mystery novels or true crime studies, dating up to the year 1959. Along with books dealing with Latin America, mysteries were Todd's most notable area of interest, at least in terms of the sheer quantity of volumes in his library. Before the 1930s, Todd's crime collection was dominated by Edgar Wallace thrillers (in 1974 Todd's library included a staggering sixty-five volumes by Wallace). However, during the 1930s, when Todd was reviewing crime fiction for the *Daily Oklahoman*, the mystery authors he most collected were, for the most part, true detective novelists, both male and female, American and British: John Dickson Carr, Rufus King, Ellery Queen, Agatha Christie, Mignon Eberhart, Hugh Austin, Anthony Berkeley, Eden Phillpotts, Anthony Wynne, John Street (John Rhode/Miles Burton), H. C. Bailey and G. D. H. and Margaret Cole. There also are omnibus volumes by Dashiell Hammett, Mary Roberts Rinehart and Dorothy L. Sayers. Only one hard-boiled author, Dashiell Hammett, appears on this list.[140]

Although during the 1930s Todd's favorite mystery writers tended to be, judging from his library, true detective novelists, Todd's holdings from the 1940s and 1950s indicate that, while he continued to buy true detective fiction during this period, he became attached as well to what was then called the "woman's suspense" novel, or, less chauvinistically, novel of psychological suspense. Along with such writers as Michael Innes and Edmund Crispin, British exponents of the "donnish detection"

Jared Lobdell, *The Detective Fiction Reviews of Charles Williams, 1930-1935* (Jefferson, NC, and London: McFarland, 2003). For an analysis of the changes that occurred in mystery fiction in the 1930s see Curtis Evans, *Masters of the Humdrum Mystery: Cecil John Charles Street, Freeman Wills Crofts, Alfred Walter Stewart and the British Detective Novel, 1920-1961* (Jefferson, NC, and London: McFarland, 2012), Chapter One.

140 In addition to Dashiell Hammett, Todd bought smaller numbers of novels by other hard-boiled authors, including three by George Harmon Coxe, two by Jonathan Latimer and one by James M. Cain—though surprisingly his library included nothing whatsoever by Raymond Chandler or Ross Macdonald.

school, and the American detective novelists Clifford Knight, Patrick Quentin, Frederic Brown (semi-hard-boiled) and Helen McCloy (who later diverged largely into tales of psychological suspense), the newer writers Todd favored in the forties and fifties were female suspense writers. In Todd's library this group was headed by the American and Canadian-American authors Dorothy B. Hughes and Margaret Millar and the English authors Ethel Lina White and Joseph Shearing (pseudonym of Gabrielle Margaret Vere Campbell, who as Marjorie Bowen also wrote horror fiction Todd purchased). Among Todd's older favorites, Mignon Eberhart and Mary Roberts Rinehart were pioneers of suspense-oriented mystery fiction and Rufus King turned to suspense in the 1940s.[141]

Todd's library thus indicates that while he enjoyed both traditional detective novels and thrillers, he also became increasingly interested in more psychologically acute crime fiction. These preferences appear as well in his 1930s mystery reviews in the *Daily Oklahoman*. Of 286 books reviewed, classical detective fiction by both American and British authors predominates, although there are also a significant number of reviews of works by hard-boiled and psychological crime writers. 56% of the books reviewed have American authors or co-authors, while 41% have British and 3% have French. 77% of the authors are men, 23% women. Nor are British women disproportionately represented compared to American women; the male-female ratio is roughly the same in both national groupings. These numbers suggest that, contrary to conventional wisdom, British women did not dominate classical detective fiction in this period (indeed, these numbers suggest precisely the opposite). However,

141 In the 1950s Todd also purchased two novels by the noted American suspense writer Charlotte Armstrong, *The Black-Eyed Stranger* (1951) and the Edgar-winning *A Dram of Poison* (1956). Additionally Todd was a great admirer of the esteemed English novelist Graham Greene, some of whose 1930s and 1940s novels have been associated with crime/espionage fiction. Among these latter works Todd owned *Orient Express* (1932) (*Stamboul Train* in England), *Brighton Rock* (1938), *The Confidential Agent* (1939) and *The Ministry of Fear* (1943).

it is true that the percentage of women authors reviewed by Todd increased substantially over time, from 18% in 1930-32 (nearly one-fifth) to 31% in 1936-37 (nearly one-third).[142]

The growing importance in thirties and forties mystery genre writing of the British Crime Queens Dorothy L. Sayers, Margery Allingham and Ngaio Marsh—along with numerous other authors, male and female, such as, from England, Georgette Heyer, Joseph Shearing, Ethel Lina White, Francis Iles, Michael Innes and Nicholas Blake, and, from the United States, Dashiell Hammett, Raymond Chandler, Rufus King and Mignon Eberhart—reflects the shift of interest in detective fiction during these years away from pure puzzle plotting toward other literary values more

142 For a statement encapsulating errors in the now conventional gynocentric view of classical Golden Age detective fiction see Erin A. Smith, *Hard-Boiled: Working-Class Readers and Pulp Magazines* (Philadelphia: Temple University Press, 2000), 39-40. "[T]here were some successful male authors of detective fiction between the wars," Professor Smith too grudgingly allows, before asserting: "[W]omen were so prominent that the occupation of mystery writing could seem as 'feminine' as teaching or nursing. . . . [American] hard-boiled texts defined themselves against feminized, classical English detective fiction. . . . What the hard-boiled writers of the '20s and '30s were doing was attempting to wrest control of a specific section of the literary marketplace for men and manly fiction from the women who had dominated the field." Here, Smith does that which is too commonly done today: She ignores the existence of classical detective novelists, both male and female, in the United States and male classical detective novelists in Britain, treating classical detective fiction in the Golden Age as an almost exclusively feminine and British demesne. Smith finds space to mention not only Agatha Christie and Dorothy L. Sayers, but Margery Allingham, Ngaio Marsh, Josephine Tey, Patricia Wentworth and Gladys Mitchell, while omitting references to British male classical detective novelists and American classical detective novelists of either sex. Smith declares that "Hard-boiled writers' reaction against female British mystery writers was part of a larger ideology . . . 'the dark legend of matricide' at the heart of the modernist impulse." In Smith's view hard-boiled books are "matricidal texts, rebelling against the figure of the all-powerful Victorian mother god and the feminization of American culture she had wrought." Smith, *Hard-Boiled*, 185. It is easier of course to draw such a conclusion if one ignores the fact that for the entire Golden Age, classical detective fiction was numerically dominated by males, in both the United States and England.

associated with mainstream fiction, such as humor and satire, greater depth of characterization and psychological realism. Todd Downing never relinquished his interest in the puzzle plot, to be sure, yet both his own fiction writing and his book reviews reflect his mental engagement with this new artistic impetus within the genre.

In a 1934 newspaper interview, Todd expressed the opinion that "the detective story has been pretty well reduced to formula. . . . The time is ripe for some writer to abandon the Poe-Doyle tradition and strike out into a new field, which will be entirely different" (see Appendix Two). Nearly a decade later Todd, in his 1943 essay "Murder is a Rather Serious Business," indicated that something of a new direction had indeed been struck (see Appendix Four). "Characterization is a phase of mystery-writing which can no longer be slighted," he noted. "Time was when one expected the characters of this type of fiction, apart from the central figure of the detective, to be cardboard people, standing for goodness or for villainy, for generosity or for avarice. The demands of today are increasingly for verisimilitude. In fact, in the hands of many widely read authors the detective story is approaching the psychological novel." This development is one that Todd's 1930s crime fiction reviews illuminate.

In Todd's crime fiction reviews, there are 25 authors who are each reviewed three or more times:

Ellery Queen (Frederic Dannay and Manfred Lee) (8)
Agatha Christie (7)
Eden Phillpotts (7)
H. C. Bailey (6)
John Dickson Carr (6)
Carolyn Wells (6)
Herbert Adams (5)
John Street (John Rhode/Miles Burton) (5)
Patricia Wentworth (5)
Anthony Wynne (5)
Mignon Eberhart (4)
Harry Stephen Keeler (4)

Rufus King (4)
Milton Propper (4)
Dorothy L. Sayers (4)
Anthony Abbot (3)
Hugh Austin (3)
G. D. H. and Margaret Cole (3)
J. S. Fletcher (3)
Walter S. Masterman (3)
Darwin Teilhet (3)
Sir Basil Thomson (3)
John V. Turner (also Nicholas Brady and David Hume) (3)
S. S. Van Dine (3)
Valentine Williams (3)

Together these authors account for 110 books, 39% of the volumes Todd reviewed in the *Daily Oklahoman* in the years from 1930 to 1937. With a few exceptions—most obviously Carolyn Wells, with whose work Todd takes an indulgent, wryly satirical attitude; significantly, his library includes none of her novels—these 27 individuals (15 British/12 American/21 male/6 female) generally can be taken as representing for Todd the cream of 1930s mystery writers.

Largely these authors represent classical detective fiction, though their books often are more colorful than the Golden Age norm.[143] Of the British authors listed above only John Street and the husband and wife team of G. D. H. and Margaret Cole have been associated with the pure puzzle, or Humdrum, school, while Milton Propper was an American disciple of the most famous British Humdrum, Freeman Wills Crofts (Todd favorably reviewed one of Crofts' books; see below). Todd's term for Humdrum writers is the much more laudable-sounding "satisfyingly sane" (or "eminently sane"). Under this rubric, Todd also included Britishers R. Austin Freeman, Henry Wade, Christopher Bush and Herbert

143 To cite some exceptions to this generalization, Harry Stephen Keeler and Walter S. Masterman belong in their own eccentric categories, while Patricia Wentworth, best known today for her cozy Miss Silver detective novels, published primarily in the 1940s and 1950s, at this time was much more a writer of thrillers.

Adams, though the latter man (listed above) also authored an occasional thriller.

In contrast with the Humdrums, writers like Ellery Queen, John Dickson Carr, Anthony Wynne and Anthony Abbot wrote more exotic bafflers (the first three of these men were noted adepts at the art of the miracle problem, or impossible crime), while Mignon Eberhart and Rufus King upped the suspense ante so greatly in some of their mystery writing that these works arguably can be seen as hybrids of detective fiction and thrillers. For their part, Dorothy L. Sayers and Eden Phillpotts wrote more "literary" detective fiction in the 1930s, with greater emphasis on the depiction of character and setting. Phillpotts was himself primarily a mainstream regional novelist of the Thomas Hardy school, while Sayers was England's most prominent exponent of converting the detective novel into the novel of manners; her best two examples of her practicing what she preached are the novels *The Nine Tailors* and *Gaudy Night* (reviews by Todd of both novels are found in this collection).[144] Nevertheless, even these authors generally wrote what would be categorized most accurately as classical detective fiction.

In keeping with his preferences Todd often voiced orthodox sentiments in his mystery reviews. For example, in a number of early reviews he condemns what he deems extraneous and excessive "love interest" in a detective novel, especially when this love interest ensnares the Great Detective himself (in these days the Great Detective usually was a he). In a statement reminiscent of Lionel Twain's (Truman Capote) "No wives!" command in the film *Murder by Death* (1976), Todd complains of the married sleuth in Armstrong Livingston's *The Murder Trap* (1931): "We prefer our sleuths without wives." "A fair novel," he concludes of *The Black Pearl Murders* (1931) by Madeleine Sharps, "but it could have been better improved by subtracting a little of the love at first sight . . . and by adding a more reasonable solution."[145]

144 On Humdrum detective novelists see Evans, *Masters*. On Sayers' views of the detective novel see ibid., 34-37.

145 See also in Appendix One Todd's review of Donn Byrne's short story collection, *Stories without Women* (1931). "The title is too good to be true,"

In detective novels Todd vastly preferred the inclusion of outré horror elements to the portrayal of young love's stirrings. "A tale of pure horror is, we are sure, a hundred times more difficult to write than one of mystery or detection," he once pronounced, in a review of Jesse Douglas Kerruish's *The Undying Monster* (1936), before going on to condemn the novel for including, in addition to frights, "such a mundane thing as love." "If Rufus King can't awaken your jaded brain cells and titillate your nerves no purveyor of mysteries can," Todd gushes in his review of *Murder on the Yacht* (1932), while of Anthony Abbot's *About the Murder of Geraldine Foster* (1931) he concludes, "What makes this story remain in the memory of the reader is the element of horror which permeates the tale." Todd's favorite writer of this sort of outré mystery was John Dickson Carr, the acknowledged master of the "locked room" detective novel. "The touch of the grotesque with which Mr. Dickson enlivens his yarns is more than usually effective in his latest offering," Todd writes approvingly of *The Unicorn Murders* (1935) (published under Carr's pseudonym, Carter Dickson), a novel in which it appears that some fantastic horned creature is killing men by puncturing their foreheads.

Yet while Todd clearly had great fondness for the more bizarre sort of baffler, he also was respectful of the more purely ratiocinative—or "satisfyingly sane"—mystery, of the sort often associated today with the British "Humdrum" school. As indicated above, Humdrum John Street was one of Todd's more reviewed authors, and the Oklahoman generally rendered favorable judgments on Street's sober detective novels. "Routine Scotland Yard investigation, with nary a thrill," writes Todd of Street's *Dead Men at the Folly* (1932), published under his "John Rhode" pseudonym. "Recommended, nevertheless." Of John Street's *Dark is the Tunnel* (1936) (*Death in the Tunnel* in England), published under Street's "Miles Burton" pseudonym, Todd noted: "Brainwork

Todd notes, "so women play parts in most of the stories. Evidently a necessary evil."

is required on this new baffler. . . . There is no excitement in the tale save that deriving from interest in the solution of the problem. The last, however, is neat, logical, and within the grasp of any alert reader." In a review of another Humdrum detective novel, Freeman Wills Crofts' *The Crime at Nornes* (1935) (in England *Crime at Guildford*), Todd writes that "Mr. Crofts . . . is perhaps the foremost exponent of the purely intellectual type of deduction. . . . [In his books] [t]here are never any attempts to create atmosphere or induce shudders. Interest in the solution—and nothing else—holds the reader." Todd praised *Nornes* on this level, declaring that the novel was "[a]s good an example as the reader will be able to find of a type of fiction that is growing increasingly rare."

Todd's crime fiction reviews also offer abundant examples of what was replacing pure puzzle detective fiction in the 1930s: hard-boiled and psychological crime novels. Hard-boiled works never became Todd's favorite sort of mysteries, as the author from Atoka on the whole seems to have been a bit too fastidious by nature to fully identify with the milieu ("he has never witnessed a murder and has no desire to," a newspaper story on Todd once squeamishly commented).[146] "Personally, we got a bit confused among the Mikes and the Nicks and the Petes and the various speakeasies," Todd complains of Englishman Valentine Williams' *The Clock Ticks On* (1933), which Williams set in the United States. Yet Todd consistently praised in the highest terms one of the greatest names in hard-boiled fiction, Dashiell Hammett. "The highbrows have been so enthusiastic about Mr. Hammet's latest hard-boiled mélange of dialogue, liquor and murder that we suppose it will be all right if we permit ourselves a few superlatives from the mystery fan angle," Todd modestly began in his review of Hammett's *The Thin Man* (1934). "To our mind Mr. Hammett is one of the two purveyors of mystery fiction in the United States (Rufus King is the other) who are able to combine all the required elements of a detective yarn with a startling yet pleasing originality." Concerning Hammett's fictional

146 *Daily Oklahoman*, 25 August 1935, 49.

flock of rather tough birds, Todd reminded his *Daily Oklahoman* readers that "[s]uch people do exist and do commit murder."

Four months later a friend introduced Todd to James M. Cain's classic noir tale *The Postman Always Rings Twice* (1934). Todd noted that, like Hammett, Cain was "another writer who doesn't agree with the time-honored dictum that fictional murder must be 'nice'." Cain, an impressed Todd surmised, must have had "a rather intensive course in the one-syllable aspects of that thing called Life" (something the Oklahoman himself could not claim). Todd speculated that these "enfants terrible" Cain and Hammett might well establish a permanent "school of realism in mystery fiction. And, after all, why not?"

When reviewing Jonathan Latimer's *Headed for a Hearse* the next year, 1935, Todd speculated that the hard-boiled "formula—tough talk, hard drinking, Rabelaisian humor in re sex, staccato action—is one which will wear thin over time." At the moment, however, Todd added in a bit of masculine chest-beating, the tough stuff "is a relief from the dainty, frivolous manner of dealing with slaughter to which so many of the lady writers are addicted." Latimer's book was to be recommended for its "touches of realism in the death-house scenes, the lemon squeezer torture and the taxicab banter." Similarly, the next year Todd praised Whitman Chamber's forgotten tough tale *Thirteen Steps* as "[n]ot nice but engrossing, what with long-nosed friends, rye, bourbon, rum and profanity of one, two and three syllables."[147]

Although in his reviews Todd praised hard-boiled crime writing he evidently read more of psychological mystery fiction, where the emphasis is not so much—or not at all—on a puzzle, but rather on the thoughts and behavior of characters implicated

147 See also in Appendix One Todd's review of *Gray Shadows*, an anthology of short pieces authored by prison convicts. "The men whose writings compose this anthology were no white-collared, soft-palmed novelists, dashing off improbable tales of crime for a public ever anxious for more of the same vapid stuff," declares Todd. "Hence this book is as different from the usual book of crime as a sawed-off shotgun is from a child's popgun."

in crime. Todd's reviews of this type of genre fiction, which was often written by women, are of particular interest because so much of it has been unjustly forgotten in the modern era, a time when genre criticism has focused intensively on dividing Golden Age writers into two schools: masculine American hard-boiled and feminine English cozy. To be sure, it is generally recognized that the Golden Age English writer Anthony Berkeley Cox with his inverted novels *Malice Aforethought* (1931) and *Before the Fact* (1932), both written under the pseudonym Francis Iles, was an important figure in the development of psychological crime fiction (rather than following a detective investigating a murder, the one book emphasizes the thoughts and actions of a would-be murderer, the other those of an intended victim). However, the actual amount of psychological crime fiction published in the 1930s is greatly underappreciated today—surprisingly so, given the rise of feminist literary criticism and the fact that, as mentioned above, many of these writers were women.[148]

Psychological crime novels that Todd reviewed in the *Daily Oklahoman* include Mary Roberts Rinehart's *The Album* (1933), Winifred Peck's *The Warrielaw Jewel* (1933), Cora Jarrett's *Night over Fitch's Pond* (1934), Marie Belloc Lowndes' *The Chianti Flask* (1934), Elisabeth Sanxay Holding's *The Unfinished Crime* (1935), Ethel Lina White's *The Wheel Spins* (1936), Katharine Wolffe's *Tall Man Walking* (1937) and several tales by one of Todd's favorite writers, Mignon Eberhart. Of Mary Roberts Rinehart's *The Album*, a tale of murders in a genteel backwater neighborhood,

148 In *Bloody Murder* Julian Symons portrays the psychological crime novel mainly as the practically stillborn creature of Anthony Berkeley Cox under his Francis Iles pseudonym. "Iles' own long-term effect upon the crime story was permanent and important," writes Symons, "but for the time being his influence faded" (p. 142). Symons systematically slights the significant impact on the genre made by women writers like Mary Roberts Rinehart, Mignon Eberhart, Marie Belloc Lowndes and Ethel Lina White. (Elisabeth Sanxay Holding does not even merit a mention.) Surprisingly, feminist literary criticism has been slow to revise Symons' unsatisfactory take on these women writers, instead focusing mostly, among Golden Age authors, on the four British Crime Queens.

Todd praised the acuity of the author's portrayal of "the atmosphere of stodginess and impeccable respectability surrounding the neighborhood known as The Crescent." Todd compared Rinehart's novel to the real life Lizzie Borden case, about which he owned several books. Three months later, Todd lauded Winifred Peck's seemingly Rinehart-influenced mystery *The Warrielaw Jewel* for its "perfection of plot, sustained suspense, skillful portrayal of characters and setting and, last but not least, style."[149]

In 1934 Todd gave a strong review to Cora Jarrett's *Night over Fitch's Pond*, a tale of murder that he believed had "most of the elements of a mystery novel" yet was "primarily a study of character." Despite his categorization of the novel as more of a character study than a mystery, Todd avowed that its author "has a rare sense of the macabre quality of words and has succeeded in fashioning an uninvolved plot that for sheer excitement and constantly mounting tension has few equals in the class of fiction that openly strives for these effects." "Not a pleasant slice of life," Todd concluded of *Fitch's Pond*, "but an interesting one."[150]

149 Contrast Todd's admiring treatment of Mary Roberts Rinehart with Julian Symons' rather contemptuous dismissal of her in *Bloody Murder*, wherein after much ridicule of Rinehart as an HIBK (Had I But Known), feminine anxiety writer, Symons concludes of her novels (specifically including *The Album*): "These are the first crime stories which have the air of being written specifically for maiden aunts" (p. 100). For a much more positive assessment of *The Album*, see Catherine Ross Nickerson, *The Web of Iniquity: Early Detective Fiction by American Women* (Chapel Hill, NC: Duke University Press, 1999). On Winifred Peck's *The Warrielaw Jewel*, see Curtis Evans, "Murder in the Family: *The Warrielaw Jewel* (1933), by Winifred Peck, *The Passing Tramp*, at http://thepassingtramp.blogspot.com/2012/01/murder-in-family-warrielaw-jewel-1933.html. Like Rinehart's other mysteries, *The Album* was reprinted many times since its publication up through the 1990s; yet Winifred Peck's fine crime novel has been out-of-print for nearly eighty years, though Peck, a sister of the famed Anglo-Catholic theologian and detective novelist Ronald Knox, was an accomplished writer in her own right.

150 Cora Jarrett herself professed bemusement over those who categorized *Night Over Fitch's Pond*, her first novel, as a mystery, declaring: "It takes more than the enigmatic death of a character to make a mystery novel."

Todd compared Jarrett's book with Marie Belloc Lowndes' *The Chianti Flask* when he reviewed Lowndes' novel at the end of 1934 (Lowndes was a sister of author Hillaire Belloc). Unlike *Fitch's Pond*, *The Chianti Flask* was avowedly "a murder story," noted Todd, but it also was, he insisted, something more than that as well. "Mrs. Belloc Lowndes' interest lies in the bitter psychological aspects of murder; she is an astute interpreter of human nature and her pen is a scalpel, bright and relentlessly sharp, as she removes layer after layer of the sophistication and hypocrisy of her characters." Todd thought that the "unholy fascination of the process" should compensate mystery fiction fans "for the absence of those elements which may not after all be essentials of a murder novel—clues and red herrings and an omniscient detective."

When a couple months later, in 1935, Todd reviewed Elisabeth Sanxay Holding's inverted mystery novel *The Unfinished Crime*, he recommended that "[f]ollowers of Mrs. Belloc Lowndes should make the acquaintance of Miss Holding forthwith." Todd admired "the feminine subtlety of [Holding's] characterization and her masculine realism." In the novel were "scenes of realistic Medicean horror that will make even the Dashiell Hammett addict blink," the rather awed Oklahoman declared. Todd enthusiastically recommended the novel "to those fans who crave variety and to those scoffers who say that the mystery novel cannot attain depth."

In another review Todd lauded Ethel Lina White's 1936 suspense novel *The Wheel Spins* (filmed by Alfred Hitchcock as *The Lady Vanishes*) for its sense of "cumulative horror." "It had an effect on us which a recent yarn of werewolves and family curses by an English compatriot of Miss White's entirely failed to achieve," Todd, a confirmed fan of monster horror fiction, assured his readers.[151] Similarly, in 1937 Todd praised Katherine Wolffe's

The mystery genre, she insisted, had rules of construction governing it that "are in their way as definite as those that govern the sonnet." See Jarrett's preface to her "Faraday Keene" mystery novel, *Pattern in Black and Red* (1934).

151 Todd's reviews of four horror novels—Jesse Douglas Kerruish's *The Undyng Monster*, A. Merritt's *Burn, Witch, Burn!*, Guy Endore's *The Werewolf of*

Tall Man Walking "as one of the trickiest and most intelligent yarns of the season, put over without fingerprints, broken cufflinks or rouge-tipped cigarettes in the way of clues."

Todd greatly admired Mignon Eberhart's tales, which he came to see as psychological crime fiction. In his 1935 review of Eberhart's *The House on the Roof* he declared that "Mrs. Eberhart has outgrown the conventional mystery writer category and steps out as a full-fledged psychological novelist. Her product has a crime interest, yes, but it is rather a puzzle of character than of time and place and motive." Todd predicted *The House on the Roof* would appeal to all readers save those traditionalist "diehards who refuse to leave the atmosphere of Baker Street."

In his 1936 review of Eberhart's *Fair Warning*, Todd perceptively linked Eberhart with the Gothic novel tradition, avowing: "[S]he is as unique in her day as Mrs. Radcliffe [author of *The Mysteries of Udolpho*, 1794] was in hers." Since publishing her first novel in 1929, Nebraskan Mignon Eberhart had been one of Todd's favorite mystery genre writers. When in Mexico in 1932 conducting one of his tour parties, a pleased Todd reported in a letter to Professor Kenneth C. Kaufman of the University of Oklahoma that Eberhart's mystery *While the Patient Slept* had been translated into Spanish and was "in all the bookshops" in Mexico City. Moreover in 1934 Todd named Eberhart's *From This Dark Stairway* one of his six favorite detective novels (see Appendix

Paris and Gabriel *Marlowe's I Am Your Brother*—are included in this collection. Volumes of horror and supernatural fiction found in Todd's library, include, besides the four titles listed above, works by such authors as Algernon Blackwood, Marjorie Bowen, M. R. James and Arthur Machen. Todd was a fan of science fiction as well, and sci-fi titles published from the 1930s through the 1950s also are found in his library, including Isaac Asimov's *The Caves of Steel* (1954) and *The End of Eternity* (1955), Edwin Balmer's and Philip Wylie's *When Worlds Collide* (1933) and *After Worlds Collide* (1934), Everett Bleiler's *The Best Science Fiction Stories* (1950-1954), Leigh Brackett's *The Long Tomorrow* (1955), Ray Bradbury's *The Martian Chronicles* (1950) and *The Illustrated Man* (1951), Frederic Brown's *What Mad Universe* (1949), *Angels and Spaceships* (1954) and *Martians, Go Home* (1955), Curt Siodmak's *Donovan's Brain* (1943), A. E. van Vogt's *The Book of Ptath* (1947) and *Slan* (1951) and H. G. Wells' *Star-Begotten* (1937).

Two). His library at his death included eleven of Eberhart's novels, all published between 1929 and 1936.[152]

Although Todd in the 1930s enjoyed the trendier pleasures of hard-boiled and psychological crime fiction, he continued to draw enjoyment as well from the traditional master criminal thriller associated with older authors like Edgar Wallace and Sax Rohmer. These traditional thrillers of the Wallace-Rohmer variety comprise about 15% of the mystery fiction Todd reviewed in the *Daily Oklahoman*. Edgar Wallace in particular served as Todd's model for traditional thriller writing. Of Australian J. M. Walsh's *The Black Ghost* (1931), an admiring Todd avowed: "It is written in the best Edgar Wallace manner." Similarly, in a review of David Hume's *Dangerous Mr. Dell* (1935) Todd wrote: "English critics have been plastering labels of 'The New Edgar Wallace' upon so many pretenders to the throne of the Master of Thrills that it is not surprising to find them according Mr. Hume the same honors. While we wouldn't go quite so far, we can safely recommend him for his mad scientists, underground torture chambers and knock-out blows."

When reviewing thrillers Todd also was wont to invoke the name of Sax Rohmer, whose tales of Dr. Fu Manchu's diabolical doings had given Todd gooseflesh aplenty back in the 1910s. Todd so enjoyed F. L. Gregory's *The Cipher of Death* (1934) that he confidently declared all "Sax Rohmer fans would do well to get acquainted with Mr. Gregory. . . . He has concocted here as fantastic a plot as will come their way in a long time yet contrives to make it more credible than most Oriental menace yarns."

152 "The Detective Story," *Daily Oklahoman*, 30 September 1934, 47, 31 July 1932, 45. Among the many psychological crime novels of Joseph Shearing (pseudonym of a female author, it will be recalled) that Todd owned was one, *The Spider in the Cup* (1934) (*Album Leaf* in England), that was reviewed in the *Daily Oklahoman* not by him, but by Savoie Lottinvale, future director of the University of Oklahoma Press, evidently on the grounds that the book was deemed "a character novel" rather than a "mystery tale." *Daily Oklahoman*, 24 March 1934, 51. However, Todd did review *Ann Vickers* (1933), Sinclair Lewis' unquestionably mainstream novel about an unorthodox woman (see Appendix One).

Todd rather wistfully recognized that these sorts of naïve adventure tales, which were of a piece with the books that in the 1910s had fired his adolescent imagination, were fading in the 1930s in the face of demands for tougher (both physically and psychologically), avowedly more realistic crime fiction fare. In 1936 Todd sounded a distinctly nostalgic valedictory note for the traditional thriller when reviewing Reginald Davis' retrograde "shocker" *The Crowing Hen*:

> When we come across a yarn like this one we rejoice that the old-fashioned thriller hasn't been displaced altogether by the new hard-boiled, side-of-the-mouth type of fiction and that there are still haunted houses such as Dane's Priory, wherein the bells toll mysteriously at midnight, subterranean passages are revealed at the proper touch and effigies appear and disappear bewilderingly.

While Todd embraced much of the change in the mystery genre in the 1930s (even as he regretted the decline of the traditional detective novel and thriller), he eschewed the French detective novel, madcap mysteries and female-authored Americana mysteries dependent on "quaint" local color and the heavy use of "picturesque" dialect. (Today Phoebe Atwood Taylor is probably the best recalled author of this sort of Grandma Moses mystery fiction.) Perhaps surprisingly, given Todd's fluency in the French language and his admiration for such French novelists as André Gide and Pierre Loti, the peculiar charms of most modern French mystery writing eluded him. For a few years in the early 1930s a wave of French mystery novels, hopefully translated into English, splashed into the United States, rather in the manner of Scandinavian crime fiction today. Todd stuck his toe into this literature, but on the whole he did not find the water lovely. Even the much-ballyhooed Georges Simenon failed to awe Todd. The Oklahoman dismissed Simenon's novel *The Crossroad Murders* (1933) as "too absurdly theatrical for even the Grand Guignol." (He was more favorable to Simenon's *The*

Strange Case of Peter the Lett, 1933.) Over Simenon Todd preferred Stanislas-André Steeman, an author virtually unknown today in the Anglo-American world but with admirers among informed connoisseurs. Todd deemed Steeman's novel *The Night of the 12th-13th* (1933) the "[h]ighwater mark in the current penchant for things Gallic in the murder line." Other French mystery writers reviewed by Todd—Roger Francis Didelot, Simone d'Erigny and Jean Toussaint-Samat—did not fare as well even as Simenon. "French mystery yarns, by all standards, are inferior to English and American products," Todd declared flatly in his review of Toussaint-Samat's *The Dead Man at the Window* (1934). "We wish that some Francophile would come to the defense of the French mystery story and aid us in our benightment," Todd added, tongue presumably in cheek. "So many French fans can't be wrong."[153]

Todd highlighted his dislike of the madcap, or wacky, school of farcical mystery in his 1943 essay on mystery fiction, "Murder is a Rather Serious Business," when he speculated that the mystery reading public would not "tolerate much longer those authors of the so-called 'wacky' school . . . whose entertainment value lies almost wholly in the wisecracks of their characters." In his *Daily Oklahoman* reviews Todd's dislike of what he saw as excessive humor in mysteries came through mostly in his 1936 reviews of two tales by English writer Georgette Heyer, who was best known for her witty Regency romance novels. Although he commended both of Heyer's books, *Why Shoot a Butler?* and *Behold, Here's Poison!*, Todd did not think much of the levity in them. "Readers whose taste is more Anglicized than ours will get many a chuckle out of the repartee," he notes of *Behold, Here's Poison!*

153 Todd's comment "So many French fans can't be wrong" likely is a humorous reference to the 1927 hit song "Fifty Million Frenchmen Can't Be Wrong," which inspired the Cole Porter musical *Fifty Million Frenchmen* (1929) and the 1931 film of the same title. On Stanislas-André Steeman, see Xavier Lechard, "Lost in Translation: Stanslas-André Steeman," *At the Villa Rose*, http://atthevillarose.blogspot.com/2010/10/lost-in-translation-stanislas-andre.html. On his mystery *L'Assassin habite 21*, see Patrick Ohl, "Mr. Smith = ?," *At the Scene of the Crime*, http://at-scene-of-crime.blogspot.ca/2012/04/mr-smith.html.

Despite his disparagement of Heyer's humor, however, Todd actually seems to have gradually reconciled himself to British mirth. Beginning with *Lament for a Maker* in 1938 and ending with *Hare Sitting Up* in 1959 (going by year of publication, apparently the last mystery novel Todd bought), Todd acquired 22 Michael Innes mysteries for his library; he also bought three of Edmund Crispin's detective novels between 1946 and 1949. Both Innes and Crispin were key figures in the "donnish detection" school, known for its academic wit and frequently absurd situations.[154]

Like many another American mystery fan in the Golden Age of detective fiction Todd became a great devotee of English mystery, belying a surprising, stray comment he made in one 1931 review: "I never did think much of the English." By 1933 Todd pronounced (in a review of a Dorothy L. Sayers short story collection): "A murder that is discussed in the bar-parlour of the Pig and Pewter at Mugbury is bound to be a good one." Verily, Todd liked a classic English murder.[155]

Besides the thriller writers Edgar Wallace and Sax Rohmer, other English mystery authors Todd greatly admired were Agatha Christie, Dorothy L. Sayers, H. C. Bailey, Eden Phillpotts, Anthony Wynne, Sir Basil Thomson and Patricia Wentworth. Todd much enjoyed both the mystery novels and short story collections of H. C. Bailey and speculated of Bailey's detective Reggie Fortune that "he is probably the only sleuth active today who meets with the approval of every mystery fan of our acquaintance." Eden Phillpotts Todd commended for his powerful portrayal of Dartmoor characters and settings, while Anthony Wynne received high marks from Todd for his incredible locked room murders (Wynne's *The Silver Scale Mystery,* 1931—*Murder of a Lady* in England—made the list of Todd's six favorite detective novels).

154 Todd also evidently greatly enjoyed the satirical humor of Evelyn Waugh, for his library included eighteen of Waugh's books, including even *Mexico: An Object Lesson* (1939), which, contra Todd's *The Mexican Earth*, took a decidedly dim view of Mexico under the administration of President Lazaro Cardenas.

155 Evidence that Todd's literary Anglophilia had become quite an advanced condition by the 1940s and 1950s is found in the fact that his library at his death included twenty-nine mainstream novels by Angela Thirkell.

Sir Basil Thomson, a former head of the Criminal Investigation Department (CID) at New Scotland Yard, Todd greatly esteemed as an expert on sober police procedure. In his review of Thomson's *The Case of the Dead Diplomat* (1935), Todd, ever mindful of his genre *bête noire*, the French, advised: "Before sending us any more of their wares French mystery writers might read to advantage this tale of manhunting as it should be conducted on the banks of the Seine." As for Patricia Wentworth and her cozy thrillers, Todd somewhat bemusedly ruminated that "[t]here's something about Miss Wentworth's yarns that is contagious. . . . Maybe it's the restful familiarity of the formula; maybe it's the writer's real skill in narration; maybe it's a taste on our part for vicarious something or other. . . . Serious-minded fans can pass it by."

No doubt of especial interest to many will be Todd's praise of Agatha Christie and Dorothy L. Sayers, both writers very much still in print today. Like so many others mystery fans then and now, Todd thought Agatha Christie's plotting ingenuity simply remarkable. Christie's *Murder on the Orient Express* (1934) he deemed a masterpiece on par with her famous 1926 tale, *The Murder of Roger Ackroyd* (another of the novels on Todd's list of six favorites). As mentioned earlier, *Murder on the Orient Express* probably inspired Todd to write one of his finest novels, *Vultures in the Sky*. For the cleverness of Christie's *The A.B.C. Murders* (1936), Todd could not contain his enthusiasm. "Hats off to Miss Christie and her positively uncanny ingenuity in devising plots to entertain her readers!" he joyfully exclaimed. "Skillfully plotted and told in her best vein, *The A.B.C. Murders* will brighten the life of any mystery fan."

That Christie was an ingenious puzzler would come as no surprise to the Queen of Crime's many modern fans, but Todd deserves kudos, I think, for in 1931 heralding the arrival of a noteworthy new detective on the mystery scene, a certain Miss Jane Marple, a genteel, elderly lady from an obscure English village, St. Mary Mead. After having noted that one of the characters in Christie's *The Murder at the Vicarage* (1930) is "a local spinster," Todd explains that the murderer in the novel "is finally apprehended through the efforts of the spinster, whose reasoning would do justice to the famous Dupin of Poe's 'The Purloined Letter'." When fully two years later he reviewed Christie's short story collection *The Tuesday Club Murders* (1932) (*The Thirteen Problems* in England), Todd happily noted the "[r]eappearance of Aunt Jane, the delightfully naïve and no-end quick-witted spinster of *The Murder at the Vicarage*." Clearly the spinster from St. Mary Mead had made an impression on Todd, who in his own life had a more than passing acquaintance with an incisive elderly lady, his grandmother Awilda Miller.

Todd also gave due to Dorothy L. Sayers' manifold talents, particularly her formidable learning. "Miss Sayers is undoubtedly the most respected authority on the history of mystery fiction," declared Todd in a review of an omnibus collection of three of her Lord Peter Wimsey detective novels. Nevertheless, Todd found Sayers' mystery *The Nine Tailors* (1934) a mite *too* erudite. He complained that the detail about bell-ringing "left us feeling as if we had tried to master a correspondence lesson in calculus." "Frankly," he admitted, "we skipped a great deal of the bell-ringing minutiae." Despite Todd's reservations about *The Nine Tailors*, however, he wholeheartedly praised Sayers' *Gaudy Night* (1935), considered a landmark in the effort to transform the English detective novel from a puzzle story into a more realistic novel of manners. Todd praised everything that he might have deemed extraneous in 1930 or 1931: the quoting of the poetry of John Donne, the meditations on "the cloistered peace of Oxford," even "the wooing by Lord Peter of Harriet Vane, the writer of mystery yarns." Outside of E. C. Bentley's *Trent's Last Case* (1913), Todd avowed, he could think of no instance where an "amorous sleuth" had been portrayed so convincingly and appealingly. *Gaudy Night* likely influenced Todd's final two Hugh Rennert novels (both published in 1937), in which Todd attempted, with considerable success, to give his own series detective something of a deeper emotional life.

Of course Todd enjoyed the domestic vintage as well and such American writers as Ellery Queen, John Dickson Carr, Rufus King, Mignon Eberhart, Mary Roberts Rinehart and S. S. Van Dine he ranked fully on par with Christie and Sayers. It might surprise modern fans, however, to learn that Todd named as his favorite detective novelist neither Queen nor Carr, Christie nor Sayers, but rather an author who has been out of print for nearly half a century, Rufus King. In addition to including King's *Murder by Latitude* (1930) on his list of six favorite detective novels, Todd pronounced King, in his review of the author's *The Case of the Constant God* (1936) "the best living writer of mystery stories." To be sure, other writers had their particular merits, Todd allowed, but in his opinion King surpassed all the rest for "all-round excellence: ingenuity in plot construction, skill in etching his characters with light, revealing touches, his style, the gently disturbing afflatus of horror."

Writers Todd had a poorer opinion of he let down gently, on the whole, rather than batter them with cruel barbs. For the rather daft books of Carolyn Wells, for example, Todd seems to have had genuine affection of a sort, probably on the order of that of Bill Pronzini, who memorably includes Wells in his classic genre study *Gun in Cheek* (1982), a tribute to "alternative" classics (books enjoyable by virtue of how bad they are). Perhaps the funniest review Todd wrote is the one he gave to Wells' novel *The Clue of the Eyelash* (1933), in the form of a mock newspaper society item. "A pleasant time was had by all in adjusting artificial eyelashes, drinking cocktails and discussing the murder of Mr. Vane and the blonde stenographer," the review wittily closes, making sufficiently clear that Wells' novel is the sort of wealth-fawning frippery mystery that Raymond Chandler scorned in his famous critical essay "The Simple Art of Murder" (1944). About mystery writer Means Davis (a woman) Todd delicately observed, in his review of Davis' *Murder without Weapon* (1934), "Mr. Davis has what critics call a vigorous style, although in our opinion it needs, like Peter, an occasional sobering douche [Peter is the tippling nephew in the novel]. We liked 'sudden gusts of terror, like darting sharks beneath a summer sea'; were so-so about 'his voice tip-toed into her intensity'; and blinked at 'her eyes glowed like ripe olives'." Probably Todd's harshest put-down of an author (after one thinks about it for a few seconds) is found in his review of Ruth Burr Sanborn's *Murder on the Aphrodite* (1935): "We are reminded of a sign seen over a five-foot pile of mysteries at a department store: 'The Ideal Gift for Your Week-end Hostess'." Harsh but still subtle—and quite amusing.

As should be sufficiently clear by now, Todd Downing, like writers as diverse as Dorothy L. Sayers and Dashiell Hammett, wanted the mystery novel to be taken more seriously; yet he sometimes approached this subject with a certain diffidence, seemingly hampered by his awareness of the contempt in which the genre was held by some literary highbrows (as a college instructor he presumably was more likely than most thirties mystery writers to have personally encountered these fearsome creatures). "There are two kinds of people in the world—those who read detective stories and those who don't," Todd observed in his review of a 1931 detective short story collection, *Sleuths*. "The latter have had all the innings so far, as evidenced by the sheepish and apologetic air which the reader of detective fiction . . . assumes when he is caught coming out of the bookstore with a lurid-covered tale of murder under his arm. Things are looking brighter for those of us belonging to that happy first class, however. In time we may be able to return some of the sneers that have been cast at us." Yet a dozen years later in his essay "Murder is a Rather Serious Business" Todd modestly concludes with the admonition to would-be mystery writers that, whatever loftier literary pretensions might be found in particular novels within the genre, mysteries were "nothing else than the literature of escape." Whether today we judge mystery genre writing as "mere" escapist fare, a branch of fiction with the full potential to scale the highest pinnacles of Art, or, perhaps, something in between these two extremes, we should value the genre work of Todd Downing, both his finely crafted detective novels and his illuminating mystery reviews. Just as literature enriched the life of Todd Downing, Todd Downing's life enriched the world of literature.

CHAPTER ONE
REVIEWS, 1930-1932

"CHARMING MURDER WITH THE COCKTAIL"
October 12, 1930, p. 53

THE CHARMING MURDER, BY FRANK SHAY

COCKTAILS and murders vie for chief interest in this story of New York night life, written by an author well known as the editor of various collections of drinking songs. The host at a very convivial party walks out with his unsteady friends to attend a show, where he is the subject of an impersonation on the stage. When they return with him to his apartment, they discover his dead body.

Each member of the party is found to have ample reason for murdering the host. The usual array of gangsters and bootleggers is involved. The author has shown originality only in letting the New York police force solve the mystery without the aid of a clever detective. If the reader can keep his mind off the cocktails, he will find this as interesting as the average mystery novel.—Todd Downing.[1]

1 Among Frank Shay's books we find *My Pious Friends and Drunken Companions: Songs and Ballads of Conviviality* (1927), *More Pious Friends and Drunken Companions: Songs and Ballads of Conviviality* (1928) and *Drawn from the Wood: Consolations in Words and Music for Pious Friends and Drunken Companions* (1929). Clearly a detective novel about Shay's pious

"TORCH MURDER IS A SLOW MYSTERY"
December 7, 1930, p. 64

The Torch Murder, by Charles Reed Jones

Of all the detective types conceived by the brains of authors laboring to produce a novelty, Leighton Swift, "man of the world, connoisseur and scientific criminologist," is one of the most tiresome. The popularity of this brand of hero, perfected by S. S. Van Dine, seems to be on the wane, and it is high time if we are to have any more Leighton Swifts. That the author has used Philo Vance for a model is apparent. Swift arises languidly at noon, sips a cocktail of a "beautifully delicate pink," then condescends to aid a baffled police department in the solution of a murder mystery, meanwhile displaying his erudition by lectures on the habits of the female Eperides ("Never use an understandable word like 'spider'" is Swift's motto).

The plot, evidently inspired by the Snyder-Gray murder, is worthy of a better detective to solve it. The charred body of a young woman is found by the roadside. It is identified as that of Mrs. Pembroke, recently estranged from her husband. The eternal triangle develops several new angles and, if the reader can endure Leighton Swift through 255 pages, he will probably be surprised at the solution.—Todd Downing.[2]

friends and drunken companions was the obvious next step. Shay's *The Charming Murder* anticipated Dashiell Hammett's hugely popular drinking and detecting mystery, *The Thin Man*, by four years.

2 At the time of Downing's review, S. S. Van Dine had published five hugely successful detective novels, all detailing the exploits of his pretentious, "g"-dropping gentleman amateur detective, Philo Vance: *The Benson Murder Case* (1926), *The Canary Murder Case* (1927), *The Greene Murder Case* (1928), *The Bishop Murder Case* (1929) and *The Scarab Murder Case* (1930). Although Van Dine's most famous acolyte, Ellery Queen (pseudonym of the cousins Frederick Dannay and Manfred Bennington Lee), had commenced his long-running and popular detective series with *The Roman Hat Mystery* a year earlier in 1929, Downing was correct in his assessment in his review: Van Dine's popularity had peaked and his Philo Vance in the 1930s would become less of a model for aspiring American detective fiction writers. Van Dine himself died, an embittered anachronism,

"BACK-FENCE GOSSIP AND POLITICAL FIGHT"
December 14, 1930, p. 57

THE MOONHILL MYSTERY, BY MRS. WILSON WOODROW

THE reader who demands the presence of a certain amount of literary qualities, combined with a not too improbable plot, in the novels in which he seeks relaxation has learned that he is reasonably sure of finding these things in the books of Mrs. Wilson Woodrow. A little New England town, with its bridge clubs, back-fence gossipers and political squabbles, furnishes the setting for this novel.

A murder and a jewel robbery set South Ridge in a hub-bub. Unless the murderer and thief is discovered before the election, Judge Curtis' political chances will be ruined, as the murdered man was found in the home of the judge's fiancée, Anne Morton. The insurance detective, assigned to recover the stolen gems, seeks the aid of a friend of Anne's in untangling the complicated clews which connect the two crimes. Between them they unearth deep, dark secrets in the pasts of most of the principals in the case and arrest the criminal, whom of course no one had suspected.

The device of using a staid, elderly lady as the medium of story-telling—a device employed so effectively by Mary Roberts Rinehart in *The Door*—maintains an atmosphere of reality about the rather hackneyed plot.—Todd Downing.[3]

in 1939. See John Loughery, *Alias S. S. Van Dine: The Man Who Created Philo Vance* (New York: Scribner, 1992). Charles Reed Jones, one-time managing editor of the film fan magazines *Photoplay* and *Filmplay* and editor of the Hollywood how-to book *Breaking into the Movies* (1927), wrote only a short-lived series of four detective novels, all, as Downing indicates, synthetic imitations of Van Dine: *The King Murder* (1929), *The Torch Murder* (1930), *The Van Norton Murders* (1931) and *The Rum Row Murders* (1931). On The Snyder-Gray case, a brutal "triangle" affair that was the press murder sensation of 1927, see Gerald Leinwand, *1927: High Tide of the Twenties* (Basic Books, 2001), 131-132.

3 "Mrs. Wilson Woodrow" was Nancy Mann (Waddel) Woodrow (c.1870 to 1935), one-time assistant editor of the *Chillicothe (Ohio) Daily News* and estranged wife of Dr. James Wilson Woodrow, a distant cousin of former President Woodrow Wilson. Beginning her career as a mainstream writer

"PRIESTLEY INVESTIGATES"
January 4, 1931, p. 49

DR. PRIESTLEY INVESTIGATES, BY JOHN RHODE

IN the good old days when Sherlock Holmes lived in Baker Street, murdered men always had black pasts in the gold fields of Australia or the convict barracks of the Andaman Isles. After they had settled down to a peaceful life in the English countryside, a former comrade invariably turned up to claim a share in ill-gotten fortune. Nowadays, when no murder is complete without a few night club hostesses and society bootleggers, men and women with shady pasts have become too common to furnish the oldtime thrill.

John Rhode has read his Doyle. When the drunken sailor, "an elderly man with an enormous red face, almost entirely covered with hair," enters the gates of Pinehurst, announcing, "I want to see Cap'n Cloutsham," one almost expects to see Sherlock step from behind a bush. For Mr. Coningsworth, alias Cloutsham, the owner of Pinehurst Manor and of a particularly dark past, has met death under circumstances which lead Doctor Priestley, a professor who occasionally lends his hand to crime detection, to suspect foul play. The murdered man's past, as revealed by the drunken sailor, is as black as any past uncovered by Sherlock Holmes in his best days.

The murder of old Mr. Coningsworth is an ingenious one, but the author has not shown equal ingenuity in concealing the identity of the murderer. If the reader cannot identify him before he has read half the book, he had better quit reading detective stories.—Todd Downing.[4]

in 1901 after separating from her husband, Mrs. Wilson Woodrow apparently turned to writing mystery fiction when the genre exploded in popularity after World War One. (Her distant cousin-in-law Woodrow Wilson himself was a mystery reader.) Her mystery novels from this period are *Burned Evidence* (1925), *Come Alone* (1929), *The Moonhill Mystery* (1930) and *Pawns of Murder* (1932). *Saturday Review* (20 June 1925, 841) called *Burned Evidence* "a thoroughly first rate detective story, rapid, absorbing and credible."

4 "John Rhode" is a pseudonym of Major Cecil John Charles Street (1884-1964), one of the most prolific and well-regarded traditional British

"SECRET ADVERSARY WELL WORTH READING"

January 18, 1931, p. 49

THE SECRET ADVERSARY, BY AGATHA CHRISTIE

THE reader of mystery stories has learned that he has about nine chances out of ten of obtaining a good yarn when he buys a book with Agatha Christie's name on the cover. This novel, "dedicated to all those who lead monotonous lives, in the hope that they may experience at second hand the delights and dangers of adventure," keeps up the author's batting average. It is the type of novel usually associated with the name of E. Phillips Oppenheim.

There is a sinister house in Soho, where the henchmen of the Master Criminal of the Age hold clandestine meetings; there are papers upon the recovery of which depends the fate of the British Empire; there are two young adventurers who obligingly fall into the hands of the enemy when interest in the novel begins to lag. All this, seasoned with considerable love interest, makes a fast-moving story, which, if the reader is not surfeited with such fare, will make him forget his monotone life for a whole evening—and that is all he can reasonably expect.—Todd Downing.[5]

detective novelists of his day. The John Rhode books were most noted for their ingenious murder methods. *Dr. Priestley Investigates* (in Britain, *Pinehurst*) indeed is one of Major Street's most Holmesian tales.

5 In his review of *The Secret Adversary*, a tale of "the delights and dangers of adventure," Downing is unstinting in his praise of Agatha Christie (1890-1976), then in the early phase of her long, lauded and lucrative crime writing career. "The reader of mystery stories has learned that he has about nine chances out of ten of obtaining a good yarn when he buys a book with Agatha Christie's name on the cover," he declares. Agatha Christie's second mystery novel, *The Secret Adversary* was originally published in 1922. It is a master criminal, political conspiracy tale, in the manner of such then hugely popular English thriller writers as E. Phillips Oppenheim, Edgar Wallace and Sapper (H. C. McNeile). Though Downing finds Christie's novel seasoned with "considerable love interest," he nevertheless recommends it to the reader who wants to "forget his monotone life for a whole evening."

"THE MURDER TRAP"
February 8, 1931, p. 47

The Murder Trap, by Armstrong Livingston

If the murderer of Charles Brett had been a stranger the dog would have growled, but because the dog barked that night, surely then the criminal was a member of the household. So argued Jimmy Traynor, the young and unconventional detective called in by the murdered man's mother. But to identify him was a difficult matter. Brett's niece and nephew both inherited fortunes. His secretary was in love with the niece. The nephew was enamored of a dashing brunette in New York. Numerous others benefited by Brett's demise. And who was the woman who had made the assignation with him in the quarry where he met his death? Jimmy set a trap for the murderer and was as surprised at the result, although not as disappointed, as the reader will be.

The Murder Trap is an interesting tale, in which the author does his best to be humorous—and sometimes succeeds. Jimmy Traynor, in spite of his wisecracking, is a detective with whom we hope to become better acquainted in future stories. We prefer our sleuths without wives and maiden aunts, however.—Todd Downing.[6]

"ABOUT THE MURDER OF GERALDINE FOSTER"
March 1, 1931, p. 50

About the Murder of Geraldine Foster, by Anthony Abbot

This is the first of a new series to be known as the Thatcher Colt mysteries, by Anthony Abbot, who served as secretary to Mr. Colt during the time the latter was police commissioner of New

6 The prominent New York relations of the mystery novelist Armstrong Livingston (1885-1959) included the Roosevelts. In his review of *The Murder Trap*, Downing expresses the then conventional views that detecting on the whole should be serious business and that the detective should not be encumbered with the accoutrements of a personal life. Jacques Barzun

York City. Mr Abbot's commendable purpose is to destroy the popular fallacy that the police force is helpless when faced with a clever crime and that without the aid of a brilliant amateur detective they would perforce leave unsolved many a crime or arrest innocent persons.

Colt here solves the mystery of the death of a beautiful girl whose body was found hacked with an axe and buried nude behind a bungalow in the woods. He does this with the aid of third degree methods on suspects, it is true, but nevertheless [he] shows remarkable ingenuity in tracking down the killer. But if the police are here vindicated of the charge of stupidity, the shoe has merely been placed on the other foot. The district attorney plays the part of a foil to Thatcher Colt's brilliant mind. Abbot has accomplished his purpose only by creating what the reader will feel is just as unfair an impression of district attorneys.

In this book there are few, if any, departures from the general formula employed by nine-tenths of all detective story writers. Even the "Lie Detector" and the "Truth Drug" will have a familiar sound to the reader who remembers Arthur B. Reeve's Craig Kennedy stories. The reader is led astray by just as many false clues and will probably be just as far from the solution.

What makes this story remain in the memory of the reader is the element of horror which permeates the tale, from the finding of the several dead pigeons to the final revelation of the manner in which Geraldine met her death. The pigeons have died from drinking the blood of the dead girl, but the medical examiner has said that she has been dead only two days, while the pigeons have been dead ten. With this clue as a starting point, Colt

and Wendell Hertig Taylor in their magisterial survey of detective fiction, *A Catalogue of Crime*, reached a similar assessment of this author, judging from their entry on his *Night of Crime* (1938): "Quite impossible country house murders solved by Jimmy Traynor, his wife Denise, his aunt *a la* Miss Withers, and his brother-in-law. Never have so many detected to such little purpose, despite some clues and some wit, sprinkled with a spare hand over many pages." Jacques Barzun and Wendell Hertig Taylor, *A Catalogue of Crime* (1971; rev. ed., New York: Harper & Row, 1989), 348-349.

uncovers one the most fiendish crimes ever committed in fact or fiction.—Todd Downing.[7]

"THE 13TH MURDER"
March 1, 1931, p. 50

THE 13TH MURDER, BY FREDERICK G. EBERHARD

THE author of this "unlucky lucky mystery" is a surgeon who has used his medical knowledge to introduce unusual thrills into his story. The criminal whose misdeeds send shivers up and down the reader's spine is known as the "Boner." He deliberately leaves fingerprints and other clues behind him, labeled for the benefit of the police. His thirteenth murder is that of Dr. Ashcraft, a professor of anatomy known for his experiments with revivification of the dead. The fingerprints on the gun are those of a man who has been dead for three months. When the police finally receive

7 Though today Charles Fulton Oursler (1893-1952) is best known for writing *The Greatest Story Ever Told* (1949), an account of the life of Christ later adapted into an Oscar-nominated film, under his Anthony Abbot pseudonym, Oursler wrote a half dozen *About the Murder of* . . . Thatcher Colt detective novels between 1931 and 1937. The first two, both of which Downing reviewed quite favorably (see p. 161 for the second review), are generally the most highly regarded. In this first review Downing deprecates Thatcher Colt's use of third degree interrogation methods, dismisses the originality of the science employed in the investigation and points out the inherent problem of the "idiot friend," or Watson figure, being used to emphasize the genius of the detective; yet he seems to have greatly enjoyed the tale, primarily, one concludes, for its atmosphere of horror. Downing's predilection for horror in the detective tale would again be seen in additional, later reviews and in his own detective novel series, which he would launch in 1933. Arthur B. Reeve (1880-1936), alluded to by Downing in the review, was an American mystery writer best known for his eighty-two Craig Kennedy stories, originally published in *Cosmopolitan* between 1910 and 1918. Reeve's stories had a great influence on a younger generation of male American mystery writers, who read his tales, like Downing, as boys and were impressed by their imaginative scope, notwithstanding deficiencies in writing and characterization. (For Reeve's influence on Downing, see pages 35-36.)

a letter from the "Boner" notifying them that he will commit suicide, they breathe a sigh of relief, only to be more mystified than ever at the finding of the body. After much meandering though sliding panels, secret passages and haunted houses a newspaper reporter and police inspector make a surprising discovery about the "Boner."

Although full of improbabilities, *The 13th Murder* is well worth the attention of the mystery story fan. He will probably read it through in one sitting and wish that it were longer.—Todd Downing.[8]

"BARON'S BOOK STARTS WELL, ENDS SLOWLY"
March 8, 1931, p. 47

THE ROUND TABLE MURDERS, BY PETER BARON

THE opening chapters of this book arouse hope of finding that rare thing nowadays—a well-written, interesting and plausible detective story. George Teyst, alias the colonel, the oldest of four brothers, steals the Marcovian crown jewels from the American millionaire who has just purchased them. Shot while making his escape, George hides his loot, writes down the directions for finding it and then tears the paper into three pieces, sending one to each of his brothers. He dies believing that by this means

8 Frederick George Eberhard (1889-?), the only child of Eli L. Eberhard (1857-1920), a prominent Indiana doctor, graduated from Culver Military Academy, the University of Chicago and Northwestern University Medical School. See Samuel P. Kaler and R. H. Maring, *History of Whitley County, Indiana* (B. F. Bowe & Co., 1907), 838-840. As a crime writer he authored five novels: *The 13th Murder*, *The Secret of the Morgue* (1932), *Super-Gangster* (1932), *The Skeleton Talks* (1933) and *The Microbe Murders* (1935). In his books Eberhard evinced a penchant for gruesome serial killers, like *The 13th Murder*'s "Boner," who seems rather like something of a forerunner of Hannibal Lecter. In a Goodreads review, Samantha Glasser, sounding much like Todd Downing eighty-one years earlier, enthusiastically praises *The 13th Murder*, avowing that it "keeps the reader interested and guessing . . . until the very last minute," when Eberhard unveils "a thrilling and satisfying conclusion leaving the reader wanting more."

he will bring the others peacefully together at last. Instead, each brother tried to collect the missing scraps of paper for himself. So far so good, but when a mysterious person, known as the Poacher, aids in the bloody work and Inspector Keating of Scotland Yard falls in love with the beautiful Barbara, it all resolves itself into a question of how long it will be to the end.

As if a love sick inspector were not bad enough, there is a police superintendent who quotes classic poets and cannot resist the temptation to make a pun in every other sentence. The author assures us that the characters in his book are entirely fictitious. It is a relief to know that so many tiresome people do not really exist.—Todd Downing.[9]

"BAFFLING MYSTERIES END WITH SURPRISES"
March 15, 1931, p. 51

The Murder at the Vicarage, by Agatha Christie

Readers who like to match wits with the author in the solution of baffling mysteries should not fail to read Miss Christie's latest novel. Although she gives every opportunity of identifying the murderer, readers who are accustomed to the ordinary run of detective stories will fail as completely as do the police in solving the mystery of who shot Colonel Protheroe. One of the red herrings drawn across the path of the would-be Sherlock is sure to lead him astray.

When the Vicar of St. Mary Mead, a dear old gentleman with but two weaknesses—his beautiful young wife and detective thrillers—discovers the colonel's body in his study, he decides to do

9 "Peter Baron" was the pseudonym of Leonard Worswick Clyde (1906-1987), youthful author of *Who?* (1927), *Jerry the Lag* (1928), and *The Poacher* (1929). The first two novels were reprinted in the United States by Macaulay as, respectively, *The Opium Murders* (1930) and *Murder in Wax* (1931). *The Round Table Murders*, reviewed above by Downing, was the title of Macaulay's edition of *The Poacher*. Macaulay proclaimed Peter Baron "the rising star among the mystery writers of our time" and insisted that "*The Round Table Murders*, swiftly, vividly written, probing the inmost nerves of fear, is his highest achievement." Todd Downing had a differing

some amateur sleuthing. The deceased was a man of violent temper, with at least seven enemies who would rejoice at his demise. The vicar, aided by a local spinster, uncovers several conjugal infidelities among his flock, further complicating the plot. Even Caesar's wife is not above suspicion. The murderer is finally apprehended through the efforts of the spinster, whose reasoning would do justice to the famous Dupin of Poe's "The Purloined Letter." The vicar's wife whispers in his ear that the stork will shortly pay them a visit and everything ends happily, except of course for the murderer.

The Murder at the Vicarage is recommended to anyone looking for a well-constructed, interesting tale, with a surprising conclusion.—Todd Downing.[10]

"MYSTERY ABOUNDS IN ACCOUNT OF 'BLACK GHOST'"

March 22, 1931, p. 46

THE BLACK GHOST, BY J. M. WALSH

FOR five years the Black Ghost has terrorized England, despite the efforts or the police to track him down. Then he suddenly ceased his activities and for 18 months was not heard of. Our story opens with the release of a certain George Hillerby from prison and simultaneous reappearance of the Black Ghost. Inspector Field of Scotland Yard is shot down from ambush while trailing Hillerby. Tim the shopper, who was responsible for Hillerby's prison sentence, is killed outside the latter's lodgings. The reader is from the first in doubt as to Hillerby's guilt and, as the tale moves on, is more bewildered than ever. Things

opinion, demonstrating in particular a marked aversion to love interest in mystery tales. (We will see more of this in additional reviews.)

10 In comparing the deductive capacities of Agatha Christie's second most important series detective, Miss Jane Marple ("a local spinster"), to those of Edgar Allan Poe's seminal C. Auguste Dupin, Downing showed acute perception and prescience. He also neatly summed up the sources of Christie's powerful perennial appeal: neat, logical plot, lightly humorous characters and a surprise at the end.

become even more complicated with the introduction of two girls, both of whom fall in love with Hillerby. The Black Ghost is finally brought down by the efforts of Norah, the gangster's daughter, and the story ends to the accompaniment of wedding bells.

The reader who likes plenty of action in his mysteries should read *The Black Ghost*. It is written in the best Edgar Wallace manner. Mr. Walsh has written 50 novels since 1923 and, if this is a fair sample of his work, readers in this country have been missing something good in the line of detective stories.—Todd Downing.[11]

"ORGAN LOFT IS SCENE OF LATEST THRILLER"
April 12, 1931, p. 51

THE HYMN TUNE MYSTERY, BY GEORGE A. BIRMINGHAM

MURDERS have been staged, for the benefit of the great fraternity of mystery fans, in New York night clubs and Scottish moors, on trans-Atlantic liners and in Arctic snows, but it has remained for George A. Birmingham (in real life Canon Hannay of Mells Rectory) to choose the organ loft of a cathedral for his latest thriller. Carminster cathedral had already had considerable scandal and basking in the limelight several years before our story opens and the love affairs of a medieval bishop and the theft of the Carminster emeralds play an important part in the solution of the mystery surrounding the death of the cathedral organist.

It is seldom that a murder story contains such well-drawn characters as this one: The lovable old dean, translating Latin drinking songs and being nagged by his daughter, one of those efficient women with a mission in life; Elsie Hill, a gay young person of doubtful quality, whose father has died in prison after concealing a message in a hymn tune; and, best of all, a young

11 The extremely prolific James Morgan Walsh (1897-1952) was an Australian who later settled in England. He wrote under several pseudonyms. His most enticing story title surely is *The Mystery of the Green Caterpillars* (1929).

Irish precentor who, with the aid of Inspector Smallways and a jug of beer, solves the mystery.

Those superior persons who scorn mystery stories are urged to read this one. If they remain unconverted, they are hopeless.—Todd Downing.[12]

"NEW OPPENHEIM BOOK MUCH LIKE OTHERS"
April 12, 1931, p. 51

THE LION AND THE LAMB, BY E. PHILLIPS OPPENHEIM

ALTHOUGH the jacket advertises this book as a representative of the new Oppenheim, it is little different from the kind of novels this prolific author has been writing for 40 years. He has merely ransacked the storeroom wherein lie his worn out plots, dusted and put them together, and the result is *The Lion and the Lamb*. It lacks the novelty of plot of *Up the Ladder of Gold* and its villains are mere amateurs compared to the arch-criminal of *The Million Pound Deposit*, which, by the way, is our favorite Oppenheim.

12 George A. Birmingham was the pseudonym of Reverend James Owen Hannay (1865-1950), an Irish Anglican clergyman who attained a fair amount of fame as a novelist and playwright over a long writing career lasting from 1905 to 1950, the year of his death. Mystery stories and thrillers make only a comparatively small amount of his total fiction output. His best mystery tale is generally considered to be *The Hymn Tune Mystery*. One of Hannay's sons, James Frederick Wynne Hannay (1906-1984), also wrote several fine crime novels, including *The Thirteenth Floor* (1931), set in Dallas, Texas, while one of Hannay's daughters, Theodosia Frances Wynne (Hannay) Hickey (1910-?), published *The Corpse in the Church* (1930) and two schoolgirl mysteries, *Bulldog Sheila* (1936) and *The Hand* (1937). In his review of *The Hymn Tune Mystery*, Downing stresses a theme that would grow increasingly common in thirties mystery criticism: the desirability of more serious, novelistic treatment of characters and situations. To those "superior persons who scorn mystery novels," Downing urges perusal of *The Hymn Tune Mystery*, on the grounds that it reads like a good mainstream novel. Barzun and Taylor in *A Catalogue of Crime* agreed, declaring Birmingham's tale "a delight. Intelligence, humor, character, and prose are in equipoise." Barzun and Taylor, *Catalogue of Crime*, 51.

This tale concerns another of those rich and adventurous young Englishmen, an earl this time, who wages a private war on a gang of criminals known as the Lambs, who were responsible for his serving a prison term. This particular Oppenheim hero cuts a rather poor figure, in our opinion. He forgets where he hid "The Virgin's Tear," a valuable diamond, and has to be rescued from a ticklish place by the police. He does not even take the lead in his own courtship.

When all is said, however, Oppenheim at his worst is still better than most writers of adventure stories at their best.—Todd Downing.[13]

"REVIEWER IS BORED BY GHOSTLY MYSTERY"
April 26, 1931, p. 51

MURDER FROM BEYOND, BY R. FRANCIS FOSTER

WHEN Tom Manning, cub reporter for the *London Planet*, visits his uncle, the rector of the quiet village of Stanmead, he expects a restful vacation. Instead he is at once thrown into the middle of a series of mysterious murders. Two are by hypodermic injections of aconitine in the neck; the other is by shooting. Manning's friend, Ravenhill, whom readers of *The Moat House Mystery* will remember without any particular enthusiasm, joins him and does some high-powered sleuthing, which leads him into a spiritualistic seance. At this point the reader will probably become completely confused as to what it is all about. Ghosts flit about under the trees and some of the characters, we are authoritatively informed, are possessed by devils—or maybe obsessed, as there seems to be a difference. Anyhow it turns out that a devil is responsible for all the bloodshed, which is at least something new in detective fiction.

13 E. Phillips Oppenheim (1866-1946), the so-called "prince of storytellers," wrote some 150 thrillers. He is considered a key pioneer of the espionage tale. See Robert Standish, *The Prince of Storytellers: The Life of E. Phillips Oppenheim* (Peter Davies, 1957).

The author is said to be a Franciscan monk, an ex-soldier, and the author of eight mystery stories. Our advice to him is to devote his time to the cloister hereafter.—Todd Downing.[14]

"NARCOTIC TRADE IS BASIS FOR MYSTERY"
May 10, 1931, p. 45

JUROR NO. 17, BY C. C. WADDELL

A BEAUTIFUL girl about to give information on the dope racket to the grand jury is shot by a gunman and dies in the aristocratic arms of Gregory Van Sweyn (Juror No. 17), gasping, "Sixty—get Sixty—at the head of it all."

Gregory, just returned from Asia and having plenty of time and money on his hands, joins Agent McCall of the narcotics bureau in tracking down the mysterious "Sixty." The chase takes him from a New York apartment house to a quiet little Georgia town where he spends a rather nerve-wracking night in a graveyard full of rattlesnakes and incidentally falls in love with a southern maiden who is suspected of complicity in the dope business. After the reader has picked every character in the book to be the elusive "Sixty," the latter turns out to be the least likely one, as usually happens in these stories.

As a novel of the activities of the big dope rings, *Juror No. 17* is a rattling good yarn. As a mystery story, it is just another book.

14 Beginning in 1924, Reginald Francis Foster (1896-1975), a former World War One military cleric, wrote nine detective novels, his last being *Something Wrong at Chillery*, which appeared only a year after the Downing-maligned *Murder from Beyond*. Barzun and Taylor agreed with Downing's assessment that the latter tale is confusing and muddled: "Three hundred pages of mystery-mongering with three murders, two murderers, spiritualism, two official detectives and one unofficial (a London crime reporter) and, of course, a lovelorn pair. The author likes clues and detection but muddles badly." Barzun and Taylor, *Catalogue of Crime* (2nd ed.), 207-208. Downing may have liked supernatural trappings in a detective novel, but he also liked clarity in the investigation and solution, something lacking in *Murder from Beyond*.

The reader will not be able to work up any particular interest as to the identity of "Sixty" and still less as to the outcome of the love affair between the hero and the heroine.—Todd Downing.[15]

"MURDER IN LIBRARY"
May 17, 1931, p. 49

Murder in a Library, by Charles J. Dutton

A library is no place for a murder to take place and the elderly Reference Librarian who was strangled to death in her office had no enemies. Within sound of her voice had been at least 50 persons, none of whom could throw any light on the tragedy. No wonder the police of the city were at a loss to solve the mystery. Things are still more complicated by the assault upon the young reporter who found the body at the library desk; by the death of the librarian, under circumstances that point to murder; and by the attempted killing of one of the library staff.

The man who finally solves the mystery is Harley Manners, a young professor of abnormal psychology, who has figured in Mr. Dutton's last two novels. Just when Manners teaches classes is somewhat of a mystery in itself, but as a detective he is one of our favorites. He uses psychology in identifying the criminal, but he does not bore the reader with too many lectures on the subject.

This is our nomination for the detective story-of-the-week. The plot is logical and the characters act and talk like human beings. Suspense is well-sustained.—Todd Downing.[16]

15 A prolific writer for the pulps, Charles Carey Waddell (1868-1930) also authored (with Carroll John Daly) *Two-Gun Gerta: A Western Story* (1926) and *Breaking into Print: The Waddell System of Story-Writing* (1919).

16 Charles Judson Dutton (1888-1964), a Unitarian minister, published fourteen detective novels between 1921 and 1934, six with detective Harley Manners, who was introduced in *Streaked with Crimson* in 1929. In this review, Downing reveals his preferences for a fair amount of realism ("the characters act and talk like human beings"); a logical plot and suspenseful narrative; and an intelligent detective who nevertheless does not overwhelm the reader with his erudition in the Philo Vance manner.

"THE CLERGYMAN'S MISTRESS"
May 31, 1931, p. 45

ABOUT THE MURDER OF THE CLERGYMAN'S MISTRESS, BY ANTHONY ABBOT
TO borrow the favorite expression of District Attorney Dougherty, "Hell and hot water, things are popping" in this fast-moving tale of love and slaughter in New York's select church circles. Those who read Mr. Abbot's first book, *About the Murder of Geraldine Foster* will need no urging to buy his second contribution to detective fiction. Thatcher Colt, a Police Commissioner of New York City, is here presented to even better advantage than in the previous book.

The Halls-Mills case has served fiction writers as a model before, but never as well here. The bodies of the Reverend Timothy Beazeley and his mistress, the beautiful choir singer, Evelyn Saunders, are found, not under a crab-apple tree, but in a boat floating down the East river. Clues present in the boat are a love letter, a leaf from the Tree of Heaven, and a Manx cat. With these as a starting point, Colt unravels a tangled skein of love, hate, jealously, fear, and several other emotions. Those readers who appreciate unusual situations in their murder stories will find one to their liking in the room from which the cat had walked with blood-stained paws, but which showed no traces of blood. It is equal to those blood-gorged pigeons in the Geraldine Foster case.

The publishers have divulged a secret that we suspected all along—Anthony Abbot is the pseudonym of a well-known novelist and music critic. Clues to his identity are that he never rises before noon (lucky man!), smokes Lucky Strikes, and does not like red-headed women. We are not going to waste any time worrying over who he is. He can write good detective stories and that is enough for us. Watch for *About the Murder on the Fifteenth Floor* and *About the Murder of the Night-Club Lady*.—Todd Downing.[17]

17 The notorious Halls-Mills Case concerned the 1922 murder of an Episcopal priest and his mistress, a member of his choir. In this review, Downing again reveals his affinity for touches of horror in detective stories.

"JIMGRIM"
June 28, 1931, p. 41

JIMGRIM, BY TALBOT MUNDY

TALBOT Mundy knows how to write adventure stories with a punch; witness *King of the Khyber Rifles*. Maj. James Schuyler Grim—known as Jimgrim to the secret services of the world—has all the makings of a he-man hero and a number of stories about him ran successfully in *Adventure* magazine. The plot of this novel is a good one—the menace to Occidental civilization of an Oriental king of the world who has unearthed forgotten secrets in buried cities of Tibet. And the scenes through which the readers is hurried are romance in themselves—harbor dives of Marseilles, hidden cellars of Cairo, secret tombs in the great pyramids, black dens in Delhi and finally a valley, "beyond the Kwen-lun mountains, to the north and west of Koko Nor."

Yet *Jimgrim* is a little disappointing, perhaps because Sax Rohmer has done the same thing so much better. Dorje is a mere amateur beside Doctor Fu-Manchu and the Princess Baltis has evidently lost most of her vamping abilities through too many reincarnations (She has been the Queen of Sheba, a concubine of Cyrus, and Anne Boleyn). The Babu Chullunder Ghose slows the action considerably, too, with a great deal of talk about nothing in particular.

Just the same, here's hoping that Mundy tries it again soon.—Todd Downing.[18]

"ONLY SEVEN MURDERS TOLD IN ONE VOLUME"
July 5, 1931, p. 41

THE BLACK PEARL MURDERS, BY MADELEINE SHARPS

UNLESS I have overlooked a few, there are only seven murders in

18 "Talbot Mundy" was the pseudonym of Englishman William Lancaster Gribbon (1879-1940), prolific pulps writer and novelist. Downing contrasts Mundy unfavorably with Sax Rohmer, creator of the premier nefarious "Oriental criminal mastermind," Dr. Fu Manchu.

this book. Before the story opens, Walter Vaughan, his father and his wife have died under mysterious circumstances. In the first chapter Demorest Vaughan, a millionaire charity worker, is found murdered in Chinatown, a black pearl in his mouth. Across his corpse is lying the body of a working girl, appropriately named Poppy. Then the scene shifts to the little town of Foreston, where old Doc Blaine, a village character, is killed. In his mouth is another black pearl. Then Inspector Ryan, on the trail of the slayer, is done away with in a nasty manner. It does not take much ingenuity to guess that somebody has a grudge against the Vaughan family and intends to wipe them off the map.

Captain Leigh and his head detective Fred Irons get on the job, each following his own private clues. As a result, they bump into each other in the dark several times, but finally get their man.

A fair novel, but it could have been better improved by subtracting a little of the love at first sight (Captain Leigh and the aristocratic Constance Ingleby are the victims) and by adding a more reasonable solution.—Todd Downing.[19]

"FOUND DROWNED IS WORTH YOUR TIME"
July 5, 1931, p. 41

Found Drowned, by Eden Phillpotts

This novel is recommended to those who like their detective stories with a minimum of bloodshed and horror and a maximum of deductive reasoning. Doctor Meredith, a retired surgeon living in a little English seaside village, has his suspicions about a "suicide" found on the beach. He succeeds in proving to his own satisfaction that the police are mistaken as to the identity of the dead man and that furthermore the cause of death was poison, not drowning. Feeling the need for some means of occupying

19 Madeleine Sharps Buchanan, a contributor to the Street & Smith line of pulp fiction, published six detective novels between 1926 and 1930. In his review of *The Black Pearl Murders*, Downing amusingly reveals his distaste for overmuch love interest in detective fiction.

his time, he prevails upon Inspector Forbes to give him a free rein in his investigation. With the aid of several lucky breaks and some clever guessing, the doctor, who tells his story in the first person, discovers a clue or two which leads him to the truth. The solution is one which has been used in a dozen or so of these novels recently.

This is one of those stories in which the reader is expected to be so engrossed in following the detective that he is not tempted to do any sleuthing on his own. No opportunity of identifying the person who did away with the unknown is given. According to my taste, this makes rather tame reading. I am always more interested in the murderer than in the detective, perhaps because most of the murderers one meets in books are so much less tiresome than most detectives; perhaps because I prefer my own guessing.

Anyway, *Found Drowned* will furnish a pleasant evening's reading.—Todd Downing.[20]

"MURDERS"
July 5, 1931, p. 41

The Bell Street Murders, by S. Fowler Wright

Mr. Wright's previous attempt at detective fiction, *The Case of Anne Bickerton*, seems to have met with enough success to encourage him to try it again. This is not a tame murder like the one for which Anne was tried, however. There is plenty of gore here for the most bloodthirsty reader.

20 The respected and venerable mainstream English regional novelist Eden Phillpotts (1862-1960) began regularly publishing detective fiction at the age of nearly sixty, with his mystery novel *The Grey Room* (1921). Especially in the 1920s, Phillpotts' mysteries were highly acclaimed, particularly in the United States. However, today Phillpotts is best known in the mystery world for having encouraged a young Devon neighbor of his, a certain Agatha Christie, to stick with the writing racket. Downing clearly found *Drowned* rather on the dull side (in part because he thought that Phillpotts did not attempt to "play fair" with the reader, but also because

The trouble starts with an invention "that will revolutionize the whole film industry and imprison the record of any phase of human activity in stone." The inventor and his black sheep brother are murdered in an abandoned factory. The only clues are a message scrawled in milk on the floor and the screen which has registered the murders—if anyone can get the right combination. The fair Evelyn plays a large, though useless, part in the excitement, losing a little finger in the barrage.

The ending is unsatisfactory, the villain going scot-free, on promising to reveal some inside information on the dope racket (I forgot to mention that opium, cocaine, morphine and other trifles are thrown in for good measure). Some mystery fans may like this book.—Todd Downing.[21]

"THE LONELY HOUSE"
July 19, 1931, p. 43

THE LONELY HOUSE, BY ARTHUR GASK

GILBERT Larose is the supersleuth of this manhunt staged in South Australia. His efforts are directed toward finding the hiding place of one Miles Fallon, a bad hombre who has escaped from the stockade at Adelaide. Gilbert is good at finding clues, one must admit that. He is also quick on the trigger, bagging two men without half trying. In fact, if he had not been given to too much soliloquizing he might not have been such a disappointment. Every now and then he has to stop and "frown" such remarks as: "Now I'll think out what I must do." "Now don't get excited Gilbert. Take plenty of time and keep your cool!" After feeding a man to

the author's solution in his view was one "used in a dozen or so of these novels recently"), yet the young Oklahoman nevertheless soon came to greatly admire the older Englishman's writing.

21 Sydney Fowler Wright (1874-1965) was by far best known for his best-selling 1928 apocalyptic novel, *Deluge*, republished in 2003 by Wesleyan University Press. Yet he was an extremely prolific author who also penned a large amount of detective and science fiction.

the sharks, he takes time out to do a strange interlude: "Fate! Fate! It is fate. I was destined to be the avenger."

As if this were not bad enough, not only Gilbert, but the mysterious Doctor Steyne, have to fall in love and fill page after page with a lot of hooey. The author gets real "sexey" himself and throws in some atmosphere with outbursts like this: "There were flowers of wondrous beauty all around them in that fairy garden, but none was half as beautiful as the passion-flowers that were twining round their hearts." The last chapter is devoted to recording the births of the offspring, in case the reader is still awake.

Mr. Gask, an Australian surgeon, is said to be threatening Edgar Wallace's popularity in England, where his stories are creating a "sensation." I never did have a very high opinion of the English.—Todd Downing.[22]

"DANGER CALLING"
August 16, 1931, p. 43

DANGER CALLING, BY PATRICIA WENTWORTH

"HOW would you like to die for your country?" When Benbow Collingwood Horatio Smith, high mogul of the foreign office, asked Lindsay Trevor this question, the young author and publisher had just been jilted by his sweetheart. In a reckless mood he accepts the job, which entails a pretended death in the English Channel and a resurrection, with hair dyed red, as Froth, his cousin. The object of all this secrecy is to obtain information about a mysterious personage who is plotting to plunge the world

22 Arthur Gask (1869-1951) was an Australian dentist turned crime writer who produced over thirty crime genre novels between 1923 and 1952. In his review of Gask's *The Lonely House*, Downing again demonstrates his distaste for love interest in mysteries ("a lot of hooey"), but his gratuitous insult of the English is surprising, given that English mystery novels comprised much of his reading material (in the 1930s he also became a decades-long devotee of the conservative English country life novels of Angela Thirkell).

into another war. Is this arch-villain Algerius Redstow, the millionaire whose secretary Lindsay becomes? Or is Drayton, Redstow's librarian, the man who has the governments of the world in such a state of excitement? And who is the Vulture? And why does Lindsay's former sweetheart visit Drayton's office by night? And what does one do when one awakes in the dead of night to find one of those deadly East Indian snakes known as a "karait" sharing one's pillow? And what does Gogo, the Parisian apache, know?

Just when it begins to look like a perfect evening for the mystery fan, the authoress become tangled up in her own web and things fall flat. Even the voluptuous snake-charmer Gloria Paravicini and a pair of cobras affectionately known as Romeo and Juliet cannot prevent the reader from yawning as he looks to see how many pages are left. E. Phillips Oppenheim and Edgar Wallace cannot be beaten for this kind of novel.—Todd Downing.[23]

"ADELE AND CO."
August 23, 1931, p. 41

ADELE AND CO., BY DORFORD YATES

THE author, an Englishman living in southern France, has won considerable success with his stories of adventure. Particularly successful have been those which recount the experiences of *Berry & Co.* and *Jonah & Co.* This novel is dedicated to "all those who have been so kind as to write and ask me for 'more Berry'." This reviewer hereby petitions Mr. Yates for even more. As a rule

23 British author Patricia Wentworth (1878-1961) is best known for her thirty-two cozy Miss Silver mysteries, many of which are still in print today. Miss Silver, a genteel spinster in the Miss Marple mode (though in novel form she appeared shortly prior to Miss Marple, in 1928) remains the author's most famous fictional creation. However, from 1923, with *The Astonishing Adventures of Jane Smith*, to 1945, with *Silence in Court*, Wentworth published as well thirty-three non-series thrillers, often ladylike cloak and dagger romances like *Danger Calling*. Initially Downing found her too tame compared to his beloved Edgar Wallace, but his opinion of her work improved over time.

fictional wise-crackers are terrible bores, but Berry is an exception. He is good.

This novel concerns the efforts of a party of vacationists in France to recover their jewels, stolen after a wild party at which the champagne had been doped. Their leisurely chase after the thieves takes them into the highways and byways of the chateau country and across the Spanish frontier. A Chicago fence is likewise after the jewels and adds spice to the pursuit.

Here is everything that readers of adventure stories crave: espionage on the housetops of Tours, disguises, pearls hidden in tree-trunks, apaches with scowling faces, beer, champagne and a villain named Casca de Palk. As an antidote for an Oklahoma summer, *Adele & Co.* is unexcelled.—Todd Downing.[24]

"MOUSETRAP"
September 20, 1931, p. 47

MOUSETRAP, BY M. N. A. MESSER

A LONELY house on the moor is the favorite spot for fiction writers to sequestrate their heroines, in order that they may be rescued by heroic young Englishmen. In this novel the author has introduced a slight change in the formula by making the old and musty Chateau des Bois Profonds, outside Tours, the prison of the wealthy Jennifer Talbot. The sinister villain who springs the mousetrap on Jennifer is Le Vicomte des Champs-Nouveaux, who is aided in his machinations by la Comtesse du Bois, a weather-beaten antique, with designs on Jennifer's fortune. Other characters are le Comte Philippe du Bois, weak but willing to marry

24 Dornford Yates was the pseudonym of Cecil William Mercer (1885-1960), who left the bar to become a hugely popular fiction writer. Downing's admiration for Yates' reactionary British thriller (which he read in Oklahoma after his 1931 summer trip to Mexico was canceled) casts into doubt his earlier claim of not having a "very high opinion of the English." On Yates, see Richard Usborne, *Clubland Heroes: A Nostalgic Study of the Recurrent Characters in the Romantic Fiction of Dornford Yates, John Buchan and "Sapper"* (1953; rev. ed., Hutchinson, 1983).

Jennifer; M. Sentier, an artist and counterfeiter; Mirepoint, henchman of des Champs-Nouveaux; and, last but not least, Jervis Quentin, the ubiquitous young Englishman who rescues Jennifer.

The author has striven desperately to create a *Castle of Otranto* atmosphere, with mediocre success. His villains are double-dyed, however, and there is enough meandering through secret passages and sliding panels to satisfy the most exacting reader of mystery stories. Le Vicomete escapes, threatening to provide more devilment for a sequel to this tale.—Todd Downing.[25]

"SLEUTHS"
September 20, 1931, p. 47

SLEUTHS, EDITED BY KENNETH MACGOWAN

THERE are two kinds of people in the world—those who read detective stories and those who don't. The latter have had all the innings so far, as evidence[d] by the sheepish and apologetic air which the reader of detective fiction ("that odd combination of small boy and riddle-riddling scientist," Mr. Macgowan calls him) assumes when he is caught coming out of a bookstore with a lurid-covered tale of murder under his arm. Things are looking brighter for those of us belonging to that happy first class, however. In time we may be able to return some of the sneers that have been cast at us. For detective fiction (which of course

25 "M. N. A. Messer" was a pseudonym of Anne Hocking (1890-1966), daughter of Joseph Hocking and niece of Silas Hocking, both once-famous English Methodist religious novelists. Anne Hocking wrote 41 thrillers and detective novels between 1931 and 1962 (a final tale was posthumously published in 1968), all but *Mousetrap* under her own name. As "Mona Messer," she wrote mainstream novels as well. Downing's rather tongue-in-cheek review of *Mousetrap* suggests his scorn for the traditional girl in peril British thriller, wherein a daring rescue is effected by the clean-limbed, public-schooled hero. Hocking herself was to go on to better things in her genre writing. Downing's reference to Hocking striving "desperately to create a Castle of Otranto atmosphere" is an allusion to Horace Walpole's 1764 tale, *The Castle of Otranto*, generally viewed as the first Gothic novel and a key forerunner of the modern suspense genre.

is not the same as mystery fiction) is beginning to assume the dignity of such accepted hobbies as bridge and philately. Dorothy Sayers and Willard Huntingdon Wright have given us historical accounts of its development and studies of its esthetic problems. Now comes Macgowan with an anthology, not of detective stories, but of the great detectives of fiction.

His gallery begins with such old standbys as Poe's Auguste Dupin and Doyle's Sherlock Holmes and ends with such lesser, but no less interesting, lights as O'Higgins' Detective Duff and Stribling's Henry Poggioli. Except in cases where death has made it impossible, the authors have chosen for Macgowan the stories which they think most characteristic of the detectives. Besides a bibliography of detective fiction, there is an unusual feature—a "Who's Who" of each detective, giving details of birth and education, hobbies and tastes, the chief interests of his life, and a list of his most important cases. It's a book no detective fan can afford to miss.—Todd Downing.[26]

"ANOTHER MYSTERY"
October 4, 1931, p. 47

The Silver Scale Mystery, by Anthony Wynne

Mr. Wynne specializes in murders committed under peculiar circumstances, usually in rooms with doors and windows locked

26 By 1930, when Downing wrote his review of *Sleuths*, both Dorothy L. Sayers and Willard Huntingdon Wright (the man behind "S. S. Van Dine") had published significant essays on the detective novel. Sayers' introduction to *Great Tales of Detection, Mystery and Horror* (1928) had appeared in the United States in 1929 as the introduction to *The Omnibus of Crime*, while Wright's introduction to *The Great Detective Stories* was first published in 1927. Wright also had laid down "Twenty Rules for Writing Detective Stories" in 1928. Downing's review is of particular interest for the defensive stance assumed by him in regard to "those who don't" read detective stories. Downing, an instructor at the University of Oklahoma and a confirmed murder yarn fancier, seems eager to establish detective fiction as a respectable intellectual hobby, at least; and he

on the inside. *The Blue Vesuvius* was one such tale. Here is an even better one. Miss Mary Gregor is stabbed to death in a locked and barred room in an old Scottish castle. On her breast is found the scar of a similar wound inflicted years before. Doctor Hailey is called in and finds the clue of the herring's scale embedded in the wound. Police Detective Dundas then appears on the scene and takes over the case. Just as he has proven to his own satisfaction that the lady's nephew has murdered her for her money, the murderer strikes again and Dundas lies dead. Yet it was impossible for the murderer to have entered the room! Another detective takes over the baffling case. He finds a new trail of evidence, pointing to the village doctor. As he is about to effect an arrest, he too is killed—in plain view of witnesses who see the flash of the weapon, but no murderer.

All the detectives out of the way, Doctor Hailey is free to carry on, in accordance with his method of "proceeding from the people to the crime rather than from the crime to the people." There is a great deal of character study and a solution that will knock you cold. This is a book that is worth $2 of anybody's money.—Todd Downing.[27]

looks forward to being "able to return some of the sneers" cast at mystery readers like himself.

27 Downing would later cite Anthony Wynne's *The Silver Scale Mystery* (in Britain, *Murder of a Lady*) as one of his all-time favorite detective novels (see Appendix Two: "The Detective Story: An Interview between Kenneth C. Kaufman and Todd Downing"). "Anthony Wynne" was the pseudonym of Robert McNair Wilson (1882-1963), a Scottish-born London physician and lay economist who published twenty-seven detective novels between 1925 and 1950. Wilson is still known today in some quarters for his conservative treatises on world finance, which influenced fascist poet Ezra Pound (the two men maintained a correspondence for a quarter century, from 1934 to 1958). The Wynne mysteries usually involve so-called "miracle problems," such as murders in locked rooms, that appealed to Downing's romantic imagination. Another American admirer of Wynne was Harry Stephen Keeler, a quite eccentric mystery writer reviewed by Downing a mere two months after he reviewed Wynne (see p. 175). On Keeler and Wynne, see the *Bulletin of the Harry Stephen Keeler Society* 59 (October 2006): 7-10. Wynne's *The Blue Vesuvius* was deemed a "detective story of the better sort" by Kenneth C. Kaufman (see *Daily Oklahoman*, 12 April 1931, p. 51).

"MR. FORTUNE SPEAKING"
November 8, 1931, p. 41

MR. FORTUNE SPEAKING, BY H. C. BAILEY

BLAND, imperturbable Reggie Fortune has more competitors in the field of detection now than when Mr. Bailey introduced him many years ago. But he manages to hold his own among newcomers, many of whom have borrowed his mannerisms. While on the whole the eight stories in this volume are slightly below par, they are certain to be hailed with delight by Reggie's numerous admirers among mystery fans.

Some of Mr. Fortune's most unusual cases are here recounted. That baffling affair of the Painted Pebbles, for instance, in which archaeology and criminality are mingled. And the curious case of The Woman in the Wood, in which the detective, true to his course of action in previous adventures, sends the malefactor to his grave. In the affair of the Lion Fish, as well, Reggie assumes the role of executioner. In the puzzling mater of the Hazel Ice the scene switches to the Swiss Alps and gives Reggie an opportunity to do some mountain climbing, much against this will.

This volume is recommended for old admirers of Mr. Fortune. Those who have not yet made his acquaintance should read one of the earlier books first, in order to appreciate him.—Todd Downing.[28]

"MORE MYSTERY"
November 22, 1931, p. 45

MURDER IN FOUR DEGREES, BY J. S. FLETCHER

BY writing some forty-odd consistently successful mysteries, Mr. Fletcher has acquired an easy, effortless touch that makes his

28 Henry Christopher Bailey (1878-1961) in 1920 created the highly mannered and amazingly intuitive Reggie Fortune, one of the great Golden Age English sleuths (though mostly forgotten today). Between 1920 and 1948 Reggie appeared not only in short story collections but novels as well, twenty-one volumes all together.

stories move without a halt from the discovery of the body to the manacling of the murderer. His popularity, equaled probably only by Edgar Wallace, would indicate that mystery fans who like to rack their brains over problems in deduction are in a minority, as compared with those who read to pass the time away.

This, entry number two in the casebook of Ronald Camberwell, the now famous sleuth who made his debut in the Wrides Park affair, is a typical Fletcher book. From the moment that the body of Thomas Hannington, editor of Lord Cheverdale's paper, the *Daily Sentinel*, is found on the grounds of his lordship's residence in Regent's Park, there is little doubt as to who did the deed. The rest of the book is devoted to an account of the chase staged by William Chaney, former C. I. D. and Camberwell's chronicler.

The plot wears rather thin in places, despite the introduction of several more murders and sundry suspicious characters, among them a veiled female carrying "the papers," but the guilty man is finally caught in a swimming pool and identified by the snake tattooed on his arm. And by that time it's time to go to bed.—Todd Downing.[29]

29 The numerous mostly uninspired detective novels written by the tremendously prolific British writer Joseph Smith Fletcher (1863-1935) typically produced a blasé reaction among 1930s crime fiction reviewers, though Fletcher enjoyed a substantial following in the United States, from 1919, when he was quite successfully promoted by his publisher as Woodrow Wilson's favorite mystery writer, through the 1920s and into the 1930s. As Downing's review indicates, Fletcher's novels tended to offer mild mystery, rather than the intricate plotting and challenging detection of Anthony Wynne's *The Silver Scale Mystery*, say, or the novels of Ellery Queen (soon to be reviewed by Downing), for crime fiction fans merely wanting to keep themselves dozily occupied in the evenings until bedtime. Downing speculates that "mystery fans who like to rack their brains over problems in deduction are in a minority."

"UMBRELLA MURDER"
November 29, 1931, p. 41

The Umbrella Murder, by Carolyn Wells

Murder of the nicer sort is described by Miss Wells in her latest. The victim is the rich and popular heiress Janet Converse, who is jabbed (in a rather indelicate spot) with a hypodermic needle filled with prussic acid, as she sits alone under a gay umbrella on the sands of the fashionable Club Spindrift. All the nice young people of her set are suspected, as well as some others not so nice. "Mercifulation!" exclaims the Irish housekeeper, Molly Mulvaney, "What a coil! All the kickooin' ther'll be straightenin' of it all out."

Molly's prediction comes true when a ha'ant wails through Terror Turret, calling on Janet's aunt to "give up the treasure." The aunt disappears, the debonair Stacpoole Meade is murdered, and Fleming Stone, Miss Wells' favorite sleuth, arouses himself from his lethargy and identifies the murderer by studying his cranium. All this accompanied by descriptions of the latest styles in beach pajamas.

By no means the worst of Miss Wells' imposing list of mysteries.—Todd Downing.[30]

30 By all means among Downing's best reviews are those of novels by Carolyn Wells (1862-1942), at this time along with Mary Roberts Rinehart the grande dame of American mystery. Wells published her first detective novel, *The Clue*, in 1909, when she was forty-seven, and produced eighty-one more between that year and 1942, when she died at the age of seventy-nine. Though Wells published a still well-regarded treatise on detective fiction, *The Technique of the Mystery Story* (1913, rev. ed., 1929), the reputation of her mystery novels has not held up well. "When it came to constructing a plausible mystery," scoffs Bill Pronzini, Wells "was . . . helpless." See Bill Pronzini, *Gun in Cheek: A Study of "Alternative" Crime Fiction* (1982; repr., New York: Mysterious Press, 1982), 43. Similarly, Barzun and Taylor allow of Wells that "the author was not a stupid woman," before concluding that "in almost all her novels of crime she supplies the reader with very little he can get a grip on: the situations are silly, the characters unbelievable, and the detection so at odds with the foolishness as to seem intrusive when it appears." See Barzun and Taylor, *Catalogue of Crime*, 541. The typical Wells book involves a country house

"THE HUNTER MURDER"
December 6, 1931, p. 50

THE MATILDA HUNTER MURDER, BY HARRY STEPHEN KEELER

MR. Keeler is said to be on contract with E. P. Dutton & Co. to furnish them with one 110,000-word novel every 90 days. This time he must have forgotten when the 90 days were up, for in this leviathan volume of 741 pages there are enough thrills, clues, deductions, and whatnot to satisfy the most avid mystery fan.

It all starts with the arrival at Mrs. Hunter's boarding house of a new boarder, carrying a mysterious black leather case tightly closed with stitches of silver wire. The boarder disappears, Mrs. Hunter gets curious, and suffers the fate of the proverbial cat. Enter Japanese spies, X-rays, atoms, Chicago prostitutes, insurance policies, fires, and a brand new detective, Mr. Tuddleton Trotter, with empty pockets and an encyclopedic brain, and the author of *Crime—Always a Motived Social Reaction as Well as a Motivated One*.

It is all first-class, A1 mystery and Mr. Keeler is an acknowledged master in this field, but my personal opinion is that it is too long, too complicated, too scientific, for anyone but a Robinson Crusoe. Everyone to whom I have loaned it, including an anthropologist, has returned it unfinished.—Todd Downing.[31]

populated by idly wealthy northeastern society people who never seem to take the murders in their midst seriously and servants who are objects of heavy-handed, "humorous" treatment by the author. In his review of *The Umbrella Murder*, Downing amusingly mocks the utter artificiality of the typical Wells murder milieu before concluding devastatingly that the tale is "by no means the worst" of the author's many mysteries.

31 Harry Stephen Keeler (1890-1967), an eccentric American author of bizarre mystery tales, died in obscurity but today enjoys a small but extremely devoted cult following. Keeler's publisher, Ramble House, deems the author a "victim of a plot by publishers to weed out all writers who don't write swift, easy-to-read, dumbed-down prose for the masses." See "Harry Stephen Keeler (1890-1967)" at http://www.ramblehouse.com/HarryKeeler.htm. Of *The Matilda Hunter Murder*, Ramble House warns, "An odyssey that only a died-in-the-wool Keelerite could handle. . . . Otherwise you might want to try another Keeler before tackling this one."

"THE DUTCH SHOE MYSTERY"
June 26, 1932, p. 36

THE DUTCH SHOE MYSTERY, BY ELLERY QUEEN

WITH the publication of *The Roman Hat Mystery* three years ago, the unknown owner of the pen-name Ellery Queen leaped full-fledged into the front rank of detective story writers. With his *The French Powder Mystery* the following year, he outdistanced all but a few of his competitors in this country. This is the third adventure of the questing Queen to be presented to the public and, if the public knows good detective stories when it reads them, S. S. Van Dine's phenomenal success will be repeated.

For the publishers are correct in calling this a problem of deduction. The reader is given all the facts in the sensational murder of the rich and famous Abigail Doorn in the anteroom of the main operating theater of the Dutch Memorial Hospital, just before she was to go under the knife. A varied array of suspects is lined up for questioning: Dr. Janney, Abigail's protégé; Sarah Fuller, her disagreeable companion; Hendrik Doorn, the playboy of Broadway; Philip Morehouse, her attorney. And don't overlook Michael Cudahy, the gangster (although he was under the ether at the time of the murder) or the hospital staff, some of whom have pasts that will bear looking into.

The solution seems simple after Ellery explains it, but when the reader receives his challenge on page 253, it's dollars to doughnuts that he is completely at sea as to the identity of the murderer. If your brain needs exercise buy, borrow or steal a copy of this book.—Todd Downing.[32]

Evidently *Matilda Hunter* defeated both Todd Downing and his OU anthropologist friend, Professor Forrest E. Clements.

32 Another of Downing's very favorite authors makes his first appearance in the young Oklahoman's review column. Along with John Dickson Carr, "Ellery Queen" (pseudonym of cousins Frederic Dannay and Manfred Bennington Lee, 1905-1982/1901-1971) would soon eclipse the waning S. S. Van Dine as the greatest American exponent of the classical clue puzzle mystery.

"DETECTIVE ELLERY"

Aug. 14, 1932, p. 41

THE GREEK COFFIN MYSTERY, BY ELLERY QUEEN

ELLERY Queen's fourth and best baffler. The action antedates in point of time the other investigations in which the suave Ellery aided his father, Inspector Queen of the New York Police. Here we meet a young, more carefree and cocksure Ellery, but one whose theories of deduction, although embryonic, lead him to the truth in the strange circumstances surrounding the death of George Kalkis, blind art dealer, in his palatial New York residence. Highly recommended.—Todd Downing.[33]

"DEATH'S SERVANT"

October 16, 1932, page 53

THE SERVANT OF DEATH, BY J. H. WALLIS

A MYSTERY story in reverse. Instead of running with the hounds the reader is chased with the hare. He sees a man commit the almost perfect crime—no clues for the police, no false step to give him away—and watches the murderer's own conscience and caution lead to his undoing. Another appearance of Inspector Jacks, the likeable sleuth of *Murder by Formula* and *The Capital City Mystery*.—Todd Downing.[34]

33 Queen's *The Greek Coffin Mystery* often is listed as Queen's best pure puzzle novel.

34 Between 1931 and 1934, James Harold Wallis (1885-1958) published six tales of the detections of the "likeable" Inspector Wilton Jacks. He also wrote four additional crime novels, including *Once Off Guard* (1942), filmed by Fritz Lang as *The Woman in the Window* (1944). Born in Dubuque, Iowa, Wallis was a graduate of Yale University, where he edited the *Yale Courant* and the *Yale Literary Magazine*. After graduating he returned to Dubuque, where he became a newspaper publisher and editor. He later moved to Scarsdale, New York, where he devoted himself to writing fiction. See "James Harold Wallis," Encyclopedia Dubuque, http://www.encyclopediadubuque.org/index.php?title=WALLIS%2C_James_Harold

"CLUES, CORPSES" (REVIEWED BY TODD DOWNING)[35]
November 6, 1932, p. 52

The Egyptian Cross Mystery, by Ellery Queen

The suave Ellery's fondness for gore increases with every book. In his last, *The Greek Coffin Mystery*, it dripped; here it gushes all over the pages. The source is the headless trunk of a West Virginia schoolmaster, found crucified on a signpost. Keep your eye on Harakht, a reincarnated god of Pharoanic Egypt; Paul Romaine, who conducts a nudist colony on a lonely island; and Professor Yardley, an antiquary who may not be as innocent as he looks. And leave the light on when you go to sleep.—Todd Downing.[36]

Red Shadow, by Patricia Wentworth

Those darned Russians are at it again! This time they have their clutches on Jim Mackenzie and are going to shoot him unless his sweetheart Laura marries Vassili Stefanoff and appoints him to the boards of all the firms in the Hallingdon combine, to which combine Laura has fallen heir. What does the poor girl do?[37]

Find the Motive, by Jack Woodford

". . . . and the one who plans to take my life is seated at this table. I will not tell you the person's name just yet; but I will explain the motive. The motive is. . . ." A blinding flash and the lights in the dining room went out. One corpse, a dozen suspects, as many motives. Told in rapid fire journalese.[38]

35 At this point Downing's name first begins to appear above the review column. Not coincidentally, Downing's OU mentor, Professor Kenneth C. Kaufman, on this date became editor of the *Daily Oklahoman*'s literary page, where Downing's mystery book reviews appeared.

36 Downing's love of Ellery Queen and outré shudders continues.

37 Downing's tone in his review of *Red Shadow* (*Red Danger* in Britain) suggests he found, reasonably enough, the anti-Communist thriller of the period quite silly. Yet his romantic heart seems to have had a soft spot for Patricia Wentworth tales, judging by later reviews.

38 Josiah Pitts Woolfolk (1894-1971) was a journalist turned prolific and

"MURDER! FIRE!"
(REVIEWED BY TODD DOWNING)
November 13, 1932, p. 47

MURDER ON THE YACHT, BY RUFUS KING

IF Rufus King can't awaken your jaded brain cells and titillate your nerves, no purveyor of mysteries can. In his latest, reminiscent of and fully as good as [his] *Murder by Latitude*, he bewilders with several new tricks—a spiritualistic medium, a disappearing corpse (which may not be a corpse) and a dummy which comes to life—all on a sinking yacht.

THE FIRE AT GREYCOMBE FARM, BY JOHN RHODE

"AY, 'tis a bad business indeed," opined Farmer Jim as he watched his barn burn. "There's all my stock of cider gone." The next day Farmer Jim discovers a heap of charred human bones in the ruins and [he] calls in the chief constable. The C. C. scratches his head and calls in our old friend, Doctor Priestley.[39]

popular novelist and short story writer who published under a number of pseudonyms, most prominently Jack Woodford. Many of his books were considered quite salacious for the day. His single best known work is *Trial and Error* (1933), a blunt and caustic tome advising prospective writers on how to get published.

39 Downing's contrasting treatment of novels by American Rufus King and Britisher John Rhode suggests a difference in American and British national temperaments. A greater contrast between King's tale of spiritualism, a sinking yacht, a disappearing corpse and an animated dummy and Rhode's story of bones found in Farmer Jim's cider barn is hard to imagine. It is easy to see Downing preferred King's tense, sophisticated tale to Rhode's laconic, rural one, though he did label Rhode's detective, Dr. Priestley, an "old friend." Rufus King (1893-1966) published twenty-two detective novels between 1927 and 1951 (three volumes of short stories appeared between 1958 and 1964). In the 1930s critics considered him a major figure in American detective fiction. His early novels *Murder by the Clock* (1929) and *Murder by Latitude* (1931) were especially heralded. His works have been out of print since his death, however.

"CLUES AND CORPSES"[40]
(REVIEWED BY TODD DOWNING)
November 20, 1932, p. 42

No Friendly Drop, by Henry Wade

An injudicious mixture of di-dial (a derivative of barbituric acid), scopolamine (one of the Atropine group of vegetable poisons, more generally known as hyoscine), claret, port and brandy did in Lord Grayle (of the Tassart Grayles). "Sounds a bit ticklish, certainly," remarks Inspector Poole. For fans who know their pharmacopoeia.[41]

The Harness of Death, by W. Stanley Sykes

The whole is greater than its parts, said Euclid, but he wasn't present at the Southbourne police station when the checkroom clerk brought in a grip containing a severed leg. The distracted police forgot all about the whole corpse in Reinhold's foundry. Replete with Edgar Wallace thrills, tunny fishing and Inspector Drury.[42]

"CLUES AND CORPSES"
(REVIEWED BY TODD DOWNING)
November 27, 1932, p. 43

The Student Fraternity Murder, by Milton Propper

No, Uncle Abner, that's not a lynchin' you hear. It's those snooty Mu Beta Sigma fraternity boys over on Locust Street. They were having one of those things they call initiations—candle light and robes and oaths—and one of 'em dropped dead. Tommy Rankin

40 Through May 1934 this served as the title of Downing's mystery review column.

41 "Henry Wade" (1887-1969) was the pseudonym of Henry Lancelot Aubrey-Fletcher, one of the great Golden Age English detective novelists.

42 W. Stanley Sykes (1894-1960) was a physician and acknowledged authority on anesthesia. Besides *The Harness of Death*, Sykes published an acclaimed detective novel, reprinted in paperback by Penguin, *The Missing Moneylender* (1931).

(you remember he solved *The Boudoir Murder*) has been put on the case and is trying to find a clue in the ritual. Between you and me, I never did trust the dean of men.[43]

About the Murder of the Circus Queen, by Anthony Abbot

With big-lipped Ubangia, black magic and sawdust at his disposal, Mr, Abbot (still pseudonymous) should have concocted another tale of horror like *The Murder of Geraldine Foster* (remember those pigeons?). As it is, even Thatcher Colt seems a trifle bored with the investigation of the death of Josie La Tour in Madison Square Garden. You'll enjoy the animals.[44]

The Conjure-Man Dies, by Rudolph Fisher

The conjure man who dies or doesn't die or maybe dies and yet lives (one never knows about fictional corpses these days) is one Frimbo of West One Hundred and Thirtieth street. Suspects

43 Milton Propper (1906-1962), an American follower of the orthodox timetable and alibi mysteries of Freeman Wills Crofts, published fourteen Tommy Rankin detective novels between 1929 and 1943. Unable to publish his work after 1943 and harassed over his homosexuality, Propper descended into poverty and committed suicide in 1962. See Francis M. Nevins, "The World of Milton Propper," *The Armchair Detective* 10 (July 1977): 196-203. Propper made a fair-sized splash with his 1929 debut novel, *The Strange Disappearance of Mary Young*, which he published at the relatively precocious age (for an author) of twenty-three, the year he graduated with honors from University of Pennsylvania Law School. Propper's tales of murder among Philadelphia's upper crust have been harshly criticized as elitist by Nevins; yet in his review of *The Student Fraternity Murder*, Downing, who participated in Greek functions at the University of Oklahoma, more lightly pokes fun, in the voice of a country rube, at arcane fraternity initiation ceremonies (as Downing implies, the robed men on the Bobbs-Merrill dust jacket look unnervingly like Ku Klux Klan members). Downing's reference to "Uncle Abner" likely was deliberate, Uncle Abner being the detective in the celebrated Melville Davisson Post short stories, which were published between 1913 and 1918 and likely perused by Downing as a teenager.

44 Clearly Abbot disappointed Downing with a tale that lacked any real horror trappings, despite boasting such exotica as an African witch doctor (indelicately referred to by Downing as "big-lipped Ubangia").

include Spider Webb (number-runner), Doty Hicks (drug addict) and Easley Jones (Pullman porter).

Wisecracks by the team of Jinx and Bubber and so-so sleuthing by Perry Dart, Negro member of the Harlem police.[45]

"CLUES AND CORPSES" (REVIEWED BY TODD DOWNING) December 4, 1932, p. 45

VALCOUR MEETS MURDER, BY RUFUS KING

SPRING in Center Street and fog, hip-high fog, shrouding a mysterious farmhouse on the Canadian border. The dachshund Jezebel stabbed with an ice pick. Professor Belding at the foot of the stairs with a broken neck. Madame Bertier, and the ice pick again ($2 worth of chills on one page). Lieutenant Valcour. And Rufus King at his baffling best.[46]

NO! NO! THE WOMAN!, BY NORMAN KLEIN

MR. Klein, formerly a Chicago and New York newspaper man, is hailed by his publishers as an author "distinctly original" who "enters the field of fiction with a resounding bang." A dull thud would be more exact. All about old lady Pollard, with her wealth and her champagne drinking, her naughty songs, her naughtier heirs: lots of gangsters, bootleggers, kidnappers, a touch of Rufus King, and another of Dashiell Hammett. And some highly picturesque language. Just medium.[47]

45 Though Downing seemed little interested in *The Conjure Man Dies*, the novel's author, Rudolph Fisher (1897-1934), was an accomplished figure in the Harlem Renaissance. *The Conjure Man Dies* is considered the first African-Amèrican detective novel and was reprinted, along with a collection of Fisher's short stories, in the early 1990s.

46 "Chills" such as the ice pick killings in *Valcour Meets Murder* continue to draw Downing's praise.

47 James Thurber deemed *New York Post* reporter Norman Klein's debut detective novel "one of the best mystery novels I've ever read" (see "A Sunday

THE KEEPER OF THE KEYS, BY EARL DERR BIGGERS

CHARLIE Chan again, this time in a palatial California country home; an opera singer who got herself bumped off; four of her former husbands. Plenty of clues, all of which lead to nowhere.

Suspicion hovering about over the whole crowd, to alight finally on the only one who could not possibly be guilty. Thrills and scenery; some ideal western characters; a pretty girl; and, of course, a satisfactory hero. Plenty of Charlie Chan's proverbs and psychology. Altogether a soul-satisfying story.[48]

"CLUES AND CORPSES" (REVIEWED BY TODD DOWNING) December 18, 1932, p.43

THE TRAGEDY OF X, BY BARNABY ROSS

PRESENTING a new sleuth—Drury Lane. Who's Who of the Drama says, according to his pseudonymous chronicler, that he is the son of actors and unmarried, specialized in Hamlet before going blind and now lives in monastic retirement on the Hudson. Despite a touch of Philo Vance-like dilettantism, Drury deserves your acquaintance. The murder takes place in a crowded street car.[49]

THE WHITE ARROW, BY ANTHONY WYNNE

THE next time you find a murdered man in a room locked on the inside, call in Doctor Hailey. That's his specialty. The victim is

Afternoon with Mr. Thurber," *New York Herald Tribune Book Review*, 2 November 1957, 2). Downing clearly found it derivative.

48 Earl Derr Biggers (1884-1933) published six Charlie Chan novels between 1925 and his premature death in 1933. Charlie Chan became, along with Sherlock Holmes and Sam Spade, one of the most famous screen detectives. On Biggers and the Charlie Chan phenomenon see Yunte Huang, *Charlie Chan: The Untold Story of the Honorable Detective and His Rendezvous with American History* (New York and London: W. W. Norton, 2010).

49 Ellery Queen's Drury Lane figured in four of their detective novels. *The Tragedy of X* is considered the best of the Drury Lane tales, and indeed

the famous millionaire Rollo Bowmark (gone insane from wondering whether Bowmark is derived from Beaumaris? Or maybe it's domestic trouble?). Colonel Wickham finds the head but it takes Doctor Hailey to find the body.[50]

THE BIRTHDAY MURDER, BY KATHLEEN SPROUL

YOUNG Dick Wilson ("Skillful butlers, squab, Burgundy and silver plate were native to him") busts into the sleuthing game when the fair Emily Justin is found dead at the wheel of her car after a birthday party. Dick cogitates and opines: "The reason for such an inhuman crime is indistinguishably bound up with its perpetrator." Just what we suspected all along.[51]

"CLUES AND CORPSES"
(REVIEWED BY TODD DOWNING)
December 25, 1932, p. 35

THE WOMAN IN BLACK, BY HERBERT ADAMS

NOT guilty was the verdict of the jury in the case of Beresford Wilson, prominent London journalist, accused of the murder of his

one of the high points of American Golden Age detective fiction. For the sake of the ingenuity of the tale, Downing was willing to forgive "a touch of Philo Vance-like dilettantism" in Drury Lane.

50 Downing's love of exotic miracle problems again finds outlet in another of Anthony Wynne's locked room tales.

51 Kathleen Sproul's writing was not only affected, Downing suggests, but, even worse, ineptly affected. An instructor of English at Rollins College, where she taught Ernest Hemingway's youngest sister, Carol, and the wife of Harold C. Sproul, head of the English department at Amherst University (and amateur cellist), Sproul authored five mystery novels, the first of which was *The Birthday Murder*. "A nervous breakdown and a decision during convalescence that there were not enough good detective stories led Kathleen Sproul . . . to write one," declared the *New York Times Book Review* in its "Book Notes" of March 1, 1932. Sproul's best known mystery was probably, appropriately enough, *Death Among the Professors* (1933). She herself would reviews books, including mysteries, for *Saturday Review* from the late 1930s into the 1950s.

estranged wife. A few hours later he was shot as he was leaving the apartment of the other woman. Jimmie Haswell, his lawyer, Inspector Sprules and a pair of sweethearts get busy. Satisfyingly sane.[52]

DEAD HANDS REACHING, BY MARION SCOTT

"NOBODY home but Mr. Keye," the old housekeeper muttered (yes, it's that kind), when Dallas Gantry, star of *Queen Anne*, returned to the house of the miser of Willow Valley to wrangle out of him a divorce.

Keye proved to be a corpse and the alcoves and curtains concealed sundry suspects. Added attractions—a face at the window and Captain Brade. Ho hum![53]

52 British mystery writer Herbert Adams (1874-1958) published fifty-one thrillers and detective novels between 1925 and 1958, the earlier ones featuring lawyer Jimmie Haswell and the later ones featuring the gentleman amateur detective Roger Bennion. Though Adams was never placed at the front rank of British mystery novelists in his day, Jacques Barzun and Wendell Hertig Taylor wrote admiringly of his work in *A Catalogue of Crime*. Downing's verdict on *The Woman in Black*—"satisfyingly sane"—he would apply more than once to competently plotted and written but not viscerally thrilling British detective novels.

53 *Dead Hands Reaching* seems to have been Marion Scott's sole detective novel—possibly a good thing, judging by Downing's review most scathing.

CHAPTER TWO: 1933 REVIEWS

"CLUES AND CORPSES"
(REVIEWED BY TODD DOWNING)
January 1, 1933

THE BOX FROM JAPAN, BY HARRY STEPHEN KEELER

"CHICAGO was Chicago: and anything could happen in Chicago!" Even in the month of Sol. 1942, when transpire the events of Mr. Keller's latest mammoth concoction of mystery, murder and what not. Fans of this indefatigable spinner of yarns hailed *The Matilda Hunter Murder* as a tour de force. Mr. Keeler, however, seems to be serious about it, judging by this 765–page volume, crammed bewilderingly with plot and counterplot.

A few of the hors d'oeuvres piled up for the reader's delectation are: an unclaimed box in an Express Company auction, Papuan cannibals, Mexican revolutions, television, D. T.'s and gangsters. Recommended.[1]

MURDER OF THE LAWYER'S CLERK, BY J. S. FLETCHER

BEING entry number five in the case-book of Chaney and Camberwell, the thoroughgoing, cricket-playing, rather colorless firm

1 Downing's taste for the bizarre continues to attract him to the odd works of Harry Stephen Keeler. Publisher Fender Tucker of Ramble House calls *The Box from Japan* possibly "the damnedest mystery novel ever written." See the description of the novel at http://www.ramblehouse.com/boxfromjapan.htm.

of private inquiry agents to the chronicling of whose activities Mr. Fletcher is now devoting himself.

The leisurely, non-brain-taxing plot concerns the missing "papers" which may or may not have been concealed in the library of a murdered antiquarian. Add a will, heirs and Superintendent Bailiss ("Bailiss," observed Chaney, "is improving. Ideas are coming into his head.") Typically Fletcher.[2]

"CLUES AND CORPSES" (REVIEWED BY TODD DOWNING)

January 8, 1933, p. 41

THE NAMELESS CRIME, BY WALTER S. MASTERMAN

WHEN is a murder not a murder? How long can a man remain alive after his corpse has been cremated? What was the sinister purpose of the Film Services Corp.? And who was Count Ginburg of the Holy Roman Empire? Trust Superintendent Sinclair to find out. The heroine is a blue-eyed doll who probably believes in the stork, and the villain is that dastardly that the horrible justice finally meted out to him is guaranteed to send a thrill of righteous satisfaction up your spine. And don't forget the noble self-sacrifice of Captain Stanley. Not much room for brain-teasing, but thoroughly satisfactory in every other respect. Recommended.[3]

DEATH RIDES THE DRAGON, BY EUGENE THOMAS

"KU ku ti ki tak no kong," hissed Lai Ching, prince of Inner Mongolia and emperor-to-be of Central Asia. "You will never leave

2 "Typically Fletcher," Downing yawns of the banally titled *Murder of the Lawyer's Clerk*. To this novel that astute English reviewer Charles Williams afforded two clever, cutting lines: "Mr. Fletcher—is Mr. Fletcher. His admirers will admire him, and others have no need to interfere." See Jared C. Lobdell, ed., *The Detective Fiction Reviews of Charles Williams, 1930-1935* (McFarland, 2003), 94.

3 Downing continues to reveal that he very much enjoyed a good shocker. Walter S. Masterman (1876-1946) wrote some two dozen mystery novels of sorts, usually infused with horror elements.

New York alive," whispered the girl of mystery as she vanished in a taxicab. And young Lorry Carter, far eastern diplomat on leave, grasped his automatic. Easily digestible and satisfying.[4]

"CLUES AND CORPSES" (REVIEWED BY TODD DOWNING)

January 15, 1933, p. 39

THE KENNEL MURDER CASE, BY S. S. VAN DINE

"THAT'S dashed interestin'," our incorrigible friend Philo Vance murmurs as he withdraws his finger from the interior of the Chinese vase (a piece of later Ting Yao—from the Yung Cheng era). "Blood!"

Or, if you prefer dogs, there's a wounded Scottie. "A dog, like a painting or a piece of sculpture, must have free movement in three dimensions, balance, organization, rhythm."

Or, if you insist on murder, there's one Archer Coe—stabbed, shot and struck with a poker—in a room bolted on the inside. Shall we say the event of the present murder season?[5]

BRED IN THE BONE, BY EDEN PHILLPOTTS

A MURDER, but not a mystery. Mr. Phillpotts, who divides his time between regular mystery stories and pleasant English country novels, has here contrived a complicated novel of character, which makes slow reading because he takes the reader into his confidence from the beginning. We know who murdered Peter Bryden, how and why; and the obscure processes by which his murderer's stamina is undermined grows stale before his self-inflicted end. We should like to suggest that Mr. Phillpotts stick

4 Described by a bookseller as "a mystery thriller involving a jade dragon, Mongolians, Japanese and Park Avenue debutantes," Eugene Thomas' "Yellow Peril" thriller *Death Rides a Dragon* receives indulgent treatment from Downing.

5 Philo Vance had palled on some readers in the 1930s (Ogden Nash memorably declared that the amateur sleuth needed a "kick in the pance"), but not, however, on Downing, who continued to view Vance as *sui generis*.

to the two lines in which he is an acknowledged master and not try to mix the two.[6]

"CLUES AND CORPSES" (REVIEWED BY TODD DOWNING)

January 22, 1933, p. 37

MURDER IN FULL FLIGHT, BY MARCUS MAGILL

GETTING off to a slow start by devoting five chapters to family tit-tat, Magill, author of the much-touted *Murder out of Tune*, concocts a plausible, not-too-ingenious tale of aeronautics and murder (mostly aeronautics). The victim is one Simon Nicholson, inventor of the Eagle Energizer, which has something to do with aeroplanes and the unpatented plans for which are being sought by a dark Jew with foreign accents (suspect No. 1). Other suspects: (2) a nice old lady from South Africa; (3) Howard Millburne, a cranky neighbor; (4) a dubious botanist among the buttercups; (5) Patsy (aged seven), who stands on her head. Solved by David Leroy, detective, who recovered Mrs. What's-her-name's pearls. Better than the average.[7]

I'LL TELL YOU EVERYTHING, BY J. B. PRIESTLEY AND GERALD BULLETT

SIMON Heath, lecturer at Cambridge and as nice a young scholar as you would ever hope to meet, was suddenly and mysteriously

6 In his review of this crime novel by the respected mainstream writer (and more than occasional spinner of mysteries) Eden Phillpotts, Downing reveals skepticism that the mystery tale can be fully merged with the mainstream novel. Over the years he nevertheless was to prove a strong admirer of Phillpotts' genre fiction.

7 "Marcus Magill" was the pseudonym of (Leonard) Brian Hill (1896-1979) and Joanna E. Giles (1893-1952). Born in London, Brian Hill later attended Oxford University and became assistant publicity manger of the Gas Council (headquarters of the British petroleum industry). Besides five detective novels novels—*Who Shall Hang?* (1929), *Death-in-the-Box* (1929), *I Like a Good Murder* (1930), *Murder Out of Tune* (1931) and *Murder in Full Flight* (1932)—and a thriller, *Hide, and I'll Find You!* (1933), Hill wrote and translated poetry. His translations included works by Rimbaud, Verlaine,

handed a steel casket, which might have contained anything from a bomb to smuggled dope, and requested to get it into London. Then things began to happen: various mysterious gentlemen waylaid him; a devastatingly beautiful young girl, no less charming for being mysterious, ransacked his room. He went on the most absurd wild goose chases, and all the time that steel box kept bobbing up to create hilarious, intriguing and dangerous situations. A mystery without a detective (that is one who really clicks), without violence, with plenty of real humor, and absolutely unsolvable.[8]

"CLUES AND CORPSES" (REVIEWED BY TODD DOWNING)
February 5, 1933, p. 36

THE COTSWOLD CASE, BY ANTHONY WYNNE

"ANOTHER Dr. Hailey detective novel" on the jacket is enough of a review for seasoned mystery fans, who have learned what to expect from Mr. Wynne's pen: a corpse in a sealed room (this time Scotland Yard and Doctor Hailey stand outside the door and hear the shot); painstaking reconstruction of the murdered man's character, wherein, repeats Dr. Hailey, lies the key to every murder; good, solid chunks of roast beef ("The gentry are the gentry still in England." Doctor Hailey pauses to take snuff. "God

Heredeia, Nerval and Gautier. He may be the same Brian Hill, born in 1896, who served in World War One as a 2nd lieutenant with the Durham Light Infantry and wrote the poem "Salonika in November," published in Kyle Galloway, ed., *More Songs by the Fighting Men: Soldier Poets* (Second Series) (London: Erskine Macdonald, 1917) ("Up above the cold gray hills the wheeling birds are flying/Brother calls to brother, as they pass in restless flight/Lost souls, dead souls, voices of the dying/Circle o'er the hills of Greece and wail into the night")—though, contrastingly, the quality most noted in the Magill mysteries is their lightly humorous touch.

8 John Boynton Priestley (1894-1984), English novelist and playwright, and Gerald William Bullett (1893-1958), novelist, essayist, short story writer and poet, both dabbled occasionally in crime/mystery fiction. In this instance they dabbled jointly.

grant that it may be so always!"); an unhurried unemotional style (gone the horror and the flirting with the supernatural that made *The Silver Scale Mystery* one of the best thrillers ever written); and, last but not least, a surprise at the end.

In other words, just about everything that a murder story should be.[9]

DEAD MEN AT THE FOLLY, BY JOHN RHODE

SUICIDE, said the village constable. Accident, opined the coroner. But Inspector Hanslet wasn't satisfied about the woman in the automobile that was seen near Tilling's Folly (a stone tower, by the way), nor about the torn telegram, nor about Mr. and Mrs. Illingfield's family squabbles. So he called in Dr. Priestley. It proved, of course, to be murder. Routine Scotland Yard investigation, with nary a thrill. Recommended, nevertheless.[10]

"CLUES AND CORPSES"
(REVIEWED BY TODD DOWNING)
February 12, 1933, p. 25

MARY ROBERTS RINEHART'S CRIME BOOK, BY MARY ROBERTS RINEHART

"A HODGE-PODGE of characters, motives, passions, all working together toward that terrible night of August twelfth, 1911, when hell seemed loose on a painted sea."

9 Downing's admiration for Anthony Wynne continues nearly unbounded ("just about everything that a murder story should be"), though he misses the quasi-supernatural trappings that in his view made *The Silver Scale Mystery* "one of the best thrillers ever written." Downing even looks indulgently on Wynne's "good, solid chunks of roast beef"—i.e., English gentry hagiography. Like the great G. K. Chesterton, creator of Father Brown, Wynne was a traditionalist Catholic who romanticized the feudal, agrarian social order of medieval Europe.

10 Downing's comments on this John Rhode novel ("Routine Scotland Yard investigation, with nary a thrill. Recommended, nevertheless.") suggests his keenness even for what Julian Symons called the British "Humdrum" mystery.

And, human curiosity being what it is, the ready-to-be-tempted reader delays turning off the bed lamp until he reaches the night of August twelfth. Then, seeing the solution dangled tantalizingly before him, he has to read on to the last page—and gets up yawning the next morning.

Therein, and in the more or less adroit use of the machinery of horror (rats fleeing from a deserted ship, presentiments, dying goldfish, creaking old houses, black cats even) lies the secret of the perennial popularity of Mrs. Rinehart's mystery stories.

In this omnibus volume are included two of her best known hair-raisers—*The After House*, a novelization of the unsolved Mate Bram case, the full possibilities of which were realized by Rufus King in *Murder by Latitude*, and *The Red Lamp*, one of the most successful skirtings about the supernatural ever penned; a (deservedly) little known novel of love, murder and politics, *The Window at the White Cat*; and two novelettes, presenting again the red-headed nurse of *Miss Pinkerton* fame, *The Buckled Bag* and *Locked Doors* (the latter especially recommended).

Literary critics may raise tufted eyebrows, Rufus King and Mrs. Eberhart may succeed in wringing new shudders out of old tricks—but Mrs. Rinehart has taught them all more than they will probably admit. Which is to say I don't know of a bigger $2 worth for the mystery fan than this volume.[11]

"CLUES AND CORPSES"
(REVIEWED BY TODD DOWNING)
February 19, 1933, p. 35

Murder at Cypress Hall, by O'Connor Stacey

Wherein are recorded the strange doings at Cypress Hall, way down in the Santee district of the South Carolina Low Country,

11 "These are the first crime stories which have the air of being written specifically for maiden aunts," writes Julian Symons contemptuously of the tremendously popular mystery novels and stories of Mary Roberts Rinehart in his genre survey, *Bloody Murder* (see page 100 of the 1992

where, if we are to believe the author (and he evidently knows his stuff), true love still flourishes, men are still men and drink their corn out of fruit jars, and murdered squires still leave wills that cast suspicion upon all the heirs.

Mr. Stacey is another pseudonymous author and if his first detective story is a sample of his abilities, you should hear more of him. His pages are slightly overweighed with premonitions but he's refreshingly different.[12]

THE CROSSROAD MURDERS, BY GEORGES SIMENON

RECENT ballyhoo concerning M. Simenon (of whom this is the third novel to be translated into English and the first to reach the reviewer) aroused interest in an addict of the fantastic, finesse, frémissements, etc., commonly associated with the French mystery yarn.

The result is, to speak mildly, disappointing. The night of terror at the Crossroads of the Three Widows outside Paris (shootings, poisonings, free-for-all fights including a desperate battle at the bottom of a well) is too absurdly theatrical for even the Grand Guignol. An incense-perfumed boudoir scene between the doughty Inspector Maigret and the divan-draped Else is too forcedly sex-y for even La Vie Parisienne. The translator has

Mysterious Press edition). For his part, Todd Downing—no maiden aunt he—unashamedly makes clear that he holds Mary Roberts Rinehart's works is quite high esteem. And he again reveals his partiality in the mystery tale for what he terms "the machinery of horror."

12 "O'Connor Stacey" was a pseudonym of William Rollins, Jr. (1897-1950). Rollins, a pulp detective writer published in *Black Mask*, produced three mystery novels, *Midnight Treasure* (1929), *Murder at Cypress Hall* (1933) and *The Ring and the Lamp* (1947). A Marxist and homosexual, Rollins also wrote the left-wing novels *The Shadow Before* (1934) (about a textile factory strike and lavishly praised by Lillian Hellman, Dashiell Hammett, John Dos Passos and Edmund Wilson) and *The Wall of Men* (1938) (about the Spanish Civil War), as well as *The Obelisk* (1930), "a novel of adolescence somewhat influenced by [James] Joyce." See Alan Wald, "American Writers on the Left," *glbtq: An Encyclopedia of Gay, Lesbian, Bisexual, Transgender and Queer Culture*, http://www.glbtq.com/literature/am_mawriters_left.html. Downing seems to have been perceptive in noting this author as something "refreshingly different."

slung together Parisian argot, Edgar Wallace toff talk and Chicago gangster slang. As M. Oscar so succinctly remarks, "boloney."[13]

"CLUES AND CORPSES" (REVIEWED BY TODD DOWNING)

February 26, 1933, p. 40

BURN, WITCH, BURN!, BY A. MERRITT

FIVE star item for former H. Rider Haggard fans who still crave the scalp-tickling sensation which comes from bed lamp expeditions into the borderland between illusion and reality and have grown a bit surfeited with recent novelistic devices to attain such end. In this fast-moving yarn centering around Mme. Mandilip and her dolls, her fish-white niece and the epidemic of inexplicable deaths that baffle New York medical authorities, Mr. Merritt has given us a thriller equal to his *Seven Footprints to Satan*. Chapter 11, "A Doll Kills," joins that chapter in Rufus King's *Murder on the Yacht* in which the dummy moves on our own recommended list for hard-to-thrill readers.[14]

THE IMPERFECT CRIME, BY BRUCE GRAEME

ADD to your list of favorite fictional detectives Inspector Pierre Allain, of the French Sûreté Générale, who made his bow in *A Murder of Some Importance* and who now returns to master further female hearts and to punish another murderer in his own ruthless, direct manner, thereby scandalizing the stolid, uxorious

13 One of the most striking of Todd Downing's reviews is this one in which he categorically dismisses Belgian-French crime writer Georges Simenon (1903-1989), now considered one of the greatest figures in the history of the genre. As we will see, Downing did not think much of modern French crime writing in general. Downing finds the relatively frank sex unenticing and the whole thing, in a memorable statement, "too absurdly theatrical for even the Grand Guignol."

14 Journalist Abraham Grace Merritt (1884-1943) was a highly influential fantasy and horror writer of the 1920s and 1930s.

Stevens of Scotland Yard. Done in the best Maurice Leblanc–Gaston Leroux manner, with a thumbing of the nose at some of the conventions which trammel mystery fiction, the book is a welcome change from the average run of such fair.[15]

DOCUMENTS OF MURDER, BY T. C. H. JACOBS

"THE papers were easily obtained?" Kharkov shivered and looked away from those cold, merciless eyes (it was the job down by the Thames that made him so nervous). "Quite easily." The big man shrugged his shoulders. Kharkov shivered again. "And the girl—?"

Secret treaties, Russian spies and Jimmie Osborne of the Foreign Office, by a worthy rival of E. Phillips Oppenheim.[16]

"CLUES AND CORPSES"
(REVIEWED BY TODD DOWNING)
March 12, 1933, p. 33

THE CIRCLE OF DEATH, BY CHARLES J. DUTTON

ONE of the slicker sleuths, in our opinion, is Harley Manners, professor of abnormal psychology, authority on eighteenth-century French prints and pre-Volstead Scotch, who appeared in *Murder in a Library* and *Poison Unknown*. The motive behind the

15 "Bruce Graeme" was a pseudonym for Graham Montague Jeffries (1900-1982), an extremely prolific crime writer who published some 100 novels and short story collections between 1925 and 1980. Jeffries mostly wrote thrillers—his most famous character was the gentleman crook turned crime fighter "Blackshirt"—but he also produced some works more properly seen as detective novels.

16 Thomas Curtis Hicks Jacobs (1899-1976) under a myriad of pen names produced over 100 novels between 1930 and 1974, including romances, westerns and, of course, thrillers. Downing may have enjoyed *Documents of Murder*, but not everyone agreed. In a satirical 1939 poem titled "You Cad, Why Don't You Cringe?" Ogden Nash memorably mocked both Jacobs and the morally ingenuous Golden Age thriller that Jacobs represented. Inspired by his noticing that in two different places in his novel *The Thirteenth Chime* Jacobs made the observation "Like most knaves he was a coward at heart . . .", Nash declared: "Ah, if none but the good were

mysterious deaths in the rich Kimball family and the anonymous telephone calls is, to our knowledge, one that has never been used in detective fiction. And that makes up for an occasional literary lapse on the part of the author.[17]

CORRUPTION, BY RICHARD CURLE

REMINISCENT, in its foreshadowing of tragedy, of that sinister line in Keats' *Isabella*—"so the two brothers and their murdered man rode past fair Florence"—is this inverted mystery story. The reader sees the murder conceived and its execution developed, while he remains in considerable of a daze as to just what it's all about. When he begins to lose interest he is reminded that there is an already dug grave in the shrubbery. Effective, but a bit prolonged.[18]

THE CLUE OF THE EYELASH, BY CAROLYN WELLS

SOCIETY item (Golden Sands, L. I. Tattler): Mrs. Wiley Vane of Greencastle House, entertained at a Fourth of July house party the following guests: Miss Rose Kortz ("great big girl, and no end handsome"); Dr. Cameron ("a jolly looking chap"); Aunt Miranday ("thin-lipped and cynical, but wise as they come"); and Fleming Stone, the famous detecatif ("Oh, Mr. Stone, you're

brave/How well would the bad behave!/Yes, if none but the bad were poltroons/Life for the good would be all cakes and ale and ice cream and macaroons/And the world would be less hag-ridden/And the air-waves less whatever-is-to-follow-Prague-ridden/The future would be more wonderful/And less blood and thunderful/And very much less Nazi/And so very much more hotsy-totsy." Ogden Nash, *The Face is Familiar: The Selected Verse of Ogden Nash* (Garden City, NY: Garden City Publishing, 1941), 77-78.

17 Downing continues to enjoy the traditional detective novels of Charles Dutton, soon to retire from the field.

18 Richard Curle (1883-1968) was an American author of a number of literary studies, including several about his friend Joseph Conrad. He also wrote this one crime novel, *Corruption*, an inverted mystery. Inverted mysteries were popularized in the 1930s by English mystery writer Anthony Berkeley Cox, under his pseudonym Francis Iles. John Keats' *Isabella, or the Pot of Basil* (1818) is a narrative poem about love and murder in medieval Italy.

just heavenly, when you want to be, aren't you?" said Sally saucily; to pique Dr. Cameron she sat with her arms around the private secretary). A pleasant time was had by all in adjusting artificial eyelashes, drinking cocktails and discussing the murder of Mr. Vane and the blonde stenographer.[19]

"CLUES AND CORPSES"
(REVIEWED BY TODD DOWNING)
March 26, 1933, p. 39

The Tuesday Club Murders, by Agatha Christie

Reappearance of Aunt Jane, the delightfully naïve and no end quick-witted spinster of *The Murder at the Vicarage*, with her guests, in a Scheherazade-like story competition. Each propounds a problem of which he has personal knowledge and to which he knows the answer. Although nothing ever happens in little St. Mary Mead, Aunt Jane never fails to find a village parallel. Miss Christie is always recommended.[20]

The Hanging Captain, by Henry Wade

Mr. Wade, who earned our plaudits with *No Friendly Drop*, gives us another eminently sane yarn written in the King's English. Captain Sterron is found hanging from a curtain rod in his study. It looks like suicide, but there's the mark on the rod to be explained, a peculiar bruise of the flesh over the man's right hip, and (shush!) a man's muddy footprint in the wife's bedroom. Starring Inspector Lott of Scotland Yard and Superintendent Dawle of the county constabulary.[21]

19 Downing continues to have a pleasant time gently mocking the mystery novels of Carolyn Wells.

20 Downing shows perception in again lauding Agatha Christie's then relatively little-known Miss Marple, this time as that "no end quick-witted spinster."

21 Henry Wade's latest novel earns commendation from Downing as an "eminently sane yarn written in the King's English"—his customary words of praise for sober, classical British detection.

RED WARNING, BY VIRGIL MARKHAM

H. ASHTON-WOLFE recital of dark doings at the Paris Opera house, on the 22:20 Rapide from the Gare de Lyon to Avignon and in the Wood of Faire-Joyeux, avowedly written by the detective "Gaillard" and translated, with the omission of some thousand dashes, by Mr. Markham. The solution may be a trifle tall (the singing assassin is "the result of his glands") but the creeping horror injected into the opening pages carries through. For shudder addicts.[22]

DR. PRIESTLEY LAYS A TRAP, BY JOHN RHODE

THE mileage reading on the Comet ZV9694 was 5,022 when it was stolen from Denham; 5,127 when it was left in Moorchester in the British Motor-Car Rally; and 5,142 when it crashed into a

22 "Creeping horror" again wins Downing's commendation, despite a reservation about a "trifle tall" solution. Virgil Markham (1899-1973) graduated from Columbia University and was awarded an M. A. from the University of California at Berkeley (his 1923 thesis was *The Satirical Method of Addison and Steele*). He was the son of (Charles) Edwin (Anson) Markham (1852-1940), a poet and man of letters best known for his paean to the manual laborer, "The Man with the Hoe" (1898). In 1909 Edwin Markham settled with his wife and son on Staten Island. His house became a noted literary salon and repository for his collection of 15,000 books. With this background Virgil Markham could hardly help but be literary. In addition to teaching what was said to be the first class on mystery literature (at UC-Berkeley in 1929)—see *Berkeley Daily Gazette*, 3 October 1929, 5—Virgil Markham wrote eight highly original (some would say eccentric) crime novels between 1928 and 1936. Blogger TomCat asserts of Markham's first novel, *Death in the Dusk* (1928), that it rivals "Joel Townsley Rogers' *The Red Right Hand* (1945) and Frederic Brown's *Night of the Jabberwock* (1950) in the race for most outlandish detective story ever contrived." See "The Grim Fairy-Tale of Parson Lolly," *Detection by Moonlight*, http://moonlight-detective.blogspot.com/2011/07/grim-fairy-tale-of-parson-lolly.html. Of *Red Warning*, the *New York Times Book Review* (22 January 1933) complained: "[T]he story is so hopelessly confused that it resembles a nightmare. One suspects that Mr. Markham has been studying the novels of the wilder and more sensational French mystery writers and decided to go them one better." Harry Ashton-Wolfe, to whom Downing alludes in his review, was a Scottish-born criminologist, formerly attached to the Sûreté.

ditch outside Westerham. Add and subtract with Dr. Priestley and learn who removed the steering pin and thus murdered the two motorists. For mechanically-minded folk.[23]

"CLUES AND CORPSES" (REVIEWED BY TODD DOWNING)

April 23, 1933, p. 43

THE NIGHT OF THE 12TH-13TH, BY ANDRÉ STEEMAN

HIGHWATER mark in the current penchant for things Gallic in the murder line. M. Stanislas-André Steeman won the *Prix du Roman d'Aventures* in 1931 with *Six Dead Men* and has pounded out another yarn inferior to the first but still worth perusal by fans who crave to be mystified whether or no. A *sine qua non* of these French items is "une femme fatale" (according to the translator *a fatal woman*) and she's here in the person of Floriane Aboody, who on the night her husband is murdered disappears in the company of the private secretary, a clerk in a Chinese antique shop, and several cops. Readers who remember Mrs. Endicott of Rufus King's *Murder by the Clock* are warned to keep their minds on the clues as Floriane descends a staircase.[24]

THE MYSTERY PUZZLE BOOK, BY WREN AND MCKAY

A BOON to the distracted host whose party is going flat as well as to the serious-minded addict of solitary cerebration is this new compilation of brain-teasers by the authors of the "Baffle Books."

23 This John Rhode (*The Motor Rally Mystery* in Britain) proved rather too mathematical and mechanical for Downing.

24 Downing bucks modern critical opinion by greatly preferring the mostly forgotten Stanislas-André Steeman (1898-1960) over Georges Simenon. In 2010, blogger Xavier Lechard called Steeman "arguably one of the greatest mystery writers of all time." See "Lost in Translation: Stanislas-André Steeman," 10 October 2011, *At the Villa Rose*, http://atthevillarose.blogspot.com/2010/10/lost-in-translation-stanislas-andre.html. If nothing else, Steeman apparently introduced many American readers, including Downing, to the term *femme fatale*!

The diagrams, documents, clues and essential facts of twenty-eight actual and hypothetical puzzle-cases from the annals of crime, detection and espionage are presented in succinct form, with solutions at the back of the book. Timorous addicts of this time-wasting game will find their consciences salved by S. S. Van Dine's erudite introduction, in which he invokes Sho-ngi, Chong-kie, I-go and "the vicissitudes of the present great epochal world change which we euphemistically call a *depression*."[25]

THE LAUGHING PERIL, BY H. L. GATES

STACCATO thrills for satiated Sax Rohmer fans, that begin when Meng Fu, faithful (?) Oriental manservant, unlocks the front door of John Farley's apartment for a "pletty lady." But pletty lady not allee same Mees Sylvia, it turns out, so the white race has added to its other worries the poppy scorpions, kiff hashish and demoniac tortures in Shantung gardens. Mr. Gates, whose stuff, by the way, is unadulterated, is the author of *Easy Lady*, *Lipstick* and *Auction of Souls*.[26]

25 In a fine feat of pseudonymity, John T. Colter wrote three *Baffle Books* and *The Mystery Puzzle Book* as a purported duo, Lassiter Wren and Randle McKay.

26 Downing's snide tone in this review is matched by that in the *Saturday Review* (Summing Up: "Allee samee velly old stuff but allee samee packee samee punch for those who want thrills and nothing else but/Verdict: Bleh!"). See *Saturday Review*, 29 April 1933, 569. Author Henry Leyford Gates (1880-1937) made something of a specialty of would-be titillating "Yellow Peril" thrillers. The publisher of the novel (Macaulay again!) describes *The Laughing Peril* as the story of "an Oriental demon who would marry a white girl to a half human monster, treat a Chinese girl with obscene, inhuman tortures, and work for the destruction of the whole white race by his gigantic international scheme for the use of kiff and hashish." In *Son of Gun in Cheek* (Mysterious Press, 1987), Bill Pronzini calls Gates' publisher Macaulay "the very first, and certainly the greatest, of the schlock houses." He gives three of Gates' novels, including *The Laughing Peril*, places in his Alternative Classic Hall of Fame (books so bad they're good). See Chapter 2 and pp. 214-215. In a serious vein, Gates also wrote *Ravished Armenia: The Story of Aurora Mardiganian, the Christian Girl Who Lived through the Great Massacres* (1918), about the infamous Armenian Genocide of 1915-18.

"CLUES AND CORPSES"
(REVIEWED BY TODD DOWNING)
May 7, 1933, p. 42

THE AMERICAN GUN MYSTERY, BY ELLERY QUEEN

THE sixth opus of the w. k. Queen saga cycle puts the suave Ellery and his indefatigable chronicler, in our humble opinion, definitely in the front rank of those purveyors of detective fare who go in for cerebral exercise, as contrasted with the manipulators of adjectival atmosphere like the subtle Rufus King, with designs on the reader's spine rather than his brain.

Hailed by the publishers as "perhaps the most characteristic American crime ever committed between the covers of a book," Ellery himself describes his new *chef-d'ouvre* as follows: "It deals with lariats, hosses, alfalfa, chaps—and lest you think I have gone west to the great divide on you, let me hasten to add that this epic of the plains takes place—as it did—in the heart of New York City, with that fair metropolis' not unpleasing ha-cha as a sort of Greek chorus to the rattle of musketry."

Problem: How did the .25 calibre automatic which killed Buck Horne at the rodeo disappear from New York's crowded colosseum?[27]

MURDER ON SHADOW ISLAND, BY GARNETT WESTON

MULTIPLE murders on an island in the St. Lawrence related in more than usually gruesome details by a newcomer to the detective story ranks. Besides the time-worn devices for inducing shudders there are demoniac peals of laughter echoing throughout the forest after each murder, a medical student with black glasses (one of the heirs to the Holland millions), Indian war-hoops and a man who screamed two hours after he was murdered. A strain on the credulity, but most people like them that way.[28]

27 Downing places Ellery Queen in the front rank of pure, unadulterated detective novelists, purveyors of "cerebral exercise."

28 Like Henry Gates, Garnett Weston (1890-1980) was a novelist and Hollywood screenwriter. He probably is best known today for writing the script for the 1932 Bela Lugosi horror film *White Zombie*.

"CLUES AND CORPSES" (REVIEWED BY TODD DOWNING)

May 21, 1933, p. 43

WIND OF THE EAST, BY ANNA ROBESON BURR

THE cream of the week's literature of escape, almost too high-brow for this department. Mrs. Burr, author of a murder story popular back in 1924 and of several romances, has chosen as the setting of her latest, the glamorous island of Rhodes, Graustarkian hodge-podge of cultures—Greek, Levantine, Crusader.

A swift-moving plot involving the usual American girl on her own, mysterious treasure (Byron's lost memoir, dedicated to "The Scandalmongers of Europe"), Turkish spies and three table-spoonfuls of Love. Names that "haunt, startle and waylay"—Lindos, Corfu, Isfahan, Cos, Skyros, Iskanderun. Crete, vague, distant, veiled-in rainbows. The painted palace of Hadhramaut, Magdalenian cave-prints, crimson mutilated human hands. Asphodel, fezzes, white wines, nargilehs and Levantine mistresses. Suleiman's mosque and radio and a grim Italian cruiser in the bay. The political episode on which the story is based took place in Cyprus, in 1931.[29]

THE GOLF HOUSE MURDER, BY HERBERT ADAMS

ANOTHER sane but unexciting item by the author of *The Crime in the Dutch Garden*, involving sweet young Susan Heriot, who returns from a West Indian trip to find her foster father dead and herself penniless because he had unaccountably altered his will in favor of a bunch of worthless relatives a few days before his death. Bob, the lawyer's son, proposes to Susan, but, as the blurbist sings, "when the dangerously beautiful Angel leans

29 Anna Robeson Burr (1873-1941), novelist and biographer, lived in affluent and intellectual Bryn Mawr, Pennsylvania. Note Downing's ironic, self-deprecating comment on Burr's novel: "almost too highbrow for this department." Downing's use of the term "Graustarkian" is a reference to the fictional Eastern European country Graustark, from the novels of George Barr McCutcheon (1866-1928).

close to him, will her nearness blind him—lull his suspicions?" An incidental corpse on page 140 and some talk of greens, mashies, bunkers, etc.[30]

"CLUES AND CORPSES" (REVIEWED BY TODD DOWNING) May 28, 1933, p. 42

MURDER AT THE WORLD'S FAIR, BY MARY PLUM

PROSPECTIVE visitors to Chicago this summer should consult this recital by a former Oklahoma Cityan of the highly incredible adventures of certain visitors to the fair. Involving a corpse in the Pavilion of the Belgranian Exhibition, vengeful Soviet agents, a shattered vase, a kidnapped blonde and sleuthing by the purposefully colorless John Smith, private detecatif. Enough of Harold MacGrath, E. Phillips Oppenheim and Edgar Wallace to provide a thrill per page.[31]

FOG, BY VALENTINE WILLIAMS AND DOROTHY RICE SIMS

SIX spade bids by Mrs. Sims and corpses by Mr. Williams, veteran dispenser of thrills. The murders take place on a transatlantic line and are obviously inspired by Rufus King's *Murder on the Yacht*. The fog provides the suspense which the hurricane lent to the latter yarn and Madame Alva, the medium who foretells her own death, is almost as creepy as Carlotta Bale. Recommended.[32]

30 "Sane but unexciting" is Downing's praiseful verdict on yet another of Herbert Adams' traditional British mysteries.

31 Downing continues to be drawn to the Oppenheim-Wallace thrills formula, this time in the hands of the much forgotten Mary Plum (c.1904-c.1981). Harold MacGrath (1871-1932) was a popular American novelist and screenwriter.

32 George Valentine Williams (1883-1946), creator of the arch-villain Clubfoot, published over two dozen crime genre tales between 1918 and 1946. His books were popular both with lay readers and critics. Williams' co-author of *Fog*, Dorothy Rice Sims (1889-1960) was a sculptor, painter, aviator, motorcyclist and noted bridge expert who told her own story in *Curiouser and Curiouser* (1940). *Fog* was adapted into a film in 1933.

The White Cockatoo, by Mignon G. Eberhart

In *The Mystery of Hunting's End* it was the drifting snow, in *While the Patient Slept*, the slowly ticking clock, in *From This Dark Stairway*, the heat and imminent storm. In Mrs. Eberhart's latest best-seller the properties of horror are furnished by the mistral, swirling into the dark little courtyard of Mr. Lovschiem's hotel in A—(it might be Avignon and it might be Arles) and ruffling the feathers of the crest of the white cockatoo perched upon the shoulders of the swarthy Lovscheim, as James Sundean, engineer lately of Moscow, inscribes his name upon the register. Nurse Keate does not appear.[33]

The Case of the Frightened Lady, by Edgar Wallace

Heralded as the last of the posthumous Wallace publications, this one upholds its author's reputation, what with mysterious stranglings in an English country house, secret passageways, beer drinking cops, and family skeletons rattling in all the cupboards. It appeared in *Collier's* and enjoyed quite a run on the Broadway stage under the title *Criminal at Large*.[34]

33 One of America's most popular mystery writers, Mignon Good Eberhart (1899-1996) published sixty crime novels between 1929 and 1988. Although the series character Nurse Sarah Keate appeared in Eberhart's first five detective novels and two later ones, the great majority of Eberhart's works concern highly distressed and not overly perceptive young women plunged into deadly *affaires des morts*. Eberhart is historically important within the genre for helping to popularize love and suspense in the modern detective novel form. Downing may not have cared much for love in his murder mystery reading, but he clearly did enjoy the suspense. The particular Eberhart novel reviewed here by Downing, *The White Cockatoo*, is singular in Eberhart's body of work in having a male protagonist.

34 After referencing Edgar Wallace a number of times in his reviews, Downing finally reviews a book by him, albeit one posthumously published. The astonishingly prolific Richard Horatio Edgar Wallace (1875-1932), the king of the Golden Age thriller, published an estimated 175 books (novels and short story collections). He was the most popular writer in England at the time (supposedly one of every four books then read in England was a Wallace). Wallace's many mystery thriller plays, such as *The Ringer*, enjoyed great success as well. Like many other mystery fans, Downing

"CLUES AND CORPSES" (REVIEWED BY TODD DOWNING)

June 4, 1933, p. 41

A Case for Mr. Paul Savoy, by Jackson Gregory

Second appearance of Mr. Gregory's favorite sleuth, who made his debut in *The House of the Opal*. Having missed said debut, we were slightly bewildered by references thereto in the first pages, but gradually got our bearings. The theory of crime detection advocated by Mr. Savoy (a rather unpleasant fellow, in our opinion) is that clues aren't necessary, after all. Detective Gateway of the San Francisco police calls his hand in the case of the naked corpse found in a taxicab whose driver did not know it was there. Fortuitous circumstances lead Mr. Savoy into a goofy, J. K. Huysmans-like atmosphere of decadent multimillionaires with penchants for purple lights; bitter, disillusioned artists; sinister Chinese mandarins; tragic princesses and wealthy widows with husband-filled pasts. It gave us the jitters and we didn't guess the murderer.[35]

The Werewolf of Paris, by Guy Endore

A shudder classic which, if it lacks the terrible tenacity of *Dracula*, gains reality by the use of purportedly authentic documents recounting the life of one Bertand, illegitimate son of a peasant girl and a priest whose heritage had a werewolf taint. When old Madame Didier discovers hair on the palms of baby Bertrand's hands, she divines something of the dreadful state in store for him. Bertrand escapes surveillance and goes to Paris, leaving

read a tremendous number of Wallace books in the 1920s; and they clearly kept a grip on his creative imagination in the 1930s.

35 Jackson Gregory (1882-1943) was primarily a writer (extremely prolific and popular) of Westerns, but he also, according to http://www.violetbooks.com/western-bios/jackson-gregory.html, "dabbled at fantasy, mysteries, & south seas adventure." French novelist Joris Karl Huysman (1848-1907) was a key figure in the Decadent movement in literature. His famous novel *A rebours* (*Against Nature/Against the Grain*) (1884) was castigated as a "sodomitical" book at the trials of Oscar Wilde in 1895.

behind him a trail of mangled lambs and humans and desecrated graves. Follow the bloody days of the Commune, when Bertrand is but one werewolf among many. Not to be taken before meals.[36]

"CLUES AND CORPSES" (REVIEWED BY TODD DOWNING)

June 11, 1933, p. 41

OUTRAGEOUS FORTUNE, BY PATRICIA WENTWORTH

CHARACTERISTIC Wentworth English countryside adventure concoction, easily skimmed through. A sufferer from amnesia, picked up on the Sussex coast after the wreck of the good ship Alice Arden, babbles of children's beads and the reader soon tumbles to the fact that he's talking about the ubiquitous emeralds of Atahualpa, the last Inca, stolen from Mr. Elmer K. Van Berg, American millionaire. Some mystification about identity and poetry by Patsy Ann, spinster.

MURDER AT ENDOR, BY WILLIAM ALMON WOLFF

MEET Jeremy Tyler, ex-reporter, son of a reputedly rich father, and hopelessly in love with Judith Pryor, whose father had committed suicide at the time of the big crash in 1929. And now Judith's uncle is mysteriously murdered and the tracks lead right up Jerry's alley. But we know and Jerry knew that he didn't do it. Meet also a keen, but not too keen, Jersey district attorney and a much keener Jersey detective. Meet also Lieutenant Mitchell of the New York homicide squad, whose hand is as big as a ham and whose heart is as big as a football. And finally meet Scott Ramsey, also in love with Judith. Scott is entirely too much of a gentleman to be real. Here is a detective story with everything: Newspaper lingo, typical bulls, suspense, attempted murders of

36 Samuel Guy Endore (born Samuel Goldstein) (1900-1970) was a novelist and Oscar-nominated scriptwriter. His best-known novel is the classic horror tale *The Werewolf of Paris*, which obviously greatly appealed to Downing's love of the shudders.

material witnesses, human interest and a profoundly satisfactory finish. One of the best.[37]

"CLUES AND CORPSES" (REVIEWED BY TODD DOWNING) June 18, 1933, p. 29

THE ALBUM, BY MARY ROBERTS RINEHART

THAT hardy perennial among American *causes célèbres*, the Lizzie Borden case, seems to be in even fuller bloom this spring, what with Lillian Gish playing the part of the Fall River hacker in *Nine Pine Street* and Mrs. Rinehart giving it the fictional treatment it has so long deserved. Not that superficially the plot of *The Album* has further resemblance to the Borden tragedy than that a rather disagreeable old lady is murdered with an axe on a hot August afternoon, presumably by her stepdaughter.

As the story proceeds and the pages become cluttered with cadavers, each gorier than the last, the similarity is rather with Jack the Ripper or the Ruth Judd case. It is in the atmosphere of stodginess and impeccable respectability surrounding the neighborhood known as the Crescent that one sees the parallel to the atmosphere which made Lizzie run amuck.

With the possible exception of *The Red Lamp* it is the best mystery novel that Mrs. Rinehart has written. Read on a hot nerve-frazzling afternoon. It makes one almost sympathetic with Lizzie and her hated curling irons.[38]

37 Novelist William Almon Wolff (1885-1933) was born in Brooklyn and attended school in England. He died from a heart attack in his home in Barnstable, Massachusetts, less than a month after Downing reviewed (and raved) *Murder at Endor*, his final novel.

38 Julian Symons wrote dismissively of *The Album*, yet Dorothy L. Sayers' appraisal of the novel was as high as that of Downing's (she thought it had the spaciousness of Victorian sensation novels, while Downing compared it to a classic Victorian true crime). The novel more recently has been subjected to serious academic analysis in Catherine Ross Nickerson's *The Web of Iniquity: Early Detective Fiction by American Women* (Duke

WHO SPOKE LAST?, BY JOHN V. TURNER

REAPPEARANCE of Amos Petrie alternately mildly unobtrusive solicitor and fisherman and hardboiled sleuth of *First Round Murder* fame. Horatio Bedlay (chairman of the defunct Bedlay's Atlantic Trust) is found in his study with a knife through the back of his neck the morning after a heated argument among the board of directors.

"There was an awful row," the housekeeper says, "and as sure as I stand here the last one to talk to the master was the one who did the murder." Lots of revocation deeds re L. W. R., ramps, preference shares, call options, rods, reels, perch, pike and gudgeons—for them as understands such things.[39]

"CLUES AND CORPSES" (REVIEWED BY TODD DOWNING) June 25, 1933, p. 39

OBELISTS AT SEA, BY C. DALY KING

WE'RE still gasping over this one! Written by the author of such heavy fare as *Beyond Behaviorism*, *Integrative Psychology*, and

University Press, 1999). Downing, who read several books on the Lizzie Borden case, obviously found fascinating the incongruity of savagely violent slayings in genteel and emotionally repressed surroundings, such as that of the Crescent, the wealthy neighborhood that is the setting in *The Album*. In *Bloody Murder*, on the other hand, Symons scolded that, while people died in the novel, "this is not important, because in relation to the real world none of them was ever alive. Nobody is ever doing any work. . . ." (p. 101). The Ruth Judd case, to which Downing also refers, was a notorious 1931-1932 case involving an accused "trunk murderess," Winnie Ruth Mckinnell Judd (1905-1998), who allegedly killed and dismembered two other women in 1931. The play *Nine Pine Street*, which dramatized the Lizzie Borden case (as the story of Effie Holden), opened in New York City less than two months before Todd Downing reviewed *The Album*. See Amnon Kabatchnik, *Blood on the Stage: Milestone Plays of Crime, Mystery and Detection* (Scarecrow Press, 2008), 347-348.

39 John Victor Turner (1904-1945) published nearly fifty detective novels and thrillers between 1932 and 1946. He was best known for his David Hume thrillers with tough guy ex-cop Mick Cardby. However he also produced

Psychology of Consciousness, it includes, besides a triple dose of blood, bafflement and corpses, a brand new set of gadgets, such as sphygmomanometers, galvanometers, dynamometers, pneumographs and chronoscopes; antithetical inferior-superior expressions, psychic maladies, distorted egos, ab-reactions, conspiracy delusions, voice-keys ("Hello"–"Hello"), stimulus words ("shady"—"hippopotamus"); sex (psychological, physiological and sentimental—"Now, my doctor," Madame Sudeau smiled and patted Doctor Pon's hand; had she been masculine, the pat would have been plainly avuncular. "You will tell me all about those so charming love responses, *n'est-ce pas?*)"; and ocean sunsets.

The plot (the murder of an American millionaire in the crowded smoking room of the S. S. Meganaut—two bullets in the heart and only one wound, yet neither of the bullets caused death) is complicated enough for half a dozen novels. The detection is by four eminent psychologists, bound for a European convention (a behaviorist, a psycho-analyst, an integrative psychologist, a middle-grounder). Each meets with varying degrees of success in applying his pet theory to a practical end, but each finds his major premise false. It remains for another passenger (try and identify him before page 392) to solve the mystery by the good old method of deduction from objective clues. The clue finder, at the end of the book, cites the 36 places in the text where the identity of the culprit has been revealed. Whatever your taste in murder fare, Mr. King belongs on your list.[40]

Death of a Star, by G. D. H. and M. Cole

The Coles can always be relied upon for a smooth-flowing, logical yarn with no creakings in the joints and no striving for effect. Their latest concerns the discovery in a taxicab near

amateur sleuths Amos Petrie and Reverend Ebenezer Buckle, under, respectively, the pseudonyms J. V. Turner and Nicholas Brady (see pages 234-235, 311).

40 American Psychologist Charles Daly King (1895-1963) published six extremely complicated detective novels and one book of mystery short stories between 1932 and 1940.

Hammersmith Bridge of a severed head that turns out to be that of Rita Morning, film star. Suspects (mostly discarded lovers): Gavin McLeod, son of Lord Aberfeldy, "amiably a bit of a moron," who paid Rita's rent; Wilbert Coxon, impresario, "a moist manner"; A. Gapp, piano tuner; Hubert Phipps, lived upstairs, cross and unwilling to talk; Maxy Ikeman, film producer. Sleuthing by Inspector Walling and Chief Inspector Camp of Scotland Yard.[41]

"CLUES AND CORPSES"
(REVIEWED BY TODD DOWNING)
July 2, 1933

THE STRANGE CASE OF PETER THE LETT, BY GEORGE SIMENON

REMEMBERING our recent derogatory remarks anent *The Cross-road Murders*, we feel that we owe the prolific M. Simenon a word or two of apology. With true Gallic inventiveness and élan he has dashed off doubtless as rapidly as his English confrere, Edgar Wallace, an extremely complicated, not too incredible *roman policier*, crammed with anonymous corpses, double identities, dangerous females and man-hunts by Inspector Maigret, not the least of whose feats is the draining of a stein of beer at one swallow. The opening—"ICCP to the SÛRETÉ PARIS"—and the ending—"At Pskov, an old lady wearing the national bonnet pulled tightly over her head and face, would be going to church in a sled that glided smoothly over the snow, while the drunken coachman cracked his whip over the ears of the toy pony"—makes one wish that M. Simenon's yarns didn't sell as well as they do. Perhaps then he would take more pains with them and

41 George Douglas Howard Cole and his wife Margaret (Postgate) Cole (1889-1959/1893-1980) were prominent English socialists. Douglas Cole taught at Oxford and was an influential leftist political theoretician and economist from the 1920s through the 1950s. After a single detective novel was published by Douglas Cole in 1923, the couple went on to produce twenty-eight detective novels and novellas between 1925 and 1945. Though the later books are credited to both authors, in fact they were individually composed. *Death of a Star* was by Margaret Cole.

not rely entirely on a kaleidoscope succession of scenes. As they are, they are worth reading.[42]

MURDER AT CAMBRIDGE, BY Q. PATRICK

BREEZY tale told in the first person by a former Cambridge student. It concerns the murder in All Saints College of a youth from South Africa, whose real name may or may not be John Baumann. Replete with a secondary corpse, not-too-obnoxious love at first sight, poetry by William Blake, ghost stories, an escaped lunatic, and a glossary of Cambridge colloquialisms. Perhaps a trifle too much sentimentality about dear old Cambridge and the author's favorite masters there, but that was probably unavoidable. Worth two hours of your time.[43]

SHOES THAT HAD WALKED TWICE, BY JEAN TOUSSAINT-SAMAT

THE winner of the French *Prix du Roman d'Aventures* for 1932, translated with oaths, picon-grenadine, bouillabaisse and oh, la, la! by Elizabeth Abbott. Of the type popularized by Georges Simenon and Andrée Steeman. It involves some bloody doings down in Provence.

The discovery of the body of Miss Gilchrist, a tall, athletic Englishwoman who painted landscapes, her features destroyed by her two half-mad police dogs. Soviet agents and Romanoff refugees among the oil refineries. The disappearance of Fanny the Greek. Sleuthing by Inspector 109 of the counter espionage service. The Marseillaise. Sonia Pavolva Garitzina in the arms of Inspector 109. The villain unmasked. "Now it was finished! The

42 Downing affords some praise to Simenon here, though he accuses the author of over-hasty composition.

43 "Q. Patrick" at the time of the writing of *Murder at Cambridge* (*Murder at the 'Varsity* in England) was solely the pseudonym of English-born pharmaceutical executive Richard Wilson Webb (1901-1966). However, Webb wrote eleven additional Q. Patrick detective novels between 1931 and 1952, with several different collaborative partners, the most significant of whom was Hugh Callingham Wheeler (1912-1987). Webb and Wheeler also collaborated as "Patrick Quentin" and "Jonathan Stagge." The work of all these various incarnations was well-received.

French had the upper hand! He was beaten!" An odor of bitter almonds filled the room.[44]

"CLUES AND CORPSES"
(REVIEWED BY TODD DOWNING)
July 9, 1933

DEATH ON MY LEFT, BY PHILIP MACDONALD

RECOMMENDED recital of the strange death of Kim Kinnaird, cruiserweight champion of the world, in the gymnasium of Leo Petrass' training camp at Perry Down, the fruitless inquest and the interest and sudden lack of interest displayed in the case by Anthony Gethryn, sleuth of *Rope to Spare*, *The Noose*, and a long line of thrillers. Divided into four parts: Effect—the discovery of the body by Hooky Flynn; Cause—the life of Kim from his first acquaintance with Petrass in 1921 to the eve of his fight with the giant Argentinian, Carlo Ferrara; Question—Who murdered Kim and why did the latter have a trunk in his room with a box of shoe brushes in it? Answer—supplied and suppressed by Colonel Gethryn.

Mr. MacDonald has succeeded in putting into his novel that rare element in the genre—emotion that is an integral part of the story and yet not sloppy. The solution is neither original nor hackneyed. For prize fight fans and anyone who enjoys a good detective yarn.[45]

44 The French mystery tale seems to have left Downing distinctly blasé. Evidently the translation—with its "oaths, picon-grenadine, bouillabasse and oh, la, la!"—did not help matters.

45 Philip Macdonald (1900-1980) was a lively (Barzun and Taylor thought rather too lively) British detective fiction writer, who entered the Golden Age lists early on and at a young age with *The Rasp* (1924). In the late 1920s and early 1930s, Macdonald became one of the most popular and prolific English mystery writers, producing sixteen additional mystery genre novels (three under the pseudonym Martin Porlock) in the six years that spanned from 1928 to 1933. Like Edgar Wallace he moved to Hollywood in 1931 and became a screenwriter. Wallace died the next year, but

Death is a Stowaway, by Wesley Price

Yet another rehash of the strange events that Rufus King chronicled in his justly popular maritime murder yarns. The millionaire's yacht that slips southward in the darkness on an unexplained mission in southern seas. The last minute discovery of a corpse aboard. The smashed radio. The disappearance of the corpse. The missing hypodermic syringe and another murder in the offing. A few of the characters: James Wick, detacatif of Miami, whose detecting is somewhat interfered with by seasickness; Theo M. Cogswill, financier of New York, who owns the yacht; Charlie, his son, who drinks too much; Professor Renfrew of Columbia University, who has found something or other in an old Mexican manuscript; Elinor Chastain, alias Mlle. Le Marr, third from the end at Minky's; and old Dave, stowaway. Thrills for those who missed *Murder by Latitude* and *Murder on the Yacht*.[46]

Macdonald remained in the United States the rest of his life, ending his days in a Woodland Hills, California, nursing home in 1980. After 1933, he produced only three crime novels, including the celebrated *Warrant for X* (1938) (in the United States, *The Nursemaid Who Disappeared*) and *The List of Adrian Messenger* (1959). Macdonald also wrote some non-mystery novels, such as the war tale *Patrol* (1927), made into a popular film, and *Likeness of Exe* (1929). *Death on My Left*, which Downing praised for incorporating "that rare element in the genre—emotion that is an integral part of the story yet not sloppy" reflected Macdonald's interest in transcending the perceived artistic limitations of detective fiction. Of his twenty mystery genre novels it is the closest in form to a conventional novel.

46 The reader may have noticed by now that in his reviews Downing invariably compared any mystery involving sailcraft mayhem to Rufus King's maritime mysteries *Murder by Latitude* (1931) and *Murder on the Yacht* (1932), novels that made a terrific impression on him. Wesley Price's *Death is a Stowaway* was, according to Bill Pronzini, the first mystery novel published by William Godwin, Inc., "best known for the soft-core sex novels they published between 1931-38." Godwin's mystery series was short-lived. See Bill Pronzini, "William Godwin, Inc.," http://www.lendinglibmystery.com/Godwin/Covers.html.

"CLUES AND CORPSES"
(REVIEWED BY TODD DOWNING)
July 16, 1933, p. 39

TAKE UP THE BODIES, BY K. T. KNOBLOCK

". . . AND they died." The book's final words sum up the plot of this nightmarish compound of Hamlet and mad Ophelia, the Ku Klux Klan and the Mer Rouge murders, sawed-off shotguns and Ol' Man Mississippi and breaking levees—all against a William Faulkner background of lust and dubious paternity. David Dane, a young Jew who has been forced by the disappearance of his father to abandon his studies at Harvard and go to work in the store in Iberville, Goula Parish, La., turns from bidding his mother and stepfather farewell on their honeymoon to see grappling hooks lifting from the swollen river the bullet-riddled body of his father. Follow Dashiell Hammett third degrees, seduction, duels, hangings, suicide and madness. "They were mad, then, as the word is, if this be not madness which knew neither hawk nor handsaw nor camel nor compass, nor anything but everything."

Mr. Knoblock, author of *There's Been Murder Done*, is a former New Orleans newspaperman who is said to be fond of Proust, Faulkner, Lewisohn, and Muenchner beer. Admirers of Faulkner, as well as murder fans in search of something different, yet violent, should get acquainted with him.[47]

47 Between 1931 and 1933 Louisiana journalist Kenneth Thomas Knoblock (1898-1946) authored three crime novels, all visceral exercises in southern Grand Guignol. In these novels one can discern the influence of both Faulkner and Proust (one opens with two pages describing a pool of blood flowing under a door and down a stairway). Knoblock's wife, Adaline Katz, in the early 1920s had been a close confidant of the novelist Sherwood Anderson. See John Shelton Reed, *Dixie Bohemia: A French Quarter Circle in the 1920s* (LSU Press, 2012), 42, 100, 274. Ludwig Lewisohn (1882-1955) was a prominent American Zionist novelist and literary critic in the 1930s. The brazen 1922 Mer Rouge, Louisiana, torture-mutilation murders of two white men by Ku Klux Klan members provoked national outrage when Downing was a young man. See James Ruiz, *The Black Hood of the Ku Klux Klan* (Austin & Winfield, 1997).

The Case of the April Fools, by Christopher Bush

Ludovic Travers, young man about town, loved nosing things out. "And," the author goes on, "let it be understood about Travers, whatever his eccentricities and his don't-give-a-damn attitude toward the conventions, and whatever the hilarity of the garb he chose to assume, there was always something about him that told you he was a somebody." Hence his activities in the investigations of the murders at The Covers, Marbury, on April Fool's day. Typical ingenious, unexciting Bush tale, with lots of checking of alibis, double identities and English countrysides.[48]

"CLUES AND CORPSES" (REVIEWED BY TODD DOWNING) August 20, 1933, p. 36

Inspector Rusby's Finale, by Virgil Markham

Prologue in the Riviera with all sorts of ladies showering Mrs. Cade-Jack with gloves of the same make and size. Mrs. Cade-Jack inviting Inspector Rusby to a week-end party at Stoke New Place, hinting at some mysterious problem, which she wishes his help to solve. House full of people; strange snatches of conversation. Next morning, house empty; hostess, guests and all, vanished into thin air. All except absolutely strange corpse hidden away in a closet. Mrs. Cade-Jack's gloves scattered around in queer hiding-places. Inspector Rusby in love with Mrs. Cade-Jack. Dark past of a multi-millionaire, recently elevated to the peerage. Discovery of a body, apparently that of Mrs. Cade-Jack, in the garden of Stoke New Place. High falutin' and mysterious home for mental patients. Discovery that the two corpses were two

48 Surely Downing's quotations from Christopher Bush's novel on the high-falutin' character of Bush's sleuth Ludovic (Ludo) Travers suggest a sardonic attitude on Downing's part concerning the British gentleman amateur detective, yet Downing admits he finds this "unexciting Bush tale" to be "ingenious."

other fellows. Complete breakdown of the C. I. D. Tremendous anti-climax, would-be thrills turn out to be near-obscenities.[49]

He Arrived at Dusk, by R. C. Ashby

Here is the lineal descendant of *The Hound of the Baskervilles*. Foggy, wind-swept Northumbrian moor, with Colonel Barr stricken by mysterious disease, two of his brothers recently dead under mysterious circumstances, a young American nephew, of whom little is known, a tight-lipped young nurse in charge and a young London antiquarian called in to value the furniture of the old house. Add to this a mad doctor and a golden-haired dazzler with blue eyes. And the ghost. The ghost of a Roman soldier, who had an unpleasant propensity for stabbing people in the back with a Roman gladius. And a feeling of evil in the house: tangible, palpable evil which grew and grew until the young Londoner almost went off his nut. But fortunately there was a solid, beef-eating detective inspector in the background, and the whole thing finished with an extremely unspiritual arrest. For cleverness, thrills and water-tight structure, this is one of the best in a long time. Conan Doyle would have been proud to have written this one. Should not be read after dark.[50]

49 Apparently *Inspector Rusby's Finale* played around too much with the strictures of the classical form for Downing's taste. In *A Catalogue of Crime*, on the other hand, Barzun and Taylor write of the novel: "The denouement . . . is a bit hard to swallow, but the author manages it with virtuosity and the reader has all the pleasure" (p. 381).

50 "R. C. Ashby" was the pseudonym of Ruth Constance Ashby Ferguson (1899-1966), who wrote children's books, romances and a small number of supernatural-tinged mysteries. Given Downing's taste for horror, it is not surprising that he found the novel *He Arrived at Dusk* "one of the best in a long time." Blogger John Norris deems the novel "a classic of its kind," effectively blending "the supernatural and detective genres." See his review at Mystery*File, 27 November 2010, http://mysteryfile.com/blog/?p=6225.

"CLUES AND CORPSES" (REVIEWED BY TODD DOWNING) September 17, 1933, p. 43

The Captain's Curio, by Eden Phillpotts

Not who? but how? and why? are the perplexing questions propounded by Mr. Phillpotts when he recounts the circumstances surrounding the murder of old Martin Knox, erstwhile pawnbroker, at his cottage on Daleham-on-Exe, and the theft of a pair of rubies of fabulous value. Suspects are four in number and all are portrayed with Mr. Phillpotts' usual skill: Miss Hoddy, the housekeeper, who gets 10,000 pounds under the will; Dr. Wilson, a Socialist, who is the deceased's oldest friend; Sabine Knox, a nephew and residuary legatee; and a probably apocryphal colored man seen lurking about the village.

Though the identity of the criminal will probably be apparent to the attentive reader early in the game, the motive and particularly the death gadget will provide bafflement until the end. Commonsense sleuthing by Inspector Midwinter; secondary characters including Captain Palk, retired sea captain, who owns the curio, and Mr. Blake, verbose coroner and pig breeder; and a great deal of Devonshire local color that adds charm to the book without distracting from the interest in the plot.[51]

The Case of Marie Corwin, by Gregory Dean

Two hundred and sixty-five pages of investigation by the New York police department of the murder of the beautiful Marie Corwin in her luxurious apartment on the West Seventies prepare the way for a last chapter swivel chair solution of the mystery by Benjamin Simon, deputy commissioner of the department, and protagonist of a new series of murder tales. Marie, it would seem, was a decidedly interesting young lady and somewhat of a paradox.

51 Downing admired Phillpotts' adept characterization and local color, which in this case he thought added "charm to the book without distracting from the interest in the plot."

She blackmailed right and left, and then she spent the money on such charities as a tuberculosis sanitarium in Denver. Simon's identification of her murderer will bring to the lips of the reader that exclamation which is the mystery writer's laurels: "Why, I never thought of that person!" Were we a detective we should be tempted to draw conclusions from the similarity of Mr. Dean's style and that of Mr. Anthony Abbot's.[52]

THE TOWNSEND MURDER MYSTERY, BY OCTAVUS ROY COHEN

THE text of the radio serial broadcast over the network of the National Broadcasting Co. beginning Feb. 14, 1933. Mr. Cohen, known to the wide public as a writer of detective stories and of Negro dialect tales, acknowledges in his introduction the difficulties inherent in such writing: the dependence on dialog alone and the consequent translation of action into speech.

Judged solely from the reader's standpoint, therefore, the result is a little disappointing. For one interested in the rapidly developing field of radio-writing, however, the book should be invaluable.[53]

52 "Gregory Dean" was the pseudonym of Jacob D. Posner (1883-?), who wrote three Benjamin Simon mysteries. Downing's comparison of Dean to Anthony Abbot was high praise indeed, given Downing's great regard for Abbot.

53 Octavus Roy Cohen (1891-1959) was an American writer best known for his southern local color humor stories in the *Saturday Evening Post*, but he also published mystery tales. Critic and mystery writer Jon L. Breen concurs with Downing concerning *The Townshend Murder Mystery*. "In an unusual and unsuccessful experiment, Cohen's radio serial *The Townshend Murder Mystery* was published in book form the same year it was broadcast coast-to-coast . . . on NBC," writes Breen. "However it played on air, it doesn't work as a print mystery." See Jon L. Breen, "A Note on Octavus Roy Cohen," *Mystery*File*, http://mysteryfile.com/blog/?p=6225

"CLUES AND CORPSES"
(REVIEWED BY TODD DOWNING)
September 24, 1933

THE WARRIELAW JEWEL, BY WINIFRED PECK

ON most of the counts that go to make up a good mystery yarn (perfection of plot, sustained suspense, skillful portrayal of characters and setting and, last but not least, style) *The Warrielaw Jewel* is one of the best that has come our way during the past year and not unworthy of comparison with *Trent's Last Case*.

Of Mrs. Peck we know nothing except what this book reveals—that she writes as few of our mystery writers can and that she knows the technique of the genre from corpse to handcuffs. From the first premonitory line to the final flashback to "the library where the two sisters sat once, in silent hatred, over their eternal embroidery," the saga of the decadent Scottish family in the Edinburgh of twenty years ago moves swiftly through dissension and murder to its climax.

The young English wife of an Edinburgh lawyer tells the story of the murder of the elder sister, the theft of the jewel and the investigation by the police and a likeable young amateur detective, Bob Stuart. Fans will miss this one to their loss.[54]

MURDER IN BERMUDA, BY WILLOUGHBY SHARP

INTERESTING yarn by a well-known magazine writer, with the scene among the bicycles and barrooms of Bermuda. The corpse is a beautiful girl found one Easter morning on Snake Road. There are

54 Lady Winifred (Knox) Peck (1882-1962) was a sister of Ronald Knox (1889-1957), the noted Catholic priest and theologian. In a minor sideline to his distinguished career, Father Knox authored six Golden Age detective novels and the "Detective Fiction Decalogue," one of the most important sets of rules from the period for the writing of detective fiction. Though overshadowed by her famous brother, Winifred Peck in her own right was an accomplished writer, mostly of mainstream novels. In my view Lady Peck's first novel, *The Warrielaw Jewel*—one of two mystery novels that she wrote—surpasses her brother's detective fiction. Downing's praise may sound extravagant—he compares the novel to the E. C. Bentley

tourist ships in the harbor and clues scattered about, including a bunch of Madonna lilies clasped in the girl's hand (Inspector Welch, local sleuth, finds in *Our Garden Flowers* the following: "The Madonna lily, or *lilium candidum*, unlike the Bermuda Easter lily, blooms in June, not April").

Watch the New York newspapers that give details of the Marsden kidnapping and the suspicious Mrs. Bigelow, who precipitates the inquisitive inspector into a reservoir beneath her cottage. Ingenious and speedier than the average.[55]

MURDER IN THE BATH, BY ROGER FRANCIS DIDELOT

TRANSLATIONS of murder items from the French are coming thick and fast these days, so that fans must like them. This one concerns the discovery of Betty Smithson, Detroit, U. S. A., strangled in her bath in a Paris hotel and is told, according to the blurbist, "in that vivacious *joie de vivre* way that only the French have." Really, it is not as naughty as it sounds. Hectic sleuthing by Inspector Lecain of the Sûreté and glimpses of Montparnasse and those places.[56]

"CLUES AND CORPSES" (REVIEWED BY TODD DOWNING) October 8, 1933, p. 45

HANGMAN'S HOLIDAY, BY DOROTHY L. SAYERS

THE innumerable admirers of Miss Sayers' punctilious sleuth, Lord Peter Wimsey, will find him featured in four of the twelve tales that

mystery classic, *Trent's Last Case* (1913)—but on the whole I am in agreement with him. See my article "Murder in the Family: The Warrielaw Jewel (1933), by Winifred Peck," *The Passing Tramp*, http://thepassingtramp.blogspot.com/2012/01/murder-in-family-warrielaw-jewel-1933.html.

55 Willoughby Sharp (1900-1955), wealthy New York City stockbroker and publisher, wrote two detective novels, *Murder in Bermuda* (1933) and *Murder of the Honest Broker* (1934), both reviewed by Downing.

56 Downing seems not to have thought much of "that vivacious *joie de vivre* way that only the French have," particularly in this *roman policier* by Roger Francis Didelot (1902-1985).

make up this volume. Lord Peter solves the mystery of the doppelganger ("uncommonly disagreeable," he says); of the bewitched wife of the American physician living in a little village in the Pyrenees ("A more abominable crime it has never been my fortune to discover"); of the purloined pearls; and of the murder of Charmian Grayle at Sir Charles Deverill's ball ("a very hefty bit of work").

Six of the tales introduce a new detective, of whom Miss Sayers seems to be rather proud. And justly. Mr. Montague Egg is a wine-merchant's traveler and combines some rather clever ferretting out of clues with close attention to business. A murder that is discussed in the bar-parlour of the Pig and Pewter at Mugbury is bound to be a good one.

Two additional yarns complete a book that is recommended to fans without reservation.[57]

THE PARACHUTE MURDER, BY LEBBEUS MITCHELL

LIVELY and fairly ingenious yarn by a native of Arkansas who became a New York newspaper man. "Body of Chadwick Morne Floated to Earth by Parachute: Was He Already Dead or Was Crime Committed after His Descent?" inquires a headline in the *Sun*. The corpse was an actor, star of the Broadway success, "The Wife's Turn," and disliked by various and sundry, including leading ladies, an Italian racketeer and a Jap valet (What is the meaning of the latter's words: "Watash Kereo Korosu Jo?"). Sleuthing by another actor, Kirk Kemerson, whose specialty is disguise. Surprisingly sane, despite such chapter headings as "The Captive Lovers" and "Whose Child?"[58]

57 Downing held both the detective fiction and the literary criticism of British Golden Age Crime Queen Dorothy L. Sayers (1893-1957) in high esteem. His comment that a "murder that is discussed in the bar-parlour of the Pig and Pewter at Mugbury is bound to be a good one" suggests Downing had developed pronounced Anglophilic tendencies by this time.

58 Lebbeus Mitchell (1879-?) published only one novel in book form, *The Parachute Murder*, but he also wrote crime tales for the pulps, including the novel-length *Murder of the Resurrected Man* (1935). Downing's reference to the tale's "Jap valet" is indelicate, but indicative of many Americans' attitudes in the 1930s.

"CLUES AND CORPSES" (REVIEWED BY TODD DOWNING) October 29, 1933, p. 41

THE DRAGON MURDER CASE, BY S. S. VAN DINE

"OF all the cases I have thus far recorded," says Philo Vance's chronicler truthfully, "none was as exciting, as weird, as apparently unrelated to all rational thinking as the dragon murder. The darkest chapters in the ethnological records of the human race were reviewed within sight of the skyscrapers of Manhattan; and so powerful was the effect of these resuscitations that even scientists searched for some biological explanation of the grotesque phenomena that held the country enthralled during the days following the uncanny and incomprehensible death of Sanford Montague."

For Montague, at a house party at the Stamm estate in Inwood had dived into a swimming pool one night—and failed to rise to the surface. The swimming pool, known as the Dragon Pool, was reputedly the haunt of Amangemokdom, the devil-monster of the Lenape Indians. Among those present in the party: Rudolph Stamm, aquarist who is drunk most of the time; his mother who has hallucinations; Gale Leland, halfbreed Algonkian; and Ruby Steele, an actress. Philo Vance, District Attorney Markham and Sergeant Heath run true to form.

We liked it better than any of the Van Dine novels except *The Greene Case* and *The Bishop Case*.[59]

"CLUES AND CORPSES" (REVIEWED BY TODD DOWNING) November 12, 1933, p. 38

THE CLOCK TICKS ON, BY VALENTINE WILLIAMS

THE fans seem unusually enthusiastic about Mr. Williams' sixteenth thriller (during one week it was one of the four bestsellers

59 S. S. Van Dine's latest baroque effort appealed greatly to Downing, confirmed lover of Golden Age baroque.

among such fare), probably owing to the effective device for creating suspense which he has employed. Young Trevor Dene of Scotland Yard believes that an innocent man has been sentenced to death in the Oldham Priory case and starts off on his own to America to track down the real culprit.

Follow beautiful girls in distress in New York night clubs, basilisk-eyed gunmen, nocturnal chases through Long Island and a corpse in the tonneau. With an interlude for cocktails at Mrs. Benzler's place at Rosemount. And the clock ticks on, ever shortening the 72 hours which Dene has at his disposal for identifying the man whose arrest will save Gerry Cloan from the gallows! Personally, we got a bit confused among the Mikes and the Nicks and the Petes and the various speakeasies.[60]

THE STRANGE MURDER OF HATTON, K. C., BY HERBERT ADAMS

MR. ADAMS' mysteries are consistently good, despite his slightly disconcerting departure from the routine method of narration. His latest is up to the standard of *The Golf House Murder* and *The Woman in Black* and includes a full $2 worth of bafflement, including stolen emeralds, a corpse with a dagger in the eye, blackmail, incendiarism and garbled French.

Dramatis personae include: Wilfred Hatton (the corpse) who recently acquired a young and beautiful French wife; the latter's cousin, whose kisses in the dark may or may not be platonic; Janet and Ruth Hatton, the former in love with an actor and the latter with—whom? The attentive millionaire or the penniless young surgeon? It all happened at a house party at Fullock Park, Surrey.[61]

RED RHAPSODY, BY CORTLAND FITZSIMMONS

ANOTHER house party, this time at Cliff Side, the remodeled house out on the lake which the rich Blandells have bought. It seems

60 Here Downing shows a little restiveness with the busy and boozy sort of American mystery novel, with its Mikes and Nicks and Petes and its "various speakeasies."

61 Downing's love affair with the classical British mystery novel that Herbert Adams represented continues.

that the house boasts a ghost ("Can the Blandell money, new decorations and modern plumbing stop long tenure of famous ghost which for more than 30 years has been sole occupant of grim old house on lake?" queries the local newspaper). A musician, Phil Ryder, is stabbed in the back while at the piano and most of the book is devoted to questions by Harry Curtis, detecatif. Who sat where? Who put out the lights? What happened then? And so forth. Jonah, the poetess' rabbit, plays an important part, as does Stephen Braden, mystery writer. Mr. Fitzsimmons, in case you forgot, wrote *70,000 Witnesses*.[62]

Drury Lane's Last Case, by Barnaby Ross

We are somewhat at a loss to predict the fan's reaction to this, the volume that completes the much-discussed Drury Lane tetralogy—the successive tragedies of X, Y, and Z. . . .

Suffice it to say that this is not an *ex post facto* examination of a crime already committed, but a search for evidence of a murder committed in 1599, and that the murders, kidnappings, bombings, etc., which take place in 1933 are themselves a part of the tragedy of 1599. Clues: the cipher 3HS wM inscribed upon a piece of paper left with Inspector Thumm by a man with a blue beard; 17 elderly Indiana school teachers; and a purloined copy of the first edition of *The Passionate Pilgrim*, fraudulently assigned by the Elizabethan printer William Jaggard to Shakespeare. . . .[63]

62 Cortland Fitzsimmons (1893-1949) worked in publishing before establishing himself in the 1930s as a detective novelist and screenwriter. His greatest success, alluded to by Todd Downing, was *70,000 Witnesses* (1931), which concerned murder committed on the playing field during a football game (it was filmed the next year; unsurprisingly, Fitzsimmons mystery yarns about baseball and hockey followed). Despite Fitzimmons' successes, reviewers did not place him in the front rank of detective fiction writers. Downing's tone and use of the word "detecatif" signal that he was something less than enthralled with *Red Rhapsody*.

66 Downing seems to have enjoyed *Drury Lane's Last Case* (written by Ellery Queen, under their Barnaby Ross pseudonym), though he thought it might alienate traditionalists, for reasons I have edited from the review. (Downing came a little close to "spoiling" here, in my opinion.)

Murder at Bayside, by Raymond Robins

A treat for lovers of Colt .45's and students of ballistics ("The science of interior ballistics began its so-called modern development about the middle of the last century. Before that time, we had smooth-bore weapons, which fired a round, ball-shaped bullet which had no rotation or spin to it. In order to get greater accuracy at long range the projectile was elongated with a point at one end and a flat surface at the other").

Which encyclopedic quotation is occasioned by the murder of old Cyrus Evans in his Maryland estate. In the gunroom is a rare collection of firearms and in the study are disgruntled nephews and adopted sons and presumptive heirs. The author is a graduate of West Point and the Massachusetts Institute of Technology. His motto: "More plunder can be gained by the pen than by the sword." Well worth perusal if a penchant for premonitions can tide you over the opening pages.[64]

Thirteen at Dinner, by Agatha Christie

The fans were unusually enthusiastic about Mrs. Christie's sophisticated tale of London stage folk when it ran in *The American Magazine* this summer. Those who missed the latest exhibition by Hercule Poirot of the working of the "little gray cells" are urged to obtain it at once.

"She'd kill as easily as she'd drink her morning tea," says Bryan Martin of the famous actress, Jane Wilkinson. A few days later Lord Edgware, Jane's eccentric and irascible husband, is found murdered in his study at Regent Gate. To Inspector Japp of Scotland Yard the case is a clear one against Jane. Two more murders complicate things, however, and Poirot is almost run over by a bus when the solution comes to him in the middle of the street.[65]

64 Lieutenant Raymond Robins was born in Michigan in 1900 and graduated from West Point in 1924.

65 Agatha Christie's modern detractors no doubt would scorn the notion that her novels could be seen as "sophisticated," but in fact this was true of *Thirteen at Dinner* (*Lord Edgware Dies* in Britain), with its setting in the theatrical world.

"CLUES AND CORPSES"
(REVIEWED BY TODD DOWNING)
November 26, 1933, p. 45

THE MASTER MURDERER, BY CAROLYN WELLS

SIMILAR in many respects to the recent Hayter murder mystery in Lawton, Okla., is the unusual situation which confronts Fleming Stone, Miss Wells' favorite sleuth, at the aristocratic home of the Everett family on one of the East Sixties, New York City. The entire Everett family is wiped out overnight—each by a different means. Were there four murderers or was someone clever enough to move so stealthily as to commit four murders within a few minutes of each other? The first, that of old Phoebe Everett (dying of cancer), was evidently a mercy death. But what about the will, with its peculiar conditions? And what about the Arizona hunting trip alibi of the inheritor of the Everett fortune? And the pink feathers found on the rug? Solved by Stone though his insistence upon the importance of clues. Casting our mind back over the thirty-odd Wells yarns, this strikes us as one of the best.[66]

DR. THORNDYKE INTERVENES, BY R. AUSTIN FREEMAN

BEGINNING with the discovery of a severed head in a box in the cloak room at Fenchurch Street Station in London and soon involving the suit of Mr. Christopher Pippet, American, to presume the death of the Earl of Winsborough, Mr. Freeman's latest contribution to the chronicles of Dr. Thorndyke is every bit as good as his numerous others, depending upon intricacy of plot rather than thrills. There is the problem, for instance, of Mr. Pippett's claim to be heir presumptive to the Earldom, for instance. And of how a valuable shipment of platinum was stolen from the

66 Given his previous reviews of her books, Downing is surprisingly generous to this Carolyn Wells murder tale. The "Hayter murder mystery" to which Downing refers concerned the early November 1933 slayings of three members of the Hayter family—mother, son and daughter—in their house in Lawton, Oklahoma. Mrs. Hayter and her son had been shot, the daughter bludgeoned to death with a baseball bat.

waterfront at Riga. And of the comparative melting point of platinum and of cast iron. Not to mention calligraphy, coffins (1843 or 1933) and a corpse in a dene hole. "When in doubt," says Christopher Morley, "stick to Dr. Thorndyke." Sage advice for sober-minded fans.[67]

THE MONKEY WRENCH, BY JASON GRIFFITH

"YOUNG master," says the desert dervish to young Larry Reynolds, "guard well your head and heart. I see for you a thorny path. Beware of the three fair forms. Allah be with you!" But Larry's uncle falls ill in Cairo and it's up to Larry to follow Hamid Hassa to the Chateau Marguay northeast of Paris and to obtain from him the formula for synthetic rubber before unscrupulous rival interests get busy. The three fair forms turn out to be Mademoiselle Helene, self-styled Parisian actress (Room 288 on the Alexandria-Marseilles steamer); Patricia Carroll, late of Salt Lake City (in Larry's compartment on the Paris-Lagny sur Marne express); and Susan Squibbs, daughter of Larry's host at the secret-ridden chateau. Truly, as ye blurbist sings, "Light, fantastic, yet thrilling."[68]

67 R. Austin Freeman (1862-1943), creator of the great medical detective Dr. John Thorndyke and father of the so-called Golden Age pure puzzle (or "humdrum," as crime writer and critic Julian Symons put it) school of mystery, which put absolute primacy in a story on the ratiocination of a murder problem, is given his due here by Downing as just the thing for "sober-minded fans." American writer Christopher Morley (1890-1957) authored over 100 novels and essay and poetry collections.

68 The *nom de plume* "Jason Griffith" concealed a husband-and-wife writing team, Mr. and Mrs. E. G. Griffith of Portland, Oregon. The couple conceived *The Monkey Wrench* as a humorous novel and Downing seems to have taken it as such in his wry review. Judge Lynch (William C. Weber) of the *Saturday Review* was not amused, however, in his review complaining that the novel's "trick ending" caused him "to coise viciously." He thunderingly rendered the verdict of "Dumm." A month later the *Saturday Review* published a letter from Mr. Griffith, in which Griffith complained of the unjustness of Judge Lynch's review, asserting that *The Monkey Wrench* was a "satirical comedy" mocking "the vogue for mystery stories." "We accuse your detective story reviewer of having no sense of humor," retorted Mr. Griffith. Judge Lynch responded that *The Monkey*

"CLUES AND CORPSES" (REVIEWED BY TODD DOWNING) December 15, 1933, p. 45

THE SIAMESE TWIN MYSTERY, BY ELLERY QUEEN

THIS takes its place upon our gooseflesh shelf between Rufus King's *Murder by Latitude*, and Mignon Eberhart's *From This Dark Stairway*. The fans can't afford to miss it.

It all happens on an "isolated peak of iniquity" known as Arrow Mountain, in the Tepees, in the heart of the ancient Indian country. Ellery and his father are trapped in a forest fire which encircles the mountain and are forced to take refuge in the forbidding house of Dr. Xavier ("His God is Science"), which stands upon the brink of a precipice. The first night the Inspector is startled by two sights: a giant crab-like thing which scuttles (grand word!) into a dark doorway; and a female upon the balcony (Marie Carreau—"bluest of the blue . . . pots of money . . . supposed to be in Europe").

Chapters entitled "The Queer People," "Blood on the Sun" and "Xiphophagus," then Dr. Xavier is found in his swivel chair, shot, with half of the six of spades in his hand (six—and the medico's wife is named Sarah Isere Xavier!). Another murder and the corpse's hand holds half of the knave of diamonds (Carreau means "diamond" in French!). As Ellery remarks, "it's so far removed from the ordinary realm of observation and simple deduction as to partake of something out of *Alice in Wonderland*."

The trick by which Ellery conceals the identity of the murderer and baffles the reader is worthy of Agatha Christie. The best of the Queen crop.[69]

Wrench was not any good as a satire either. On the great *Monkey Wrench* kerfuffle, see *Saturday Review* 18 November 1933, p. 272 and 23 December 1933, p. 368.

69 Elevating Ellery Queen's *The Siamese Twin Mystery* to the status of *Murder by Latitude* and *From This Dark Stairway* is high praise indeed coming from Downing, as the latter two novels he named in 1934 as two of his six favorite mysteries. It also indicates just how much he enjoyed what might be termed gooseflesh detection.

THE EX-DETECTIVE, BY E. PHILLIPS OPPENHEIM

BEING, unless we lost count, Mr. Oppenheim's 129th published tome. It introduces a typically Oppenheim sleuth—Malcolm Grossett, who quits Scotland Yard in a huff and sets up as a private investigator with offices in Macadam Street. His specialty is the investigation of cases involving innocent men accused of various and sundry crimes. We liked particularly "The Killing of Monica Quayles," wherein Malcolm saves a man's life; "The Battles of the Suites," involving another of those Oriental jewels; "The Cinema Murder," wherein Malcolm and his beautiful wife (who looks like Marlene Dietrich) are present at the slaughter; "Captain Bronsen's Cargo," with adventure on the Thames; and "The Mystery Ticket," which has a particularly agreeable touch of gruesomeness. And six other stories—all told in the good old Oppenheim manner.

THE MENACE, BY SYDNEY HORLER

"HORLER for Excitement" recommend the publishers. This item concerns the blackmailing activities of a gentleman who signs his letters "The Menace." Among those trying to unmask him are: Stephen Brandell, newspaper proprietor from America; his daughter Mary ("She had—oh, ridiculous and yet fascinating miracle—fallen in love!"). Philip Cranston, Mayfair solicitor with a past; Mrs. Montagu ("has slid down the slippery slopes of Avernus"); Lady Dahle ("'My dear,' she said, looking down at him, 'at this very moment I believe I would sell what remains of my soul for you. . . . Well?'"); and Sir Harcourt Bruce, of Scotland Yard. The more rabid of the fans will like it.[70]

70 In *1001 Midnights* Bill Pronzini deems the novels of English thriller writer Sydney Horler "high camp by today's standards . . . for their hilarious prose, pomposity, and absurd plots" (p. 381). Downing's choice of quotations and his observation that the "more rabid" thriller fans would like *The Menace* suggest that he shared Pronzini's assessment of Horler. For his part, Judge Lynch in *Saturday Review* (25 November 1933, p. 297) rendered the verdict "awful" on *The Menace*.

CHAPTER THREE: 1934 REVIEWS

"FITCH'S POND"

January 14, 1934, p. 37

NIGHT OVER FITCH'S POND, BY CORA JARRETT

TO a lonely, almost inaccessible mountain lake come for three successive summers a—at first glance—commonplace group of people. Three staid middle-aged college professors, two of them with their wives, the other unmarried.

The novel opens at the end of the third summer, when Julius Nettleton is dead by drowning. Accident or suicide? That is the question which occupies the mind of Walter Drake, the bachelor member of the party, as he watches through the long night beside the body of his friend. Seeking for a clue to the truth, his thoughts play over the circumstances that led two such oddly assorted couples to spend the summers together on the shores of the solitary lake. Incidents, seemingly insignificant before, take on new meaning and bit by bit he reconstructs the real story of the tragedy until at last he finds the hidden reason for Nettleton's magnificent gesture of death and atonement. These thoughts of Drake's constitute the novel.

While it has most of the elements of a mystery novel (including some excellent deduction by the protagonist from a pile of wet salt) it is primarily a study of character. Mary and Eloise, the wives, smiling and sewing and fighting a quarterless duel;

Rolf, his resistance to his wife's worldly ambitions gradually wearing away under the drip-drip-drip of a persistence worse than the Chinese water torture; Julius, tyrannical, self-centered, yet atoning for his shortcomings by his death; the narrator (like Maugham's character in *Of Human Bondage*, symbolically crippled) living in a world that belongs to other people, who must be placated—or dodged. And, last, the dark still waters of the lake, waiting patiently for their foreordained victim.

The author, whose first novel this is, has a rare sense of the macabre quality of words and has succeeded in fashioning an uninvolved plot that for sheer excitement and constantly mounting tension has few equals in the class of fiction that openly strives for these effects. She writes with admirable restraint and sees, as does her character Walter Drake, "the terrible little things that give people away."

Not a pleasant slice of life, but an interesting one.—Todd Downing[1]

1 Todd Downing gives a longer than usual (355 words) and more serious review to a book that in his view "has most of the elements of a mystery novel" yet, in fact, is not one. Notably, this review was not part of his "Clues and Corpses" column. Like many a crime reviewer today, Downing seems tempted to embrace a mainstream novel as a mystery (today we would say "crime novel"); however, he qualifies his claim by conceding that *Night over Fitch's Pond* (1933) is "primarily a study of character." Cora Jarrett herself specialized in psychological character studies that were seen as occupying a place on the borderland of mystery, though she herself professed bemusement over this. In the preface to the one self-admitted mystery that she wrote (under the pseudonym Faraday Keene), *Pattern in Black and Red* (1934), Jarrett confessed her "astonishment" that "in certain bookstores" *Night over Fitch's Pond* "was offered for sale as a 'mystery'." She noted wryly that "with readers devoted to this fascinating genre, of which the rules are in their way as definite as those that govern the sonnet, [*Night over Fitch's Pond*] had little success." Jarrett believed that "it takes more than the enigmatic death of a character to make a mystery-novel." Cora Hardy Jarrett (1877-1969), a native of Norfolk, Virginia, enjoyed an elite education, attending Bryn Mawr, Oxford and the Sorbonne. She married Edward Seton Jarrett, a civil engineer, and had three children. *Night over Fitch's Pond* was her first novel, though she earlier had published short stories. Besides *Pond*

"CLUES AND CORPSES" (REVIEWED BY TODD DOWNING)
January 21, 1934, p. 45

THE CASE OF THE GOLD COINS, BY ANTHONY WYNNE

VARIATIONS upon the sealed room motif seem to come endlessly from the fertile brain of Mr. Anthony Wynne (Question for the fans who are interested in such matters: Who is Anthony Wynne? It is said to be a pseudonym). This time it is the body of Lord Wallace of Eastsea Manor, Northumberland, who is found lying on a wide expanse of untrodden sand, free from footprint of any kind. Yet there is evidence that the man had been stabbed and died instantly on the spot where he lay. Follow in short order two more murders (Henry the footman and Mrs. Pykewood, a neighbor).

Dr. Hailey's only clues are the gold sovereigns which are found beside the bodies of the victims. The usual suspects, including Colonel Bolton, red-faced, who had quarreled with the deceased over a mill; his daughter, Pamela, who attempts to commit suicide; Peter Ingram, whose jack-knife is found in Lord Wallace's back and who is engaged to the fair Pamela; Mr. Pykewood, who may or may not be insane, etc. Altogether, as ingenious a puzzler as Mr. Wynne ever concocted and told in his unexcited fashion with an extra-large dose of thrills.[2]

THE DARK GARDEN, BY MIGNON G. EBERHART

WE have been an Eberhart fan ever since her first, *While the Patient Slept*, appeared and we consider *From this Dark Stairway* the most skillful mélange of gruesome horror and straight detection in recent years, hence superlatives are to be expected when a new Eberhart novel appears.

and *Pattern*, her works are the novels *The Ginko Tree* (1935), *Strange Houses* (1936), *The Silver String* (1938) and *Return in December* (1951) and the short story collections *Peccadilloes* (1929, under the Faraday Keene pseudonym) and *I Asked No Other Thing* (1937).

2 Anthony Wynne continues to provide Downing with what he wants in a detective novel: an "ingenious" puzzler with "an extra-large does of thrills."

The Dark Garden, which appeared in *The Red Book* under the title *The Figure in the Fog*, is Mrs. Eberhart's long-promised Chicago murder mystery. It concerns the usual houseful of relatives who are assembled to await the death of the old woman who controls the purse strings of the family. Concentrate on the words "grape hair" overheard in the fog, the tinkling of crystal in the dining room, the old German shopkeeper found murdered on the beach and the fog-shrouded figure in the garden. Our candidate for the best spine-chiller of the season.[3]

Mr. Fortune Wonders, by H. C. Bailey

Reggie Fortune addicts (and in our opinion all mystery fans worthy of the name belong in this category) are afforded a new treat in the shape of eight brand new bafflers, written in the well-known serio-comic Bailey vein. We liked particularly "The Cigarette Case," concerning the tragic demise of young Mr. Fyfield, a curate of Wanshire (we probably preferred this because it has a sinister mansion and a beautiful girl with a past); "The Yellow Diamonds," bluebells and blood; "The Lilies of St. Gabriel's," barbituric acid; and "The Gypsy Moth," strangling. To our mind Reggie improves on acquaintance and we welcomed his biography, which Mr. Bailey obligingly contributes to this volume. Reggie likes poetry, chocolate ice cream, his wife, his garden and his laboratory. And as a sleuth, he's one of our favorites.

The Carnival Murder, by Nicholas Brady

Who would want to murder the fat woman in a carnival show? And why? And who was the Hungarian who pretended to be a famous physician and wasn't? And how are freaks made? All of these questions perplexed Inspector Doby of the local police, and it took that irresponsible, lovable, whimsical and intensely cerebral clergyman, the Rev. Ebenezer Buckle, who loved flowers and crime better than anything else in the world, to find the answers.

3 Mignon Eberhart continues to send chills Downing's spine, much to his pleasure.

Ebenezer is one of the coming detectives in fiction. If he can keep up his whimsicalities, his common sense, and his capacity for knowing exactly where to go to find out what it is that nobody else knows, and which knowledge is the one essential clue to the identity of the culprit, he should become one of the classics. You'll like.[4]

"CLUES AND CORPSES"
(REVIEWED BY TODD DOWNING)
February 4, 1934, p. 39

A Shadow Passes, by Eden Phillpotts

In *Bred in the Bone* and *Witch's Cauldron* Mr. Phillpotts recounted, somewhat in the nature of a case history, the story of Avis Bryden—conscienceless, calculating and indifferent to the judgments of the world—and of the murder which she committed that her son might benefit.

In this, the concluding volume of the Book of Avis, we find Peter Bryden burdened by the knowledge of his mother's guilt and forced to keep his knowledge a secret even from his young wife, whose admiration for Avis he does not dare to shake. Avis

4 Much better known for his David Hume crime thrillers, John Victor Turner also wrote, among other genre books, five detective novels about the investigations of amateur detective Reverend Ebenezer Buckle: *The House of Strange Guests* (1932); *Fair Murder* (1933) (*The Carnival Murder* in the United States); *Week-End Murder* (1933); *Ebenezer Investigates* (1934); and a late bloom on the plant, *Coupons for Death* (1944). On the character of Ebenezer Buckle, see Philip Grosset, "The Rev Ebenezer Buckle," *Clerical Detectives*, http://www.detecs.org/buckle.html. Although Downing's enthusiasm for Buckle is pronounced, it must be admitted that Buckle did not become one of the classic detectives in mystery fiction. Yet Bill Pronzini described the Buckle tales as "Golden Age fair-play mysteries with more spice than is usual in the breed." Specifically, Pronzini shares Downing's admiration for *The Carnival Murder*, deeming it "a first-rate macabre puzzler." See Steve Lewis, "Once Again with J. V. Turner a/k/a David Hume," 7 March 2007, *Mystery*File*, http://mysteryfile.com/blog/?p=107.

despises him as a weakling and to test his mettle puts him into a position which requires of him the sort of courage she herself has always shown. But Peter, conditioned as he is by his God-fearing Dartmoor environment, can think of his mother and her deeds only with horror. Realizing this, Avis leaves this world in a manner befitting her passage through it.

This tale is complete in itself without the preceding volumes. While not a mystery novel in the ordinary sense, fans will find in its pages some of Mr. Phillpotts' best end-of-a-chapter technique ("Is there somebody coming to meet us tonight?" "No, my son. There's somebody waiting for us at North Wood." "What do you want me to do about him, then?" he asked. "Help bury him," she answered). The author's craftsmanship, polished perfection of style and intimate knowledge of the Dartmoor countryside are too well known to need comment here.[5]

Two O'clock Courage, by Gelett Burgess

Offering the fans something new in the way of bafflement. The narrator finds himself upon a Brookline street, a bump on his head and his memory gone, a pistol in his pocket and blood on his clothes, and the newsboys crying: "Extra! John Saxon Murdered! Proprietor of the Imperial Theater shot down in his Brookline Home by an Unknown Hand!" Aided by an heiress, a starving waif and a garrulous reporter our hero has three mysteries to solve: Who is he? Did he kill Saxon? If not, who did?

An unusually intricate plot, recounted in swift unadorned prose. We admit that we failed to experience the "nightmare shudder" which ye blurbist predicted and we are sure that any trained mystery fan will spot the murderer at once; but we recommend the book for its staccato conversation, if for nothing else (as a wit Mr. Burgess is said to have contributed more argot to our language than any other man of our times). Watch Maurice

5 Although Downing had been somewhat ambivalent about the first volume of Eden Phillpotts' *Book of Avis*, with the final volume, *A Shadow Passes*, he embraces the trilogy wholeheartedly. Downing's final judgment is astute, as the Avis Bryden trilogy is one of Phillpotts' finest achievements and a supreme example of the 1930s British crime novel.

Bellinghampton ("the characterization of a distinguished and successful New York playwright"); Sidney Jetland, philandering clubman; Olga Biscom ("voluptuous brunette with reptilian green eyes"); Lily Cloyed ("irrefutable blonde, with 22-carat hair"); and the housekeeper, who doesn't allow her daughter to keep company with the boys. Try it for your next tired evening.[6]

"ABOUT CLUES AND CORPSES" (REVIEWED BY TODD DOWNING)

February 18, 1934, p. 41

THE MYSTERIOUS MADAMES, BY SIMONE D'ERIGNY

TRANSLATIONS of French mystery yarns continue to come (a note in this one to the effect that "others are in preparation") so some of the fans must like them. We may be lacking in appreciation of the Gallic genius or prejudiced in favor of Scotland Yard and Center Street, but they just don't click with us. However, not to discourage those whose tastes differ, this won last year's *Prix du Roman d'Aventures* and certainly lacks for nothing in the way of mustached detectives, taxicab dashes across Paris and women of mystery who leave behind them anonymous correspondence, whiffs of exotic perfume and other knickknacks. The most interesting character is Dr. Silas Lorrain, of the French medical academy and author of *Superhuman Will Power*, who believes that there is an unknown and terrifying force emanating from his brain. It certainly worked on the condemned prisoner at Orleans, but what about the medico's colleague, Dr. Myrte Renouard (fatally stabbed), who had been indulging in a liaison with Mme. Lorrain? No strain on the brain, which may be a recommendation.[7]

6 Gelett Burgess (1866-1951), poet, humorist, artist, critic, is probably best known for being the creator of the Goops children's books and the author of the nonsense verse "The Purple Cow." *Two O'Clock Courage* was filmed twice, in 1936 and 1945.

7 Noting, like Downing, that *The Mysterious Madames* had won a major French literary award, Judge Lynch of the *Saturday Review* fervently declared that he hoped "nobody publishes the runners-up." *Saturday Review*, 3 February 1934, 460.

THE THIN MAN, BY DASHIELL HAMMETT

THE highbrows have been so enthusiastic about Mr. Hammett's latest hard-boiled mélange of dialogue, liquor and murder that we suppose it will be all right if we permit ourself a few superlatives from the mystery fan angle. To our mind Mr. Hammett is one of the two purveyors of mystery fiction in the United States (Rufus King is the other) who are able to combine all the required elements of the detective yarn with a startling yet pleasing originality.

This concerns the visit to New York of a retired private detective, Nick Charles, referred to by his wife as "that Greek louse." A visit to a speakeasy involves Nick in the murder of Julia Wolf, confidential secretary to a missing inventor. This about Julia: "Her old man booted her out when she was 15 or 16 and got in some kind of a jam with a high school teacher and she took up with a guy called Face Peppler, a smart kid if he didn't talk too much. They stuck together till they got nailed trying to shake down some bird from Toronto," etc. Follow more slaughter, third degree and a passage from Duke's *Criminal Cases* entitled "Alfred G. Parker, the Maneater," "who murdered his five companions in the mountains of Colorado, ate their bodies and stole their money." Nobody sobers up for any lucid intervals, and, as one of the characters expresses it, "they're all sex crazy and it backs up into their heads"; but that's one of the things that makes the book different. Such people do exist and do commit murder.[8]

8 Hard-boiled crime writer Dashiell Hammett (1894-1961), one of the landmark figures in American crime fiction (he "took murder out of the Venetian vase and dropped it in the alley," wrote an admiring Raymond Chandler in his 1944 essay, "The Simple Art of Murder"), published his last of five detective novels with *The Thin Man*. Though some critics over the years have viewed *The Thin Man* as something of a sell-out novel, lacking the brutal street authenticity of *Red Harvest* (1929), *The Maltese Falcon* (1930) or *The Glass Key* (1931), it was extremely well-received at the time, both by critics and lay readers, and spawned the hugely popular "Thin Man" series of films, starring William Powell and Myrna Loy as Nick and Nora Charles. *The Thin Man* also inspired numerous imitators, who penned derivative tales of wisecracking, hard-drinking couples cockily confronting crime. Downing certainly seems to have enjoyed Hammett's tale, comparing the author to his own beloved Rufus King.

MURDER DAY BY DAY, BY IRVIN S. COBB

THE only faults one can find with Mr. Cobb's incursion into the blood and bafflement field are on the score of lack of originality and obvious padding. The devise for concealing the identity of the murderer was effective the first time used (by Agatha Christie) and will deceive only those trusting fans who do not expect it to be used again; the method of murder is avowedly a steal from [L. T.] Meade and [Robert] Eustace (with minor improvements in technique); the method of disposal of the corpse will be spotted at once by readers of [J. H.] Wallis' *The Servant of Death*. Pages filled with typical Cobb descriptions of county landscapes, Long Island bayman dialect, and journalistic reminiscences are likely to cause impatience in the reader anxious to get ahead with the tale.

But maybe we are expecting too much of Mr. Cobb. The yarn is well written and there is no lack of gore and goofy suspects. Find the slayer of mean old Uncle Cresap and his henchman Wong Gee among these: Manuel Sabino, Mexican-Apache dwarf; Haw Verity, homegrown handyman; Olsen, the Swedish chauffeur; T. Cheever Pettigrew, dipsomaniac; Tony Tontini, Sicilian rum-runner; and sweet young Florence Dane, who inherits the deceased's fortune.—Todd Downing.[9]

"Such people do exist and do commit murder," Downing assured his Oklahoma readers of Hammett's gallery of big-city bad'uns.

9 Originally from Paducah, Kentucky, Irvin Shewsbury Cobb (1876-1944) was a prolific and popular American author and journalist. Cobb was best known for his local color humor stories, but he also wrote horror tales (some of which influenced H. P. Lovecraft) and, as we see from Downing's review, one detective novel. In his review of *Murder Day By Day*, Downing reveals his ample knowledge of detective fiction, casually referencing a novel by Agatha Christie (in something of a spoiler), a story by L. T. Meade and Robert Eustace and J. H. Wallis' *The Servant of Death*, previously reviewed by Downing (see p. 177).

"MYSTERIES AND MURDERS" (REVIEWED BY TODD DOWNING) February 25, 1934, p. 47

THE EIGHT OF SWORDS, BY JOHN DICKSON CARR

FOR something different in the mystery line, try this recommended baffler by the author of *The Mad Hatter Mystery*, *Poison in Jest*, etc. It would seem that a poltergeist (German for "racketing spirit") is playing pranks at the Grange, Gloucestershire residence of Colonel Standish, or else the Bishop of Mappleham, amateur criminologist, has gone loony. The worthy clergyman is reported to have slid down a bannister, thrown an ink-well at the Vicar of Primley and choked a housemaid. Scotland Yard is more amused than disturbed until one of the Colonel's neighbors, Septimus Depping, scholar, gourmet and owner of a dark past, is found murdered in his study. Dr. Gideon Fell, devious-minded sleuth of whom Mr. Carr should be proud, views the corpse, the Eight of Swords from a taroc pack, the partially eaten dinner and the buttonhook which had been used to blow the fuses—and spots the murderer.

Questions for less nimble-minded fans: Why did the deceased leave his favorite soup untouched? Why did he open instead of close the windows when the rain began? Who purloined the old shoes from the attic: Harry Morgan, detective story writer; Burke, his publisher ("frequently drunk and always at ease"); or Lady Standish ("I demand to know why this house has been filled with these objectionable people")? Extremely well written.[10]

10 As one can sense from this review, John Dickson Carr (1906-1977), a towering figure from the Golden Age of the detective novel, was quickly to become one of Downing's very favorite mystery writers. In the 1930s Carr emerged as the greatest master of the "miracle problem" or "impossible crime" mystery—typically involving a murderer perpetrating foul play within a locked room. Carr's mysteries also often involve the sort of shuddery, pseudo-supernatural and horror elements that powerfully appealed to Downing's imagination. Under his own name and the pseudonym Carter Dickson, Carr produced over seventy detective novels between 1930 and 1972.

THE WEEPING-WILLOW MURDERS, BY CHARLES KOONCE

MR. Koonce, a former Oklahoman, is a newcomer to the mystery story ranks who deserves the attention of the fans. He writes in the Mignon Eberhart-gooseflesh manner and sprinkles his pages with a generous allowance of premonitions. Some of his attempts at atmospherics (such as the chapter-heading "The hands! The hands!") are obvious but we liked them.

The plot is stereotyped and the fans will know what to expect when the heroine-narrator goes up to the attic in the dead of night; Finch ("criminologist, psychiatrist, psychologist and the Lord knows what else") doesn't quite live up to his reputation; the ending is a bit disappointing. But Mr. Koonce calls his book a "mystery-farce" so doesn't take it too seriously.

Some of his characters he describes thus: Grandfather Asa Yarr—"a devil on wheels"; Clarence Reid—"a good-lookin' cuss"; Fritz—"the handsome homosexualist, plays a minor part in order that this story may not be naughty"; Mrs. Greer—"a cook—her thyroid does things." For less serious fans.[11]

IN THE TIGER'S CAGE, BY CAROLYN WELLS

FLEMING Stone again, this time investigating the death of lovely Marcia Moore, who is found upon the floor of the cage of Bluebell, Bengal tigress. Our suave Fleming suspects that all is not as it appears and orders an autopsy performed. It develops, of course, that the tiger didn't really kill her, but that she was dead when put in the cage. And—again of course—there is a house-party going on, so as to provide suspects. For example, Pamela, "an interesting youngster of 17"; Reid, wild animal painter; Sara Lamb, known as "the Lambkin." And don't forget Ballyhoo, the chimpanzee. A great deal of wild animal lore which sounds

11 *The Weeping Willow Murders* apparently was Charles Koonce's sole foray into fiction. One wonders what Downing's readers, if they perused the book, made of Fritz, "the handsome homosexualist." Downing seems to have been amused with this effort by his fellow Oklahoma native, who wrote in the "Mignon Eberhart-gooseflesh manner"—with his tongue in cheek.

authentic, cocktails and general philandering upon the sunporch. Wells fans (and there are lots of them) will like it.[12]

"CLUES AND CORPSES" (REVIEWED BY TODD DOWNING) March 4, 1934, p. 58

MURDER IN THE CALAIS COACH, BY AGATHA CHRISTIE

HAVING read this novel serially in *The Saturday Evening Post* and having maintained stubborn arguments with several fans about its merits ever since, we are even surer that it deserves our applause after rereading it in book form. The phenomenally popular *Thirteen at Dinner* can't, we insist, hold the proverbial candle to this.

The scene—the Orient express, halted by snow-drifts high in the mountains of Jugoslavia. In one compartment of the Calais coach, by curious coincidence full despite an off season, Hercule Poirot; in another the body of a murdered man. That particular coach was shut off from the rest of the train; there had been no stops since the victim had last been seen alive; there were no tracks in the snow. *Alors*, as Hercule Poirot would say, the murderer was still aboard.

For once a blurbist's superlatives, in our opinion, are justified: "And thus commences a case that will take a place second to none in the annals of fictional crime. With *Murder in the Calais Coach* Agatha Christie has matched her world-famous *Murder of Roger Ackroyd*." To say more would be to give away the secret (it has been done once already in this review) so we confine ourselves to unhesitating recommendation of *Murder in the Calais Coach*. We venture to predict that if the reader is honest he will agree with us—after he gets over his natural resentment at having been completely, honestly and ingeniously bamboozled.[13]

12 "Wells fans . . . will like it." No more need be added!

13 Most likely reading Agatha Christie's classic *Murder on the Orient Express* (the novel's better-known English title) influenced Downing in setting his own next mystery novel, *Vultures in the Sky* (1935), on a train.

THE MYSTERY OF DEAD MAN'S HEATH, BY J. JEFFERSON FARJEON

ADVENTUROUS mystery yarn in which the usual framework of corpse-clues-solution is dressed up with generous daubings of excitement, including a beautiful girl in a negligee and a young handsome barrister with an injured foot ("All he could see were a contour of cheek and the lobe of a pink ear. He pitied the ear for the ruthless logic that was being driven into it"); a house on the heath and a corpse in the kitchen ("The hammer cracked the back of his skull." "H'm. But he's on his back." "Eh? You don't get a bruise on your forehead when you fall on your back."); a vindictive female who doesn't mince words and London lingo that sounds authentic to an Edgar Wallace fan. A favorite dictum of a discriminating fan: An Englishman makes the best corpse. And we add: English girls lead their male admirers the most useless, time-taking and thrilling chases before they finally 'fess up that weak young brother from Canada didn't really commit the murder. Well-written. Recommended for the bedside table of brain workers.[14]

FEAR BY NIGHT, BY PATRICIA WENTWORTH

THERE's something about Miss Wentworth's yarns that is contagious. We were lukewarm about *Danger Calling*, the first one we recall reading, but have grown more enthusiastic ever since. *Walk with Care* made us a Wentworth fan—just why we are not sure. It's not on the score of originality. The plot [of *Fear by Night*] boils down to this: An eccentric old uncle has left a fortune to Anne Vernon, but Anne doesn't know it. If Anne is done away with the money goes to Hilda, her cousin. So Hilda and her

14 "A favorite dictum of a discriminating fan: An Englishman makes the best corpse." With this dictum, Downing officially confirms himself as a pronounced mystery genre Anglophile. The son of popular Victorian novelist Benjamin Farjeon and a brother of beloved children's writer Eleanor Farjeon, Joseph Jefferson Farjeon (1883-1955) between 1924 and 1954 published over fifty mystery thrillers, mostly of a rather whimsical and genial nature. His most famous creation was the Cockney tramp, Ben, the lead character in eight novels and his popular play *No. 17*, later filmed by Alfred Hitchcock (as *Number 17*).

unscrupulous husband lure Anne to a lonely island in a black Scottish lake. But Charles Anstruther loves Anne, despite his haughty family's protests, etc., etc. etc. Maybe it's the restful familiarity of the formula; maybe it's the writer's real skill in narration; maybe it's taste on our part for vicarious something or other. At any rate, we—and, it would seem, many others—like books like *Fear by Night*. Serious-minded fans can pass it by.[15]

"CLUES AND CORPSES" (REVIEWED BY TODD DOWNING)

March 11, 1934, p. 47

Mr. Digwood and Mr. Lumb, by Eden Phillpotts

The Book of Avis brought to a conclusion, Mr. Phillpotts has turned his attention again to the mystery yarn pure and simple, for which fact his fans should be thankful. Phillpott's mysteries are of the problem rather than the gooseflesh variety but they do hold one's interest, being well written and presenting skillful character analyses.

Here we have the curious situation presented by two elderly bachelors who occupy adjoining properties by the lonely and deserted Heathfield Chine, Hampshire. Mr. Digweed, a man of modest means, lives only for his garden.

Mr. Lumb has a more substantial income and his only interest is his stamp collection (Note to riders of these hobbies: There is more about *Pilocerus Senilis* and *Dianthus Granticus* than perforations and watermarks in these pages). Neither cares for his fellow creatures or ever entertaining a visitor; each boasts that he possesses not a relation in the world. Mr. Lumb employs an attendant, Higgs, who, because of his interest in gardening, has become a friend of Digweed. Suddenly Digweed commits

15 As Patricia Wentworth grows on Downing, it becomes clear that Downing has a marked fondness for what Julian Symons would have classified as "maiden aunt" fiction: tales by, in addition to Wentworth, such writers as Mary Roberts Rinehart and Mignon Eberhart.

suicide by drowning, Higgs is murdered and an attempt is made upon the life of Lumb. Solved by the church organist with the same technique that he uses in the composition of a fugue. Naively told in the first person by a police sergeant in love with the organist's daughter.[16]

THE KILLING OF THE GOLDEN GOOSE, BY R. JERE BLACK

WILLS and their complement of disgruntled relatives seem to be enjoying another run of popularity, which is all right with us. The testator this time is old Roger Hilliard (rich, outspoken, and recently married to an ex-musical comedy star). "Slanderers, sneaks, sponges all!" the old man thunders at his relatives at the dinner table. "You perceive in my hands two small but momentous documents—the last wills and testaments of Roger Hilliard." One, says he, is the old will, whereupon his estate is to be divided among them. The other is a draft of the new will—to be signed upon the arrival of the lawyer—whereby they are cut off in favor of the wife. A snowstorm delays the lawyer's arrival and (you've guessed it!) Roger is done in that very night. Solved without dramatics by Christopher King, suave detective from New York, with Charles Forbes, reporter for the Mayfield (Pa) *Daily Mail* acting as the open-mouthed Watson. Well-written, according to formula, by a man who has evidently seen the snow upon the trees of Pennsylvania.[17]

MURDER STALKS THE WAKELY FAMILY, BY AUGUST DERLETH

INTRODUCING Judge Ephraim Peabody Peck of Sac Prarie, Wis., "lawyer, retired judge and terror of local law breakers." Ordinarily we don't like homespun characters in detective stories

16 Downing continues to hold Eden Phillpotts in high esteem, in large part because of the author's good writing and "skillful character analyses."

17 R. Jere Black (1892-1953) was from Mckeesport, Pennsylvania, so presumably indeed had seen the snow upon the trees there. He wrote stories for the slicks and the pulps, in addition to publishing his lone detective novel, *The Killing of the Golden Goose*, in 1934. See Terence Hanley, "R. Jere Black (1892-1953), 19 August 2011, *Tellers of Weird Tales*, http://tellersofweirdtales.blogspot.com/2011/08/r-jere-black-jr-1892-1953.html.

but Judge Peck doesn't indulge in localism of speech, isn't benevolent and knows a clue when he sees one.

The corpse is one Satterlee Wakely, an old scoundrel, found with a knife in his neck when four persons of the village answer a midnight summons from him: Doctor Considine ("last of a long line of Sac Prairie family doctors"); Julie Jennifer ("Why, Miss Jennifer, what an odd time for a lady of your standing to have an appointment!"); Rufus Wakely, half-brother of the corpse ("a bulbous nose"); and Judge Peck. Four murders, all told. We liked the chapter headings: "Enter Four Characters and Death"; "Second Entrance: Death"; "Third Entrance: Death"; and "Fourth Entrance: Death." Another will and a missing cedar box.[18]

"CLUES AND CORPSES"
(REVIEWED BY TODD DOWNING)
March 25, 1934, p. 51

EPILOGUE, BY BRUCE GRAEME

HERE'S one the highbrows can read unashamedly. Serious mystery fans have often lamented the fact that death cut short Charles Dickens' excursion into the blood and bafflement field, whither he was more or less consciously headed. How different mystery fiction might be today had he lived to finish *The Mystery of Edwin Drood* affords interesting speculation. How much sooner, for instance, might character delineation have received its proper share of attention along with sleuths, red herrings and corpses? And—most persistent question of all—who did kill young Mr. Drood?

18 August Derleth (1909-1971), Wisconsin writer of regional, supernatural and detective fiction, is best known within the latter field for his collections of Solar Pons tales, pastiches of Arthur Conan Doyle's Sherlock Holmes stories. However, he also wrote ten regional detective novels. See John Norris, "The Man on All Fours (1934)—August Derleth," 13 February 2011, *Pretty Sinister Books*, http://prettysinister.blogspot.com/2011/02/man-on-all-fours-1929-august-derleth.html.

Many clever suggestions have been made as to what Dickens' solution might have been and now comes Mr. Graeme (himself a plot fashioner of no mean ability) with another version, the most logical we recall. Our old friend Superintendent Stevens wakes up one morning with a hangover and finds himself in 1857 London and summoned by one Thomas Sapsea, Mayor of Cloisterham, to solve the disappearance of a young man named Drood. The methods of detection of the year 1933 bring about a discovery of Drood's body and the identification of his murderer. With a touch of gruesomeness that is one of the most delightful we remember, just the right amount of atmosphere, some humor, satire and thrills. Recommended to all fans, whether Dickens lovers or not.[19]

THE NINE TAILORS, BY DOROTHY L. SAYERS

IT was with some trepidation that we began Miss Sayers' latest novel. We had failed utterly and completely to make head or tail out of the two sheets of instructions for the reviewers. They concerned "the ancient and venerable art of bell-ringing" which, it seems, England alone in the world has perfected. Kent Treble, Bol Major, Grandsire Triples, Stedman Triples, the consecutive fifths of Tittums, etc., etc. left us feeling as if we had tried to master a correspondence lesson in calculus.

But with faith in Miss Sayers' ability to spin a yarn (says Dashiell Hammett: "Dorothy L. Sayers plots a detective story better than anyone I know") and the promise of another exploit of Lord Peter Wimsey, we began the book and liked it. There is an unknown corpse in Fenchurch St. Paul churchyard, East Anglian fens and some excellent sleuthing by Lord Peter, whose mannerisms don't annoy us for some reason or other. Frankly, though, we skipped a great deal of the bell-ringing minutiae, perhaps missing some of the story thereby. Anglophiles will doubtless be enthusiastic about it.[20]

19 Since 1934 other attempts have been made in novel form to solve Charles Dickens' unfinished *The Mystery of Edwin Drood*, but Bruce Graeme's *Epilogue* appears to have been the first. Downing boasts that "highbrows can read this one unashamedly."

20 Unlike Edmund Wilson, Downing seems to have enjoyed Dorothy L. Sayers *The Nine Tailors* (still beloved by many today), though he expressed

"CLUES AND CORPSES" (REVIEWED BY TODD DOWNING)

April 15, p. 51

Red Square, by Samuel Andrew Wood

We're looking now for *Bright Angel*, Mr. Wood's previous yarn. If *Red Square* is a sample of his output, we've been missing something. He knows how to tell a story without rambling down bypaths and seems to have the lowdown on life in Soviet Russia. Meet in chapter one: Prohackai, a Mongol of the Kinghan mountains, known in Manchuria and Turkestan as "The Flame Thrower"; Donald Armitage, English architect engaged under the five year plan to design the new Asiatic palace in Moscow; Lido-[?] Wei, Chinese girl revolutionary and artiste of the eastern propaganda film; "Lidoshka, on her fourteenth birthday had been stripped and slowly roasted by a drunken Chinese general somewhere outside the walls of Peking"; and Ishbel Dane of the Hampshire Danes, who has thrown up her possessions to come to Moscow. Prohackai is mudered in Ishbel's apartment, the agents of the OGPU rap at the door and the excitement begins. The best adventure yarn that has come our way in some time. Even the highbrows might take a look at Mr. Wood's prose.[21]

The Portcullis Room, by Valentine Williams

A red letter week this, with our vicarious adventuring ending in a Scottish castle. Our liking is doubtless colored by early initiation into Walter Scott (a portcullis is linked ineluctably in our mind with *Marmion*), but if there is any better place for a murder than an English country house it is a Scottish castle. Here we have the mist-bound stronghold of the Torays on the west coast

reservations about its emphasis on "bell-ringing minutiae."

21 Between 1925 and 1955 British author and journalist Samuel Andrew Wood (c. 1887-1967) published over fifty science fiction novels and thrillers, many under his pseudonym Robin Temple. Downing finds Wood's take on the Soviets much more convincing than that of Patricia Wentworth in *Red Shadow*.

of the Highlands, filled with oubliettes, faded tapestries, dour retainers and legends. Not to mention a ghost that stalks the room where, in 1739, an enemy of the clan was found murdered, with a dirk in his back.

Stephen Garrison, American millionaire, comes to view the castle with an eye to its purchase and experiences agreeable shudders when an uninvited guest is found murdered in the ghost room. There's a family secret too in connection with the French kepi in the tower and the son who died in the Foreign Legion. A treat for fans who have a penchant for atmosphere. Much better than *The Clock Ticks On*.[22]

"CLUES AND CORPSES"
(REVIEWED BY TODD DOWNING)
May 20, 1934, p. 49

THE CIPHER OF DEATH, BY F. L. GREGORY

SAX Rohmer fans will do well to get acquainted with Mr. Gregory, a much touted newcomer to the mystery story ranks. He has concocted here as fantastic a plot as will come their way in a long time yet contrives to make it more credible than most Oriental menace yarns. Back in the twelfth century, you'll find if you look in the encyclopedia, there existed in Persia a sect known as the Hashishites or assassins, whose leader Shaykh-al-Jebal, or Old Man of the Mountains, gained considerable proficiency

22 "[I]f there is any better place for a murder than an English country house it is a Scottish castle." Tellingly, Downing much preferred Valentine Williams' 1934 tale of shuddery shenanigans in a Scottish castle, *The Portcullis Room*, to Williams' 1933 novel *The Clock Ticks On*, which was filled to the brim with, in Downing's wry words, "the Mikes and the Nicks and the Petes and the various speakeasies." In praising *The Portcullis Room* Downing confesses his own youthful immersion in Atoka in the romantic works of Sir Walter Scott, specifically Scott's 1808 epic poem *Marmion* ("Then to the castle's lower ward/Sped forty yeoman tall/The iron-studded gates unbarr'd/Raised the portcullis' ponderous guard/The lofty palisade unsparr'd/And let the drawbridge fall").

in the murder line. When the members of a scientific-cinematic expedition begin to die under mysterious circumstances after their return from Persia to the U. S., it looks as if the Old Man of the Mountains were busy again.

Beside each body is a silver dagger, engraved with the victim's name, and his murderer, a hashish-filled youth, is found dead within a few hours. M. Saul Bouvard, who holds the chair for criminal research with the University of Paris, solves the case with a series of equations. M. Bouvard's Gallicisms bear too much resemblance, perhaps, to those of Hercule Poirot, but we prefer him to the probably more authentic French sleuths recently popularized in translation. Offhand, we can't remember a yarn since *Five Fatal Words* that gets the same atmosphere of other-dimensional doom. Try it.[23]

The Divorce Court Murder, by Milton Propper

Mr. Propper, author of *The Strange Disappearance of Mary Young* and *The Student Fraternity Murder*, has found another unusual setting for his latest baffler. This time it is the offices of Dawson, MacQuire and Locke, the prominent Philadelphia attorneys, where six people are discussing the case of Rowland vs. Rowland. Mr. Rowland is resisting his wife's libel for divorce and things are rather strained when a witness, Mrs. Mortimer Keith (of the Philadelphia Keiths) is found strangled in an inner office. Our old friend, Tommy Rankin, is summoned from headquarters and begins to inquire into such things as time of death, movements of suspects,

23 Born in Iowa, where he graduated with a degree in journalism from the University of Iowa, Franklin Long Gregory (1905-1985) worked as a journalist for Philadelphia and Newark newspapers for over forty years. In the 1940s and 1950s he was a frequent contributor to mystery, adventure and science fiction pulps. Besides *The Cipher of Death*, he published *Murder at Four Dot Ranch* (1936), set in Wyoming, and *The White Wolf* (1941), a supernatural horror novel of lycanthropy. *Icons of Horror and the Supernatural* (2006), edited by S. T. Joshi, lists *The White Wolf* as one of the "Ten Essential Werewolf Novels." *Five Fatal Words* is a 1932 crime novel by Edwin Balmer and Philip Wylie, authors of the classic science fiction novel *When Worlds Collide* (1933). It tells of multiple mysterious murders in Cornwall, England.

etc., etc. Incidentally, he uncovers considerable dirt about Philadelphia's leading families and he has to go to a roadhouse. Mr. Propper attempts no gymnastics of style and (to our mind) overloads his pages at times with minutiae, but his novels are well worth reading at that for those who like their murders straight.[24]

The Clutching Hand, by Arthur B. Reeve

The jacket brings back memories of days when we used to wait each Saturday night for the 6 o'clock train to bring a big-town newspaper containing the latest installment of a yarn by Mr. Reeve. Later, it ran for endless weeks as a movie serial, starring, if memory serves, Pearl White. The title was *The Clutching Hand*. More or less consciously ever since we have been comparing our thrillers with these chapters read between the railway station and home. We followed Mr. Reeve and his sleuth, Craig Kennedy, though magazine after magazine, until the formula wore thin. We have known that he was still sending Craig Kennedy out on murder-quests but this is the first of his yarns we have dipped into for years.

It begins with television and "rolang," which in Tibet means a corpse that dances; goes on to Aunt Cathie's "gompa" or temple of the occult near Oyster Bay; and in the third chapter lets the reader in on the secret that the Clutching Hand didn't die after all but was merely in suspended animation in Long Sin's subterranean chambers. Yawns began to punctuate our reading at this point and grew more frequent. We wonder whether Mr. Reeve has lost his grip or whether we have grown up. Better let The Clutching Hand rest in his glass coffin, Mr. Reeve![25]

24 Milton Propper, American detective fiction's most devoted follower of Alibi King Freeman Wills Crofts, tended to prove on the dull side for Downing, though he nevertheless recommends Propper's book to "those who like their murders straight."

25 Downing is actually thinking of *The Exploits of Elaine*, a 1914 film serial based on the Arthur B. Reeve book of the same name. Downing would have been twelve when he saw the film. *The Exploits of Elaine* starred Pearl White as the titular character, Elaine Dodge, and pitted her against "The Clutching Hand," considered the first "mystery villain" to appear in

NO HEADLINE
June 17, 1934, p. 51

THE POSTMAN ALWAYS RINGS TWICE, BY JAMES M. CAIN
OUR recent enthusiasm for Dashiell Hammett's *The Thin Man* was echoed by a friend who brings us now the work of another writer who doesn't agree with the time-honored dictum that fictional murders must be "nice." Mr. Cain's checkered career as a student, soldier, newspaperman and short story writer included, one would surmise, a rather intensive course in the one-syllable aspects of that thing called Life.

Centered about a hot-dog stand in southern California, the Greek proprietor, his wife and a young bum, the plot, as ye blurbist truthfully says, "rushes, plunges ahead." With three touches of gruesomeness that deserved our rereading: the dead man's echo; a sexual-vinous interlude; and this: "When I came out of it I was wedged down beside the wheel with my back to the front of the car, but I began to moan from the awfulness of what I heard. It was like the rain on a tin roof, but that wasn't it. It was her blood, pouring down on the hood, where she went through the windshield."

If they keep on, these *enfants terrible* who persist in thumbing their noses at the conventions of the genre, it is entirely possible that we shall have in a few years a definite school of realism in mystery fiction. And, after all, why not?—Todd Downing.[26]

film serials. This charming nostalgic review clearly reveals the powerful impact Downing's youthful immersion in thrillers had upon him. Downing may have outgrown Arthur B. Reeve's tales, but the hands of many other traditionalist thriller writers continue to clutch him. Arthur Benjamin Reeve (1880-1936) published eighty-two Professor Craig Kennedy stories between 1910 and 1918, earning Kennedy the perhaps over-generous sobriquet "the American Sherlock Holmes."

26 Noir pioneer James M. Cain (1892-1977) is best known for his novels *The Postman Always Rings Twice* (1934), *Mildred Pierce* (1941), and *Double Indemnity* (1943). Cain's detractors—who included, interestingly, Raymond Chandler—condemned the sexual seediness of the novels, but they made a great impression on critics and the lay public alike, both in print and in 1940s film adaptations. Though probably rather sheltered himself, Downing welcomes the possible arrival of "a definite school of realism in mystery

"MR. PINKERTON"
June 24, 1934, p. 47

MR. PINKERTON GOES TO SCOTLAND YARD, BY DAVID FROME

MR. Frome's timid little gray Welshman has become such a favorite with his inventor that the latter seems inclined to neglect his erstwhile sleuth, Inspector J. Humphrey Bull, who occupied the entire stage in *The Hammersmith Murders*. The domineering Mrs. Pinkerton has been removed from the scene, too, so that her once browbeaten spouse is now free to spend ninepence whenever he feels like it and to run with the hounds of Scotland Yard when occasion offers.

Mr. Pinkerton's latest exploit is the result of a conversation overheard on a Richmond park bench. "Do you think they're really feedin' 'er poison," asks Mrs. Higgins of Mrs. Richards. The latter agrees that old Mrs. Ripley is doubtless being done away with in this manner either by her son or one of her two daughters. It being a Bank Holiday, Mr. Pinkerton decides to investigate and uncovers quite a scandal in the Ripley family when the mother dies from arsenic poisoning. The old lady was quite a virago and had just signed a new will, so there are suspects aplenty.

Mr. Frome is one of the few writers of detective yarns who can infuse humor into his tales without aggravating the reader avid for clues. His characterization is excellent. Recommended for those who want a sane, entertaining yarn.—Todd Downing.[27]

"FAMILY AFFAIRS"
July 1, 1934, p. 53

EYES IN THE WALL, BY CAROLYN WELLS

FLEMING Stone again, dapper as ever, investigating the death of Mark Mason, art critic noted for his vitriolic pen, in the studio of

fiction," written by men familiar with what he suggestively terms "the one-syllable aspects of that thing called Life."

27 "David Frome" was a pseudonym of Zenith Jones Brown (1898-1983), wife of an English professor at St. John's College, Annapolis, Maryland.

Ellis Kane. Kane is competing for the commission to paint the portrait of a prominent philanthropist, as are several of his guests, including Ann Murdock, who belongs to a new school and is suspect number one until she is found dead in her bed in chapter eleven. Among the puzzlers: Who stepped on Mason's foot while the cocktails were being passed? Who sat next to whom? Who is in love with whom? Is Maggie, the cook, telling the truth about the black-mustached plumber who visited the basement the day before Ann died? What secret does Mrs. Grover, the landlady, know? And—is our detecatif going to fall for the fascinatingly wicked Lily Dana ("With an inward injunction to himself to be careful, Fleming Stone let himself go")? With strophanthin, anonymous letters and studio parties, Wells fans will like it.—Todd Downing.[28]

"MURDER TRAP"
July 8, 1934, p. 50

THE EMERALD MURDER TRAP, BY JACKSON GREGORY

ONE never knows what is going to come next from Mr. Gregory's typewriter. He alternates first-rate detective yarns with fast-moving westerns, with an occasional Stone Age love idyll thrown in. In this one he has returned (to this reviewer's pleasure) to his favorite sleuth, Mr. Paul Savoy, whose earlier exploits he recounted in *The House of the Opal* and *A Case for Mr. Paul Savoy*. Savoy, you will remember, is one of the more urbane sleuths, with less dilettantism than Philo Vance and more Olympianism than Reggie Fortune.

Mr. Gregory has let himself go a bit more in this than in previous bafflers and we have in fantastic mélange Sylvester

Between 1929 and 1950, she wrote fifteen David Frome tales of the doings of mild-mannered Mr. Pinkerton. In addition to these formal exercises in classical British detection, Brown as "Leslie Ford" published thirty-one mysteries, more in the psychological suspense thriller style of Mignon Eberhart.

28 "Wells fans will like it." Indeed.

Paradene, eccentric and sinister millionaire, and his guests in an isolated mountain mansion—the Lady Nepthys, daughter of Egypt, with night-black eyes; Maj. Harry Quoin, soldier of fortune; Hugo, dumb Negro; Amos Laufer-Hirth, jeweler who brings an emerald of fabulous value; Justine Jefferson, who lisps but can take care of herself—and, last but not least, Savoy and Gateway of the San Francisco homicide squad. The plot is about as wildly improbable as could have been concocted but Mr. Gregory evidently intended it to be just that. Some of the shivers are worthy of Edgar Wallace.—Todd Downing.[29]

NO HEADLINE

July 15, 1934, p. 49

CARTWRIGHT IS DEAD, SIR!, BY HUGH BAKER

IF you are skeptical about thrillers of which the publishers say, "You cannot lay it down until you have read the last page," try this one by a (to us) new author and be convinced that such yarns do exist.

Mr. Baker can write and he knows all the gadgets of the maritime mystery which Rufus King made popular. To mention but a few, there are: the fruit steamer *Napoc* en route from New Orleans to Puerto de Oro, somewhere in Central America; the quartermaster slumped in death beside the wheel; radio messages signed M. O. D. and threatening further disaster unless the ship's course is directed into unknown waters; death after death—the ship's doctor, the radio operator—from some inexplicable cause, as the orders of M. O. D. are disobeyed; the missing copper luck piece of the owner's daughter; seasick Mr. Saddler who cannot endure the smell of oranges and exotic Señora Alcobar singing the Shadow Song from *Dinorah*; some hard-boiled dialogue that would be a credit to Dashiell Hammett.

Set against a background of Central American politics and fruit company rivalries, it is that *rara avis* among detective

29 "[S]hivers . . . worthy of Edgar Wallace"—some of the highest praise that could come from Downing!

yarns—something different. The solution is no taller than most. We hope that Mr. Baker will continue to cultivate this field.—Todd Downing.[30]

NO HEADLINE
July 15, 1934, p. 49

DEATH IN THE STATE HOUSE, BY TIMOTHY KNOX

Factory-made baffler divulging dirty doings at the statehouse in an eastern capital. Governor Ransom is found in his private office late one night in the regulation position—slumped forward over his desk, with a knife protruding from the back of his neck. The governor, it seems, was quite a stepper at times, so besides Senator Ryder, political rival, we have as suspects Molly Shayne, alias Mrs. Merritt, in pink negligee; Theodore Manius, gambler, who knew Molly when; Doctor Kromback, who knows her now—when the governor is not in town; Podder Cottringer, blank-eyed gambler who wears a Stetson hat, and Mrs. Ransom, who does a bit of spying upon his honor when the latter is in one of his playful moods. With sleuthing by Van Brunner, superintendent of police, who spends his time trying to develop a new type of apple when not showing up the metropolitan cops. A clever solution saves it.—Todd Downing.[31]

30 Hugh Baker was a pseudonym of Hermann Baker Deutsch (1889-1970) and Donald Hugh Higgins (1891-1960). Deutsch was a native of Brux, Austria-Hungary, but grew up in Cincinnati, Ohio, where he moved with his family in 1891. After earning a Ph.D. (in botany) at the University of Chicago, Deutsch moved to New Orleans, where he became a prominent journalist. In addition to several novels, he published *The Huey Long Murder Case* (1963), a study of the assassination of the notorious populist Louisiana governor. His collaboration with Higgins, a shipboard mystery thriller, unsurprisingly induces an admiring Downing to invoke the sainted name of one of his favored mystery idols, Rufus King. On Deutsch, see the biographical note to the Hermann B. Deutsch Collection, Earl K. Long Library, University of New Orleans.

31 Timothy Knox was the pseudonym of journalists Elizabeth Read and Charles Fisher. Downing seems not have thought the late governor's steppings-out of much interest.

"RANSOM"
August 12, 1934, p. 43

RANSOM, BY CHARLES FRANCIS COE

IN that hard-fisted coterie whose specialty is the gangster yarn Coe's supremacy as a deft handler of lingo and plot is challenged, probably, only by Dashiell Hammett. While a suggestion of the Sunday school tract crops up in the philosophizing of Coe's characters and while retribution can be depended upon to follow misdeeds as unfailingly as in the detective story proper, the action is not slowed.

And action is the essence of *Ransom* as of *About 2 A.M.*, *The River Pirate* and other yarns which have appeared serially in the *Saturday Evening Post*. It is the story of one Alec Danvers, born and raised over his father's saloon and educated for life in a reform school. In time he plans the "perfect" kidnapping and executes it perfectly. He kidnaps a baby girl and sends her father part of her clothes, half of her ring and one set of her fingerprints. The same day he gives her to a German family to keep for him for two years. But the unexpected happens: He is convicted of another crime and thrown into a Canadian jail for twenty years. When he comes out he discovers that the underworld has changed, has been modernized and that the obtaining of the ransom money involves warfare with the gangs that are in the saddle. One of Coe's best stories.[32]

"SHE MET BILL"
August 19, 1934, p. 43

MYSTERY AND MINETTE, BY HERBERT ADAMS

"DID the temptation come to Minette as she lay in her bath, or had she really made up her mind days before?"

32 Charles Francis Coe (1890-1956) was a man of many talents: a Navy veteran, boxer, radio sports announcer, author of boxing and crime stories, screenwriter, attorney, and newspaper editor and publisher.

Minette is the daughter of the riding-master at Madame Sagesse's *Academie des Jeunes Filles* at Lyons and the temptation that assails her among the bath salts is the by no means novel one of impersonating a pupil of the academy and spending two glorious weeks with the latter's rich uncle and aunt from America. Follow kidnapping plots (kidnapping, by the way, is becoming a *sine qua non* of every mystery mongers' bag of tricks); robberies; roulette at Dinard; crystal gazing; envious hangers-on of the *nouveaux riches* Carters ("Carter's Catsup for Economy"); and, finally, Bill. As the blurbist puts it, "Minette incurred great risk, but without doing so she would never have met Bill."

Mr. Adams, you may remember, is the author of a whole string of first-rate detective yarns: *The Woman in Black*; *The Golf House Murder*; *The Strange Murder of Hatton, K. C.*, etc. While *Mystery and Minette* is entertaining reading for a hot summer afternoon, we hope that the author goes back to the detective story for his next.—Todd Downing.[33]

"HONEST BROKER SLAIN"
August 26, 1934, p. 45

Murder of the Honest Broker, by Willoughby Sharp

Curare, once popular fictional means of hastening the demise of *patres familias* about to sign new wills, has been frowned upon in recent years, along with venomous spiders, blowgun darts and Medici rings. It's like meeting a long lost friend, then, to find the erstwhile Brazilian standby playing a noxious part in an up-to-date mystery yarn. Up-to-the-minute, because the setting is Wall Street, which is becoming a favorite locale for murder. It's axiomatic with mystery writers that readers like to vent spleen vicariously upon the corpse, so what's more welcome these days than a nice, well-fed financier?

33 Evidently Downing found this lightweight mystery thriller by a favored author too lightweight to be very thrilling.

The brokers die within a few minutes of each other, one on the Stock Exchange, the other in an office on the Eleventh floor. The problem is how the poison entered their bloodstreams—by means of a pencil or an irate female's fingernails? The Canadian quintuplets, ticker tape and Jesuit priests who settled in Paraguay in 1605 come in for consideration by Inspector Bullock. The Inspector doesn't think much of detectives in fiction. "I'd like to run up against one of those mincing, namby-pamby, know-it-alls just once," says he. "Detectives! Bah!"

Mr. Sharp, in case you've forgotten, is the author of *Murder in Bermuda*. His next offering, already announced, bears the curiosity-arousing title *The Mystery of the Multiplying Mules*.—Todd Downing.[34]

"DEATH OF A BANKER"
August 26, 1934, p. 45

Death of a Banker, by Anthony Wynne

Intrigue in a Graustarkian kingdom on the Baltic, international banking and political theory combine to add color and a note of seriousness to Anthony Wynne's latest Doctor Hailey baffler. Doctor Hailey, as all fans know, is one of the most unobtrusive and at the same time versatile detectives in fiction. His words on capitalism and Communism may sound a bit Victorian but they are worthy of thought—and they bear directly on the question in hand, the murder of Hall, the international baker, at the Huythington Hunt.

Wynne must spend his entire time between books thinking up variants on the traditional sealed-chamber theme, one of the many gifts of Poe to mystery fiction. Here's his latest poser: The

34 "[W]hat's more welcome [as a murder mystery victim] these days," cuttingly asks Downing in the midst of the Depression-wracked 1930s, "than a nice, well-fed financier?" Former stockbroker Willoughby Sharp seems to have appreciated the temper of the times. (Sadly, however, *The Mystery of the Multiplying Mules* never actually appeared in print.)

victim is seen by 14 persons to jump his horse over a five-foot gate, gallop into the middle of a field and fall off. They rush to his side and find a hunting knife protruding between his shoulders. It has pierced his heart and he is dead—murdered at the spot. The knife couldn't have been part way in and then knocked through his heart in the fall, for there is almost no blood on his clothes; it couldn't have been thrown, for the nearest cover was too far away and Hall was in plain sight of witnesses. And yet a man with a knife through his heart couldn't jump a fence and ride a horse at a gallop. It is as neat and baffling a problem as Doctor Hailey and Colonel Wickham have ever been called on to solve. All in all, the sanest yarn that has come our way this summer.—Todd Downing.[35]

"THE DEAD MAN"
September 16, 1934, p. 47

THE DEAD MAN AT THE WINDOW, BY JEAN TOUSSAINT-SAMAT

THE second of M. Toussaint-Samat's novels to be translated into English (*Shoes That Had Walked Twice* was the other) but reaffirms out humble opinion that French mystery yarns, by all standards, are inferior to English and American products.

The opening pages of *The Dead Man at the Window* contain all the properties of horror and bafflement that the most exacting devotee of the genre could ask: an unidentified corpse among the chrysanthemums on a terrace in a small provincial town; naked footprints coming out of the sea; the moon at its full; and the discovery by M. Levert, Police Commissioner of

35 Downing's esteem for Anthony Wynne and the miracle problem remains as high as ever as he reviews his second Wynne novel of the year. He also deems Wynne's hostile opinions of both Communism and modern corporate capitalism "worthy of thought." On this latter aspect of Anthony Wynne's writing, see Curtis Evans, "*Death of a Banker* (1934), by Anthony Wynne," *The Passing Tramp*, at http://thepassingtramp.blogspot.com/2012/07/death-of-banker-1934-by-anthony-wynne.html.

Matigues, that within the past thirty years six others have died in the same place under the same circumstance—the moon always at its full.

But, as almost always happens in Gallic mysteries, the author's ingenuity fails and *dei ex machina* clutter the final pages—a journey to the wilds of South America in the company of a frail fair maiden whose mother is none other than the last Inca; jools buried under the altar of sacrifice in the Temple of the Moon Goddess; ancient curses and incantations of vengeful deities in a jumbled Inca, Aztec, Toltec pantheon. Love, theology and fishing lore add to the confusion.

We wish that some Francophile would come to the defense of the French mystery story and aid us in our benightment. So many French fans can't be wrong.—Todd Downing.[36]

"WAX FACE"

September 16, 1934, p. 47

THE MAN WITH THE WAX FACE, BY RICHARD WORMSER

MURDER in Wall Street, with this admonition from the author: "If this book has a hero, it is not Detective Sergeant Dixon. It is not any one man, but it is the whole New York police department: the two accountants going over the books at Graydon & Hanley; third grade Detective Cline kidding along Helene Mallin, telephone operator, and picking up little bits of information; Joyce, who was shortly destined to trail Marjory Ross, typist; and some 19,000 other men taking fingerprints, making photographs, patrolling beats."

Also John Linley of the *Daily Mail*, sleepy-eyed because the *Mail* has a rule against reporters drinking during business hours

36 Confronting this tale by Jean Toussaint-Samat, deemed "very French and very improbable" by *Kirkus Reviews* (12 July 1934), Downing finally begs some kindly "Francophile" to help him understand the popularity of modern French mysteries. He seems especially dismissive of Toussaint-Samat's "jumbled Incan, Aztec, Toltec pantheon."'

and he has to stay up most of the night making up for lost time; Erika Strindberg, Communist, of the staff of *Wall Street Inside Out* ("To hell with the proletariat!" yells Erika, drunk, in a Greenwich village nightclub, "My boyfriend's left me and I'm all alone!"); and Richard Sigfrid Wolf, who has gone into the jewelry business but who wants to be a detective. With what seems to be an authentic Centre Street atmosphere and Dashiell Hammett dialogue.—Todd Downing.[37]

"SECRET WAYS"
September 23, 1934, p. 21

SECRET WAYS, BY ANDREW SOUTAR

OUR first acquaintance with Mr. Soutar, who, it seems, is the author of a formidable list of yarns, including such intriguing titles as *The Hanging Sword*, *Kharduni*, and *Thirty Pieces of Silver*. *Secret Ways* is a decidedly intelligent detective novel which we recommend unhesitatingly to serious fans who like a considerable seasoning of Edgar Wallace atmosphere and who don't object to the young-lovers-separated-by-a-secret-sugar-coating to the all-important business of murder.

Fabricated on the standard lines of problem plus red herrings that successfully conceal the honest to goodness clues, the author has managed nevertheless to drag the aforementioned

37 What Downing emphasizes in *The Man with the Wax Face* is not the novel's puzzle plot, but its colorful characters (including Erika Strindberg, the soused and boyfriend-bereft Greenwich Village Communist), "Dashiell Hammett dialogue" and authentic police procedural detail. For its part, the *New York Times Book Review* (12 August 1934) noted that the cast of characters in *The Man with the Wax Face* "is thoroughly representative of the seamy side of New York. It includes racketeers, dope sellers and users, women of easy virtue or of no virtue at all, a drunken reporter, some Communists and other persons who . . . are at odds with law and order. . . . much too rough to be recommended for circulation in Sunday School libraries." Downing seems not to have minded. After two years at Princeton University, Richard Wormser (1908-1977) became a writer of pulp fiction (an estimated 300 short stories and 200 novelettes), detective

Clupeidae (as Philo Vance would say) across the path of the armchair sleuth in a novel and entertaining fashion. Old Judge Cringle is the unorthodox detective who solves the problem of the murder of Ambrose Merriman, diamond merchant, the missing jewels and the secret panel in the death chamber. The old judge is one of the most successful attempts by the purveyors of mystery fiction to create the lovable, doddering type of sleuth.

While some fans may find fault with the not infrequent carelessness of style and the resort to such a hackneyed device as a secret passage, they will be disposed to lenient.—Todd Downing.[38]

"THE NO. 1 LADY DETECTIVE"
September 30, 1934, p. 47

The Dorothy L. Sayers Omnibus, by Dorothy L. Sayers

When and if detective fiction establishes its right to the dignity of critical studies, some bespectacled student will find material for a thesis in the subject of femininity in the genre. For some reason (tradition probably) readers of mystery yarns are predominantly masculine (We are referring to the hardened fan who must have his fare of blood and bafflement as regularly as his morning coffee, not to the occasional reader who takes up a mystery for want of something better). It is a cause for some surprise, then, to find women producing consistently some of the very best work done in the field. Dorothy L. Sayers, Mary Roberts Rinehart, Mignon Eberhart, Agatha Christie, Carolyn

and western novels and Hollywood screenplays. Some of his crime stories were adapted into films, one of the best known of which is *The Big Steal* (1949). Wormser won two Spur Awards from the Western Writers of America and an Edgar in 1973 from the Mystery Writers of America for his paperback original novel *The Intruder*. Erika Strindberg, John Linley and Detective Sergeant Jocelyn "Joyce" Dixon feature in two Wormser detective novels, *The Man with the Wax Face* and its sequel, *The Communist's Corpse* (1935). Wormser engagingly told the story of his life in a post-humously published memoir, *How to Become a Complete Nonentity* (2006).

38 Andrew Soutar (1879-1941) was a prolific popular novelist.

Wells come at once to the mind of anyone at all acquainted with the literature of detection.

Miss Sayers is undoubtedly the most respected authority on the history of mystery fiction, her introduction to that masterpiece of anthology, *The Omnibus of Crime*, being the most comprehensive essay on the subject. Since 1923 she has been writing highly successful novels: her favorite sleuth, Lord Peter Wimsey, shares with Philo Vance and Reggie Fortune the honors in the dilettante tradition.

The omnibus idea seems to be growing in popularity—and if anyone deserves such an honor it is Miss Sayers. Here we have three full-length novels which have been read and enjoyed by thousands of her admirers and a perusal of which is a treat that no fan should miss. *Whose Body?* subtitled *The Singular Affair of the Man with the Golden Pince-Nez*, was her first venture into the field and introduced Lord Peter. *The Unpleasantness at the Bellona Club*, published in 1928, reveals Lord Peter in his full stride, solving the mystery of the death of George Fentiman's uncle at the fireside. *Suspicious Characters*, which came out in 1931, poses the neat little problem of Campbell, the landscape painter, who the doctors say has been dead 10 or 12 hours, although he was seen painting only a few hours before the discovery of his body.

From the standpoint of either quantity or quality, as good a buy as the fans will find.—Todd Downing.[39]

39 This prescient review of work by the great English Crime Queen Dorothy L. Sayers speculates that in the future there will be scholarly interest in the subject of the rise of female crime writers (how true indeed!). In contravention of modern-day critical wisdom, Downing asserts that the most devout mid-1930s mystery readers are "predominantly masculine" (I think Downing was right on this), yet he declares that women writers produce "some of the very best work done in the field" (his list of the women writers consists of, besides Sayers, Agatha Christie, Mary Roberts Rinehart, Mignon Eberhart and, surprisingly, Carolyn Wells). Although he probably preferred Christie, Rinehart and Eberhart to Sayers, Downing clearly was greatly impressed with Sayers' critical writing on the mystery genre, and here he takes the opportunity to pay tribute to her as "the most respected authority on the history of mystery fiction."

"WHO KILLED IT?"
October 21, 1934, p. 49

THE CLUE OF THE DEAD GOLDFISH, BY VICTOR MCCLURE

SCOTLAND Yard puzzler in the leisurely yet dead-serious Freeman Wills Crofts–Austin Freeman manner. Inspector Burford is the debonair young sleuth who wrestles with the problem presented by the discovery of the charred body of the young engineer in the debris of his burnt-out drawing office. The doctor confirms the inspector's suspicion that a bullet was the cause of death. As the blurbist truthfully says: "The whole case is presented in the first chapter and then Burford's careful investigations follow step-by-step." The young man's partner is missing so qualifies as suspect number one. Geraldine, young charmer who lives in the house on the hill, saw the fire first and gave the alarm (although somewhat tardily). The inspector, being of sterner stuff than the reader, is not averse to questioning the fair Geraldine about the squashed goldfish found by a lily-pond and about her relations with the young engineers.

No frills or thrills, but then a large number of fans seem to like them that way. Mr. McClure will be remembered as the author of *The Counterfeit Murders* and *Death Behind the Door*.—Todd Downing.[40]

"STAGE MURDER"
October 21, 1934, p. 49

DEATH IN THE THEATER, BY J. R. WILMOT

THE play was "The Ace of Diamonds" at the Phoenix Theater and Inspector McNeeve of Scotland Yard went there at the recommendation of a waiter at Peter Pepper's. "I've heard, sir," says

40 Victor Maclure (1883-1967) was an English writer who veered into mystery for a time in the 1930s, producing seven mysteries, probably the best known of which were *Death Behind the Door* and *Death on the Set*. Downing places *The Clue of the Dead Goldfish* in the "leisurely yet dead-serious category" of Freeman Wills Crofts and R. Austin Freeman, concluding that while no "frills or thrills" are offered, "a large number of fans seem to like them that way."

the waiter, "that it's drawing crowded houses. A crook play, I believe it is, sir—deals with jewel robberies."

So we have Inspector McNeeve sitting in a well-upholstered seat in the stalls when the curtain goes up on act one of *The Ace of Diamonds*. His contempt for fictional crime and its counterpart, the stage presentation, has a considerable jolt when the man in the stall next to his is found dead at the end of the act. The doctor suggests heart failure but the Inspector has other ideas and is engaged in following them up when he is poisoned. Scotland Yard finds that the identity of the murderer is tangled up with the problem of the missing jewels, which may or may not be somewhere about the theater. For some reason or other we found ourselves more interested in the location of the jewels than in the identity of the criminal.

Mr. Wilmot has written a yarn that is well above the average. He is unfortunate in that two masters have preceded him among the grease paint and footlights—Ellery Queen in *The Roman Hat Mystery* and Agatha Christie more recently in *Murder in Three Acts*.—Todd Downing.[41]

41 Downing concedes that this detective novel by James Reginald Wilmot (1897-?) was "well above the average"—but then he undermines this concession by declaring it inferior to Ellery Queen's and Agatha Christie's theatrical mystery efforts (this is setting a high bar). Interestingly, the *New York Times* reviewer positively gushed over the novel (23 September 1934). "Seldom does the novel of detection contain as liberal, satisfying and ingenious entertainment as this one affords," he declared. "The book has about everything that the exacting mystery addict could demand—high-keyed suspense, exciting action, freshness of plot, novelty of crime problem, first-rate sleuthing and excellently portrayed characters." Wilmot was a prolific mystery writer under his pseudonym "Ralph Trevor." Unfortunately, the Ralph Trevor mysteries are regarded as mere hack-work. Under the Ralph Trevor pseudonym, Wilmot published thirty mysteries in the eight years from 1935 through 1942, yet under his own name he wrote merely one additional mystery, *Night Tide* (1936). None of these titles were reprinted in the United States. The *New York Times Book Review* proclaimed Wilmot "a master of the mystery craft whose work one should hope to see frequently hereafter." What we saw more was Ralph Trevor.

"BLIND BARBER"
November 4, 1934, p. 51

THE BLIND BARBER, BY JOHN DICKSON CARR

"MR. Carr can lead us away from the small, artificial, brightly-lit stage of the ordinary detective plot into the menace of outer darkness. He can create atmosphere with an adjective . . . alarm with an illusion or delight with a rollicking absurdity. . . . In short he can write." So stated unequivocally no less an authority than Dorothy L. Sayers. And far be it for us to dispute her.

Those who read and liked his *The Eight of Swords* and wondered if this were but a brilliant flash in the pan can now rest assured of having another standby to fall back upon when others disappoint.

In *The Blind Barber* Mr. Carr jams his tongue into his cheek and propels the reader headfirst into as intricate, baffling and subtly worked-out a plot as ever Harry Stephen Keeler concocted. The action transpires on board a transatlantic liner, with our old friend Henry Morgan, detective story writer, Peggy Glenn, secretary to a marionette maker, Curtis Warren, nephew of a certain Great Personage in the U. S. A., and Captain Valvick, Norwegian ex-skipper, all entangled in a comedy of terrors which involves stolen moving picture film and a stolen emerald elephant, champagne, bug-powder guns and The Song of Roland. The murder and Dr. Fell's armchair deductions as to the Blind Barber's identity are, we must admit, rather incidental to the fun-making, but there are bits of as grisly frozen horror as the most hardened fan could ask.

The Blind Barber is one that we're planning to read again.—Todd Downing.[42]

42 For Dorothy L. Sayers' review of John Dickson Carr's *The Mad Hatter Mystery* (1933), quoted above, see the *Sunday Times* (24 September 1933). Carr's combination of "intricate, baffling and subtly worked-out" plot with bits of "grisly frozen horror" naturally proved irresistible to Downing.

"VISITING VILLAIN"
November 4, 1934, p. 51

THE VISITING VILLAIN, BY CAROLYN WELLS

ECCENTRICITIES are always to be expected, of course, in a corpus delecti, when the latter happens to have been a millionaire with a will and heirs in the offing; yet Bruce Dunbar, in Miss Wells' latest baffler, is our nomination for the most obliging when it comes to furnishing motive, opportunity and clues.

In the first place, he keeps a pet cobra (fangs not extracted) in his bedroom. When his valet finds him dead in bed, with two little red marks on his neck, a member of the household remarks casually over a cocktail: "He'd probably gone to bed and was playing with his pet, perhaps playing a little flute." The benevolent old fellow had three nieces and a nephew, all with an eye on his cash, and he insisted on their coming to Saturday night dinners with him, upon which occasion he would whisper to each that he or she was going to inherit.

After the slaughter (Fleming Stone does some millimeter measuring and finds that Streamline's fangs couldn't have made the red marks) three lawyers turn up with as many wills made by Dunbar on the same afternoon, each leaving his fortune to a different niece and each invalidating the former will in favor of the nephew. "For Heaven's sake!—well—well!" muses Stone and, after a "pleasantly selected and carefully prepared dinner" proceeds to unmask the fiend. It's a relief when a cop gives vent to a good, rotund "Hell!"—Todd Downing.[43]

"LAUGHING CORPSE"
November 4, 1934, p. 51

A GIRL DIED LAUGHING, BY VIOLA PARADISE

WE were rather surprised to see a serious-minded friend who is inclined to cast a kindly yet paralyzing eye upon our weakness

43 According to Downing, Carolyn Wells reaches new heights (depths?) of sublime daftness in *The Visiting Villain*.

in the direction of mystery fiction, glance over the first chapter of this one and plunge on to the end without looking up. Impressed, we waited our turn, and found ourselves just as engrossed.

The reason is a simple one—there is simply no stopping place. Miss Paradise, whose first mystery yarn this is, knows how to tell a tale without useless expenditure of words. The plot is so intricate, yet so close-knit, that the reader is hurried on from page to page and from chapter to chapter almost without his knowledge. On close inspection, some of the properties are decidedly stage-worn, but this makes no difference during the reading. Even the usual young-lover-falsely-accused is characterized so well that one finds oneself interested in his fate and afraid that everything will not turn out all right in the end. Young Joey, the bellhop, seemed in the way at first, but soon proved himself as essential to the goings-on as District Attorney Alby.

The corpse is a girl with violet eyes, found lying in a pool of her own blood in the apartment of a couple who claimed never to have seen her before. Sheridan Dinard, young archaeologist, had heard the girl's laughter cut off suddenly as he waited in the hall for his fiancée. Recommend for those who demand sanity in their mystery fiction.—Todd Downing.[44]

"THE GOLDEN HOARD"
December 2, 1934, p. 53

THE GOLDEN HOARD, BY EDWIN BALMER AND PHILIP WYLIE

LEAVING their star-wanderers marooned on far Bronson Beta, these prolific contributors take time off to spin a yarn in lighter vein, a tale of love and murder and not much else.

44 Like Todd Downing's sister, Ruth, Viola Isabel Paradise (1887-1980) was a social worker. After graduating from the University of Chicago in 1908, Paradise worked at Jane Addams' famous Hull House. She was a co-founder of the Immigrants' Protective League, which assisted immigrants in adjusting to life in the United States. Paradise published numerous sympathetic articles on immigrants in American magazines, and she also wrote novels and plays. Though she lived for over four decades after the

The corpse is Horace Denslow, aged eccentric who has exchanged all his wealth for gold and then sped by plane to his Georgia estate to cache it. His attorney learns of a plot to plunder the plane and kill the occupants. He attempts to reach Denslow by phone but can establish communication only with Linda Telfair, daughter of one of those poor but proud Georgia families one reads about. Linda goes to the Denslow house, sees a masked man descend the stairs, find a corpse in the library and another in a tree, and on the floor a torn message incriminating none other than Gregory, son of the dead man and object of Linda's affections. Old Lucius, Negro servant, sees men digging in the swamp by moonlight and finds a conjure stone that may be something else.

Our complaint is not with *The Golden Hoard*. It is told in the smooth Balmer-Wylie manner and makes easy and entertaining reading. But a dozen other mystery writers could have done as well or better. We belong to that group of readers (and we aver there are many of us) who impatiently scan news and bookstands for a sequel to *When Worlds Collide* and *After Worlds Collide*. With our imaginations still with Eve and Tony on Bronson Beta, doings on a Georgia plantation seem unimportant.—Todd Downing.[45]

"PLENTY GORE"
December 2, 1934, p. 53

The Family Burial Murders, by Milton Propper

Mr. Propper has built up quite a following among mystery fans since he clicked with *The Strange Disappearance of Mary Young*. If we are unable to work up much enthusiasm about his Philadelphia yarns it is because there is, to our way of thinking, too much minutiae. A detailed description of the furniture of a room

well-received *A Girl Died Laughing* appeared (when she was 47), Paradise never published another detective novel.

45 As Downing indicates, the best-known collaboration of writers Edwin Balmer (1883 to 1959) and Philip Wylie (1902-1971) was the acclaimed apocalyptic science fiction novel *When Worlds Collide* (1933) (there was also a 1934 sequel, *After Worlds Collide*).

in which the reader remains but a few minutes only serves to retard the action and to tempt the reader to skip pages—and the reader who skips pages is lost to the writer of mystery fiction.

Tommy Rankin, human and not incapable of committing precipitate arrests, is confronted with a gruesome and baffling situation when the body of David Hutton is discovered in the loose earth beside his aunt's newly made grave in the Greenlawn cemetery, West Philadelphia. With his usual attention to detail Tommy sets to work on the problem and discovers discrepancies in the alibis of several suspects (one of them necessitates the reader's concentration upon the timetables of the Reading railroad and the Lehigh Valley Transit Co. between Philadelphia and Allentown) and scraps of paper reading: "436223217" and "Honey, I can't tell you how excited I am about this little trip of ours to Montreal together."—Todd Downing.[46]

"CHIANTI FLASK"
December 9, 1934, p. 48

MURDER CALLING, BY DAVID WHITELAW

"WHY," demands Mr. Whitelaw, "drag in the members of such a hard working body of men as those of Scotland Yard, pitchfork them into a story and slaughter their reputations to make a reader's holiday? Why make these admirable public servants the butt of more or less gifted amateurs, dilettante gentlemen who mix up their criminology with mild philosophies, platitudes, cheap cynicism and wisecracks?" So he proceeds forthwith to write a mystery yarn without a sleuth, amateur or otherwise.

The first corpse is that of an unidentified man found in Regent's canal; the second, of a mysterious individual posing as Stephen Droon of Tiflis, Pernambuco, Delgoa Bay and Bechuanaland. With

46 The emphasis of Milton Propper upon what Downing deems "minutiae" prevents Downing from working up "much enthusiasm" about Propper's "Philadelphia yarns." Downing's complaint about a superfluity of detail about room furnishings in detective novels has been echoed by critics of the modern four-hundred-page-plus detective novel, as typified by a currently reigning British Crime Queen, P. D. James.

the inventiveness of another Edgar Wallace, the author sweeps the reader into a maelstrom of excitement, to whose maw contribute the subterranean activities of Archie Bates and his partner in nefariousness, Rhoda Fraser, alias Gourlay; a white-faced woman in the shrubbery of Wynd Marches; love in the Great Horton Flying Club; and abduction in a lonely house on Romney Marsh (Since Dorothy L. Sayers wrote so harshly of them, mystery writers have been constrained to abandon lonely houses on English marshes. We hope that this marks their return to popularity).

Hypercritical readers may think there is too much straining for shuddery effects, but we—for one—liked it.—Todd Downing.[47]

"CHIANTI FLASK"
December 9, 1934, p. 48

The Chianti Flask, by Marie Belloc Lowndes

Not since Rufus King's *Murder by the Clock*, has there come into our hands a mystery novel—avowedly such—with the restraint, the subtlety of character analysis of *The Chianti Flask* (Cora Jarrett's *Night Over Fitch's Pond*, the publishers and the author insisted, did not belong in this category—causing one to inquire: when is a novel of murder not a murder novel?).

The Chianti Flask is a murder story, most readers will say, only because it deals with violent death and because the identity of the culprit is in doubt until the end. It is the story of Laura Dousland's trial for the poisoning of her husband, of her speedy acquittal and of her ill-starred love for Mark Scrutton, the young doctor who testified on her behalf. Thus baldly put, the novel would seem to be but another of those lachrymose courtroom dramas that have recently enjoyed much popularity. But it is more than that. Mrs. Belloc-Lowndes' interest lies in the bitter psychological aspects of murder: she is an astute interpreter of human nature and her pen is a scalpel, bright and relentlessly sharp, as she

47 David Whitelaw (1875-1970) was a prolific English thriller writer, better known in England than in the United States. Comparing Whitelaw's inventiveness to that of his beloved Edgar Wallace, Downing gives *Murder Calling* a rave.

removes layer after layer of the sophistication and hypocrisy of her characters. The unholy fascination of the process should compensate the reader for the absence of those elements which may not after all be essentials of a murder novel—clues and red herrings and an omniscient detective.—Todd Downing.[48]

"FOR THE HANGMAN"
December 16, 1934, p. 42

FOR THE HANGMAN, BY JOHN STEPHEN STRANGE

BALTIMORE, recently discovered by writers as "a pleasant and inexpensive place to live," is the scene for the latest baffler by the author of *The Strangler Fig* and other yarns, all of them eminently sane and satisfactory. Boyd Jenkins, contributor to the *Baltimore Scurrilities*, scandal sheet, is found shot to death in the vestibule of Mrs. Henry Clapp (of the Baltimore Clapps). There are motives and suspects galore so that Mordaunt Peel, Mrs. Strange's favorite sleuth, is hard put to it to solve the riddles of the anonymous pink letters ("Ask Jenkins what he knows about *Madame Butterfly*"), the broken watch chain, the elusive man in the brown coat and the illustrated lecture on Soviet Russia by a man who hadn't been there. A puzzler for fans: Why should a man purchase an outboard motor costing $92.85 and pay for it in stamps? The second murder is satisfactorily gory. This is the current Crime Club selection.—Todd Downing.[49]

48 Though Downing does not use the term in his review, *The Chianti Flask* is a "crime novel"—a novel where, as Downing puts it, the author's "interest lies in the bitter psychological aspects of murder." Though today remembered almost exclusively for her much-filmed Jack-the-Ripper novel *The Lodger* (1913), Marie Adelaide Belloc Lowndes (1868-1947), a sister of writer Hillaire Belloc, is an important figure in the development of the psychological crime novel. Important titles by her include *The Chink in the Armor* (1912)—along with *The Lodger* highly praised by Ernest Hemingway—*The End of Her Honeymoon* (1913), *What Really Happened* (1926), *The Story of Ivy* (1927), *Letty Lynton* (1931) and *Lizzie Borden: A Study in Conjecture* (1939).

49 "John Stephen Strange" was the pseudonym of Dorothy Stockbridge Tillett (1896-1983), the wife of William Smith Tillett (1892-1974), a prominent

NO HEADLINE
Dec. 23 1934, p. 47

Death Rides the Air Line, by William Sutherland

An unusual structural design sets this apart from the usual run of mystery novels and makes it well worth the attention of the fan who appreciates good writing and who is more interested in characterization than in clues.

Walter Schlaf, president of Metropolitan Newspapers, Inc., is stabbed in the cabin of an air liner making its scheduled journey between Boston and Newark. Six passengers are on board, as well as the pilot and co-pilot. Which one murdered Sclhaf?

At this point Sutherland leaves Detective Inspector Grady to his routine investigations and gives the reader flashbacks into the pasts of the principal suspects, somewhat in the manner of *Lightship* and other recent successes. Schlaf himself, unscrupulous opportunist; Judge Dewitt, whose staid life has known but one interlude of passion; Marguerite Rose, in the corner drug store, in a business office, in a burlesque show and finally in a Rolls-Royce; Tim Cowley, gangster; and Gus Jensen, who left an Indiana farm for adventure in the air; strangely the lives of each have become interlocked with that of Schalf. Had the author not insisted upon the beginning and the ending of a mystery yarn, *Death Rides the Air Line* would have been a capital novel of manners.—Todd Downing.[50]

physician and medical researcher. Between 1929 and 1962 she produced twenty-one mystery novels, followed by a last tale in 1976. Downing deems her tales "eminently sane and satisfactory," meaning that they offered an emphasis on puzzles, solidly constructed in the classic tradition.

50 *Lightship* (1934), by Archie Binns, was described in the *New York Times Book Review* (August 26, 1934) as a novel about "the lives of nine men cooped up together on a ship heaving eternally to the sea, yet never getting anywhere." In recommending *Death Rides the Air Line* to fans "more interested in characterization than clues" Downing was taking note of a demographic that was to become increasingly important among mystery genre readers in the 1930s. Yet Downing himself seems somewhat dubious about commingling the detective novel and the "novel of manners," something Dorothy L. Sayers called for with ever more urgency over the course of the 1930s.

CHAPTER FOUR: 1935 REVIEWS

"PROBABLY TALKED TO DEATH"

January 13, 1935, p. 45

MURDER WITHOUT WEAPON, BY MEANS DAVIS

A LATE entrant in the ether and scalpel division, Mr. Davis keeps on with hospital mysteries, which, the fans will recall, enjoyed quite a flurry of popularity not so long ago. We missed his debut with *The Hospital Murders* and so opened this one with interest.

The opening chapters bewildered us but after we got over the shock of meeting Miss Violet Jowett (exophthalmic goiter), her maiden sister Dolly (angina pectoris), their niece Eva (sent to the psychiatric clinic in Chapter 4) and Peter, the nephew (sobering up with the aid of a stomach pump) and after Dr. Hall-Simpson explained to us that "the nastiest thing in the world and when coupled with immense wealth the strongest single force among English-speaking peoples" is life-long virginity, things went more smoothly. Dolly dies screaming "Vi's eyes!" and subsequent chapters are entitled "She Saw Something," "Lil Parkins Says She Saw It," "The Wildcat Sees It Too" and "Everybody Sees It."

Sleuthing is in charge of Matt Higgins (undergoing cystoscopic treatment) and his assistants Snod Smooty and Lil Parkins. We recommend this trio—they don't talk like most of the detectives one reads about.

Mr. Davis has what critics call a vigorous style, although in our opinion it needs, like Peter, an occasional sobering douche.

We liked "sudden gusts of terror, like darting sharks beneath a summer sea"; were so-so about "his voice tiptoed into her intensity"; and blinked at "her eyes glowed like ripe olives."

Recommended for those who liked Mignon Eberhart's *From This Dark Stairway*.—Todd Downing.[1]

"MURDERED TWICE"
January 27, 1935, p. 49

CRIMSON ICE, BY CORTLAND FITZSIMMONS

FITZSIMMONS (he looks like a college professor) created quite a furor among the fans with his mélange of football and murder in *70,000 Witnesses*. Next he turned his attention to baseball with *Death on the Diamond*. Now it's hockey, "scientific mayhem on skates," he calls it. During the game between the Blue Devils from Quebec and the Boston Cougars, Gaston Lemaire, star player of the Canadians, falls dead on the ice. There's a knife in his back, but the Doc suspects poison. A neat problem having been posed, Fitzsimmons seems rather hard put to fill up 300 pages of the book and resorts to the young lover falsely accused, a bright-faced juvenile sleuth and a hunt for a gold mine in Arizona with ferocious redskins guarding the secret of their people. One good touch: the powdered ice turned pink as a colored snowball by the blood. For hockey addicts only.—Todd Downing.[2]

1 Means Davis was actually a woman, Augusta Tucker Townshend (1904-1999). She wrote three mystery novels: *The Hospital Murders* (1934); *Murder without Weapon* (1935) and *The Chess Murders* (1937). Seventy-five years after Downing's review of the novel, Bill Pronzini pronounced *Murder without Weapon* "awful." See *Mystery*File*, 13 June 2010 http://mysteryfile.com/blog/?p=2119. In Downing's defense, let us allow that, his weakness for Rinehart-Eberhart thrills and chills notwithstanding, he wryly conceded that Means Davis' "vigorous style" needed, like the character Peter, "an occasional sobering douche."

2 Downing once again deems a Cortland Fitzsimmons tale ho-hum. The presence of "ferocious redskins guarding the secret of their people" probably did not enhance the book's appeal for Downing.

"ASSORTED CORPSES"
February 10, 1935, p. 49

CRIME AT CHRISTMAS, BY C. H. B. KITCHIN

MR. Kitchin, author of the successful *Death of My Aunt*, makes a belated return to a mystery field a bit satiated with bickering relatives and house parties in English estates. Malcolm Warren, the previous narrator, here appears as the guest of the financier Quisberg. On Christmas morning he wakes to find the body of the mother of his host's secretary impaled upon the railing of the balcony outside his window. With the aid of Inspector Parris (who says: "I am dying for some tea") he does some leisurely sleuthing, finds another corpse in the bracken and is present at some startling last chapter revelations.

The plot is satisfactory enough but the reader is likely to lose patience with Warren's frequent soliloquies, with the propensity of the guests to faint and with the author's fidelity in quoting Mr. Quisberg: "de deat(h) of de moder of my poor little secretary."—Todd Downing.[3]

"SERIOUS MURDER"
February 17, 1935, p. 53

THE UNFINISHED CRIME, ELISABETH SANXAY HOLDING

FOLLOWERS of Mrs. Belloc Lowndes should make the acquaintance of Mrs. Holding forthwith. Having missed her earlier opus, *The Death Wish*, we were unprepared for the unconventionality of her

3 Clifford Henry Benn Kitchin (1895-1967) was an independently wealthy gay author of modernist novels, as well as four detective stories starring as the lead character/amateur detective stockbroker Malcolm Warren: *Death of My Aunt* (1929), *Crime at Christmas* (1934), *Death of His Uncle* (1939) and *The Cornish Fox* (1949). Downing seems something less than enraptured with *Crime at Christmas*, faulting the novel for, among other things, its clichéd country house part setting and its determinedly self-absorbed lead character. However, a number of other critics then and since have applauded Kitchin's tales of detection for their novelistic qualities

technique, the feminine subtlety of her characterization and her masculine realism—the latter not unakin to the Faulkner–Caldwell school of shock.

There are lacking here practically all the ingredients of the detective yarn: fingerprints, weapons, alibis, a detective even. There is no doubt as to the identity of the criminal, the reader watching him as he plots and executes his deeds. Yet the psychological reactions driving Andrew Branscombe, gentleman of leisure and litterateur, from a normal humdrum life to desperate emotions and acts furnish a suspense that is seldom accomplished in the who-did-it? tale. There are scenes of realistic Medicean horror that will make even the Dashiell Hammett addict blink.

The Unfinished Crime is recommended enthusiastically to those fans who crave variety and to those scoffers who say that the mystery novel cannot attain depth.—Todd Downing.[4]

"WEIRD CLUES"
February 17, 1935, p. 53

DEATH BLEW OUT THE MATCH, BY KATHLEEN MOORE KNIGHT

WHEN the Crime Club judges recommend this one for February, they don't go far wrong. It's quite the best of the current output, as far as we are concerned, and should not be missed by those

and air of everyday realism. In particular, *Death of My Aunt* has been deemed a genre classic by, for example, Jacques Barzun and H. R. F. Keating.

4 Though we might quibble at Downing's binary categories of "feminine subtlety of characterization" and "masculine realism," his praise of the work of Elisabeth Sanxay Holding (1889-1955) is acute, as is his coupling of her name with Marie Belloc Lowndes. Holding's eighteen mystery genre novels, published between 1929 and 1953, are notable early efforts in realistic, psychological crime fiction. Again revealing his sensitivity about "scoffers who say that the mystery novel cannot attain depth," Downing suggests these anti-mystery highbrows give Holding a look. His mention of "the Faulkner-Caldwell school of shock" references the recently published, highly controversial William Faulkner novel *Sanctuary* (1931) and Erskine Caldwell's then scandalous *Tobacco Road* (1932) and *God's Little Acre* (1933).

fans who like the homespun characters of Phoebe Atwood Taylor and the tenseness of Mignon Eberhart's plots.

The narrative is by Anne Waldron, erstwhile copy-writer who is spending a vacation in a cottage on the Cape Cod Island of Penberthy. Miss Knight maintains a fast pace throughout and manages to cram into her pages more than the usual number of thrills, including the customary corpse (Marya Van Wyck, playwright, found in the living room of her summer home); strange signal lights flashed from the sea; abduction; assault and battery upon Wing Lo, the Chinese cook; and—oh, yes—an innocuous enough love affair. The solution will probably catch the most practiced follower of clues napping. Watch the silver buckle upon the window sill, the burnt match in the corpse's fingers and the wad of gum on the floor.—Todd Downing.[5]

"WHO KILLED COWDIN?"
March 1, 1935, p. 73

THE WHIP-POOR-WILL MYSTERY, BY HULBERT FOOTNER

MR. Footner is at his best when he leaves Madame Storey and her sleuthing and lets himself go in a rapid-fire adventure yarn, such as this one.

Who cares who murdered Lee Cowdin, scion of an aristocratic Maryland family? We know it wasn't his daughter Leila, although she was found nailing together his coffin on the upper floor of the old house with the Corinthian pillars. We know it wasn't young Wier Lambert, Yankee editor of the *Kent County Witness*, who followed up the advertisement in his paper: "Personal, the whip-poor-will: I am alone. Come to me. I need help. The girl on the hill."

5 Kathleen Moore Knight (1890-1984) published nearly forty mystery novels between 1935 and 1960. The Elisha Macomber series, which ran from 1935 to 1959, accounted for sixteen of the Knight tales, including *Death Blew out the Match* (though Downing does not mention by name the "homespun" sleuth Macomber). Today she is much overshadowed by that other Golden Age Cape Cod local color mystery writer, Phoebe Atwood

The questions that keep the night-light burning are: Will the bloodhounds get Wier and Leila in the swamp? What saved Wier from the clutches of the night-riders? Will Frank Baer, the sheriff, choose between friendship for Wier and adherence to duty?

Although it sounds familiar, you'll probably read it and like it.[6]

"ON THE GREEN"
March 1, 1935, p. 73

The Body in the Bunker, by Herbert Adams

Mr. Adams, author of *The Golf House Murder*, has evidently found a following among golf addicts, for he appears with yet another yarn of evil doings on the green. It begins at 9 o'clock on a Monday morning, which is all to the good, for we can't think of a better time for murder. Stuart Slade's ball rolls into a deep bunker. He follows it up and finds it nestling against the elbow of a corpse. He is a suspect, of course, as well as other members of the Barrington Golf club. The remainder is routine stuff, including the complication, amorous and otherwise, brought about by Sylvia Wilston, divorced wife of the deceased. Sleuthing by Simon Ross, young barrister on holiday.

If we can't honestly recommend this except to golfers, it doesn't mean that it isn't a baffler as good as the average. We got along very well by skipping a great deal that was incomprehensible to us (including the entire first chapter). We wish that Mr.

Taylor, (1909-1976), yet Knight in her own right was a notable Golden Age regional crime novelist. What Downing seems to admire in Knight's novel is not so much the local color, however, as the quirky clues and, especially, the "fast pace" of the narrative, which reminds him of one of his favorite mystery writers, Mignon Eberhart.

6 The years from 1918 and 1945 saw the publication of over forty detective novels and crime thrillers by William Hulbert Footner (1879-1944). Today he is best known for his series detective Madame Rosika Storey (who appeared in both novels and short stories), though later in his career he dropped her and introduced another detective, Amos Lee Mappin. He also wrote a good number of standalone mysteries, often more in the nature of thrillers, to which Downing alludes.

Adams would do another tense courtroom yarn like *The Woman in Black*.—Todd Downing.[7]

"NIGHTMARE HORRORS"
March 1, 1935, p. 73

I AM YOUR BROTHER, BY GABRIEL MARLOWE

UNHERALDED, a new invoker of horror makes his debut with a tale which, unless we are badly mistaken, will take its place beside *Dracula*, *Frankenstein* and *The Werewolf of Paris*. The publishers profess to know nothing of Mr. Marlowe other than that he is a musician who has lived in London and can write with astonishing vigor and subtlety. This much, they say, they have learned from the internal evidence of the book.

It is the story of the brilliant composer Julian, who lives in a house with his mother and—upstairs in the attic, his presence unsuspected at first—another. The heavy tread upon the attic boards heralds the madness that approaches just as Julian is reaching the height of his powers.

For effect the author has not depended alone on the eternal fascination of the nightmare country between sanity and madness. With nice discrimination he had added bits of undigested realism demanded by the "Werewolf" public and has given the whole a note of uncanny fantasy by juxtaposition with the lives of a troupe of music hall artists. His style is singularly like that of Virginia Woolf.

After page 64 we deliberately opiated our conscience and took a peek at the last page.—Todd Downing.[8]

7 Today golf mysteries are a highly collectible sub-genre, but there was altogether too much golf in this tale for Downing. However, I once came across a copy of Miles Burton's *Tragedy at the Thirteenth Hole* (1933) that was filled with marginalia from a disgruntled reader carping about the author's technical errors in his portrayal of golfing—so evidently some readers took the golf in detective novels quite seriously!

8 *I am Your Brother* made something of a cult sensation on its appearance in 1935, yet its author, Gabriel Marlowe, remains shrouded in mystery, allegedly having disappeared in Norway in 1940 during the Nazi invasion (Marlowe

"WEIRD DOINGS"
March 1, 1935, p. 73

BULLDOG DRUMMOND AT BAY, BY H. C. MCNEILE ("SAPPER")
TOPS in the gentleman amateur division go unanimously to Hugh "Bulldog" Drummond, as far as we are concerned. And now that "successors to Edgar Wallace" are being touted on every hand, we venture to nominate for this honor Bulldog's creator, Mr. McNeile.

The high-hat classic detective novel looks askance at certain devices as shop-worn. Anything goes in the thriller. A lonely house in the English countryside; out of the night a stone wrapped in a blood-stained paper bearing the message "Mary Jane. Urgent. G. G. Pont. A-3"; a lovely damsel who unexpectedly flavors our hero's tea with a sleeping potion; tension in the chancelleries of Europe; stabbings in Genoa and in the Harwich-Hook of Holland boat and missing submarine drawings; a secret society, the Key Club; a brand-new torture in a rat-infested dungeon; an occasional cliché which will make seasoned readers of this fare grow reminiscent. Just about all the essential ingredients of an A-1 thriller are present in the current Crime Club Selection. We recommended it heartily for the left wing of the fans.—Todd Downing.[9]

supposedly was Jewish). See "The Marlowe Mystery," at http://www.nsl.com/papers/marlowe.htm. Today copies of the book are extremely rare.

9 Between 1915 and 1937 Herman Cyril McNeile (1888-1937) published over thirty novels and short story collections under the pen name "Sapper." Along with such titans as Edgar Wallace, Sax Rohmer and E. Phillips Oppenheim, Sapper was one of England's most popular crime and mystery genre writers in the 1920s and 1930s. His most famous character is the high-spirited, public school hero Bulldog Drummond, who with extreme gusto battles diabolical villains menacing the safety and security of England. Fifteen Bulldog Drummond films were made between 1922 and 1939, with such prominent names as Ronald Colman, Ralph Richardson and Ray Milland playing the title role. McNeile's tales tend to find disfavor now, but they made a great impression on readers in their heyday, as attested by Richard Usborne in his *Clubland Heroes: A Nostalgic Study of Some Recurrent Characters in the Romantic Fiction of Dornford Yates, John Buchan and Sapper* (1953; rev. ed., London: Barrie & Jenkins,

"LYRICAL MURDER"
March 17, 1935, p. 35

How Strange a Thing, by Dorothy Bennett

Miss Bennett has a fine lyric gift. She knows, as well, the formulae for suspense, bafflement and successful characterization. In a daring experiment she has attempted to wed starry-eyed verse with virile murder. The result, a detective story in the form of a narrative poem, may be a nine days wonder but we doubt whether it will inspire imitators. Lovers of poetry will find it hard to stomach the third degree. Mystery fans will not want to stop for an interpolated sonnet that contains clues. The plot itself, concerning the murder of Mary Thayer, leader of San Francisco's bohemian set, is satisfactory enough and could, we venture, have been told very well in the conventional form.

More than once, reading Miss Bennett's lines, we were reminded of Rufus King. Mr. King writes prose. It might pay Miss Bennett to study some of the effects he attains with it.—Todd Downing.[10]

"NAWSTY BUSINESS"
April 7, 1935, p. 51

Big Business Murder, by G. D. H. and Margaret Cole

A prodigious couple, the Coles. They alternate skillfully plotted mysteries of the Scotland Yard genus with weighty tomes on economics. They occupy the unique position of having two

1983). Distinguishing Sapper's sort of cheerily cliché-ridden crime thrillers from the "high-hat classic detective novel," Downing reaches back to the French Revolution and wryly recommends the author's latest Bulldog Drummond tale for "the left wing of the [mystery] fans"—i.e., the rabble (he evidently includes himself in this category, at least at times).

10 The general critical view seemed to be that Dorothy Bennett's attempt to fuse poetry and detective fiction was a failure. Downing recommends to Bennett that she study the work of his sainted Rufus King. The same year Bennett also published a "straight" detective novel, *Murder Unleashed*.

separate groups of readers, with little in common. In their latest offering they attempt to interest both groups.

The critical murder fan should not be disheartened by the opening chapter, wherein he sits at a meeting of the board of directors of Arrow Investments, Inc. A few terse words from Kingsley Manson, managing director, and murder is scented in the offing. Manson admits brazenly that he hasn't been any too scrupulous in the management of the Arrow funds and challenges the members of the board to do something about it. Rather than accompany him to Dartmoor they agree to stand behind him. All except Wilfred Cathorne, who is going to the public prosecutor. He is murdered, of course, before he can do so. Superintendent Wilson interrupts a birthday celebration to settle the mess.

Chatty writer-to-reader narrative (more than once we were reminded of Edgar Wallace); just enough sex to give interest but not to distract; and suspense until the end. A good yarn.—Todd Downing.[11]

"DEATH FOLLOWS A FORMULA"
April 7, 1935, p. 51

Death Follows a Formula, by Newton Gayle

A better example of the faithfulness with which mystery writers follow their formula (the fifty-year-old Doyle tradition) could not be found. The wind is veering now in the direction of a change but the combination of Downing Street bafflement plus a brilliant amateur and a slow-witted admiring Watson is one that the majority of fans still rely on.

Maybe it's because the reader is never in doubt that what he's reading is pure fiction, written only to entertain. He is merely invited to "kid" himself for a couple of hours into believing that the fate of the empire hangs on the recovery of stolen papers.

11 Downing again invokes the name of Edgar Wallace in praising this "good yarn" by the Coles, "with just enough sex to give interest but not distract."

He knows that his newspapers will never tell him of the discovery by a dutiful butler of Lord Bridgdale's body in the study of Harley Gardens, Kensington. He can read on, blissfully happy in a fictional environment as familiar and restful as the slippers in which his toes have worn their grooves.

Michael O'Donnell, American scientist, is en route to England with a formula for a gasoline substitute. He is murdered at Plymouth and the formula disappears. The Foreign Office, distressed, calls in Scotland Yard, which in turn calls on young James Greer, erstwhile M. I. D. standby. "As I greeted Greer delightedly," exclaims the narrator, "I was struck once again by his absolute conformity to type, the English sport-loving, wellborn type."

But how, we ask ourselves, could an English novelist (such we supposed Newton Gayle to be) know about Oklahoma oil men, Ponca flint knives, sod houses and the Crazy Snake rebellion? The mystery was explained by the discovery that this is the work of two collaborators, one of them a well-known Oklahoma author, whose identity we are not yet at liberty to reveal. It is to be hoped that she will make another excursion outside her regular field of authorship.—Todd Downing.[12]

12 In reviewing this debut novel by Newton Gayle, Downing interestingly speculates on the popularity of the "formula" detective novel (which he believes that "the majority of fans still rely on," despite wind "veering now in the direction of a change"). Downing thinks that popularity rests upon the sheer capacity for cozy entertainment of "pure fiction, written only to entertain." As Downing indicates, Newton Gayle was the pseudonym of two joint writers, Muna Lee (1895-1965) and Maurice Guiness. Muna Lee was born in Mississippi but spent seven of her childhood years in Oklahoma. A published poet, Lee later married Luis Muñoz Marin (1898-1980), a Puerto Rican poet and journalist who became one of the leading political figures in Puerto Rico. Lee later worked for the State Department in cultural affairs and was an outspoken advocate of women's rights. Maurice Guiness was a Shell Oil Executive who met Lee when he was stationed in San Juan. The pair produced five detective novels between 1935 and 1939. Besides *Death Follows a Formula*, these are *The Sentry-Box Murder, Murder at 28:10, Death in the Glass* and *Sinister Crag*. Guiness plotted the novels and Lee largely wrote them. All the Newton Gayle novels were published in the United States as well as in England, where "Newton Gayle" became a member of the prestigious Detection Club.

"WITHOUT A CLUE"
April 21, 1935, p. 53

Profile of a Murder, by Rufus King

The appearance of a new novel by Rufus King is, distinctly, an "event" for us. Taking everything into consideration—originality of plot, suspense, skill in character delineation, perfection of style, plus a subtle injection of his own personality into whatever he writes—he is by far the best mystery writer today in our opinion.

In his latest he has returned to the restrained manner of *Murder by the Clock* and has given us an insight into the thoughts and emotions of a worthy sister of Mrs. Endicott. In the transcript of the inquest on Beatrice Mundy, heiress murdered at her estate in a remote part of the Adirondacks, Lieutenant Valcour sees four discrepancies that show him, beyond a shadow of a doubt, the identity of the murderer. Since there is no shred of evidence by which to fasten the crime upon this individual, he decides upon a fatal game of tag—which must end in death for someone. The death shall come, he calculates, at exactly 2 o'clock in the morning. It does. The reader watches it come.

We would advise the publishers to become better acquainted with their new acquisition. *Murder by the Clock*, in 1929, was not Mr. King's first mystery novel. Three successful ones preceded this. Also, they fail to triple-star among his later books that harrowing tale of malignant nature, *Murder on the Yacht*.—Todd Downing.[13]

"WAS IT MURDER?"
April 21, 1935, p. 53

Was It Murder? By James Hilton

We are always a bit skeptical when a blurbist confides that a

13 "[B]y far the best mystery writer today in our opinion": Todd Downing welcomes Rufus King back to the lists!

mystery writer's pseudonym conceals the identity of an exceedingly highbrow author. But really and truly Glen Trevor, whose *Murder at School* was published in England in 1933, is none other than James Hilton, without a talking knowledge of whose *Goodbye, Mr. Chips* and *Lost Horizon* you can't go out into society these days. We recommend the American edition to fans, although we can't honestly predict that it will create the sensation among the more seasoned of them that Hilton's novels have done among the ladies' club reviewers. Those footsteps on the stairs that stiffen every hair on our hero's head and send perspiration streaming down his forehead are not in the best odor nowadays.

The plot is a carefully constructed one having to so with a series of strange deaths in an English boys' school. Those characters are those that one would expect to find in such a locale: no gangsters, no foreign spies, no sinister Orientals. "Delightfully written" and "free from goofiness" were judgments of the critics when the book first appeared. That pretty well summarizes everything that needs to be said about it.—Todd Downing.[14]

"HUNGER FOR DETECTIVE STORIES SATISFIED"

May 5, 1935, p. 53

(Review by Savoie Lottinville of *The Poacher*, by H. E. Bates, omitted)

MR. FORTUNE OBJECTS, BY H. C. BAILEY

THE really good detective short story is becoming hard to find, now that magazine editors are constricting length. One by one mystery writers are seeking the greater freedom of the novel. Of the short story standbys Mr. Bailey is easily the best. He attains an atmosphere of suspense with light deft touches. His crimes have the psychological complexity that modern readers are demanding.

14 With his references to "an exceedingly highbrow author" and "the ladies' club reviewers" Downing sounds perhaps slightly hostile to this mystery by the lauded mainstream novelist James Hilton (1900-1954), author of the best-selling *Lost Horizon* (1933) and *Goodbye, Mr. Chips* (1934).

Six of Reggie's cases are here presented. We liked particularly "The Broken Toad," a study of which is necessary to a liberal education; "The Angel's Eye," wherein is solved the 134-year-old mystery of the death of "the blushing bride of Letley" as well as a current puzzler; and "The Long Dinner," with an artist's dirty linen leading Reggie to a primitive Breton goddess, the woman of Sarn, and as diabolical a scheme for organized murder as was ever devised. Then there are "The Little Finger," "The Three Bears," and "The Yellow Slugs," all guaranteed to make the discriminating fan wriggle with delight as he feels that "cold and authentic shiver in the spine."—Todd Browning.[15]

"AIRPLANE MURDER"
May 19, 1935, p. 49

Death in the Air, by Agatha Christie

If you noticed an unusual number of knitted brows during the month of February they were occasioned doubtless by brains at work upon this neat puzzler by the clever and indefatigable Miss Christie in the *Saturday Evening Post*.

Madame Giselle, notorious moneylender, dies in the airliner *Prometheus* midway between Paris and London. She was killed, apparently, by a poison dart shot from a blowpipe. Suspects: Jane Grey, a young hair-dresser; Norman Gale, a young dentist; two English peeresses; two French archaeologists; a detective writer; a physician; a businessman and—our old friend Hercule Poirot.

Hints to the would-be emulator of the little Belgian: watch the wasp that was buzzing about the plane at the time of the murder, the blowpipe wedged behind M. Poirot's seat, the clay pipe in the hand of the archaeologist, the flute which Dr. Bryant

15 "His crimes have the psychological complexity that modern readers are demanding," says Downing of H. C. Bailey in this review of a fine collection of Bailey's Reggie Fortune short stories. "[T]ales that deal in a mature, thoughtful way with the existence of evil in the world," I say in my review of *Mr. Fortune Objects*, at Mystery*File, 10 November 2010, http://mysteryfile.com/blog/?p=5762.

was holding and the inexplicable item among one of the passenger's effects—and remember that you're not reading a routine clue and confusion concoction but are pitting your wits against the cleverest baffler in the field of detective fiction.

We are glad to see that Miss Christie is going in for the X-ray fashion of peeking into character's minds.—Todd Downing.[16]

"CAPE MYSTERY"
May 19, 1935, p. 49

THE SPANISH CAPE MYSTERY, BY ELLERY QUEEN

TOO much eavesdropping on the part of our old friend Ellery is the main fault we have to find with *The Spanish Cape Mystery*. Really, Ellery's forte is dignified deduction, not snooping behind pillars to spy on his subjects. Such goings-on may add to the interest of the story but it's not quite what one expects, don't y'know.

The murders on Spanish Cape present a very neat problem, however, and the trick by which the identity of the culprit is concealed is worthy of Agatha Christie. There is assembled the usual house party of jealous females, philandering males and parted lovers. David Kumber, brother-in-law of the host, and his niece Rosa are abducted. Then a guest—Don Marco, a gallant straight out of Lope de Vega—is found murdered. He is sitting on the terrace. Except for his hat and black cloak he is naked. "Not," says Ellery, "three-quarters naked, not half-naked, not almost naked. He was naked as the day he had been born." Keep in mind the problem of the corpse's clothing in *The Chinese Orange Mystery* and try to solve that one!

Old Inspector Queen does not appear, which is a shame to our way of thinking. He was always a greater favorite of ours than Ellery.—Todd Downing.[17]

16 "[Y]ou're not reading a routine clue and confusion concoction but are pitting your wits against the cleverest baffler in the field of detective fiction," pronounces Downing of Agatha Christie—a judgment certainly validated by the Crime Queen's phenomenal popular duration.

17 Downing deems that this title involving a country house and a naked male corpse presents "a very neat problem," one aspect of which is "worthy

"HOUSE ON ROOF"
May 19, 1935, p. 49

The House on the Roof, by Mignon G. Eberhart

Mrs. Eberhart has outgrown the conventional mystery writer category and steps out as a full-fledged psychological novelist. Her product has a crime interest, yes, but it is rather a puzzle of character than of time and place and motive. It will be eminently satisfactory to the general reader who appreciates a good tale as well as to all the fans, save those diehards who refuse to leave the atmosphere of Baker Street.

The setting is Chicago, a city which Mrs. Eberhart seems to have adopted definitely. "It is a city of the unexpected," she writes in her foreword. "This story might have taken place. A woman in maroon velvet might have waited at a door—I'm not sure she didn't. A girl might have paused upon a slippery fire escape to listen for footsteps that stopped. A man might have hurried through fog-marked streets." And by the end of the first chapter Mrs. Eberhart has set the reader to wondering if maybe she weren't actually present in that little penthouse on the roof when the old prima donna stared into the shadows. A characteristic Eberhart touch, the overheard telephone conversation: "I wasn't in her house when it happened, but they told me. I had to clean up the blood. . . . And I went to the hospital every day to inquire. I was there the night you died."—Todd Downing.[18]

of Agatha Christie"; yet he seems to be tiring somewhat of his "old friend" Ellery Queen. Playwright and poet Felix Arturo Lope de Vega y Carpio (1562-1635) is one of the great figures of Spanish literature.

18 Downing lavishly praises Mignon Eberhart as someone who has "outgrown the conventional mystery writer category" to become "a full-fledged psychological novelist." He believes her works will appeal to all but those traditionalist "diehards who refuse to leave the atmosphere of Baker Street." Today a similarly-minded critic no doubt would proclaim that Eberhart had "transcended the genre."

"MIRTHFUL MURDER"
May 19, 1935, p. 49

THE DEADLY DOWAGER, BY EDWIN GREENWOOD

"THE great combination in all real literature," says Arthur Machen in a foreword, "is the combination of murder with mirth. . . . *The Deadly Dowager* is compounded on the true and ancient recipe; it mixes mirth and murder with immense spirit and success."

We agree wholeheartedly with Mr. Machen. Not since Victoria Lincoln's *February Hill*, have we spent such a hilarious and altogether mirthful evening as the one we spent getting acquainted with the old Dowager Arabella, Lady Engleton, and watching her insure the lives of her relatives and then start killing them. In the killing she shows a detail of inventiveness that puts to shame those sissies who make away with their victims by pouring boiling oil in their ears, poisoning them with a cat's claws and stabbing them with icicles.

The Deadly Dowager is not a mystery novel, but we suggest that fans take time off and meet Arabella.—Todd Downing.[19]

19 In his review of *The Deadly Dowager*, Downing—like Arthur Machen (1863-1947), the great supernatural horror writer—evinces a taste for humor of the more macabre sort. Theodore Edwin Greenwood (1895-1939) directed thirty silent films between 1923 and 1929. A friend of Alfred Hitchcock, Greenwood co-wrote the scenario for the great director's *The Man Who Knew Too Much* (1934) and contributed to the screenplay for *Young and Innocent* (1937), Hitchcock's very loose adaptation of Josephine Tey's detective novel *A Shilling for Candles* (1936). In the 1930s Greenwood wrote a series of satirical novels, including the following, all of which have a crime interest: *Skin and Bone* (1934) (*The Deadly Dowager* in the United States), *Pins and Needles* (1935) (*The Fair Devil* in the United States), *French Farce* (1937) and *Dark Understudy* (1939). The last of these tales is, as the title implies, much darker than the rest, a story of a sex-obsessed serial killer in the modern mode. One of his novels, *Old Goat* (1938), Greenwood dedicated (ironically?) "To Alfred Hitchcock ("Hitch"): Good Maker of Good Pictures, Good Judge of Good Things, Good Friend." Sadly, Hitchcock has been blamed for Greenwood's premature death. Greenwood appeared in a bit part as a regency dandy in Hitchcock's film *Jamaica Inn* (1939). According to director Sidney Gilliat, during the filming of a stormy scene on the set Greenwood contracted pneumonia, from which he died at the age of 43. "I feel that could have been avoided and

"ART AND MURDER"
May 26, 1935, p. 59

Most Beautiful Lady, by Dorothea Brande

Just why such an experienced writer as Miss Brande should insist that her novel is a mystery is beyond us. There is a corpse, yes, but it doesn't show up (isn't even hinted at) until page 300. What goes before is simply an entertaining story about three artists who journey to a strange and lovely villa in the north of Italy to make likenesses of Rossi Pechot, the beautiful young wife of a fabulously rich Frenchman. Such complications as there are arise from artistic temperament, love and such puzzles as these: Who stole the key to the art gallery? Who flashed a light in the Fothergill bedroom? Where has Mrs. Fothergill seen Mme Pechot before? Even the huge chest across the door of la Pechot's room and the discovery of the piece of raw meat nearby didn't quite make up for the delayed entrance of the corpse.—Todd Downing.[20]

"SECRET FORMULA"
May 26, 1935, p. 59

The Bannerman Case, by Jeremy Lord

It looks as if no mystery writer's bag of tricks were complete nowadays without a secret formula for synthetic something or

that Hitch was to blame for what happened," declared Gilliat. See Patrick Mcgilligan, *Alfred Hitchcock: A Life in Darkness and Light* (New York: Regan Books, 2003), 160, 225. Victoria Lincoln's novel *February Hill* (1934), which Downing lauds in his review of *The Deadly Dowager*, was a well-received comic tale of a New England family headed by an amiable prostitute mother and a tippling, genteel father. Today Victoria Lincoln is best known as the author of *A Private Disgrace: Lizzie Borden by Daylight* (1967). The latter book was in Downing's library at his death. Downing was fascinated with the Lizzie Borden case.

20 Downing finds *Most Beautiful Lady* more a mainstream novel than a mystery. Dorothea Brande (1893-1948) was a writer best known for her inspirational bestseller *Wake Up and Live!* (1936). She married Seward Collins (1899-1952), a wealthy New York socialite, bookstore owner and

other. Fans who are still in the era of wills, revenge and blackmail had better read Mr. Lord's offering and get up to date.

Mr. Colin Bannerman, inventor, dies in a mysterious explosion which engulfs his laboratory. Who is the sinister C—about whom Sir Colin was writing at the time of his demise? Is it the same individual to whom Lillian Kennion (actress, "gorgeous legs") was telephoning at 5:50 p.m. (and whose mistress is Lillian, anyway)? The second and third corpses are Josef Zeyer, electrical expert, and Dr. Henry Webb, brain specialist.

The case is solved by a brand new sleuth, whom we predict will make many successful appearances: Col. Winston Creevy, D.D.O. The colonel is a "slightly plump, military gentleman, who lost his left eye when, as a slim young subaltern, he charged with the Twenty-first Lancers against the dervish hosts of the Khalifa of Omraman." The Glory of the Empire stuff is soft-pedaled, however, and one doesn't have to be an Anglophile to appreciate him.—Todd Downing.[21]

publisher of *The Bookman* and *American Review*. In the 1930s Collins controversially became a vocal defender of Hitler and Mussolini.

21 As "Jeremy Lord" writer, editor and critic Ben Ray Redman (1896-1961) wrote the novels *The Bannerman Case* (1935) and *69 Diamonds* (1940), both starring ex-service British sleuth Winston Creevy, as well as the 1928 short story "The Perfect Crime," televised as a memorable 1957 episode of *Alfred Hitchcock Presents* (co-starring Vincent Price) and reprinted in 2001 in Tony Hillerman's and Otto Penzler's *The Best American Mystery Stories of the Century*. A prolific writer of book reviews, Redman was long closely associated with the *Saturday Review* and contributed pieces as well to the *New York Times*, *Harper's* and the *American Mercury*. According to "The Greenwich Village Bookshop Door: A Portal to Bohemia, 1920-1925," an exhibition at the Harry Ransom Center at the University of Texas at Austin, Redman "was described upon his death as a debonair gentleman-scholar type, an authentic bookman who was born for a part in a Noel Coward play." See http://norman.hrc.utexas.edu/bookshopdoor/signature.cfm? item=54#1. The *Saturday Review* (perhaps a biased source, admittedly) raved *The Bannerman Case*, declaring that "it out-Opps Opp [Oppenheim]." Himself an admirer, as we have seen, of E. Phillips Oppenheim's popular espionage fiction, Downing echoes the praise of *The Bannerman Case*, even adding gratefully that the "Glory of [British] Empire stuff is soft-pedaled."

"SAME OLD PLOT"
June 2, 1935, p. 53

Crime in Corn Weather, by Mary M. Atwater

Corn weather, as we didn't know, is the kind of heat that makes Iowa corn grow. "Smothering, baby-killing, soul-sickening weather." From Miss Atwater's description, just the weather to lend the proper atmosphere to murder.

William Breen, hard-hearted banker, is shot to death outside the little town of Keedora. Grandma Breen is worried when he doesn't come home to supper. Mrs. Paradise, who lives next door, phones Dr. Flagler. A church party finds a deserted car with blood on the cushions. "It's too bad the old geezer's been killed," says Kelley Price, embryo journalist, "but if you think I'm not tickled at the break for us you're crazy." But, of course, Kelly is in love.

All of which is to say the plot is run-of-the-mill stuff. What saves the book is the realistic picture that Miss Atwater has drawn of a little farm town. As a setting for laughter it is a welcome relief from weekend parties in English country houses and Long Island estates.—Todd Downing.[22]

"WIDE INTRIGUE"
June 9, 1935, p. 51

Death in Four Letters, by Francis Beeding

"It is reported," say the publishers, "that one of the central figures in *Death in Four Letters* is one of the world's best-known dictators." Come, come, Messrs. Harper, we know you mean Reichsfuehrer Hitler.

22 A granddaughter of Montgomery C. Meigs (1816-1892), Quartermaster General of the United States Army during the American Civil War, Mary Meigs Atwater (1878-1956), the "Dean of American Handweaving," was born in Illinois and raised in Iowa, later studying design at the Chicago Art Institute and in Paris. After marrying mining engineer Maxwell W. Atwater, she travelled with him around the western United States and Central and South America. While living in Montana, Mary Atwater organized a hand loom weavers' guild and taught the craft by correspondence, for which she is best known today. Perhaps surprisingly, *Crime in*

Beeding, author of *The Street of Serpents*, *Six Proud Walkers* and *Seven Sleepers*, belongs to the Oppenheim school of international intrigue and is, it seems to us, fully as good as the late master. In his latest he has chosen a timely subject, the secret activities of munitions makers. The pages recounting the German dictator's brazen challenge to the world and his piffle anent racial solidarity sound like front page news of not so long ago.

Lord Fentyman, millionaire newspaper owner, is killed in an airplane accident. The narrator, F. X. D. Dodd, correspondent of the *Daily Clarion*, witnesses the crash and finds on Fentyman's person papers which connect him with the "Syndicat International des Armements." F. X. D. carries the fight upon the connivers against world peace over most of the map of Europe.

We should say that Beeding either has been in a German detention camp or has read E. E. Cummings' *Enormous Room* to advantage. He writes about it rather feelingly.—Todd Downing.[23]

"GENTLEMAN CROOK"
June 9, 1935, p. 51

JIMMIE DALE AND THE MISSING MINUTES, BY FRANK L. PACKARD

THIS is the fifth volume through whose pages debonair Jimmie Dale has led his followers—via deserted streets, dark basements

Corn Weather, Mary Atwater's only novel, has nothing whatsoever to do with handweaving. Though Downing thinks the plot run-of-the-mill, he praises the novel as a realistic regionalist tale, as did the *New York Times* reviewer, who affirmed that the author's "picture of life in the Corn Belt is remarkably well done" (5 May 1935).

23 Francis Beeding was the pseudonym of John Leslie Palmer (1885-1944) and Hilary St. John Saunders (1898-1951), Oxford graduates who met in the early 1920s while employed at the League of Nations in Geneva, Switzerland. Their series of over thirty mystery and espionage thrillers, published between 1925 and 1946, was not pathbreaking like the novels of Eric Ambler (1909-1998). Yet the Beeding books were more realistic than was the norm for Golden Age spy novels, as Downing's review indicates. Note Downing's openly expressed contempt for the Adolf Hitler's "piffle anent racial solidarity" and his reference to E. E. Cumming's 1922 autobiographical novel about his imprisonment in France during World War One.

and lonely country roads. To our mind, Jimmie grows more likeable with every volume, cracks a safe more expertly and manages more adroitly to keep separate his different lives as Larry the Bat, Smarlinghue the dissolute artist and his daylight self, the rich young clubman.

The disappearance of his friend Carruthers is the reason for Jimmie's resumption of his role as Larry the Bat, alias the Gray Seal. He makes the decision although it entails postponement of his marriage with Marie LaSalle, who (the Packard fan will recall) has as the Tocsin and Mother Margot as many disguises as Jimmy.

If there is anything missing in the way of ingredients for the fast moving adventure yarn we didn't notice it. Just as samplers there are a hidden treasure and a map, a lonely mansion on the Hudson, gunplay in the darkness and dirty doings on the East River waterfront.

It is the Crime Club Selection for May.—Todd Downing.[24]

"WHO KILLED HER?"
June 9, 1935, p. 51

THE WILL AND THE DEED, BY DOROTHY OGBURN

HOW Miss Ogburn has occupied herself since the publication of *Ra-Ta-Plan!* we do not know but we should say that the interval was well spent if she can give us such a competent piece of writing

24 Frank L. Packard (1877-1942) was a Canadian novelist best known for his pulp fiction character Jimmie Dale, a playboy crime fighter who appeared in five novels and short story collections, published between 1917 and 1935. Though mostly forgotten today, Packard's creation Jimmie Dale, notes David Vineyard, "not only exerted a tremendous influence on the pulps he came from, but established many of the tropes of the modern superhero in comic books. From his secret lair, the Sanctuary, his multiple identities and his calling card, a gray diamond paper seal, Jimmie Dale set the pattern for the mystery men and superheroes who followed." David L. Vineyard, "Jimmie Dale, the Gray Seal, by Frank L. Packard," 14 December 2009, *Mystery*File*, http://mysteryfile.com/blog/?p=1715 . Certainly Todd Downing, who was twelve years old when the first Jimmie Dale story appeared (in the May 1914 issue of *People's Magazine*), appears to have been a longtime devout fan.

as this. She manages to inject just the right amount of supernatural spookiness into her pages and soon has even the hardened reader wondering about the call in the night that was heard just before the heiress of Stonecliff plunged off the balcony to her death. The customary group of scheming relatives gathered about the mansion is drawn with unusual skill. The chapter "A Dead Man Reads His Will" is one of the most spellbinding openings that we can recall offhand.

Followers of Mignon Eberhart should get acquainted with Miss Ogburn.—Todd Downing.[25]

"HOTEL MURDER"
June 16, 1935, p. 49

THE GREAT HOTEL MURDER, BY VINCENT STARRETT

NONE of the usual criteria for a successful murder yarn are lacking in the case of the latest tale by the chronicler of Sherlock Holmes. It appeared in the *Red Book* under the title *Recipe for Murder* and has been made (we understand) into a good movie.

It is one of those novels in which a so-so plot is made into a first-rate story by skill in the telling and able characterization. Young Riley Blackwood is a happy combination of the dilettante amateur sleuth of the Ellery Queen type and the more realistic Dashiell Hammett school of heroes. He can write dramatic criticism and drink tea with his blue-blooded aunt without being a sissy, and he can deliver a punch to the chin and still talk intelligible English.

There is plenty of variety in the settings, which switch from a large Chicago hotel, wherein a New York banker is murdered

25 Born in Atlanta, Georgia, Dorothy Stevens Ogburn (1890-1981) enjoyed a brief spate as a mystery writer in the 1930s. Besides *Ra-Ta-Plan!* (1930) and *The Will and the Deed*, Ogburn published *Death on the Mountain* (1931). She is best known, however, for her series of books—co-authored with her husband, American Federation of Labor general counsel Charlton Ogburn (1882-1962) and later her son, Charlton Ogburn II (1911-1998)—advancing the view that the plays of William Shakespeare were really written by Edward de Vere, Earl of Oxford.

while registered under an assumed name, to a private yacht on the lake and to a sinister mansion in the wilds of northern Wisconsin. The trick by which the identity of the murderer is concealed is so simple and so effective that it is surprising no one thought of it before.—Todd Downing.[26]

"REVEREND SLEUTH"
June 16, 1935, p. 49

DEATH OF AN AIRMAN, BY CHRISTOPHER ST. JOHN SPRIGG

THE most satisfactory amateur sleuth to make a bow in a long time is the Bishop of Cootamundra, Australia. He comes to England for instruction in flying, meets the manager of the Bastin Aero Club, the disconcertingly modern Sally Sackbut, and witnesses the plunge to earth of a machine, in the wreckage of which is found the corpse of Major Furnace, instructor. It looks like accident, later like suicide, but the bishop, with the acuteness of observation of Father Brown, happens on a curious circumstance which points to murder. He leaves the regulation sleuthing to Scotland Yard and stays quietly at the club, observing suspects and trying to dodge Lady Crumbles, ardent organizer of air shows.

The author has succeeded admirably in puzzling the reader until the end, whereupon the accusing finger is pointed neatly at the most unlikely suspect. He writes well and mixes mirth with murder so that neither ingredient is impaired.

(A query, Mr. Sprigg: Have we said "adieu" or "au revoir" to the bishop? That ending took us unawares.—Todd Downing).[27]

26 Writer, bibliophile and Sherlock Holmes expert Charles Vincent Emerson Starrett (1886-1974) published a small body of mystery novels and short story collections. *The Great Hotel Murder* was filmed under the same title the same year that it was published.

27 Christopher St. John Sprigg (1907-1937)—novelist, short story writer, poet, playwright and, last but certainly not least, Marxist theorist—published six delightful detective novels between 1933 and 1935: *Crime in Kensington/Pass the Body, Fatality in Fleet Street, The Perfect Alibi, Death of an Airman, The Corpse with the Sunburnt Face* and *Death of a Queen*. A final tale, *The Six Queer Things*, was published posthumously in 1937, after Sprigg

"ENGLISH MURDER"
June 23, 1935, p. 49

DEATH IN A LITTLE TOWN, BY R. C. WOODTHORPE

HAVING missed Mr. Woodthorpe's *Death Wears a Purple Shirt* we turned with interest to his second contribution and soon found ourselves engrossed in as entertaining a yarn of English small town life as any of Eden Phillpotts'. We liked particularly the elderly spinster, Matilda Perks, with her crotchety tongue; her brother, with his "queer spells," which caused him to undress casually wherever he was; and the parrot, Ramsay MacDonald, with his disconcerting remarks. In fact, at times we forgot we were reading a murder story.

This speaks well for the author's ability as a character delineator, however, as there is no dearth of mystification as to the identity of the assassin of cantankerous old Douglas Bonar, who was disliked by the entire village of Chesworth. Suspects include a novelist with a secret in his past; a married couple, one of whom has a black eye; and a pair of lovers who don't get married. The chapter in which the dead man's niece entertains at tea for her fiancée, the local rector and his retinue of spinsters is worth the price of the book in itself—because of the poignant tragedy underlying the humor.

The best of recent Crime Club selections in our opinion.—Todd Downing.[28]

was killed in action fighting for the Republican cause in the Spanish Civil War; and it very much reflects a grimmer, post-Marxian conversion sensibility. After his death Sprigg won considerable fame in Communist circles for his posthumously published Stalinist critical essays, but his detective fiction—in its day praised by, among others, Dorothy L. Sayers—still wins the admiration of those who manage to locate it (though Sprigg himself dismissed his genre work as "trash" written simply to make money).

28 "[A]t times we forgot we were reading a murder story" is Downing's high praise for this tale by Ralph Carter Woodthorpe (1886-?), a Great War veteran and public schoolmaster who published eight well-received detective novels between 1932 and 1940. Regrettably, amateur detective Miss Perks, an inspired character, appeared in only two Woodthorpe novels, *Death in a Little Town* (1935) and *The Shadow on the Downs* (1936).

"TERROR IN THE WOODS"
July 7, 1935, p. 49

By Night at Dinsmore, by John Estevan

A tale that nearly sends the reader into dithers over the evil fate that hangs over the Dinsmore family, the malignancy of the North Woods and the identity of the Crawler. Mr. Estevan is a writer of vivid imagination who has the authentic feeling for what produces horror. Were his touch just a little lighter he would give the masters of the genre a run for their money. As it is, *By Night at Dinsmore* seems to us head and shoulders above Mr. Garnett Weston's *Murder on Shadow Island*, which was boosted into Book of the Month Club fame several seasons back.

Miles Le Breton, consultant on the staff of the Bureau of Investigation, is the sleuth whose knowledge of psychology, psychiatry and criminology serves him in good stead in observing the degenerate Dinsmores. It is not only his Gallic name that puts us in mind of Rufus King's Lieutenant Valcour. Deborah Dinsmore, too, is a woman who might have stepped out of the pages of a King novel. We predict that none of the fans will be sure until the end whether or not Deborah is the assassin who is making short shrift of the family.—Todd Downing.[29]

"MURDER IN CHURCH"
July 7, 1935, p. 49

The Eleventh Hour, by J. S. Fletcher

Although we were never an ardent Fletcher fan, especially after Camberwell and Chaney, private inquiry agents, started on their

29 "John Estevan" was the pseudonym of Samuel Shellabarger (1888-1954), author of both scholarly works and historical novels, the best known of which are *Captain of Castile* (1945) and *Prince of Foxes* (1947), both successfully filmed. As "John Estevan" and "Peter Loring" he published nine mystery novels between 1928 and 1939. Sensing in Estevan the "authentic feeling for what produces horror," Downing pays the author the ultimate compliment of comparing him to Rufus King.

adventures and further adventures, we found ourselves engrossed in this one before we knew it. Even the familiarity of the Fletcher formula didn't annoy us as it usually does. Since this is his fifty-first novel any comparison with the rest of his output would be hazardous, but we can't recall any that we liked so well. It is much better than *Murder in Four Degrees* and *Murder of the Lawyer's Clerk*, for instance.

The shattered body of John Parlement, senior verger of the Cathedral of Lanchester, is found in the nave, whence he had fallen from the clerestory sixty feet above. When it is learned that he had just discovered, in a hollow crozier, the jewels of a sixteenth-century bishop and that said stones have vanished during the night, Superintendent Wansford and young Camberwell agree that it is murder. There is a complete assortment of ecclesiastical suspects, including canons, minor canons and canons-in-residence.

Incidentally, the jacket is the most attractive we have seen on a mystery novel.—Todd Downing.[30]

"BUT IT WAS"

July 21, 1935, p. 49

It Couldn't Be Murder, by Hugh Austin

Someone has said it is fortunate for the murder-monger that, whereas there is only one known way of getting born, there are endless ways of getting killed. Every once in a while a fertile brain concocts a new shortcut to the grave that others have overlooked on account of its simplicity. The method employed by Mr.

30 Like many reviewers by this point in time, Todd Downing found mostly tedious the seemingly endless succession of books rolling out of the Fletcher factory (by my count there were closer to ninety published Fletcher detective novels by 1935, rather than Downing's estimate of fifty-one—not to mention short story collections); yet he responded favorably to the cathedral town atmosphere of *The Eleventh Hour*. Fletcher, incidentally, had been dead for more than five months when Downing's review appeared; *The Eleventh Hour* was published posthumously.

Austin's fiend in doing away with two members of the ritzy Houghton family may cause the unseasoned reader several uneasy moments because of the facility with which any disgruntled relative could make use of it.

The current Crime Club selection offers for your bafflement and midsummer entertainment: the clues, plainly labeled, of the coffee pot that didn't go off and the cat that was inexplicably silent; an honest to goodness police sergeant, P. D. Quint (P. D. Q. to the force); staccato question and answer; and a 48-hour, tick-of-the-clock time schedule.—Todd Downing.[31]

"NO SHUDDERS"
July 21, 1935, p. 49

MURDER IN THE SURGERY, BY JAMES G. EDWARDS

THE author is a practicing physician who lays the scene of his venture into the mystery field in a Chicago hospital (Are the fans aware of the increasing popularity of Chicago as a setting for fictional crime?).

For us a hospital is an ideal setting for murder. The scalpels and whatnot lying about furnish both an ideal choice in modus operandi and a ready-made atmosphere of horror. We were rather disappointed, therefore, to find Nurse Stokes' neck dislocated between the fourth and fifth vertebrae by a sandbag. No scalpel.

In fact, we didn't get a single shudder from the first page, when Dr. Carson and Nurse Connie playfully spar over a boy's abdomen, to the point when Connie returns from a date with the doctor. "What happened?" her roommate asks avidly. "Nothing," she growls in disgust. There is considerable philandering, perhaps

31 Between 1935 and 1938 Hugh Austin Evans (1903-1964) published five Peter Quint detective novels, followed by a non-series mystery in 1938 and three additional mysteries in the late 1940s. The Peter Quint books have been highly praised for their ingenuity by noted genre specialists, including Anthony Boucher.

a thrill for mild readers. It made us look up Mignon Eberhart's gore-spattered *From This Dark Stairway*.—Todd Downing.[32]

"THE NAUGHTY FRENCHMAN"
August 18, 1935, p. 55

DEATH OF THE DEPUTY, BY ROGER FRANCIS DIDELOT

SINCE publishers seemed determined to popularize translations of French mystery novels we made up our mind to enjoy this one by the author of *Murder in the Bath*. It began well enough, with a body, identified as that of Deputy Holbein, discovered on a dark Montmartre street. When Inspector Lecain goes to break the news to the deputy's daughter he finds the supposed corpse entertaining guests.

Now as far as we are concerned the trick of physical resemblances went out of fashion along with false-faces and unknown oriental poisons. But, with determined tolerance for the credulity of French fans, we followed Lecain through houses of assignation until we found the inevitable veiled woman of mystery

32 In this rather bloodthirsty review, Downing once again displays his preference in detective novels for shudders over sex, or grue over goo, if you will. "James G. Edwards" was the pseudonym of James William McQueen II (1900-1954), a son of James William McQueen (1866-1925), a wealthy Birmingham, Alabama business executive (among other things, the elder McQueen was President of Sloss-Sheffield Steel and Iron Company at the time of his death). The younger McQueen became Superintendent of Birmingham's Hillman Hospital in 1936, a year after his publication, under a pseudonym, of *Murder in the Surgery*. McQueen also wrote seven other detective novels, five of which appeared by 1939. Additionally, as "Jay McHugh" McQueen published *Sex is Such Fun*, a softcore sex novel, with William Godwin, Inc., a publisher deemed "pretty steamy for their time" by Bill Pronzini. See Mrs. Annabelle Bunting MacElyea, *The McQueens of Queensdale: A Biography of Col. James McQueen and His Descendants* (Charlotte, NC: Observer Printing House, 1916), 189; Alabama Library Association, "James William McQueen, 1900-1954," *Alabama Authors*, at http://www.lib.ua.edu/Alabama_Authors/?p=1746; Bill Pronzini, "William Godwin, Inc.," in William F. Deeck, *Murder at 3 Cents a Day: An Annotated Crime Fiction Bibliography of the Lending Library Publishers, 1936-1937*, at http://www.lendinglibmystery.com.

who had flitted out of the corpse's past in South America! It was too much! We refuse to be convinced by Gallic mystery mongers that every Frenchman has a double and possesses a dark South American past.

In one of his franker moments Lecain exclaims with a twirl of his moustachios: "We are ridiculous enough for a slapstick comedy!" We aren't quite as critical as the doughty inspector, but—Todd Downing.[33]

"G MAN"
August 25, 1935, p. 49

G Man, by Charles Francis Coe

If the movies are an indication of popular taste, mystery writers will soon be abandoning the dilettantish amateur sleuth for the hard-fisted G man. England's Scotland Yard has had its day in fiction so why not the Federal Bureau of Investigation? The difficulty will be that few writers know anything about gangsters first hand. Their interpretation of underworld argot is likely to be ludicrous.

It is in this respect that Mr. Coe excels. The speech of his gangsters, One Eye Zigo, Rap Covani, Ghost Minani, Palmy Renzo and the rest, has Dictaphone authenticity.

The bootlegging racket comes in for an exposé here as did kidnapping in *Ransom*. Upon repeal, One Eye and his lieutenant split partnership, one to undersell government-taxed liquor, the other to devote himself to stickups. The story follows the usual Coe formula, with glimpses of crooked politicians, underpaid policemen and the apathetic public, and with justice triumphant though the work of the "feds." Squeamish readers can justify their perusal of it by calling it a case-history of our times. And they won't be far wrong at that.—Todd Downing.[34]

33 Downing throws up his hands over the clichés in French mystery novels and the "credulity of French [mystery] fans."

34 In his review of Charles Francis Coe's *G Man*, Downing singles out for praise the novel's "Dictaphone authenticity" in its portrayal of organized crime argot.

"CORPSE IN HAYSTACK"
August 25, 1935, p. 49

A QUESTION OF PROOF, BY NICHOLAS BLAKE

JAMES Hilton's *Was It Murder?* seems to have started a fad for boys' school mysteries in the English murder mart. This importation comes with an impressive amount of advance publicity, recommendation by the London Book Society and selection by the English Crime Club. We should say that the cheers are justified, despite the fact that we are unable to get as worked up about 13-year-olds who go muttering "I'll kill you!" as does Dorothy L. Sayers, who inquires, "Why are school mysteries always so convincingly real?"

Well, in our opinion, they aren't. As far as we are concerned, Algernon Wyvern-Wemyss, the corpse in the haystack, is just a *sine qua non* of a detective yarn—and nothing more. Likewise, we were tepid about the amateur sleuth, Nigel Strangeways—answered examination questions at Oxford with limericks, found the Duchess of Esk's diamonds, likes tea and lots of bedclothes, murmurs, "Mon dieu, quel hulerberlu! Quel, I might even say, tohobohu!"—although we are assured that "he is a simple soul, really."

As frequently happens; superlatively good writing minimizes first novel defects. We can't see why Mr. Blake isn't as good a stylist as James Hilton.[35]

35 "Nicholas Blake" was the pseudonym of Cecil Day Lewis (1904-1972), an Anglo-Irish schoolmaster, Oxford literature professor and poet. Day Lewis served as poet laureate of the United Kingdom between 1968 and 1972. Like Downing, Day Lewis reviewed crime fiction in the 1930s and decided to try his hand at it. He produced 20 crime novels between 1935 and 1968, sixteen of them tales of the doings of his insouciant amateur detective Nigel Strangeways. Though "tepid" (to say the least!) about Strangeways, Downing praised Day Lewis' "superlatively good writing" in *A Question of Proof*, comparing him favorably with the best-selling English novelist James Hilton, who in 1933 had published his own boys school mystery, recently reprinted in the United States and reviewed by Downing in April. Note also that Downing dares for once to take issue with Dorothy L. Sayers on a matter of mystery criticism. He answers Sayers' rhetorical question, "Why are school mysteries always so convincingly real?" with the retort, "Well, in our opinion, they aren't." At this time

"HARD BOILED SLEUTH"
September 8, 1935, p. 53

Headed for a Hearse, by Jonathan Latimer

Mr. Latimer, author of *Murder in the Madhouse*, is the latest addition to the hard-boiled school of detective fiction. The formula—tough talk, hard drinking, Rabelaisian humor *in re* sex, staccato action—is one which will wear thin in time but for the nonce is a relief from the dainty frivolous manner of dealing with slaughter to which so many of the lady writers are addicted.

Herein is continued the career of William Crane, private detective, whose task is to save young Robert Wantland, convicted of the murder of his wife and sentenced to be executed in six days. Miss Hogan ("a perfectly sculptured hip") opines: "I wouldn't give two bits for Westland's chances. I haven't seen 'the great detective' sober yet." Yet Crane surprises her and during the hangover that results from a mixture of bourbon, absinthe and gin solves the problem of the locked apartment, the faked telephone call and the missing automatic and provides a last-minute substitute for the chair.

There are recommended touches of realism in the death-house scenes, the lemon squeezer torture and the taxicab banter. The solution will prove, we believe, a complete surprise. The Crime Club selection for August.—Todd Downing.[36]

Sayers was about to publish her own school mystery, *Gaudy Night*, which Downing would review (very favorably) the next year.

36 Journalist, author and screenwriter Jonathan Latimer (1906-1983) is best-known in the mystery field for his series of hard-boiled William Crane detective novels, which skillfully combine ingenious plots, tough talk and action and black humor. These are: *Murder in the Madhouse* (1935), *Headed for a Hearse* (1935), *The Lady in the Morgue* (1936), *The Dead Don't Care* (1938) and *Red Gardenias* (1939). After this series ended, Latimer published *Solomon's Vineyard* (1941), controversial in its day, *Sinners and Shrouds* (1955) and *Black is the Fashion for Dying* (1959). Under the pseudonym Peter Coffin he also published the quirkily titled *The Search for My Great Uncle's Head* (1937). Downing pronounces that the hard-boiled formula represented by Latimer "will wear thin over time," but then in a shot across the bow of "cozy" women authors indicates he views it as

"MILLIONAIRE CORPSE"
September 8, 1935, p. 53

SUDDEN DEATH, BY LEE THAYER

EXCEPT for a frequently annoying resemblance to Dorothy L. Sayers' Lord Peter Wimsey and his valet, Bunter, red-headed Peter Clancy and the faithful Wiggar do well enough. We just skip the passages where "Wiggar picked up one of Peter's feet as if it were priceless bric-a-brac and decorated it imperturbably with spats."

The excitement revolves around the corpse of millionaire Marvin Hayden, found in the library with a bullet wound in his head. There is some talk of suicide but Peter, like the reader, knows that it just can't be. Didn't the beautiful young wife of the deceased wipe off the handle of the gun? And didn't his own son stand to profit to the tune of half a million in life insurance? And didn't Gillespie, the sanctimonious butler, hint at sinful goings-on between the wife and her stepson?

Whilst we couldn't agree with the blurbist that the yarn is "fiendishly ingenious," it gave us a pleasant two hours.—Todd Downing.[37]

"BRAIN TEASER"
September 15, 1935, p. 52

THE CRIME AT NORNES, BY FREEMAN WILLS CROFTS

MR. Crofts of course needs no introduction to the fans. He is one of the most painstaking of modern purveyors of detective fiction and is perhaps the foremost exponent of the purely intellectual type of deduction. His plots are always constructed with

"for the nonce . . . a relief from the dainty frivolous manner of dealing with death to which so many of the lady writers are addicted."

37 Artist and book designer Lee Thayer (1874-1973) produced over sixty detective novels between 1919 and 1966. (Her final novel was published when she was in her ninety-second year.) As Downing indicates, Thayer's characters Peter Clancy and Wiggar quite obviously aped the Lord Peter-Bunter relationship in Dorothy L. Sayers' mysteries. Critics generally have

so much care that they move with all the precision of well-oiled machinery. There are never any attempts to create atmosphere or induce shudders. Interest in the solution—and nothing else—holds the reader.

Inspector French, backed by the resources of Scotland Yard, is confronted with the double problem of the murder in a country house of the accountant of the firm of Nornes Limited, working jewelers, and of the theft of a million dollars' worth of stones from the firm's safe in London. Nornes, it develops, has been on the verge of bankruptcy and the murder took place during a week-end meeting of the directors, who were trying desperately to escape the finger of fate. Follow investigation into alibis, the mechanism of safes and the ups and downs of the jewelry business and a chase for the criminal that ends in the marts of Amsterdam.

As good an example as the reader will be able to find of a type of fiction that is growing increasingly rare.—Todd Downing.[38]

"GORY AND GROTESQUE"
October 13, 1935, p. 51

THE THREE COFFINS, BY JOHN DICKSON CARR

IT is an exceptional mystery writer nowadays who uses vampirism as atmosphere so convincingly that the reader who hasn't

deemed Thayer's books third-rate. See my review of the author's *The Scrimshaw Millions* at *Mystery*File*, 11 February 2011, http://mysteryfile.com/blog/?p=7839

38 Anglo-Irish railway engineer turned detective novelist Freeman Wills Crofts (1879-1957) is the best known of what Julian Symons called the "Humdrum" school of detective novelists: those who focused intensively on the puzzle. "There are never any attempts to create atmosphere or induce shudders," writes Downing of Crofts and other writers of "purely intellectual" ratiocinative detective fiction. "Interest in the solution—and nothing else—holds the reader." Downing praises Crofts' novels as, tellingly, among the best examples "the reader will be able to find of a type of detective fiction that is growing increasingly rare." Crofts himself published thirty-three detective novels between 1920 and 1957 (only one

yet come to the last chapter (in which he is assured that there really aren't any such critters) will start up in bed and grab at his throat in panic at the nip of a mosquito. When that same writer can bamboozle the veteran reader with two new variants on the old sealed chamber trick, he is deserving of the plaudits which Mr. Carr is getting with his latest chronicle of Dr. Fell.

Mr. Carr, still in his twenties, has a nerve about him. Before going on to elucidate the murders of Prof. Grimaud, student of low magic, in his locked study, and of Pierre Fley, illusionist, in deserted Cagliostro Street, he has Dr. Fell treat us to a discourse on "the general mechanics and development" of the sealed chamber in fiction, along with some sharp remarks about readers who decry the improbable in detective stories. It's all a matter, says he, of personal tastes and preferences. He "cannot find a story enthralling solely on the grounds that it might really have happened." He likes his murders "frequent, gory and grotesque." If your taste happens to agree with that of Dr. Fell (ours does) *The Three Coffins* is recommended to you unreservedly. You probably won't come across anything more to your liking this season.—Todd Downing.[39]

"REACTIONS"
October 13, 1935, p. 51

MURDER ON THE APHRODITE, BY RUTH BURR SANBORN

"THERE is an abnormal amount of fear and jealousy and anger seated round this table: there is one obsession, probably two: there is a split personality, at least three complexes, a dangerous inhibition . . ."

of these after 1951). For more on Freeman Wills Crofts see my book *Masters of the "Humdrum" Mystery: Cecil John Charles Street, Freeman Wills crofts, Alfred Walter Stewart and the British Detective Novel, 1920-1961* (Jefferson, NC and London: McFarland Press, 2012).

39 Like Dr. Fell, Downing likes his murders "frequent, gory and grotesque"—and he accordingly raves this landmark locked room mystery by John Dickson Carr.

The speaker is Professor Dante Gabriel Burge and the table is aboard Mrs. Van Wycke's yacht, beached on an island off the coast of Maine. To prove a theory about reactions the professor dons magenta pajamas, a Panama hat, rubber boots and a pink Angora scarf, turns off the lights and starts shooting with a revolver. A scream. When the lights are turned on la Van Wycke is a corpse and the jools are gone, including an opal that may or may not be the one Verity Insurance Company is after.

Further complications: a hero and a heroine with a secret that the reader (if he has a lick of sense) knows all the time but that the hero doesn't stumble to until page 298.

We are reminded of a sign seen over a five-foot pile of mysteries in a department store: "The Ideal Gift for Your Weekend Hostess."—Todd Downing.[40]

"REVEREND SLEUTH"
October 20, 1935, p. 51

The Scandal of Father Brown, by G. K. Chesterton

The jacket of the latest collection of Father Brown's sallies into criminology is in the way of being a compendium of tributes to the reverend sleuth and his genial creator. Rufus King, Agatha Christie, Ellery Queen and R. Austin Freeman are among those who voice praise which will probably not find a dissenting murmur among the fans. There is a mixture of cold-blooded crime, expert bafflement and ingenious intuitive detection, of psychological probing and whimsical humor which puts the Father Brown stories into that Olympian group to be reread. We don't know where else to find nowadays the modulated note of the bizarre which runs through these tales, or of another author who

40 A Radcliffe graduate, book reviewer, novelist and prolific short story writer, Ruth Burr Sanborn (1894-1942) published two mysteries, *Murder by Jury* (1932) and *Murder on the Aphrodite* (1935). She also inspired, in the final line of this review, one of Downing's most acidic comments as a book reviewer: "We are reminded of a sign seen over a five-foot pile of mysteries in a department store: 'The Ideal Gift For Your Weekend Hostess.'"

could dub his characters Agar Rock, Roger Rook and Harold Harker without a protest from the reader.

Of these eight, we liked particularly "The Blast of the Book," a satisfying tale of psychic disappearances; "The Crime of the Communist," with two men sitting horribly dead in the sunlit garden of Mandeville College; and "The Insoluble Problem," wherein a man is hung to a tulip tree and transfixed with a sword yet, according to Father Brown, there is no murder to solve.—Todd Downing.[41]

"ARCH-CRIMINAL"
October 20, 1935, p. 51

DANGEROUS MR. DELL, BY DAVID HUME

THIS is our first occasion to call attention to the aptly titled Tired Businessman's Library, wherein brain easers and teasers are conveniently if a bit dubiously sorted into Detective, Mystery and Adventure Yarns. *Dangerous Mr. Dell* falls into the first group. Cardby and Son, private detectives who starred in *They Called Him Death*, are here confronted with the triple problem of the abduction of the wife of Reuben Small (Excelsis Corn Beef), the blackmailing of a matinee idol by Sadie the Innocent and the murder of an underworld character in a dark alley. The problems soon resolve themselves into a search for the mysterious Mr. Dell, another of those sinister arch-criminals who pop up in London so frequently.

English critics have been plastering labels of "The New Edgar Wallace" upon so many pretenders to the throne of the Master of Thrills that it is not surprising to find them according Mr. Hume the same honors. While we wouldn't go quite so far, we can safely recommend him for his mad scientists, underground torture chambers and knock-out blows.—Todd Downing.[42]

41 The great English writer Gilbert Keith Chesterton (1874-1936) graced numerous literary fields, but in mystery fiction is best known for his utterly unique Father Brown stories. Downing puts these brilliant tales in "that Olympian group to be reread."

42 Though Downing feels David Hume doesn't quite measure up to his beloved Edgar Wallace, he nevertheless gives him an enthusiastic

"SLIGHTLY PURPLE"
October 20, 1935, p. 51

The Perjured Alibi, by Walter S. Masterman

Kipling's Maxim of Hafiz beginning "If there be trouble to Herward, and a lie of the blackest can clear" provides Mr. Masterman with the inspiration for this account of a man who perjured himself to save a friend from the gallows. When Sir John Barton is murdered on the eve of his wedding to the Vicar's daughter, all the evidence points to young Kenneth Darent, dissolute scion of the Darents of Crowfield Hall: the footprints in the dew; the walking-stick which was the instrument of death; frequent threats uttered in the presence of the villagers. Yet Dennis Tracey, guest at the Hall, believes Darent's protestations of innocence and concocts an alibi for him, to save him until he can find the real murderer.

Those who found some of Mr. Masterman's earlier yarns, such as *The Yellow Mistletoe*, too fantastic can safely renew their acquaintance with him. *The Perjured Alibi* is perfectly sane, with only a few slightly purple passages.—Todd Downing.[43]

"MURDER UNADORNED"
November 3, 1935, p. 55

The Norwich Victims, by Francis Beeding

Murder unadorned, we should say, is Mr. Beeding's forte and not the international brand of fiction to which he treated us in *Death in Four Letters*. A light, concise style, skillful characterization and a chronological arrangement too seldom used in mystery yarns make *The Norwich Victims* easy and exciting reading. The trick of concealing the murderer deserves applause even though it fails to come off owing to ye blurbist, who gives the show away.

recommendation as an accomplished chronicler of "mad scientists, underground torture chambers and knock-out blows."

43 Himself rather a lover of the outré, Downing assures potentially squeamish readers of this particular Walter Masterman title that it "is perfectly sane, with only a few slightly purple passages."

The scene shifts from St. Julian's, one of those English boys' preparatory schools that is so popular at present as murder locales, to Scotland Yard and the boulevards of Paris. Veronica Haslett, housekeeper at St. Julian's, starts to Paris to collect a large sum of money which she has won in a French lottery. She visits Mr. Throgmorton, London investment speculator, and is never seen again alive, although the lottery money is collected and someone wearing her clothes descends from a plane at Croydon field. Three successful murders and an attempted one are solved by Inspector Martin, young and in love with Elizabeth Orme, secretary at St. Julian's.—Todd Downing.[44]

"GARDEN MURDER"
November 17, 1935, p. 55

The Garden Murder Case, by S.S. Van Dine

Interest in the latest offering in the Philo Vance saga will be occasioned by the fact that Philo comes down from his Olympian aerie long enough to get spring fever, albeit a mild case, and to find for the first time that one of the individuals in the line-up of suspects is a woman and not merely an integer in a problem.

Horse-racing vies with romance in furnishing the trimming for the straight tale of detection which one has come to expect from the Van Dine typewriter. The scene is a skyscraper apartment over Riverside Park, where a group of enthusiasts are listening to the returns on the Rivermont handicap. Among them is Vance, who has received an anonymous phone message: "There is a most disturbing psychological tension at Professor Garden's apartment, which resists diagnosis. Read up on radioactive sodium. See Book XI of the Aeneid, line 875. Equanimity is essential." A shot is fired and the dead body of the professor's nephew is found on the roof-garden.

44 Downing argues that Francis Beeding was better suited to proper detective stories than spy thrillers, though Beeding in fact wrote many more of the latter than the former. Today the best known Beeding novel is *Death Walks in Eastrepps* (1931), a tale of classic English murder like *The Norwich Victims*.

We are glad to recommend this more heartily than any of the Van Dine output since *The Scarab Murder Case*. It will be an astute reader who is not misled by as odoriferous a red herring as Agatha Christie ever flung out.—Todd Downing.[45]

"THIRTEEN SUSPECTS"
December 1, 1935, p. 59

Terror at Compass Lake, by Tech Davis

Introducing Aubrey Nash, young bachelor of means, who goes in for amateur sleuthing at the request of his friends. An appeal to journey up to Compass Lake, near the Canadian border, to investigate the death of Jordan Powell, Wall Street broker, does not tempt him, despite the mysterious circumstances. "There were thirteen of us at the lodge," writes his correspondent. "If any man was ever sealed into a room and inaccessible, it was Powell, and yet in the six hours that we slept someone entered his den, buried a dagger in his back, and left. Before or after departing—whichever offers less affront to your credulity—he locked three windows and the single door admitting to Powell's room, on the inside." But when a telegram follows, ordering Nash to disregard the letter, since the case is insoluble and far better forgotten, he takes the next train.

The author deserves praise for creating a tense atmosphere by able characterization of the mutually suspicious inmates of the lodge and for concocting a particularly ingenious alibi. The solution is almost certain to prove a surprise.—Todd Downing.[46]

45 S. S. Van Dine continues to receive high praise from Downing, even as his general popularity was falling from its former Olympian heights (forcing Van Dine to the desperate measure of injecting mild love interest into the proceedings).

46 Edgar "Tech" Davis (1890-1974), a University of Wyoming graduate who worked as a New York City reporter, teacher and salesman, wrote his first detective novel, *Terror at Compass Lake*, on a bet. He followed it with *Full Fare for a Corpse* (1937) and *Murder on Alternate Tuesdays* (1938). Bill Pronzini describes Davis' plotting as "excellent," though he finds his prose "somewhat tedious and verbose." See William F. Deeck, "The Backward Reviewer," at *Mystery*File*, 4 January 2012, http://mysteryfile.com/

"MURDER PSYCHOLOGY"
December 1, 1935, p. 59

Murder at High Noon, by Paul McGuire

Mr. McGuire, a newcomer to the Crime Club list, should prove a favorite with those who have a liking for an insight into the psychological makeup of the characters who murder and get murdered. His gallery is admirably free of the goofiness which so many mystery writers think they have to put into their characters in order to make the readers suspect them of crime.

The story is told in the first person by a young reporter for the *London Morning Register*, who identifies a corpse found in a Dorsetshire haystack dead in a particularly grisly way, as that of Charles Diegel, financial editor of the paper. Since he knew Diegel and aided in the search for him four months previously, he is assigned to the case and proves of material aid to Superintendent Fillinger of the local police force and Chief inspector Cummings of the Yard in clearing up the mystery of the shorthand notes, the scrap of paper reading 1-P.C.-3-1, etc. and the phial of atophan found on the body. The incident of the green race ticket that should have been yellow struck us as an especially bright idea on the part of the author.

This proved popular in England under the title *Daylight Murder*.—Todd Downing.[47]

blog/?p=14291. Downing seems to have had no such qualifications, praising not only the plotting in *Terror at Compass Lake*, but the "tense atmosphere" and "able characterization."

47 Like a number of Golden Age mystery writers, Dominic Mary Paul McGuire (1903-1978) had a quite interesting career that touched only comparatively incidentally on detective fiction. An Australian Catholic, he was a leading lay figure in the church in that country, eventually rising to the post of Australia's ambassador to Italy and achieving a papal knighthood. In addition to books of Catholic thought, social analysis and Australiana, McGuire wrote sixteen mystery novels between 1931 and 1940, mostly set in England and drawing on the time he spent in that country between 1928 and 1932. His most highly regarded and original book, much praised by Jacques Barzun, is *Burial Service* (1938) (in the United States, *A Funeral in Eden*). On Paul McGuire see his entry in the *Australian Dictionary of Biography* by Katharine Massam, found at *adb.anu.edu.au/biography/*

"GOOSEFLESH"

December 1, 1935, page 59

Smoke Screen, by Christopher Hale

If Mr. Hale fails to start the gooseflesh with his first mystery it is not for lack of effort. He isolates a little community on a peninsula jutting into Black Hawk Lake by starting a rampaging forest fire; he unlooses a killer who seems determined to make a clean sweep of them; he shows that their nerves are cracking under the strain. Unfortunately, Ellery Queen used exactly the same situation in *The Siamese Twin Mystery* and *Smoke Screen* suffers a little from comparison. Too, Mr. Hale has not yet acquired the knack of telling a straightforward story. There is a great deal of aimless conversation and running hither and yon to no apparent purpose, either to carry on the plot or to heighten suspense. Some of the studied horror touches, such as the small boy eating snakes, do not come off, in our opinion. Lastly, we were not much impressed with Pete, the Indian, who says, "Why should Indian care about pale faces? Let 'em all disappear. Too damn many anyway."

In spite of all this fault-finding we must admit that a perusal of *Smoke Screen* makes one want to keep an eye out for Mr. Hale's future offerings.—Todd Downing.[48]

"EGYPTIAN STUFF"

December 8, 1935, p. 59

The Bat Flies Low, by Sax Rohmer

If you have been curious about the creator of so many Oriental masters of villainy, you will be interested to know that his likeness,

mcguire-dominic-mary-paul-10965. Striking a modern note, Downing praises McGuire for the realistic psychological insight he provides into the minds "of characters who murder and get murdered."

48 Between 1935 and 1949 eleven detective novels appeared under the name "Christopher Hale," pseudonym of Frances Moyer Ross Stevens (1895-1948). Downing thought Stevens' first mystery, *Smoke Screen*, showed

in a sufficiently exotic setting, adorns the jacket of this volume. He is dark and spare and looks a little like Sherlock Holmes.

There is likewise some resemblance to Lincoln Hayes, New York bachelor and Egyptologist, about whom the action of this thriller revolves. One of Hayes' agents has brought from Egypt a chapter of the Book of Thoth, containing a formula for producing light which has been lost to the world for ages. Enter two Egyptians, Mohammed Ahmes Bey and the beautiful Hatasu. Darkness descends upon the Hayes mansion and the papyrus vanishes. Its trail leads Hayes and his friends to London, to a hidden monastery in the Libyan Desert and back to New York for a cataclysmic climax.

This, the Crime Club selection for November, strikes us as the best of the Rohmer yarns since the early exploits of Fu Manchu. We found ourselves wishing, however, that Hayes weren't too strong and silent to use articles and pronouns. Says he: "Point is got to get reinforcements."—Todd Downing.[49]

"DEAD DIPLOMAT"
December 8, 1935, p. 59

THE CASE OF THE DEAD DIPLOMAT, BY SIR BASIL THOMSON

BEING Inspector Richardson's fourth and perhaps most lively case, as recounted by his creator, K. C. B. and former Assistant Commissioner of New Scotland Yard, in charge of the C. I. D. and Special Branch. Besides these recent ventures into fiction the titled author is responsible for such serious tomes as *The Criminal*

signs of promise, despite flaws, such as too great a similarity to Ellery Queen's earlier The *Siamese Twin Mystery* (1933) and a racially demeaning portrayal of the Indian Pete.

49 "Sax Rohmer" was not just the pseudonym but the exotic persona created by Arthur Henry Sarsfield Ward (1883-1959). One of England's most successful writers of mysteries and occult thrillers, he achieved his greatest fame as the creator of the sinister Asian criminal mastermind, Dr. Fu Manchu—the leading fictional figure in the "Yellow Peril" thriller subgenre. Downing pronounces *The Bat Flies Low* the best Sax Rohmer "yarn since the early exploits of Dr. Fu Manchu."

and *The Story of Dartmoor Prison*. No one can carp, then, at the methods employed by the inspector when he goes to Paris to help the home office and the French police solve the mystery surrounding the slaying of the young press attaché of the English embassy.

Since it all transpires in Paris the seasoned fan will know some of the things to expect: a knife bearing the Nazi swastika and threatened international complications; scandal and a Madame X in the dead man's past; swindlers and disguises in the Café Veil and a dark villa at le Pecq. Before sending us any more of their wares French mystery writers might read to advantage this tale of manhunting as it should be conducted on the banks of the Seine.—Todd Downing.[50]

"GROTESQUE CRIME"
December 22, 1935, p. 55

THE UNICORN MURDERS, BY CARTER DICKSON

THE touch of the grotesque with which Mr. Dickson enlivens his yarns is more than usually effective in his latest offering, spiced as it is with medieval lore about that fabulous beast, the unicorn. What instrument caused the curious wounds in the foreheads of the men murdered in Marseilles and in the isolated Chateau de l'Ile, near Orleans? The unicorn, you remember, could render itself invisible at will and, while three people saw the mysterious visitor die on the staircase, not one of them could say what happened.

Addicts of sleuthing are given a double opportunity to display their talents, for, among the passengers of the Marseilles-Paris plane when it is forced down, are Flamande, the super-

50 Sir Basil Home Thomson (1861-1939) served as head of the Criminal Investigation Department (CID) at New Scotland Yard between 1913 and 1921. As a genre writer he is best known for his pioneering police procedural series of eight novels, published between 1933 and 1937. Downing acidly suggests that his critical *bête noire*, French mystery writers, try reading Thomson to get some notion of what actual police procedure is like.

criminal, and his pursuer, Gasquet, of the Sûreté. Both are keeping their identities hidden. Gruff Sir Henry Merrivale, of the British intelligence service, who appeared in *The Red Widow Murders*, is likewise present.

For those who liked John Dickson Carr's *The Three Coffins*.—Todd Downing.[51]

"BREATHLESS MURDER"
December 22, 1935, p. 47

MURDER WITH PICTURES, BY GEORGE HARMON COXE

NEW members continue to enroll in Prof. Dashiell Hammett's class in hard-boiled, side-of-the-mouth fiction. The latest is Mr. Coxe, whose name is new to us but who, we are told, did his preparatory work in the pulps.

While Kent Murdoch, photographer on a Boston newspaper, is under his shower, trying to clear his head after a two-fisted drinking party in the apartment above, a beautiful, breathless girl slips in beside him and begs him to cover her with the curtain. Kent does so and in this predicament banters the policemen who enter in search of the girl. Upstairs the lawyer who threw the party to celebrate his client's acquittal on a murder charge has himself been murdered. Kent has three incentives to solve the case: he wants to shield the girl, to obtain exclusive pictures for his paper and to win the reward money, with which he can buy a divorce from his wife.

The yarn ends with the most unusual and withal satisfactory punishment for a murderer which we recall. It should appeal to those who liked Adam Hobhouse's *The Hangover Murders*,

51 The "touch of the grotesque" that appealed so much to Downing is amply present in Carter Dickson's *The Unicorn Murders*. Downing recommends the novel to those who enjoyed John Dickson Carr's *The Three Coffins*. As well he should, since John Dickson Carr was "Carter Dickson."

recently made into the movie *Remember Last Night*.—Todd Downing.[52]

52 George Harmon Coxe (1901-1984) enjoyed a successful career as an extremely prolific crime writer, producing over sixty mystery novels between 1937 and 1976. Adam Hobhouse's *The Hangover Murders*, to which Downing compares Coxe's book in his review, has been called "a jaw-dropping tour de force" by Bill Pronzini. See his review at Mystery*File, 4 October 2009, http://mysteryfile.com/blog/?p=1523. Marcia Muller's review of Coxe's *Murder with Pictures* in *1001 Midnights* is considerably less enthusiastic than Pronzini's review of *The Hangover Murders*. She praises it as one of Coxe's typically competent and satisfactory writing jobs but nothing more, with "sex that seems oddly innocent by today's standards." Bill Pronzini and Marcia Muller, *1001 Midnights: The Aficionado's Guide to Mystery and Detective Fiction* (New York: Arbor House, 1986), 164.

CHAPTER FIVE: 1936-1937 REVIEWS

"UNORTHODOX SLEUTH"
January 12, 1936, p. 49

THE SULLEN SKY MYSTERY, BY H. C. BAILEY

MOST mystery writers are satisfied with one successful sleuth. Mr. Bailey, when he feels the modish drawing-rooms through which Reginald Fortune moves too stuffy, turns to Joshua Clunk, the criminal lawyer and psalmster whom Supt. Bell called a "smug little cat" in the *Garston Murder Case*. Mr. Clunk is still a thorn, a rotund little thorn, in the side of the CID and Bell is still growling about him: "I don't mind Clunk always having five aces up his sleeve, but I do object to his telling me the Almighty put 'em there."

This last is on the occasion of Clunk's efforts to free his client, the old lag Isaac Terry, of suspicion in the murder of Alderman Layton, stabbed to death on a beach near Walden. Before long he has the local police, the CID and the London newspapers jumping through hoops for him, has broken the case with the aid of a momentary gleam of sunshine in a sullen overcast sky and has provided the police and the readers with so many murderers that they are completely befuddled. He is probably the most unorthodox sleuth on record.

The Sullen Sky Mystery is the Crime Club selection for October.—Todd Downing.[1]

"GUILTY OR NOT?
January 12, 1936, p. 49

THIRTEEN STEPS, BY WHITMAN CHAMBERS

THERE seems to be doubt in the minds of readers and reviewers alike as to whether this is a bona fide mystery yarn or a slice of life peeled off in the interests of science or sadism (take your choice!) after the manner of James Cain's *The Postman Always Rings Twice* and John O'Hara's *Butterfield 8*. We read it as a mystery and are recommending it as such, although those who enjoy the hard-boiled school of fiction won't be disappointed.

As an unnamed man mounts the steps of the gallows at San Quentin, Al Herrick of the *San Francisco Register* recalls the events leading up to the murder and speculates as to whether the condemned man is guilty or not. The flashback is for each step, with the reader free to pick out among the members of a New Year's Eve drinking party the eventual corpse as well as the murderer. The latter may even be Al himself, for he went blotto for a while after his wife hit him over the head with a candlestick.

Not nice but engrossing, what with long-nosed friends, rye, bourbon, rum and profanity of one, two and three syllables.—Todd Downing.[2]

1 H. C. Bailey's second-string detective, the surpassingly unctuous defense attorney Josiah Clunk, headlined twelve Bailey detective novels between 1930 and 1950. Downing calls Clunk "probably the most unorthodox sleuth on record" and declares that his solution befuddles not only the police but also the readers—perhaps not the best quality in a detective novel.

2 Elwyn Whitman Chambers (1896-1968) published eighteen novels between 1928 and 1950, most of which are criminous, though only a minority of them are tales of detection. His detective novels *The Campanile Murders* (1933) and *Murder for a Wanton* (1934) in the 1930s were filmed

"INGENIOUS MURDER"
January 12, 1936, p. 49

THE GREY ROOM, BY EDEN PHILLPOTTS

THE Modern Readers series has admitted Mr. Phillpotts, with his well-known haunted room yarn of some fourteen years ago, to the company of Homer and Hardy and Ibsen. It is a book which deserves to be owned by the discriminating fan, not only for the author's careful diction but also because it contains perhaps the most ingenious murder method yet devised. Highly recommended.—Todd Downing.[3]

as, respectively, *Murder on the Campus* and *Sinner Take All*. In the 1940s and 1950s he also wrote some screenplays for noir films, including *Manhandled* (1949) and *The Come-On* (1956). Of *Thirteen Steps*, which Downing deems a "not nice but engrossing" mystery genre tale, Fred T. Marsh wrote quite condescendingly in his piece on the novel in the *New York Times Book Review*, suggesting the hostile attitude held toward detective fiction in many literary quarters in the 1930s. "It swings along at a good clip," Marsh wrote of the novel, "but just as you begin to take it seriously as merely tenth-rate [Ernest] Hemingway or second-rate [P. J.] Wolfson you discover that it is only a commercial detective yarn after all and as such, to one who is an outsider in that brand of specialized fiction, as good as any of them and better than most—to judge from a limited acquaintance." Marsh complained that he thought *Thirteen Steps* "was a piece of realism and psychology until it was too late to do anything about it." He then gratuitously revealed the identity of the murderer to the unfortunate readers of his shameful, snide review. *New York Times Book Review*, 8 December 1935. On writer P. J. Wolfson, to whom Marsh alludes in the above quotation (as somewhat better then Chambers though much inferior to Hemingway), see http://www.wdors.com/the-p-j-wolfson-story-bodies-are-dust.

3 Originally published in 1921, *The Grey Room* launched Eden Phillpotts on his prolific second writing career as a Golden Age detective novelist. The story of a haunted chamber in an old English country house, *The Grey Room* was well-suited to appeal to Todd Downing's mystery reading sensibilities. Downing also clearly was impressed by the novel's inclusion—along with works by Homer, Hardy and Ibsen—in the New Directions Publishing Corporation's recently launched Modern Readers series.

"DEATH ON THE BRIDGE"
January 12, 1936, p. 49

Death on the Bridge, by Royce Howes

Bloody doings on the *Sari-Bahr*, 8000-ton freighter en route from Liverpool to New York, described with adequate attention to nautical detail by a man who knows the sea. Says the captain of the *Sari-Bahr*: "It's a bad name. It's a name stained with blood and torture, and if I were a superstitious man I'd pray it didn't taint this ship. I'd pray it didn't put murder on her cargo manifest and blood in her scuppers." That will give you an idea of the effect Mr. Howes tries to create. Whether he succeeds or not will depend on the reader's liking for this sort of thing. Adding to the excitement are: Julia Reynai, Captain Cooper's pseudo-wife; Pinzane, the steward, who has paid 250 pounds for the privilege of working on the boat; Wong Tso Wei, the Chinese cook; and Fenton, the wireless operator, drunk. For those who liked Mary Roberts Rinehart's *The After House*.—Todd Downing.[4]

"DEAD STAR"
January 12, 1936, p. 49

The Cat and the Clock, by Charles G. Booth

We recall that there was considerable enthusiasm among Oklahoma City fans a few seasons back for Mr. Booth's *Murder at High Tide*. It should be good news, then, that he is back amongst us, posing new puzzlers. Who bumped off Stella Ghent, screen star, in a Hollywood penthouse? Was the cat that Stella ran over in her Rolls black or white? Who is the ubiquitous man in the green beret? And how could Stella have danced at the première of

4 Journalist Royce Bucknam Howes (1901-1973) published eight detective novels between 1935 and 1947. In 1955 he won a Pulitzer Prize for his July 26, 1954 *Detroit Free Press* editorial, "The Cause of a Strike." In his review of Howes' first detective novel, Downing again reveals his predilection for nautical mysteries (though for once in this context he does not mention Rufus King).

Napoleon Rex's film *Gay Old Girl*, when the medical examiner insisted afterward that she had been dead two hours before she appeared on the stage?

The story sags a bit in places and the Gallicisms of Anatole Flique, agent of the French Sûreté, are too reminiscent of Hercule Poirot, but all in all it's a safe enough bet for an evening's entertainment.—Todd Downing.[5]

"DEAD SENATOR"
February 9, 1936, p. 53

THE WASHINGTON LEGATION MURDERS, BY VAN WYCK MASON

BEING Captain Hugh North's ninth case. Disregarding the dictum that a mystery writer's business is to keep the mystery reader's mind away from, not on, serious matters, Mr. Mason calls your attention imperiously to the grave dangers threatening the U. S. A. because of the absence of laws punishing peace-time espionage. A super-spy known as the Guardsman is attempting to obtain the plans for some cruisers under construction and to murder Senator Freeman, author of the anti-espionage act awaiting action in Congress. The task of thwarting him falls on North's broad shoulders. The experiences into which he is plunged should contain something to the taste of every reader: murder, footprints, and a beautiful girl in the snow; the third degree and brutality in the naval hospital; a luminous green skeleton on a fog-bound yacht; and, at the end, a rather bewildering unmasking of villains. Love, detection and adventure in about equal proportions.—Todd Downing.[6]

5 Born in England, Charles G. Booth (1896-1949) migrated to the United States, where he wrote pulp magazine stories, novels and screenplays. He won an Oscar for his story for the espionage film *The House on 92nd Street* (1945).

6 Francis Van Wyck Mason (1901-1978), like Cecil John Charles Street a Great War artillery officer (though at an unlikely age), authored numerous historical novels and mystery and espionage thrillers between 1930 and 1980 (the last was published posthumously). As an aside in his review of *The Washington Legation Murders*, Downing declares it a mystery writer's dictum that "a mystery writer's business is to keep the mystery reader's mind away from, not on, serious matters."

"GRUESOME BAFFLER"
February 9, 1936, p. 53

GAUDY NIGHT, BY DOROTHY L. SAYERS

SHELVING the "do's" and "dont's" of the mystery-writing craft, to many of which she herself has given pronouncement, Miss Sayers follows the advice of her own Peter Wimsey—"abandon the jig-saw puzzle kind of story and write about human beings for a change." The result is both a first-rate novel and the most engrossing and gruesome baffler of Miss Sayers' career.

The reader is led on a merry chase in pursuit, not of the customary murderer, but of the poltergeist or worse who is throwing the celibate ladies of Shrewsbury College, Oxford, into panic with threatening letters, obscene drawings upon the walls, capped and gowned dummies transfixed by bread knives and such tricks.

Since a detective must remain aloof from the tenderer emotions, Miss Sayers tells of the wooing by Lord Peter of Harriet Vane, the writer of mystery yarns. No one but E. C. Bentley ever drew an amorous sleuth so successfully.

There is, in the course of these 469 pages, a great deal of John Donne and the cloistered peace of Oxford, which might have become tiresome but which, skillfully injected by Miss Sayers, is an integral and interesting part of the tale.

For a long time to come, *Gaudy Night* should be the first topic of conversation when mystery fans meet.[7]

7 The headline "Gruesome Baffler" hardly does justice to either *Gaudy Night* or Todd Downing's review of the novel. Though highly controversial at the time, dividing critics into three factions (those who thought it an unqualified success, those who deemed it a failure as a mystery and those who deemed it a failure as a mainstream novel and did not care whether or not it succeeded as a mystery), *Gaudy Night* generally is seen today as a landmark work in the mystery genre, helping to transition detective stories into more mainstream novels with a crime interest (crime novels). Downing himself clearly greatly admired the book, gushing that *Gaudy Night*—both a "first-rate novel" and Sayers' "most engrossing and gruesome baffler"—"should be the first topic of conversation" among mystery fans "for a long time to come."

"MODERN PIRATES"
February 9, 1936, p. 53

SAINT OVERBOARD, BY LESLIE CHARTERIS

"I HAVE become so used to seeing the adjective 'incredible' regularly used even in the most flattering reviews of the Saint's adventures," says Mr. Charteris, "that I almost hesitate to deprive the critics of their favorite word." Whereupon he proceeds to inform sticklers for the truth that they can, if they wish, verify the facts about the modern pirate crew which is retrieving treasure on sunken ships in various quarters of the world. Our guess is that few readers will bother to look up the records as long as they have before them the prospect of 298 pages of as fascinating adventure as they will come across this season.

Simon Templar is just as dashing and even more likably human than ever as he wins the gold and the girl in this, Mr. Charteris' nineteenth book and the Crime Club selection for January.—Todd Downing.[8]

"ROUGH AND TUMBLE"
February 9, 1936, p. 53

MURDER STALKS THE MAYOR, BY R. T. M. SCOTT

IF Aurelius Smith didn't have so many admirers among radio fans, young and old, we should feel duty bound to point out that he is decidedly stereotyped, that the Sherlockian pattern belongs in the fogs of Baker Street and not in the glitter of New York night clubs, that mental gymnastics, unless they outdistance the reader, are tiresome, that the strong wasp-waisted hero is no longer monosyllabic, etc., etc. In the face of so much potential protest

8 The Anglo-Chinese author Leslie Charles Bowyer-Yin (1907-1993) attained fame and fortune as "Leslie Charteris," author of the popular series of Simon Templar ("The Saint") thrillers. Downing casts aside Charteris' expressed concern with realism in his crime story, indicating that what matters to him as a thriller reader is "the prospect of 298 pages of . . . fascinating adventure."

we had better be cautious and state our opinion that Aurelius' adventures are better heard over the air than perused on the printed page.

In his latest he saves the mayor of New York from blackmail, Madame Lola of the Club Hibou and the bomb in the billiard cue. Lovers of rough and tumble action won't feel that their $2 has been misspent.—Todd Downing.[9]

"NO HORSE RACES"
February 9, 1936, p. 53

THE SHADOW ON THE DOWNS, BY R. C. WOODTHORPE

RE-ENTER Matilda Perks, the sharp-eyed spinster who made her debut in *Death in a Little Town* (Her tea party in the latter opus remains the best comedy relief in any recent mystery yarn of our acquaintance). This time the scene is the Downs near Helmstone, whither journeys Miss Perks to visit her nephew, Herbert Winstanley. Herbert is riled because the town council is planning to destroy the bucolic quiet of the place by building a racetrack. Then the leading advocate of the track is found dead in the church soon after the villagers have been shocked by hearing the bells ring out a ribald tune.

While the plot isn't up to that of *Death in a Little Town*, and the ending will draw frowns of disapproval from fans who like to see traditions respected, it satisfied us as much as Dorothy L.

9 Reginald Thomas Maitland Scott (1882-1966) was a Canadian born engineer who moved to the United States after World War One and became a writer. He introduced his pulp fiction hero Aurelius Smith in 1920 in the appropriately titled *Adventure Magazine*. Despite the one time popularity of Aurelius Smith on radio, however, Scott is best known today for having written in 1933 the first two novels about the Spider, a pulp fiction hero (these were *The Spider Strikes!* and *The Wheel of Death*). The Spider survives today in graphic novel form. Downing seems to have found Scott's Aurelius Smith distinctly old-fashioned and hokey, despite such thrills as an exploding billiard cue and Madame Lola of the Club Hibou.

Sayers' touted success of last season, *The Nine Tailors*.—Todd Downing.[10]

"WHY NOT?"
February 23, 1936, p. 47

WHY SHOOT A BUTLER?, BY GEORGETTE HEYER

To borrow the words of ye blurbist, hilarity and homicide are the characteristics of Miss Heyer's second opus, as they were of her *Merely Murder* last season. If the hilarity, which is of the English brand, seems a bit esoteric to some readers on this side of the Atlantic, no complaint can be made of the homicide, which begins on page four and recurs with pleasing regularity until the end. Miss Heyer has the true storyteller's knack and it will be a finicky reader indeed who is not engrossed in the attempt of Frank Amberley, London barrister, to solve the mystery which clings to Norton Manor. A copy of Disraeli's *Curiosities of Literature*, a bulldog and a cable to Johannesburg play important parts. Recommended.—Todd Downing.[11]

10 Downing remains much enamored with R. C. Woodthorpe's Miss Matilda Perks, who regrettably made her final appearance in *The Shadow on the Downs*. For Downing to compare *Downs* to *The Nine Tailors* (even if he thought the latter overrated by critics) is high praise indeed.

11 Georgette Heyer (1902-1974) was a prolific author, best known for her enduringly popular Regency romances in the literate style of Jane Austen. She also wrote a smaller number of historical novels, contemporary mainstream novels and mysteries. Her dozen mystery novels, published between 1932 and 1953 and actually plotted, for the most part, by her husband, George Ronald Rougier, were well-received by audiences and critics—the latter of whom particularly praised her humorous and witty dialogue—and are still in print today. Jacques Barzun deemed Heyer the fifth Crime Queen (along with Christie, Sayers, Allingham and Marsh). Though Downing found some of the humor in *Why Shoot a Butler?* too English and esoteric, he nevertheless highly favored the tale, concluding that Heyer had "the true storyteller's knack"—a conclusion with which Heyer's many modern admirers doubtlessly would agree. *Why Shoot a Butler?* was originally published in England in 1933 and reprinted in the United States in 1936 after the success of *Merely Murder* (*Death in the Stocks* in England).

"MURDER MYSTERY"
February 23, 1936, p. 47

Death of an Eloquent Man, by Charlotte Murray Russell

If you read *Murder in the Old Stone House* you will remember Jane Amanda Edwards, the spinster who dabbles in murder mysteries to her own peril, the confusion of criminals and the enhancement of the reputation of Lieutenant Hammond of the Rockport police. In her second adventure Jane pursues the murderer of Mike McCaffery, political boss and candidate for congress. Jane doesn't go in for the subtler nuances of feeling. "That place seemed spooky," says she of a dark stairway. A treat for the milder fans, she will provoke the wrath of Mary Roberts Rinehart adherents.[12]

"MURDER ON THE MOOR"
March 1, 1936, p. 51

The Dartmoor Enigma, by Sir Basil Thompson

Sir Basil, you recall, was at one time the head of the C. I. D. of Scotland Yard. So his coppers are authentic, made-in-Britain goods. This is the fifth case of Inspector Richardson and, as in *The Case of the Dead Diplomat*, he is a quiet, efficient, human detective, who doesn't have time to rescue beautiful damsels in distress, save the country from the Reds or go prowling about night clubs, as is the wont of so many of his colleagues in fiction. This time he investigates the death of one Charles Dearborn on a lonely road in Devon.

12 Charlotte Murray Russell (1899-1992) published nineteen mystery novels between 1935 and 1952, twelve of which featured the nosy, middle-aged, Midwestern spinster Jane Amanda Edwards. Russell has been embraced in the last decade by Rue Morgue Press, who calls her "[o]ne of the most successful early exponents of the American cozy school of mystery writing" and Jane Amanda Edwards "one of the most appealing of her generation of busybody spinsters" (see "Charlotte Murray Russell," *Rue Morgue Press: Mystery Books from the Golden Age of Detective Fiction*, http://www.ruemorguepress.com/authors/russell.html). Yet Downing seems to have deemed Russell's work rather weak tea compared to that

The clue to Dearborn's past may be held by the freckled face boy who can't be found, by Jane Smith, movie actress, or by the 500-pound note sealed in the pages of a detective story. For those still faithful to the venerable Scotland Yard formula.—Todd Downing.[13]

"RAILWAY MURDERS"

March 1, 1936, p. 51

THE A. B. C. MURDERS, BY AGATHA CHRISTIE

HATS off again to Miss Christie and her positively uncanny ingenuity in devising plots with which to surprise her readers! One likes to imagine her ladylike equivalent of a whoop when the inspiration for this one came to her.

It seems that our old friend Hercule Poirot has been receiving letters from someone who signs himself A. B. C., challenging the little Belgian to a battle of wits and calling his attention to certain towns and dates. A series of brutal murders comes to light: an old woman named Ascher in Andover, a young girl named Betty Barnard in Bexhill, Sir Carmichael Clarke in Churston, etc. In each case the only clue to the murderer is an open A. B. C. railway guide near the body. Poirot accepts the challenge. And in the meantime Mr. Alexander Bonaparte Cust sits in his bedroom tortured by headaches. . . .

Skillfully plotted and told in Miss Christie's best vein, *The A. B. C. Murders* will brighten the life of any mystery fan.—Todd Downing.[14]

of Mary Roberts Rinehart, along with Anna Katharine Green the most significant founding mother of "busybody spinster" detective fiction.

13 Downing's concluding sentence—"[f]or those still faithful to the Scotland Yard formula"—suggests that by 1936 he perceived that significant numbers of readers had wavered from the pure puzzle faith.

14 Downing continues to take immense delight in Agatha Christie's work. As he indicates, *The A.B.C. Murders* is unusually inspired—even by the unusually inspired standard of Agatha Christie.

"STOLEN DOCUMENT"
March 22, 1936, p. 57

Death Turns Traitor, by Walter S. Masterman

Addicts of international intrigue, exigent as they are of secret societies which menace the peace of Europe and of ex-inspectors of Scotland Yard who thwart said plans, should devour this one. If Sir Arthur Sinclair hadn't been with his Scotch and soda by the fireside that stormy night, he wouldn't have seen the document which puzzled Mr. Oldfield, the bank manager. . . .

Those who like the straight recipe of corpse plus clues equals murderer will be disappointed, for amid all the excitement attendant on the Geneva conference Sir Arthur, as well as the author, forgets that an unexplained murder has been committed at 10 Downing Street. Mr. Masterman has a rare imaginative gift, but we wish that he would decide which field he is going to cultivate: detection, adventure or phantasy. He could be a whiz in any one of them.—Todd Downing.[15]

"NOT FOR DETECTIVES"
March 22, 1936, p. 57

The Puzzle of the Red Stallion, by Stuart Palmer

Hildegarde Withers and Inspector Piper take another bow in their maddest and merriest murder chase to date. Surfeited as we are with spinster sleuths, Hildegarde is welcome, for her caustic tongue, keen powers of observation and fondness for the terrier Dempsey.

We recommend the scenes wherein she takes a ride in the Black Maria, bets on the horses at Beulah Park and learns new stanzas to *Miss Otis Regrets*, all in the course of her investigation of the death of Violent Feverel, model, on the bridle path in

15 Downing here warns that detection can be too heavily intermingled with the fantastic, as was Walter Masterman's wont, noting that amidst the excitement in Masterman's novel the author forgets to explain one of the murders.

Central Park. Hildegarde spots the briar pipe, the curious hoe and the empty sock and opines that maybe Siwash, the red stallion, didn't kill Violet.

Of course the Inspector would be greeted with guffaws at police headquarters if any of New York's finest were aware that such a fictional prototype of theirs existed, but that consideration need not deter the reader from a good yarn. Detective yarns aren't meant for detectives.—Todd Downing.[16]

"CLASSIC MURDER"
March 29, 1936, p. 56

THE FIFTH TUMBLER, BY CLYDE B. CLASON

WHILE Theocritus Lucius Westborough, who is hereby introduced to the fans, isn't a sleuth who will dazzle anyone with his Sherlockian feats, he is likely, in our opinion, to prove a more enduring figure for that very reason. Theocritus is a professor of Roman history and his knowledge of human nature and of Tacitus aid him to link the murder of the porcine Elma Swink in a Chicago hotel room with such classical assassinations as those of Vibulenus Agrippa, the Emperor Claudius and Britannicus. Particularly praiseworthy is the characterization achieved by Mr. Clason: the gossipy old lady with the excellent ears; the hotel widow; the

16 Mystery Author and screenwriter Stuart Palmer (1905-1968) is best known for his detective novels and short stories chronicling the adventures of Miss Hildegarde Withers, one of the great spinster detectives. Although Downing complains that the mystery genre is "surfeited . . . with spinster sleuths," Downing nevertheless praises *The Puzzle of the Red Stallion* in high terms. As for the novel's lack of realism, Downing generously declares: "Detective yarns aren't made for detectives." Thirteen Hildegarde Withers novels appeared between 1931 and 1954. Additionally, a series of popular Hildegarde Withers films was made in the 1930s. On the author's mysteries, see Steven Saylor, "Stuart Palmer and Hildegarde Withers: An Appreciation," at http://www.stevensaylor.com/Stuart%20Palmer/StuartPalmerHildegardeWithers.html.

traveling salesman; the young night clerk; and all the varied types to be met with in modern caravansary.—Todd Downing.[17]

"SOME DEVILTRY"
March 29, 1936, p. 56

DEAD END STREET, BY LEE THAYER

MISS Thayer's stock in the mystery mart has been rising slowly perhaps, but steadily. To our mind her principal weakness has been one to which so many of the lady writers are prone—a tendency to flutter when giving their readers a peek into the rarefied atmosphere in which their well-valeted gentlemen eat and sleep and sometimes sleuth.

We are glad to report, therefore, that she has let red-headed Peter Clancy don the uniform of a chauffeur, soil his hands with grease and deliver a few swift upper cuts. There's some deviltry going on in the old Madison mansion, a cop has been stabbed and his body tossed into Spuyten Duyvil Creek, upper Manhattan. There's nothing in it to tax the brain, but for suspense and excitement we can safely recommend it. Miss Thayer is hereby forgiven for having let Wiggar, long ago, "lift his master's feet as if they were precious bric-a-brac."—Todd Downing.[18]

17 Between 1936 and 1941 Clyde B. Clason (1903-1987) published ten Theocritus Westborough mysteries, admired today by connoisseurs for their complex problems in detection. Interestingly, in his short review of the debut Clason detective novel Downing affords more praise for the characterization than he does for the puzzle. On Clyde B. Clason, see "Clyde B. Clason," at *Rue Morgue Press: Mystery Books from the Golden Age of Detective Fiction*, http://www.ruemorguepress.com/authors/clason.html.

18 Although he finds nothing in this Lee Thayer detective novel to "tax the brain," Downing nevertheless recommends it for its "suspense and excitement." Thayer's "bric-a-brac" comment in an earlier book still rankles Downing somewhat, however; and Downing takes this opportunity to condemn what he sees as the tendency of "so many of the lady writers" to "flutter" and fawn on their gentlemen detectives. This criticism was

"KID GANGSTERS"
April 5, 1936, p. 65

THE SLEEPING DEATH, BY G. D. H. AND MARGARET COLE
THE Coles, probably the most successful of all collaborators in the mystery field, are the latest to bow to the English fad for schoolchild murders. Santley Free School is the setting and Henrietta Zimmerman, 13, is the corpse. There has been some hanky-panky with the medicine and Henrietta took an overdose of dial. Not the least surprising thing about the school is its principal, whose name is either Spink or Cromwell and who goes in for nudism, vegetarianism and other isms. In the faculty watch Gwladys (pronounced gooladys) Bickers, a repressed spinster, and among the children are the members of The Gang, hiding in a bamboo thicket and swearing vengeance on Henrietta because she killed their mouse. We are still doubtful whether this *Mädchen in Uniform* atmosphere belongs in a mystery yarn.—Todd Downing.[19]

"GORY AND GROTESQUE"
April 12, 1936, p. 55

THE ARABIAN NIGHTS MURDER, BY JOHN DICKSON CARR
IN *The Three Coffins* Mr. Carr gave his recipe for successful mysteries: Make the murders "frequent, gory and grotesque." Since we agree with him and he grows more adept at his concoctions, we are among his most vociferous fans. Here we have the perplexing problem at the Wade Museum, stated for the benefit of Dr. Fell by three police officers: an Irishman, an Englishman and

later echoed by such critics of the British Crime Queens as Raymond Chandler, Edmund Wilson and Graham Greene. On Chandler see my three-part essay "'The Amateur Detective Just Won't Do': Raymond Chandler and British Detective Fiction," at my blog, *The Passing Tramp*.

19 Downing expresses some doubt about the "English fad for schoolchild murders." *Mädchen in Uniform* (1931) is a pioneering German film exploring lesbianism in a girls' boarding school.

a Scotchman, each "a contrast for the telling or even thinking of such a story."

It begins when the Rev. William Augustus Illingworth, of the John Knox Presbyterian Church of Edinburgh, jumps off a wall and cries to a policeman: "You killed him!" It gets more involved when a man about town is arrested in front of the museum with a note beginning: "Dear G. There has got to be a corpse." The heights of dizziness are reached with the discovery of the night watchman dancing about the coffin of Zobeide, "Missus" of Haroun al Raschid, and of the cookbook in the hand of the corpse. Doctor Fell solves the mystery of the disappearing whiskers at daylight. With close attention to clues you may do it by that time.—Todd Downing.[20]

"BEDROOM MURDER"
April 12, 1936, p. 55

THE TICKING TERROR MURDERS, BY DARWIN L. TEILHET

HAVING caught the fancy of the fans with *The Talking Sparrow Murders*, Mr. Teilhet launches a new sleuth, the Baron Franz Maximillian Karagoz von Kaz, impoverished Austrian refugee, in a series of adventures in "the barbaric states of North America." The baron is not only blood brother of a long line of literary rogues, but also a veteran of Viennese crime detection, so readers are treated to both buffoonery and expert sleuthing. Henry Kerby, Hollywood author, hires the baron to find out what is causing the ticking noises in his room at night. Kerby, it seems, is involved in an affair with Lucille Tarn, star of Solar Pictures, Inc., and fears that someone, probably Lucille's superfluous husband, is trying to drive him to suicide. Lucille is murdered in the "disappearing-woman" cabinet of the magician, Dacrokoff, and the baron sets to work in earnest.

20 Downing declares himself now a "vociferous" fan of John Dickson Carr, who "grows more adept at his concoctions."

Unusual, entertaining and, except for a proclivity of the author's to linger on bedroom scenes, fast moving.—Todd Downing.[21]

"INNOCENT PROFESSOR"

April 19, 1936, p. 61

The Long Tunnel, by Sidney Fairway

Like *Thirteen Steps*, recently reviewed on this page, *The Long Tunnel* belongs in that increasingly large category of books which are not strictly detective or mystery stories but rather novels in which the plot revolves around the question of who committed a murder. While we do not feel justified in recommending such works to the avowed fans, who object to having their plots confused by anything extraneous to the business of homicide and its detection, we do feel that there are many readers to whom they will appeal: lovers of good novelistic technique who are irked by the cut-and-dried formula of the regular mystery yarn.

The name Sidney Fairway is said to conceal the identity of a well-known London medical man. His fourth literary effort comes with the endorsement of A. J. Cronin, who feels that it deserves "a resounding success." It is the story of a professor of St. Botolph's Medical School who is acquitted of a murder charge, but who wishes to clear himself unequivocally in the eyes of his confreres. To do [so] he must unmask the real murderer.—Todd Downing.[22]

21 Between 1934 and 1940 American Darwin Teilhet (1904-1964) published, among other genre novels, five Baron von Kaz mysteries, the latter three with his wife Hildegarde Tolman: *The Talking Sparrow Murders, The Ticking Terror Murders, The Feather Cloak Murders, The Crimson Hair Murders,* and *The Broken Face Murders*. Downing seems to have greatly enjoyed *The Ticking Terror Murders*, barring the author's "proclivity . . . to linger on bedroom scenes."

22 "Sidney Fairway" was the pseudonym of Sidney Herbert Daukes (1879-1947), a Cambridge graduate and physician. Under this pseudonym he wrote at least one other crime novel, *The Yellow Viper* (1931), but he

"LOOSE ON DECK"
April 26, 1936, p. 71

The Callao Clue, by Royce Howes

You may remember Mr. Howes as the author of last season's *Death on the Bridge*, wherein he showed indubitable promise as a newcomer familiar both with mystery technique and with tramp steamers. Now we have a murderer loose on the decks of the *S. S. Corcovado*, which has been stopped at midnight in the Straits of Yucatan. Among the suspicious passengers, all bound for Peru, are: a Peruvian politico ("Eet ees my gun"); a blonde languishing lady with two black eyes; a soldier of fortune; and two rival U. S. promoters. Detective Lieutenant Brandon of the New York police investigates the corpse in the sealed room, the pair of dueling pistols, letters hinting of Peruvian intrigue and a faked appendicitis operation. Don't be frightened away by the elaborate deck drawings on the front pages. The author admits they aren't important.—Todd Downing.[23]

"MURDER AD LIB"
April 26, 1936, p. 71

Mr. Smith's Hat, by Helen Reilly

Miss Reilly, one of our ablest and most literate spinners of mystery yarns, continues the saga of Inspector McKee, of Centre Street. Admirers of this doughty Scotsman will probably like this

published primarily mainstream novels with a medical background. Though he does not use the term "crime novel" in his review of *The Long Tunnel*, it is that to which Downing essentially is referring when he distinguishes "novels in which the plot revolves around who committed a murder" from "detective and mystery stories." A[rchibald] J[oseph] Cronin (1986-1961) was a Scottish physician and bestselling mainstream novelist. One of his most popular books was the medical novel *The Citadel* (1937).

23 Royce Howes' second detective novel—another shipboard mystery—receives an equally enthusiastic review from Downing, lover of shipboard mysteries—though Downing refrains from comparing *The Callao Clue* to books written by either Mary Roberts Rinehart or Rufus King!

better than any of his previous cases, for the author has been lavish with the appurtenances of her murders.

The scene shifts rapidly: a Greenwich Village studio, where Gilbert Shannon, writer of lurid Westerns, succumbs to gin or angina; the monkey-house of a Connecticut estate, where a fake baroness is stabbed with the prong of a Betty lamp; a Manhattan penthouse, where the most promising suspect is done in with a knife. Besides the usual array of philandering husbands and wives, blackmailers and young lovers, there is a mysterious Mr. Smith lurking in the background. He it was who laughed at the funeral of the first corpse. Whatever your taste in homicides, you will find something to your liking here.—Todd Downing.[24]

"DAGGER MURDER"
April 26, 1936, p. 71

The Stars Scream Murder, by Arthur B. Reeve

It is a far cry from Craig Kennedy of the test tubes, as we knew him twenty years ago, to today's dabbler in the mumbo-jumbo of astrology, with its zodiacs, microcosms, macrocosms, fire elementals, and what not. Says Kennedy, when he learns of the death of old Maria Daskam in the burned tower of her home in Southampton: "I feel that there are actual malefic emanations surrounding this whole affair." He proceeds with faithful Jameson to pore over horoscopes until he spots the fiend who murdered Maria and maybe got away with the El Greco. Although the homicide is of the rubber dagger variety, with Dot, the slavey, in the kitchen and Nan, the sophisticate, in the living room, and That Thing lurking in the background, there are thrills for those who scare easily.—Todd Downing.[25]

24 Helen Reilly (1891-1962) wrote nearly forty detective novels between 1930 and her death in 1962, most of which chronicle the exploits of her series detective Inspector Christopher McKee. She was the mother of crime writers Ursula Curtiss and Mary McMullen.

25 In his review of *The Stars Scream Murder*, Downing's disenchantment with childhood mystery genre idol Arthur B. Reeve seems complete.

"CAPE COD MURDER"
April 26, 1936, p. 71

The Clue of the Poor Man's Shilling, by Kathleen Moore Knight

A poor man's shilling, we finally learned, is "a coin-shaped seed pod of the plant known as 'honesty,' or, more commonly, 'Peter's Pence.' It is sometimes found in old-fashioned gardens." In this instance, it is found in the shoe of a corpse by none other than Luella Page, the retired schoolmarm who, after an initial taste of adventure in *Death Blew out the Match*, has bought a house on Quontauk Island, off Cape Cod. Her assistant in detection is still easy-going Elisha Macomber, fish merchant, with his query: "Whar's the body?"

Miss Knight knows her locale, undoubtedly, and her novel will be a treat to summer visitors to Cape Cod. "Off-islanders" may find the dialog a bit difficult. Our prediction is that Miss Knight will be another Mignon Eberhart only when she chooses characters with more than a local appeal. Even the fog on the sand dunes doesn't compensate for Sheerjashub Wade, Hiram Pearse and Peleg Whitehead.—Todd Downing.[26]

"A BIT SCRAMBLED"
May 3, 1936, p. 59

The Feather Cloak Murders, by D. and H. Teilhet

Baron von Katz having met with deserved success in *The Ticking Terror Murders*, his creators carry on his adventures in their usual zestful style. The baron is on his way back to Vienna for a royalist coup when he overhears certain enigmatic words on a Honolulu bound liner and starts on the trail of the Green Lion Jade

26 Although Downing was mightily impressed with Kathleen Moore Knight's first Cape Cod tale, *Death Blew out the Match*, he deems *The Clue of the Poor Man's Shilling* rather too quaint, with such over-exotically named characters as Sheerjashub Wade and Peleg Whitehead. In Downing's view, Knight would only attain the lofty title of "another Mignon Eberhart" when she relied less on crazy quilt local color of the homespun sort and more on pure suspense.

and the feather cloak of Prince Puakini. The characters are a bit scrambled at first but they soon sort themselves out so that the reader can at least distinguish the orientals from the occidentals. There is a thrilling denouement in an ancient lava tunnel under Mauna Kea.

Inserted at the back is the opening chapter of *The Third Adventure*—so we shall be renewing the baron's acquaintance soon.—Todd Downing.

"HOMESPUN SLEUTH"
May 10, 1936, p. 55

MURDER ON THE DAY OF JUDGMENT, BY VIRGINIA RATH

HAVING missed *Death at Dayton's Folly*, it took us a few pages to figure out who Rocky Allan was and why he and his red-headed wife were bumping in an old car through the wilds of California. Rocky, it developed, is a railroader, a deputy sheriff and a woodsman from way back, with the two latter occupations occupying most of his time. He deserves your acquaintance.

To our mind the author has struck a balance between the homespun sleuth with his incomprehensible dialect, beloved by so many lady writers, and the know-it-all dilettante, with his irksome eccentricities. The goings on at Coon Hollow are guaranteed to keep you up beyond the curfew, for here Sapphira Barlow, revivalist, has gathered her satellites to await the end of the world, at 3:45 a. m., Pacific standard time, August 26. If you don't get into a dither about the fate of the world, you will about that of Sapphira's followers when she is found strangled with a scarf.—Todd Downing.[27]

27 Between 1935 and 1947 Californian Virginia Rath (1905-1950) published thirteen mystery novels, seven of which feature rural California sheriff Rocky Allan. Continuing his more recent series of digs at women crime writers, Downing observes that with her creation Rocky Allan the author had successfully "struck a balance between the homespun sleuth with his incomprehensible dialect, beloved by so many of our lady writers, and the know-it-all dilettante, with his irksome eccentricities."

"UNWANTED CORPSE"
May 10, 1936, p. 55

FAIR WARNING, BY MIGNON EBERHART

SINCE *The White Cockatoo* Mrs. Eberhart's novels have departed more and more from the category of detective yarns into a field where she is as unique in her day as Mrs. Radcliffe was in hers. If any fan is serious-minded enough to re-read *The Mysteries of Udolpho* he will realize how far the tale of terror has progressed and how much the pruning of some of the Gothic impedimenta has improved it.

When the unpleasant Ivan Godden returns to his home after a month in the hospital the seasoned reader will mark him at once as the prospective corpse. His browbeaten wife and the handsome young man next door have become enamored of each other; his spinster sister has done a great deal of spying; someone has secreted a dandelion knife, a paperweight, and a package of arsenic.

Replete with a follow-up murder, a will, a faked alibi and a rainstorm, *Fair Warning* belongs on the "must" list of every fan.—Todd Downing.[28]

"POLICE METHOD"
August 2, 1936, p. 57

X. JONES OF SCOTLAND YARD, BY HARRY STEPHEN KEELER

As his seasonal novelty Mr. Keeler presents the story of a crime told in dossier form, with photographs, letters, cables, newspaper reports, diagrams and documentary evidence, plus the "Daily Observations" of Prof. Ephraim Tulleyday, of the Northern Oklahoma College of Agriculture and Arts, at Cherokee, Okla. While the 448-volume is a sequel and necessary complement to *The Marceau Case* a reading of the earlier book is not necessary for its enjoyment.

28 Downing finds here that Eberhart out-Rads Radcliffe. His esteem for the "feminine" mystery story with terror trappings remains high.

We are still uncertain whether Mr. Keeler intends his readers to take seriously Xenias Jones' bewildering theory of crime detection but at any rate the former Yard man finally elucidates the mystery of André Marceau's strangulation in the center of his rolled lawn, of his terrified cry, "The Babe from Hell!" and of the Lilliputian footprints which began nowhere and ended nowhere.

Keeler fans, make haste to the bookstore!—Todd Downing.[29]

"MURDER IN FIJI"
August 2, 1936, p. 57

Murder in Fiji, by John W. Vandercook

Mr. Vandercook seems to be permanently enlisted in the ranks of mystery writers. Following up the success of his *Murder in Trinidad* he sends his sleuth, Bertram Lynch of the permanent central board of the United Nations, half across the world to solve a series of bizarre and seemingly unrelated slayings in the Fijian island of Viti-Levu. In a scene which arouses memories of Beatrice Grimshaw, Lynch's man Friday, Robert Deane, is abandoned on a reef in the Pacific, his legs fast in a tridacna shell. Replete with exotic atmosphere and authentic ethnological data, including the native ceremony of "yalocaki" or crime detection, this book is recommended both to mystery and adventure addicts.—Todd Downing.[30]

29 Keeler's *The Marceau Case* was earlier praised in the *Daily Oklahoman* by Stanly Vestal (1887-1957), novelist, historian and OU English professor, as a "most ingenious and spectacular yarn" (10 May 1936). By 1936 Keelerism had planted at least two flags on the OU campus.

30 Between 1933 and 1959 novelist, biographer, historian and travel writer John Womack Vandercook (1903-1963) published four tropical clime mysteries, two in the 1930s and two in the 1950s: *Murder in Trinidad* (1933), *Murder in Fiji* (1936), *Murder in Haiti* (1956) and *Murder in New Guinea* (1959). *Murder in Trinidad* was filmed three times, in 1934, 1939 and 1945. On Vandercook and his mysteries see David L. Vineyard, "John W. Vandercook and the Bertram Lynch Mysteries," *Mystery*File*, 3 April 2009, http://mysteryfile.com/blog/?p=1078. Vineyard argues that Vandercook's mystery novels offer readers the chance "to get away from the more cozy British country house and village crime without sacrificing

"ERUDITE SLEUTH"
August 9, 1936, p. 53

The Death Angel, by Clyde B. Clason

Murder continues to keep company with Theocritus Lucius Westborourgh, the mild-mannered little author of the 800-page *Trajan: His Life and Times.* The first night of his visit to Rumpelstiltzken, a Wisconsin estate, he is given a glass of whiskey doped with paraldehyde, and wakes to hear a revolver shot and to receive a threatening note from The Firefly. Arnold Bancroft, his host, has vanished; a square of black velvet has been ripped from one of Imogene Bancroft's gowns; and there is a bloody handprint on the narrow ledge of Bowen's Rock. Six days of excitement follow.

We are glad to recommend Mr. Clason's second book much more heartily than *The Fifth Tumbler*. Prof. Westborough is a bit too erudite at times, as when he discusses mathematics and mushrooms, but the fans will find him an improvement on most amateur sleuths.—Todd Downing.[31]

"TRIANGLE MURDER"
August 9, 1936, p, 53

Murder Isn't Easy, by Richard Hull

Owing to our deep distrust of detective novels, particularly those of English provenance, which bear the label "deliriously humorous," we were so ill-advised as to pass over *The Murder of My Aunt* and *Keep It Quiet!* We hereby make amends to such fans as

the fun of a formal mystery" and that they "offer thrills and solid detection," sentiments with which Downing no doubt would agree, as he recommends the book for both "mystery and adventure addicts." *Tridacna* is the scientific name for the giant clam. Beatrice Grimshaw (1870-1953) was an Irish-born novelist who lived in New Guinea for many years and favored South Seas settings for her tales.

31 Downing finds this second Clason novel superior to the first, though Clason's detective, Theocritus Lucius Westborough, he still deems "a bit too erudite at times" (yet still "an improvement on most amateur sleuths").

depend on this page for their guidance by urging them to follow our example and get on the Hull bandwagon.

Not that we consider Mr. Hull humorous. The chuckles whose echoes have found their way across the Atlantic still leave us unimpressed. We are enthusiastic, however, about his neat conversational style, his skillful characterization, his ability to tell an orthodox detective story in an unorthodox manner.

The plot concerns three members of an advertising agency who find their personalities incompatible and decide to do something about it. Partner A starts to tell the reader how and why he is going to murder Partner B. Partner B starts to tell the reader how and why he is going to murder Partner A. Partner C—

But further revelations are impossible without giving the trick away. Read it yourself.—Todd Downing.[32]

"OVERDOSE"
August 9, 1936, p. 53

MURDER OF A MATRIARCH, BY HUGH AUSTIN

SINCE it was something like a year ago that Mr. Austin made his entry into the mystery field with *It Couldn't Be Murder!* the fans should be familiar with him as the fabricator of ingenious, closely knit plots, as the master of a terse simple style and as the creator of Peter D. Quint, known as P. D. Q. to the homicide bureau of the city of Hudson.

Quint meets the members of the Farcourt household when that tyrannical old harridan, Mrs. Hortense Farcourt, summons him to investigate the poisoning of her cat. After close questioning he is inclined to take seriously the old lady's fears that the

32 Between 1934 to 1953 Richard Hull (1896-1963) published fifteen mystery novels. Although Hull never surpassed the critical acclaim afforded his first effort in the genre, the inverted crime tale *The Murder of My Aunt* (1934), arguably his greatest masterpiece in the genre is the sinister *My Own Murderer* (1941). As Downing notes, Hull had a marked "ability to tell an orthodox detective story in an unorthodox manner."

lethal dose was intended for her and is not surprised, one summer afternoon, to learn that she has been shot dead.

Sanguinary readers may object to the fact that half the book is required to lead up to the slaughter. There is plenty of excitement at the finish, however, as Quint, with his usual violence and nervous impatience, runs down the killer.—Todd Downing.

"GIGOLO MURDERER"
August 16, 1936, p. 65

Turquoise Hazard, by Alfred Betts Caldwell

Mr. Caldwell is a newcomer to mystery fiction who evidently knows the life of New York's Washington Square as well as that of Gramercy Park and who has some rather ingenious death gadgets up his sleeve. Mrs. Baldridge, a lady with "overdeveloped amorous instincts," is the corpse, presumably via the poison route, since a sixteenth century Florentine ring lies open and empty beside her. Freddy Phillpotts, an innocuous youngster with plenty of time and money, sorts over her former gigolos and semi-gigolos in his search for the killer. Meanwhile, down in Center Street, the members of the police department twiddle their thumbs and shake their heads in what writers like Mr. Caldwell would have us believe is their perpetual state of bafflement.—Todd Downing.[33]

"OIL FIELD MURDER"
August 16, 1936, p. 65

A Frame for Murder, by Kirke Mechem

This yarn will attract the attention of Oklahomans because of its setting, the oil fields about Wichita, Kansas. There's no doubt Mr. Mechem knows his petroleum.

33 About Alfred Betts Caldwell I know nothing, bar that he published three detective novels: *Turquoise Hazard* (1936), *No Tears Shed* (1937) and *Death*

Stephen Steele is the amateur sleuth who solves, competently enough, the mysteries of: the death of Ralph "Lucky" Laundon, oil operator, on top of a haystack; the sales slip for a woman's nightgown found in a deserted ranch house; and the dubious past of Reverend Van Roth, Kansas' radio parson. Those who take fright easily may be induced to believe that the critter which left the strange footprints and the tufts of brown hair escaped from the Rue Morgue. Most readers, however, will be glad when a gusher catches fire and adds excitement to a tale which is dedicated too strictly to the question: "Where were you at eight-thirty on the morning of March 16?"[34]

"MURDER: ENGLISH STYLE"
August 23, 1936, p. 55

A CLOSE CALL, BY EDEN PHILLPOTTS

WITH his usual notable mastery of English countryside and atmosphere, Mr. Phillpotts tells the story of Thomas Huntsman, police inspector of Wellbrook-on-Sea, and of his trial for the murder of his ne'er–do-well son-in-law, John Norton.

Rattle (1940). Downing seems to have admired Caldwell's employment of "rather ingenious death gadgets" in *Turquoise Hazard* even as he decried the appearance of yet another mystery novel in which the gifted and wealthy amateur detective makes the police look like fools.

34 Downing thought Kirke Mechem knew his petroleum, but rather less, unfortunately, about constructing an interesting mystery. Mechem was both a Kansas playwright (see, for example, his 1939 play *John Brown*) and Kansas State Historian. In the latter capacity he wrote the text for the fifty-six state historical markers erected in Kansas in the 1930s. Mechem's elder son James (b. 1923) is a Beat generation writer and his younger son Kirke (b. 1925) is a prominent composer (his many works include the 1980 opera *Tartuffe*). *A Frame for Murder* was Kirke Mechem's only published novel. See "James Mechem, Writer and Publisher: Interview by Denise Low," 20 October 2003, *Beats in Kansas: The Beat Generation in the Heartland*, at http://www.vlib.us/beats/mechemlow.html and "Kansas Historical Markers," *The Kansas Historical Quarterly*, http://www.kancoll.org/khq/1941/41_4_mechem.htm.

It is a placidly told tale, depending for interest on few of the usual contrivances of the mystery yarn. Speeches for the prosecution and the defense are quoted at length, with a lucid exposition of the future of psychoanalysis in English jurisprudence. Scotland Yard fails to solve the problem and justice is vindicated only by the last minute confession of the criminal. It is encouraging to see a writer of Mr. Phillpotts' stature dedicate himself so wholeheartedly to the field of detective fiction.[35]

"HAUNTED HOUSE"
September 6, 1936, p. 49

THE CROWING HEN, BY REGINALD DAVIS

WHEN we come across a yarn like this one we rejoice that the old-fashioned thriller hasn't been displaced altogether by the new hard-boiled, side-of-the-mouth type of fiction and that there are still haunted houses such as Dane's Priory, wherein bells tolled mysteriously at midnight, subterranean passages are revealed at the proper touch and effigies appear and disappear bewilderingly. What or who is the Crowing Hen and what has it to do with the old superstition that "whistling women and crowing hen are neither good for God nor men"? What is the curse which has lain upon the house of Fitz Dane since 1495 and why does it affect the fortunes of young Terry Hyland and Shirley Esdale? And how did the Buff Orpington change its identity in the grave?

There are detectives (in and out of disguise), a murderer and a few clues for those who insist on using their brains. Our advice is to read the book in an uncritical mood and enjoy it.—Todd Downing.[36]

35 Downing remains in thrall to Eden Phillpotts, declaring: "It is encouraging to see a writer of Mr. Phillpotts' stature dedicate himself so wholeheartedly to the field of detective fiction." Modern readers probably would find Downing's admission that *A Close Call* is "a placidly told tale" something of an understatement.

36 Reginald Davis authored three mystery thrillers: *The Crowing Hen* (1936), *Nine Days' Panic* (1937) and *Twelve Midnight Street* (1938). *The Crowing*

"BATHROOM MURDER"
September 6, 1936, p. 49

WHO KILLED STELLA POMEROY?, BY SIR BASIL THOMSON

THERE are no better or more authentic detective novels of the strictly Scotland Yard type than those with which Sir Basil supplies us twice yearly. As former head of the C.I.D. he knows how the Yard really functions and as the author of five previous yarns (*The Dartmoor Enigma* was the last) he has learned to adapt his knowledge to fictional requirements.

The basic problem of his latest is one which confronted California police not many years ago. Prospective renters of a bungalow find the owner working in his garden one bright morning. With the words, "I'm sure my wife will be delighted to show you over the house," he takes them within, only to find the bathroom a shambles and the wife dead from a blow on the head. The husband is suspected, arrested, and finally vindicated. While the solution is not one which could be applied to the California case, if our memory serves, it does offer interesting hypotheses.

Incidentally, our old friend Inspector Richardson gains a wife during the course of his investigation.—Todd Downing.[37]

Hen, which also has been praised by Bill Pronzini, clearly appealed to Downing's nostalgia for the "old fashioned thriller" he associated with Edgar Wallace, a type of book in the 1930s increasingly displaced "by the new hard-boiled, side-of-the-mouth type of fiction." Though the novel had "detectives . . . , a murderer and a few clues for those who insist on using their brains," Downing advised fans to "read the book in an uncritical mood and enjoy it."

37 Downing continues to find in the mystery tales of Sir Basil Thomson "no better or more authentic detective novels of the strict Scotland Yard type." His reference to a California bungalow murder of a few years earlier reveals his continued interest in true crime as well.

"HIGHBROW DETECATIF"
Sept. 6, 1936, p. 49

Death Stops the Manuscript, by Richard M. Baker

Mr. Baker, a teacher at Kent School in Connecticut, enters the field of detective fiction with the commendation of none other than S. S. Van Dine. Says Philo Vance's creator in the introduction: "I was completely fooled and nonplussed as to the correct answer. The book was simply too hard a nut for me to crack."

The Master's influence is apparent throughout: in the amateur sleuth, Franklin Russell, who dallies over morning coffee and quotes French and Latin sages while the corpse goes into rigor mortis; in the scholarly aura which surrounds the crime in the study where Professor Carson is engaged upon a translation of the *Chanson de Roland*; in the leisurely and nonchalant manner of the murderer's unmasking.

There is sound workmanship in the novel and good entertainment for fans who like to pit their wits against a criminal who is clever and determined, but not too fiendish. Welcome, Professor Baker!—Todd Downing.[38]

"ELUSIVE CORPSE"
September 20, 1936

The Lady in the Morgue, by Jonathan Latimer

The Dame in the Deadhouse becomes the title when translated into the language of William Crane, Mr. Latimer's bellicose sleuth. If you are surfeited with namby-pamby summer reading and have

38 Richard M. Baker was a longtime Master of French at a prestigious preparatory school in Connecticut. Encouraged by S. S. Van Dine, he published three detective novels in the 1930s. Later he turned his attention to Charles Dickens' unfinished novel, *The Mystery of Edwin Drood* (1870), producing a book on the subject, *The Drood Murder Case* (1951). In his review of *Death Stops the Manuscript*, Judge Lynch of the *Saturday Review* was rather less kind than Downing, paraphrasing Ogden Nash ("Philo Vance/ Needs a kick in the pance") in rendering his verdict on Baker's book: "Franklin Russell/Needs a kick in the bustle" (1 August 1936, p. 16).

some hellishness in you which you want to release vicariously, you might try the opus. At least you won't be bored.

Assisted by his doughty companions, Doc Williams and Tom O'Malley, and fortified by sundry bottles of Dewar's White Label, Niersteiner '29 and Martell cognac, plus beer and gin on the side, Crane pursues the elusive corpse of an unidentified girl who was murdered in a honky-tonk hotel in Chicago. He visits a taxi dance hall and purloins twenty dresses which aren't in use, acquires a drunken bulldog and sits in on a marihuana jag in the rear of a barroom, prowls about a cemetery at the witching hour of midnight, and is introduced to Mrs. Courtland, straight from Park Avenue. Mrs. Courtland raises a lorgnette and says: "Oh, detectives! What odd-looking men! Have the room properly aired, Chauncey."

That's probably enough to steer you straight to or from the book.—Todd Downing.[39]

"GHOST-HUNTER"
September 20, 1936, p. 59

THE UNDYING MONSTER, BY JESSE DOUGLAS KERRUISH

A TALE of pure horror is, we are sure, a hundred times more difficult to write than one of mystery or detection. The reader must be kept credulous and tense from the first page to the last; once he is allowed to relax he thinks of how silly the whole business of ha'nts really is. It is not to be expected that works like *Dracula* and *The Red Lamp* will appear every season.

We feel that it is only fair to Miss Kerruish to make this statement before we confess our lukewarmness with regard to her novel. It is well written and has all the required elements: A monster which for generations has been slaying members of the house of Hammand; an old manor house, with secret passages,

39 Do you "have some hellishness in you which you want to release vicariously?" Then Todd Downing suggests Jonathan Latimer's ribald, hard-boiled tale of raucous, hard-boozing Chicago sleuths and crooks might be just the thing for you.

sealed chambers and turret prisons; libraries filled with works on necromancy; burial mounds of Saxon chieftains. But, alas, it also has Luna, who failed to impress us. Luna is a ghost-hunter (Supersensitive to you) who is hired by the twentieth century heirs to ferret out the mystery. It is rather disillusioning to find her succumbing to such a mundane thing as love.—Todd Downing.[40]

"PLENTY SHIVERS"
September 27, 1936, p. 67

THE WHEEL SPINS, BY ETHEL LINA WHITE

THIS is unquestionably the finest example of the macabre which has come to our attention in years. A comparatively unpretentious chronicle of a railway journey, it had an effect on us which a recent yarn of werewolves and family curses by an English compatriot of Miss White's failed entirely to achieve. It unnerved us completely.

Iris Carr suffers a sunstroke on the platform of a tiny European station as she is about to board a train for home. She is traveling alone and has no knowledge of the language of the people about her. She is befriended by a colorless little English spinster, Miss Froy. Miss Froy disappears and the passengers unite in affirming that no such person existed. Iris is bewildered, uncertain whether she was suffering from a hallucination or whether there is a conspiracy afoot to do away with an innocent person.

It is impossible to give a satisfactory idea of the cumulative horror which is built up as the train speeds toward Trieste. The fabric of the plot is so delicately fashioned, the action adjusted so precisely to the revolutions of the wheels, that the book must be read to be appreciated. Don't miss it.—Todd Downing.[41]

40 Jesse Douglas Kerruish (c. 1884-1949) is best known for her lycanthrope novel, *The Undying Monster*, originally published in 1922 and filmed by director John Brahm in 1942. Note Todd's criticism of the novel's heroine, psychic detective Luna Bartendale, for "succumbing to such a mundane thing as love."

41 Bafflingly underappreciated today, Ethel Line White (1876-1944) was one of England's most important crime novelists in the 1930s. Her tales were

"KING IS KING"
Sept. 27, 1936

THE CASE OF THE CONSTANT GOD, BY RUFUS KING

To the highly unethical question, "Who, in your opinion, is the best living writer of mystery stories?" we reply without hesitation, "Rufus King." Whereupon we hold forth upon his all-around excellence: ingenuity in plot construction, skill in etching his characters with light revealing touches, his style, the gently disturbing afflatus of his horror. *The Case of the Constant God* confirms us in our conviction.

It is the story of the wealthy Todd household, the suicide of their eldest daughter and the threat to her memory which comes out of the fog in the person of Sigurd Repellen, with his new shoes, his little black bag, his prattle of a new religion. It is a chronicle of the activities of Lieutenant Valcour, of the New York police department, from the moment when he learns of the corpse on Queensboro Bridge until the night on the yacht *Amberjack* when he faces the gun that doesn't exist.

It heads our recommended list for the autumn.—Todd Downing.[42]

precursors of the psychological suspense subgenre that became increasingly important in crime fiction after World War Two. White published fourteen mystery novels between 1931 and 1944. The most popular and best reviewed of these was *The Wheel Spins,* which also was adapted into a classic suspense film by Alfred Hitchcock in 1938, under the title *The Lady Vanishes*. Downing's praise of the novel is high indeed, but many 1930s reviewers echoed his words. White's second best known novel, *Some Must Watch* (1933), was adapted into another classic suspense film, Robert Siodmak's *The Spiral Staircase,* in 1946. The "yarn of werewolves and family curses" that left Downing unmoved is Jesse Douglas Kerruish's *The Undying Monster,* which he reviewed a week earlier (see above).

42 Downing makes his supreme devotion to Rufus King patently clear, declaring "without hesitation" that Rufus King is "the best living writer of mystery stories."

"RASCALITY GALORE"
October 4, 1936, p. 63

"Trouble at Glaye," by Mrs. Baillie Reynolds

With 25 novels to her credit, Mrs. Reynolds is one of the standbys in the field of romantic adventure, trapdoor school. Mystery is really a misnomer for a book like this, for, while there is rascality galore, the reader is never in any doubt as to the perpetrators.

Adam Damarel and Denne Hereford, young London lawyers on a canoe trip, visit the ancestral home and find the usual concomitants of an English castle: scheming heirs, foreign spies and an imprisoned girl, who is being coerced into signing a will. The action, swift enough for anyone's satisfaction, shifts back and forth over the map as Adam and Denne foil the Boches and save the girl.

In England readers don't seem to consider the ubiquity of subterranean passages improbable, so why should we cavil who have never been there?—Todd Downing.[43]

"A SKEPTICAL EYE"
Oct. 11, 1936, p. 57

A Clue for Mr. Fortune, by H. C. Bailey

A treat in any season are novelettes such as these six in which Reggie Fortune is bullied and cajoled into leaving his easy chair to solve the perplexities of Superintendent Lomas of the C.I.D. "The Torn Stocking," in which he cast a skeptical eye upon the apparent suicide of a schoolgirl, dates from his earliest association with Lomas.

His interest in the gruesome murders which form the subject of "The Swimming Pool" puts him for the first time into the headlines. The others are later from his career: "The Hole in the Parchment,"

43 Mrs. Baillie Reynolds (G. M. Robins) (c.1875-1939) seems to have been primarily a romantic novelist, who strayed at times into mystery and the supernatural. Downing pithily dismisses the creakily Gothic *Trouble at Glaye* as belonging to "the field of romantic adventure, trapdoor school."

in which he comes to the aid of a bibliophile in Florence; "The Holy Well," in which he proves that Mrs. Prout didn't drown her son in a Cornish well; "The Wistful Goddess," in which he locates the despondent typist and the Bruckner diamonds; "The Dead Leaves," in which he trails the Bluebeard who climbs mountains with his victims.

The thought occurs that Reggie Fortune is probably the only sleuth active today who meets with the approval of every mystery fan of our acquaintance.—Todd Downing.[44]

"HAPPY ENDING"
November 8, 1936, p. 75

HOLE AND CORNER, BY PATRICIA WENTWORTH

THIS is the twentieth novel in which Miss Wentworth has introduced us to fair damsels whose lives are fraught with peril, to stalwart young men who bound to the rescue, to elderly millionaires who make equivocal wills, to sinister or merely avaricious villains. Her readers are numerous and loyal. For them the reviewer need merely announce the publication of "another Wentworth romance."

For the benefit of those who haven't made Miss Wentworth's acquaintance we should reveal the fact that Shirley Dale, ill-paid secretary to fussy old Mrs. Huddlestone, is in reality the heiress to the million dollar estate of William Ambrose Merewether, of New York. But Shirley is in danger of being arrested for theft. Unless it can be proved that the charge is a trumped-up one, she will lose the money, although she is sure to keep the love of Anthony Leigh, Mrs. Huddlestone's barrister nephew. There's a

44 Downing speculates that "Reggie Fortune is probably the only sleuth active today who meets the approval of every mystery fan of our acquaintance." In modern times, on the other hand, some readers have expressed no uncertain disapproval of Reggie. Julian Symons, for example, found "Fortune intolerably precious and whimsical." See *Bloody Murder: From the Detective Story to the Crime Novel* (1972; rev. ed. Mysterious Press, 1993), 183.

happy ending in sight throughout, so it need not work on your nerves.[45]

"FATAL NICOTINE"
November 29, 1936, p. 77

BEHOLD, HERE'S POISON!, BY GEORGETTE HEYER

READERS of *Merely Murder* and *Why Shoot a Butler?* have come to expect of Miss Heyer a fairly routine plot trimmed with a facile narrative style, sprightly conversation full of British humor and one character who is at the same time charming and rude. Randall Matthews is the "amiable snake" of this tale. He is a rich young scamp who scandalizes the relatives gathered to bicker and grieve about old Gregory Matthews' bier. When Gertrude Lupton, sister of the deceased, expresses doubt about the doctor's verdict of syncope and demands a post mortem, Randall says drily: "The question interests me almost as little as Aunt Gertrude's remarks." Said remarks were made when Randall told Aunt Gertrude that if he were married to her he would keep several mistresses.

Miss Heyer provides quite a bit of mystification regarding the fatal dose of nicotine (was it in the duck or the cutlets?) and springs a surprise at the finish. Readers whose taste is more Anglicized than ours will get many a chuckle out of the repartee with which she interlards the more harrowing scenes.—Todd Downing.[46]

"FOR MURDER FANS"
December 27, 1936, p. 65

THE BELL IN THE FOG, BY JOHN STEPHEN STRANGE

ONCE you have studied the map of Sowback Island, at the mouth of Penobscot Bay, and are straightened out on who is related to

45 Downing evidently found this particular Wentworth yarn quite too cozy for comfort.

46 In his review of *Behold, Here's Poison* Downing succinctly and quite accurately sums up the perennial appeal of Georgette Heyer's detective novels,

whom among the islanders, you may revel in a grade-A baffler by a writer who knows how to make the most of fog, a tolling bell, a blood-gorged jellyfish and a ghost in a cemetery.

Barney Gantt, newspaper cameraman, is the amateur sleuth who discovers the corpse on the beach at sunrise. He seeks the aid of Post Office Inspector Powell, who is investigating the theft of a letter from the mails.

It is soon evident that the stolen letter plays a part in the tangle and that Job Reardon, postmaster, knows more than he's telling. Everyone, in fact, seems to hug some secret, including Lotta Hendricks, the beautiful wife of the rabbit-eyed lighthouse keeper; John Lynch, the painter; and Mrs. Carney, Barney's landlady.

Mr. Strange shows considerable skill in combining felicitously horror and logic, simple and complex love. His book ought to satisfy fans of every taste.—Todd Downing.[47]

"MURDER MYSTERY FLAYS HYSTERIA OF THE MOB"
January 3, 1937, p. 69

DEATH IN THE DEEP SOUTH, BY WARD GREENE

THE addict of mystery fiction who inadvertently picks up this volume will find that instead of escaping from life for a couple hours he has been brought face to face with it.

Mr. Greene (southern-born, newspaperman, novelist) has written the story of the apotheosis of Mary Clay from a none-too-virtuous student in a southern business college to a cause. Mary was a 15-year-old nobody, that afternoon of Confederate Memorial Day when she returned to the classroom for her vanity case. The next morning she is a newspaper sensation, for her body—attacked, strangled, mutilated—has been found in the

while also indicating that he does not fully embrace "English" humor in mystery tales.

47 With its felicitous combination of horror and logic, *The Bell in the Fog* had just about everything Todd Downing might conceivably have desired in a detective novel.

basement. The usual Negro is tortured by the police; then, when no confession is forthcoming, framed.

But the district attorney, with eyes on the governorship, scents greater possibilities in the case. Robert Hale, a young instructor, was present in the building that afternoon. Hale is a northerner who has made derogatory remarks about the South. Mary Clay reputedly was "crazy" about him. He is arrested, the Society for the Preservation of Individual Liberty rallies to his defense and the mad screaming orgy of another "trial of the century" is on. Mary has become a cause for which mobs arise.

The whole disgusting spectacle is recorded calmly but compassionately, so that the resultant indictment of American violence is inescapable. Mr. Greene is safe from the charge of exaggeration, for it requires but a short memory to locate in our history the prototypes of Mary Clay and Robert Hale, of District Attorney Griffin and Governor Mountford, of the whole pack of sob-sisters and sadists and opportunists. Even of the lone individual who murmurs at the end: "I wonder if he really did it?"—Todd Downing.[48]

48 In reviewing *Death in the Deep South*, Downing immediately warns readers that a mystery fiction "addict" inadvertently picking it up will be disconcerted to find himself, when reading the novel, facing life rather than escaping from it. Native southern journalist and novelist Ward Greene (1893-1956) covered the Leo Frank case for the *Atlanta Journal* in 1915, when Todd Downing was thirteen years old. *Death in the Deep South*, which appeared two decades later, is clearly a barely fictionalized account of this infamous case, in which a Jewish Atlanta businessman, Leo Frank, was tried for the murder of a thirteen-year-old girl, Mary Phagan. He was found guilty and sentenced to death, but the governor commuted Frank's sentence to life in prison, whereupon Frank was taken from his jail and hanged by a lynch mob. Today Frank is almost universally believed to have been innocent and the case is viewed as a particularly shocking example of southern anti-Semitism a century ago. See Steve Oney, *And the Dead Shall Rise: The Murder of Mary Phagan and the Lynching of Leo Frank* (Pantheon, 2003). Greene's novel was adapted into the praised 1937 film *They Won't Forget*. Downing's acerbic references to the novel's effective portrayal of the "disgusting spectacle" of the trial and its "indictment of American violence" make sufficiently clear Downing's view of the Leo Frank case. Also of note is Downing's blunt reference, in

"LONDON MURDER"
January 10, 1937, p. 67

THE MURDER OF SIR EDMUND GODFREY, BY JOHN DICKSON CARR

MYSTERY addicts with acumen know that the most erudite of the writers who labor to supply them with brain-teasers is John Dickson Carr, Anglicized American, creator of Doctor Fell and adaptor of the Gothic tale to the requirements of modern taste. An essentially modest young man, Mr. Carr has for the first time donned full academic costume (with a slightly roguish air, 'tis true) and treated in the fashion of fiction the crime to which De Quincey gave his "entire approbation" as "the finest work of the seventeenth century."

On an October day in 1678 Sir Edmund Godfrey, famous London magistrate, walked out of his house and disappeared. Five days later he was found dead, beaten, strangled, and stabbed by his own sword. In recording the furor that followed—Titus Oates' cries of a Popish plot, the shouts of the Green Ribbon terror-mongers running down Catholics, the frenzy of fear which rocked the throne of Charles II—history has failed to answer the very pertinent question: Who murdered Sir Edmund Godfrey?

Mr. Carr presents all the evidence, parades a fascinating group of suspects (Queen Catherine, Samuel Pepys, Shaftesbury, etc.), draws new deductions and at the end points an accusatory finger at a person whom no one, apparently, ever considered, yet whose guilt explains all the contradictory facts. The result is a very nearly perfect detective story, faithfully extracted from history and thrillingly told.—Todd Downing.[49]

an Oklahoma newspaper in 1937, to "the usual Negro" being "tortured by the police" and then framed when "no confession is forthcoming."

49 Downing again is won over by a John Dickson Carr work, this time a recounting of a real-life murder case in seventeenth-century England. Downing deems Carr the "most erudite" of mystery writers and *The Murder of Sir Edmund Godfrey* "very nearly a perfect detective story."

"ONE MURDERED"
January 10, 1937, p. 67

One Murdered, Two Dead, by Milton Propper

This is the first of the Tommy Rankin yarns to hold our attention throughout (as a rule our interest flags when the Philadelphia sleuth, as has been his wont in the past, pores too long over time-tables or maps or such impedimenta to the action). The problem which faces Rankin here is an unusually intriguing one. Mrs. Emery, spoiled heiress of a steel king, is stabbed to death 24 hours before her child was to have been born. Was the murderer's purpose merely to do away with the woman or did he wish to prevent the appearance of another claimant for old Stephen Kent's fortune? Or was the killing the wanton act of the burglar who was arrested on the grounds with his kit of tools? Tommy unearths numerous marital triangles in the course of the investigation, flies to Florida and to Pittsburgh and says at the finish: "The solution was obvious from the beginning—there, in front of me, only I was too dull to realize it."

The plot is closely-knit, credible and fair to the reader throughout. The author of *The Strange Disappearance of Mary Young* is probably the American writer who adheres most faithfully to the Scotland Yard formula.—Todd Downing.[50]

"NOT SO ARTLESS"
January 17, 1937, p. 71

Tall Man Walking, by Katherine Wolffe

All unheralded, with one of the trickiest and most intelligent yarns of the season, put over without fingerprints, broken cuff-links or rouge-tipped cigarettes in the way of clues.

50 Later Milton Propper novels, such as the one under review here by Downing, rely less heavily on timetable minutiae (what Downing terms "impedimenta to the action"). Accordingly, *One Murdered, Two Dead* wins Downing's praise as "the first of the Tommy Rankin yarns to hold our attention throughout."

The narrator is Laure Hosmer, one of those middle-aged spinsters who have become stand-bys in the field. Her tale concerns the stabbing of Wiletta Owens a few minutes before her marriage to David Kaye. David, having come into money, is a catch for the village girls, one of whom may have done away with the prospective bride. Watch Stacy Madden, who quarreled with Wiletta, and Valerie Lane, who attempted to commit suicide, as well as Jonny Rohmer, David's jealous and neurotic foster brother. Dr. Kenneth Borden, psychiatrist, who is staying in the Rohmer home to observe Jonny, has an unexcelled opportunity to study the various suspects and analyze their emotions and reactions. He unmasks the killer in a masterly fashion.

In our opinion, Katherine Wolffe is a name to be watched in mystery fiction, where the tradition has prevailed too long that a person, to be twisted mentally, must be twisted physically. Better read this one thoughtfully. It's not as artless as it appears at first.[51]

"GENTLEMAN SLEUTH"

February 14, 1937, p. 69

THE CRIMSON HAIR MURDERS, BY D. AND H. TEILHET

THE Baron von Kaz seems to have brought his green umbrella to the mystery field to stay, so in case you missed *The Feather Cloak Murders*, you had best make his acquaintance forthwith. He doesn't fall into any one of the usual categories, being more

51 "Katherine Wolffe" is the pseudonym of Marian Gallagher Scott (1892-?). *Tall Man Walking* (*Bride of Death* in England) was so highly praised, both in the United States and in England, that it is surprising the name "Katherine Wolffe" is not remembered today. As Katherine Wolffe, Marian Scott also authored *The Attic Room* (1942) and *Death's Long Shadow* (1946), while under her own name she published *Chautauqua Caravan*, a 1939 account of her experiences as a stage performer on the Chautauqua, or lyceum, circuit with her husband, Earl Scott. Although *Tall Man Walking* involves yet another spinster-narrator, Downing deems the tale a highly original product ("one of the trickiest and most intelligent yarns of the season") and its author "a name to be watched in mystery fiction."

gentleman rogue and amateur sleuth, as well as somewhat of a Graustarkian hero. If you don't like him in one role you will in another.

We find him sampling *aguardiente* in the Mexican port of Acapulco, on his return to the "barbaric states of North America" from his beloved Austria. As a result of a telephone conversation which he inadvertently overhears, he is thrust into the intrigue surrounding Dorothy Malby, niece of the San Francisco millionaire Cyrus Fields III, and her red-headed companion. He sees a man with the head of a Botticelli angel die in the dust of a Mexican alley, from poison meant for him, and on shipboard he finds the body of the crimson-haired girl lying on the floor of his cabin, the blade of his sword sheathed in her back.

While the Teilhet style is a bit involved at times, the authors create an atmosphere which has unique qualities of terror and bring the tale to a dramatic conclusion on the new Golden Gate bridge.—Todd Downing.[52]

"LOCKED DOOR"

February 21, 1937, p. 75

Dark is the Tunnel, by Miles Burton

Brainwork is required on this new baffler by the author of *The Clue of the Silver Brush*. Sir Wilfred Saxonby, chairman of Wiegand and Bunthorne, Ltd., is shot in a locked compartment of the train that passes though Blackdown tunnel shortly after 5:29 p.m. It looks like suicide, but Inspector Arnold of the C. I. D. and his gifted friend, Desmond Merrion, want to know what became of the return half of Sir Saxonby's ticket and who flashed the red and green lights which caused the train to slow down in the middle of the tunnel.

52 True to form Downing again lauds "atmosphere which has unique qualities of terror"—even though he allows that "the Teilhet style is a bit involved."

The book divides into two parts, the first being devoted to an investigation of the method whereby the murder was committed, the second to a search for the killer. Clues seem to point to Mr. Dredger, former Manchester manager of the firm, who answers the description given by Mrs. Clutsam and her daughter of the twenty-fifth passenger with the hooked nose.

There is no excitement in the tale save that deriving from interest in the solution of the problem. The last, however, is neat, logical and within the grasp of any alert reader.—Todd Downing.[53]

"SEQUENCE OF EVIL"

May 23, 1937, p. 73

Black Land, White Land, by H. C. Bailey

According to H. C. Bailey, Reggie Fortune has a singular affection for this case, "inspired by the primeval, savage force of its sequence of evil. The first cause of it lay far off in the building of the earth. It was the harvest of warfare of thousands of years of men for the earth's good things . . ."

Which will tell Reggie's admirers that he is in fine fettle, amiable and discursive but keen-eyed enough when it comes to identifying the bones which old General Duddon found beneath a landslide in Durshire and fondly believes to be those of a giant. "Elephans meridionalis. Long extinct," murmurs Reggie and reaches for a smaller overlooked bone. "From another human family still going strong. Bit of a jaw—human, all too human. And much too new. Bone of a boy who was alive ten years ago."

53 This "humdrum" masterpiece by Cecil John Charles Street under his "Miles Burton" pseudonym in Downing's view offered "no excitement . . . save that deriving from interest in the solution of the problem." However, Downing found appealing the "neat" and "logical" problem, which, though it required "brainwork," was fair play and solvable by an "alert reader." Jacques Barzun, who at the age of twenty-eight read the novel when it was published in the United States, deemed it "a most readable affair" that "ranks very high" among railway stories. See Jacques Barzun and Wendell Hertig Taylor, *A Catalogue of Crime* (1971; rev. ed. Harper & Row, 1989), 88.

He soon discovers that the boy must have been the son of a prominent citizen of the vicinity, who went out birds'-nesting and never returned. Suspects include all the local gentry, expertly drawn, all squabbling over property rights as the Durshire proverb testifies: "Black land, white land, always at strife."

The novel will require a bit of patience for those who are meeting Reggie for the first time.—Todd Downing.[54]

"CIRCUS MURDER"
June 20, 1937, p. 71

THE UPSIDE DOWN MURDERS, BY HUGH AUSTIN

BARK Tanner, "the greatest showman since Barnum," is dead in Bonner's amusement park, and it looks like one of the troupe: Samarkinda, who shakes a wicked tambourine; Vare, who performs with Charmaine, the cosmically comical chimpanzee; or Anton the Great, etc. Yet none of their prints match the calloused thumb print on the death gun, and it is only with the aid of a man's upside down reflection in a pool of water that Peter D. Quint, head of the homicide bureau in the city of Hudson, sees the truth.

If you haven't got your eye on the wrong suspect, you are nothing less than a genius.—T. D.[55]

54 Todd Downing once again embraces his old fictional friend Reggie Fortune, though he warns readers that this novel-length Reggie adventure "will require a bit of patience for those who are meeting Reggie for the first time."

55 With this last review (signed only "T. D."), Downing pays tribute to the abiding delight of the dazzlingly devious fair play puzzles of the Golden Age of detective fiction: "If you haven't got your eye on the wrong suspect, you're nothing less than a genius." Happy sleuthing!

APPENDIX ONE

Todd Downing's 1931 Reviews of *Stories with Women* and *Gray Shadows* and 1933 Review of *Ann Vickers*

"WITHOUT WOMEN"

July 16, 1931, p. 43

Stories without Women, by Donn Byrne

"Arms and the man I sing" might have been the prelude to this book of Byrne's. These thirteen tales of "action, combat and suspense," comprising the first book of Donn Byrne's to be published in the United States, have been out of print for many years. Admirers of his later books will find here a Donn Byrne whom few know. These stories show him at his most vigorous, finding romance in strenuous adventure, in distant lands, in colorful settings.

There are two championship boxing matches, which reveal the author's love for and knowledge of the sport. There are battle scenes in Flanders, in North Africa, in Mesopotamia. There are tales of African magic, of New York racketeering, of a rhinoceros in the Bronx Zoo, of an Irish wake. Each story has a kick, which makes up for an occasional lack of polish in the style.

The title is too good to be true, so women play parts in most of the stories. Evidently a necessary evil.—Todd Downing.[1]

1 Brian Oswald Donn-Byrne (1889-1928) was an Irish novelist, poet and short story writer. *Stories without Women* was originally published in the United States in 1915, then reprinted in 1931, three years after Donn-Byrne's death in a 1928 car accident. Downing's sardonic comment about the title—"too good to be true"—is reflective of his distaste for "love interest" in novels. "Arms and the man I sing" comes from Virgil's *Aeneid*.

"PRISON TALES"
August 9, 1931, p. 41

GRAY SHADOWS, COMPILED BY JOSEPH LEWIS FRENCH

THE men whose writings compose this anthology were no white-collared, soft-palmed novelists, dashing off improbable tales of crime for a public ever anxious for more of the same vapid stuff. These men knew the crime racket from inside; their knowledge of prisons was gained from behind bars. Much of the material was written by men serving prison sentences—one of them going to his death two weeks after his article was written. Hence this book is as different from the usual book of crime as a sawed-off shotgun is different from a child's popgun.

Many of the short stories and sketches are well-known, but all of them are worth another reading. Jim Tully is represented by two powerful tales of Vagabondia from his *Shadows of Men*. "The Law Takes Its Toll," by Robert Blake, was the basis for the first act of the much discussed prison drama *The Last Mile*. Anyone who has read Jack London's "Star Rover" will be tempted to open this book to the middle, where is to be found Ed Morrell's description of life in Folsom and San Quentin prisons. Oklahomans who have not read Al Jenning's "Beating Back" will be interested particularly in his account of the robbery of the Rock Island train near Minco in 1897, the gun battle at the Spike-S ranch, and his final capture.

From a literary viewpoint, the sections are of very unequal merit, as is to be expected in material written with more attention to content than to form. Some of them are little masterpieces of realism, comparable to Gorky's "Lower Depths." Fantastic woodcuts by Roger Buck add attractiveness to a decidedly worthwhile and unusual book.[2]

2 With seemingly a touch of self-loathing, Downing strikes a blow for realism in writing when he contrasts the men whose works compose *Gray Shadows* with "white-collared, soft-palmed novelists, dashing off improbable tales of crime for a public ever anxious for more of the same vapid stuff." Al Jennings (1863-1961) was a one-time Oklahoma train robber who

NO HEADLINE

February 19, 1933, p. 35

Ann Vickers, by Sinclair Lewis

Windmill-tilting is heroic and at the same time idealism-discouraging. One's admiration for the magnificent gesture is dampened by thoughts of the hardness of the ground. And so with the life story of Ann Vickers, the dominating figure of Sinclair Lewis' new novel. Born 42 years ago to what Lewis calls "an era of fantasy known as Christian Socialism," Ann grew up on an Illinois main street.

Early she began to realize that she was somehow different from her schoolmates—the boys were a little bit afraid of her. This suspicion crystallized into knowledge when Ann (rather like Little Orphan Annie of the funny papers, it must be admitted), put out the fire at the Christmas Eve Sunday school services. Her reward was the see young Adolph Klebs, whom she worshipped, captured by a silly creature who would have stood and screamed at the sight of the fire.

Thus increasingly though life. Ann goes to college, campaigns for woman's suffrage, becomes interested in social reform and rises to the staff of a western penitentiary and head of a New York reformatory for women. Tremendously alive, filled with the uncompromising ardor of the crusader, she finds herself

later became a politician, silent film star and writer. See Jennings' entry in the *Encyclopedia of Oklahoma History & Culture*, at http://digital.library.okstate.edu/encyclopedia/entries/J/JE006.html. Jim Tully (1886-1947) was a one-time vagabond who became a celebrated writer by the 1920s and 1930s. Some saw him as a precursor to the hard-boiled school of writing. A biography and several of Tully's novels recently have been published by Kent State University Press. See Paul J. Bauer and Mark Dawidziak, *Jim Tully, American Writer, Irish Rover, Hollywood Brawler* (Kent State University Press, 2011). Robert Blake wrote "The Law Takes Its Toll" while awaiting execution for a murder committed in Texas. As Downing indicates, it was adapted in 1929 into a successful stage play, *The Last Mile* (both Clark Gable and Spencer Tracy played the lead role in productions of the play). A film version appeared in 1932. See Carlos Glarens, *Crime Movies* (Da Capo, 1997), 42. Famed Russian author Maxim Gorky's *The Lower Depths* (1902) is considered a landmark of literary social realism.

checkmated on every hand by the selfishness and stupidity of her coworkers. Mr. Lewis' pessimism concerning human nobility is none the less evident from being subordinated to the recital of Ann's numerous, varied, more or less casual experiences with men. The young college professor who attempts to seduce her; a neurotic young social worker to whom she gives herself, then refuses to marry because his offer is prompted by a mere feeling of duty; a middle-aged lawyer who marries a banker's daughter because he tells Ann later, she is "a little too big for him." Always the same. Men admire Ann, find her attractive—but marry other, shallower girls.

Ann's reaction to this realization throws her into precipitate marriage with a man too weak to hold her. Then at forty she finds herself completely in love (irony of ironies) with a Tammany politician, whose success has been built upon the violation of the very principles of social righteousness or which Ann has spent her life battling. When we take leave of her, Ann has compromised with life and we feel that she has found happiness (or its nearest possible approximation) in the middle ground between reality and idealism.

Ann Vickers has all the qualities of Mr. Lewis' other novels. He is still the thorough, clear-sighted depicter of American life; the caricaturist of hypocrisy and pretentiousness; the vivid narrator of interesting things that happen to interesting people.[3]

3 Sinclair Lewis (1885-1951) produced another bestseller in the controversial novel *Ann Vickers* (1933), though reviews of the novels were mixed, partly due to moral objections of some reviewers. (Though Downing does not mention this in his review, Ann has an abortion in the course of the novel.) *Catholic World* condemned Lewis for focusing on "the refuse, the garbage, the dumps, the cesspools of life" and urged its readers to avoid the book. The novel was filmed later that year, after much conflict with censors over content. See Gregory D. Black, *Hollywood Censored: Morality Codes, Catholics, and the Movies* (Cambridge University Press, 1996), 99-103. Downing's review of *Ann Vickers*, a novel focused on the life of an unorthodox woman, balances his earlier ones of the male-centered *Stories without Women* and *Gray Shadows*.

APPENDIX TWO

"The Detective Story": An Interview between Kenneth C. Kaufmann and Todd Downing (September 30, 1934, p. 47)

It may surprise some people who do, and some who don't, read detective stories that the rules of that branch of the writing game are far more exacting than are those of, say, the novel proper. I wanted to find out something about it, so I went to Todd Downing, Oklahoma's expert, whose latest mystery, *The Cat Screams* (Doubleday Doran), is getting a big hand from reviewers. I asked him the following questions, and these, with their answers, seem to me to sum up the whole case for the detective story:

> Where did the modern detective story start?
>
> The elements of the detective story may be found in the early folklore and literature of most peoples, detection and mystery however being connected with crime other than murder. Edgar Allan Poe is responsible for the modern mystery story, joining hitherto separate elements and laying down the rules which writers have followed ever since.[1]

1 The pioneering Edgar Allan Poe "C. Auguste Dupin" detective short stories ("tales of ratiocination") are "The Murders in the Rue Morgue" (1841), "The Mystery of Marie Roget" (1842) and "The Purloined Letter" (1844). See also "The Gold-Bug" (1843) and "Thou Art the Man" (1844).

Were Poe's stories immediately popular? Which people took him up first, the Americans, the English or the French?

Poe's five detective stories proved almost immediately popular, especially in England. While he was accepted by the French as a short story writer, it was in England that his stories—as problems in deduction and induction—were most successful.

Who were his most important followers?

Arthur Conan Doyle took the Poe formula and galvanized it into life. While practically all the elements of the Sherlock Holmes stories may be traced to Poe's work, the modern detective story would be a much more static thing had Doyle not written.

What do you find in contemporary detective fiction that is not found in Poe or Doyle?

Very few elements are present in contemporary mystery fiction that are not found in these authors. Characterization, however, receives more attention than it did with them. The personages of a detective novel are no longer black and white; gradations are present. This, of course, aids in concealing the identity of the culprit.

Does this mean that the detective novel has been reduced to formula, that every possible plot has been used and that the only changes which the modern writer can make are in setting, etc.?

It would seem that the detective story has been pretty well reduced to formula. Most of the so-called "new notes in mystery fiction" when analyzed sound decidedly familiar. The time is ripe for some writer to abandon the Poe-Doyle tradition and strike out into a new field, which will be entirely different.[2]

2 In his call for "some [mystery] writer to abandon the Poe-Doyle tradition and strike out into a new field," Downing sounds what would become an increasingly common note in the 1930s.

WHAT WOULD A DETECTIVE STORY WRITER GIVE FOR AN IDEA WHICH WOULD ENABLE HIM TO DO THIS?

Any of them would give his eye-teeth. Personally, I give my address, in case anyone has an idea to contribute.

WHAT ARE SOME OF THE THINGS THAT A DETECTIVE STORY WRITER MUST OR MUST NOT DO?

He must play fair with the reader. All the clues must be displayed so that the reader will have an opportunity to deduce the criminal's identity before the end. S. S. Van Dine has summarized the rules which govern the writing of mystery fiction. While no writer, probably, will agree with every one of the twenty rules, they remain the best presentation of what a mystery story writer must and must not do.

Among other things which Van Dine requires of the writer of this kind of fiction is that the murderer must not be a lay character, that is a servant, for example, and that the crime involved must be murder. No less a crime than murder, he says, will justify 300 pages.[3]

WHAT ABOUT THE LOVE ELEMENT IN THE DETECTIVE STORY?

The majority of writers agree that love has absolutely no place in mystery fiction; it introduces a conflict of interest. It has, however, been used, and successfully, by occasional writers, notably Earl Derr Biggers. E. C. Bentley has even succeeded in using that most difficult of situations—the detective in love.[4] Nowadays, the tendency is to keep the love element sternly in second place, if it has a place in the story.

3 S. S. Van Dine, "Twenty Rules for Writing Detective Stories" (1928). Downing refers specifically to rules #7 and #11.

4 Downing refers here to E. C. Bentley's *Trent's Last Case* (1913). Earl Derr Biggers authored the Charlie Chan series of detective novels.

WHAT ARE YOUR OWN FAVORITE MYSTERY STORIES?

Murder by Latitude, by Rufus King or any of King's maritime mystery yarns; *The Greene Murder Case* or *The Bishop Murder Case* by S. S. Van Dine; *The Murder of Roger Ackroyd* by Agatha Christie; *The Red Lamp* by Mary Roberts Rinehart as an example of a successful writer flirting with the supernatural; *The Silver Scale Mystery* by Anthony Wynne; *From This Dark Stairway* by Mignon Eberhart.[5]

5 Downing reviewed Rufus King's *Murder on a Yacht*, Anthony Wynne's *The Silver Scale Mystery* and Mignon Eberhart's *From this Dark Stairway* in the *Daily Oklahoman*. With the exception of Agatha Christie's landmark *The Murder of Roger Ackroyd*, Downing's choices for his favorite mystery stories reveal his pronounced penchant for exotic or outré elements and supernatural trappings.

APPENDIX THREE

Todd Downing's Review of *Murder for Pleasure: The Life and Times of the Detective Story* (1941), by Howard Haycraft

"A Critical Analysis for Murder Fans: A Hundred Years of Detective Story Writing and Reading" (January 25, 1942, p. 58)

Murder for Pleasure: The Life and Times of the Detective Story, by Howard Haycraft

One hundred years ago last April appeared the world's first detective story: "The Murders in the Rue Morgue" by Edgar Allan Poe. Today one out of every four new works of fiction published in the English language belongs to this category, and no less a qualified authority than Somerset Maugham has suggested that critics of the future may neglect the serious novels of our day in favor of these tales which frankly aim only to entertain.

Undoubtedly this is the outstanding literary phenomenon of modern times; and such a book as this, devoted largely to a factual outline of the main progress of the movement, is long overdue. It is by no means definitive, but for one whose interest in the subject is not exclusively academic it is the best thing of its kind in English, maybe in any language.

Mr. Haycraft is astute. He avoids both over-solemnity on his subject and that facetiousness by which so many people think to show themselves stuffed to the eyes with "culture." The result is a book that may be read with pleasure and incidental enlightenment by anyone who does not actually dislike detective fiction. For the true enthusiast here's a rare treat, for the author has been generous in tossing plums into the pudding.

Here are chapters on the rules of the game, a list of milestones in the development of the genre, a Who's Who of over a thousand fictional detectives, a comprehensive detective story quiz. Here is constructive criticism, including that which should give the *coup de grace* to the feminine "Had-I-But-Known" school. Writers are remembered along with readers, in chapters on technique and markets.

The book's one serious shortcoming was doubtless necessitated by space limitations. The line which the author draws between detective and mystery fiction cuts right through the body of the work of many authors. So far as the quality of detection is concerned, *The Arabian Nights Murder* may be a milestone in the career of John Dickson Carr; but this is one of the novels which least exemplifies his peculiar ability to evoke to macabre from his settings. How can one fully appreciate Mary Roberts Rinehart if he disregards *The Red Lamp?* Edgar Wallace, if only the J. G. Reeder tales are considered?

Mr. Haycraft is urged to give us a companion volume on mysteries.—Todd Downing.[1]

1 Although Henry Douglas Thomson's excellent *Masters of Mystery: A Study of the Detective Story* (1931) by a full decade preceded Howard Haycraft's *Murder for Pleasure: The Life and Times of the Detective Story*, Haycraft's landmark book is the first history of the genre that is still comparatively well-known today. In his review of *Murder for Pleasure*, Downing strikes a dramatic chord by pronouncing detective fiction undoubtedly "the outstanding literary phenomenon of modern times." Downing's mention of Somerset Maugham's observation that "critics of the future may neglect serious novels of our day in favor of [detective] tales which frankly aim only to entertain" was rather prescient, given the rise during the last forty years of popular culture studies. Whether Haycraft really did "give the *coup de grace* to the feminine 'Had I But Known' school" is much more disputable. Also notable is Downing's desire, as a great fan of such thriller authors as Edgar Wallace, for a companion volume dealing with more loosely-structured "mystery" stories.

APPENDIX FOUR

Todd Downing's Essay "Murder is a Rather Serious Business" (1943)

"*Pass the Poison Please!* reads as if the author has had a lot of fun writing it." That comment by a reviewer is one to make said author indulge in one of those "twisted smiles" which, if he's up on his clichés, he now forbids his characters. For the chances are that his hair is still scant from his tearing of it, his fingernails still sore from his biting of them during the ordeal of writing *Pass the Poison Please!*

Yet he has his reward for the effort which he expended in one of the sweetest bouquets that can be tossed to a mystery novel. He has given the effect of having written effortlessly.

It is this effect in successful crime fiction which beguiles so many writers, not only beginners but veterans seasoned in other fields. The former decide to turn out a murder tale as practice before they start upon the Great American Novel. The latter see here either a form of diversion between more pretentious works or a quick means of financing a vacation. In both cases they go at their writing condescendingly, often with the intention of publishing the result under a *nom de plume*; and the odds are that at the end of five or six chapters, with the corpse in the library still warm, and the detective still getting alibis from the members of house party, our unprepared author throws in the sponge—with new respect for those who do produce bafflement for the public.

There's nothing esoteric about the writing of a detective or mystery novel, but Edgar Allan Poe certainly had his tongue in his cheek when he asked: "Where is the ingenuity of unraveling a web which you yourself have woven for the express purpose of unraveling? The reader is made to confound the ingenuity of [the detective] with that of the writer of the story." It required a great deal of ingenuity to conceive *The Murders in the Rue Morgue*, and a particular brand of talent to set it down on paper. Some degree of that ingenuity and that talent must be present in the writer of today for successful cultivation of the type of fiction originated by Poe, with the added consideration that in the century of its existence this has become a highly specialized field, marshaled by the most critical and exacting group of readers in the literary world. They may pay only two or three nickels to the rental library for a book, but their attitude toward it is that of gem-buyers.

Whether one has the ingenuity and the talent to please this finical audience is a question that can't be determined in advance, of course. But I think that we may adduce one negative indication as to how the prospective baffler will fare. At writers' conferences I frequently hear this: "I'm considering writing a mystery novel. Would you kindly suggest a few of these novels for me to read beforehand?" "You aren't addicted to mysteries then?" I ask. "No," the reply will be, "although I have read some. Let's see, what was the name of that one I read on the train going to the World's Fair? . . ." Encouragement for such an individual isn't in me. People either have a taste for the police novel or they don't. I fail to see how any writer so unfortunate as to lack this taste can succeed in this genre. And I fail to see how, with one out of every four new works of fiction published in the English language dealing with crime and its detection, this taste can be present but undeveloped in any adult.

It doesn't follow that addiction to murder stories qualifies a reader to write one, but on this basis alone I would lend him encouragement if he felt the itch to try.

Further, given this addiction, one should consult his own taste when it comes to deciding on the variety of crime fiction that he is going in for: whether the straight detective story, devoted more or less exclusively to a presentation of the problem and an account of the process by which the detective reaches a solution of it; the thriller, known in England as "the shocker"; or the combination of the essential elements of the two categories in what is generally called the mystery story. One will find detective novels, thrillers and mysteries grouped together on the shelves of rental libraries and in publishers' catalogs. But there is a distinction, an understanding of which may be gained by reading Dorothy L. Sayers' introduction to her *Omnibus of Crime*. Each variety of tale has its followers, and it behooves the writer to make up his mind definitely which group he is going to strive to please. If he himself likes to whet his wits on the problems which R. Austin Freeman sets for Dr. Thorndyke, let him essay the detective novel proper. If he is one of the thousands who reveled in Edgar Wallace, let him set his cap for the audience which still misses that author. If, being inclined to yawn over Mr. Freeman's stories and finding those of Mr. Wallace too sensational, he prefers the happy medium of John Dickson Carr, who also writes under the name Carter Dickson, then his chances for success probably lie in the wide and varied field of mystery.

This may be taken as advice to be imitative in one's maiden effort. There is a premium for originality in tales of crime, as witness the popularity enjoyed by Dashiell Hammett. But this originality must lie within certain prescribed bounds, and until the writer is familiar with these he is venturing among pitfalls if he gets off the beaten path. He will find these bounds defined for him with more or less exactitude in the Dorothy L. Sayers essay mentioned above; in the "Twenty Rules for Writing Detective Stories" formulated by the late Willard Huntingdon Wright (S. S. Van Dine); and in the more recent *Murder for Pleasure* by Howard Haycraft, which listed many other references on the subject.

After reading what these authorities have to say about the requirements of the modern *roman policier*, the prospective writer will probably find himself discarding that idea for a plot which seemed so promising because surely no one has ever used it. He will throw away his notes on that rare poison which leaves no trace, and put into the hand of his murderer either some easily obtained poison or a gun or a knife. He will give up his fancies about a weird old Gothic mansion as a setting for his story and choose instead some locality near to home. He will firmly remove every suggestion of false whiskers from his characters.

This is not to say that turning out detective fiction according to pattern is an unimaginative business. For more than two decades Agatha Christie has been giving us brilliant variations on the same theme, the guilt of the least likely suspect. Rufus King has his Lieutenant Valcour follow routine police procedure but in the midst of a brooding elemental terror which keeps attracting connoisseurs back to his work, particularly that done circa 1930. Mr. King is also noteworthy for his acuteness and subtlety in delineating character, a phase of mystery-writing which can no longer be slighted. Time was when one expected the characters of this type of fiction, apart from the central figure of the detective, to be cardboard people, standing for goodness or for villainy, for generosity or for avarice. The demands of today are increasingly for verisimilitude. In fact, in the hands of many widely read authors the detective story is approaching the psychological novel. The beginner should guard against anything carrying this tendency too far, remembering always that the nub of his tale must be the duel of wits between sleuth and criminal. But he does have leeway for the exercise of his ingenuity in characterization; and, human nature being the parti-colored thing that it is, he may be ingenious without making freaks out of his *dramatis personae*. Surely this is a more fertile field for creativeness than is to be found in devising contraptions whereby a door may be unlocked from inside.

Wartime conditions, too, open up new possibilities for writers of thrillers and mysteries and to a somewhat lesser extent of straight detective stories. In *And So to Murder* and *Nine—And Death Makes Ten*, Carter Dickson has made particularly effective use of the blackout in an English countryside and on a ship during a trans-Atlantic voyage. No doubt we eventually will have a plethora of American tales with such backgrounds, but they promise to be in demand for several seasons. And over and beyond the obvious, the alert writer will discover plot material in the new stresses and strains of civilian life—and that, it is to be hoped, without feeling inspired to plant hissing spies in every dark passageway, for it would be a mistake to assume that critical standards are going by the board.

Without venturing any long-range predictions as to what the effect of the war will be on the genre of fiction under consideration, I think that one commencing a novel now would do well to anticipate a sharp emphasizing of recent tendencies toward conciseness, sprightliness and action.

Unless it is by an established author or an exceedingly promising newcomer, the manuscript of a crime story of over 80,000 words is generally frowned on by publishers. The favored length seems to be about 60,000 words, although novels have been appearing with as low as 50,000 or 40,000 words. The desideratum is that such a book should fill an evening for the reader, and prior to Pearl Harbor less than 50,000 words were scarcely adequate for this purpose. Now that the newspaper and the radio compete for his attention of an evening, however, the average reader may be expected to regard brevity in his novels with a more kindly eye.

For several years now he has been indicating that grimness in crime and its investigation is in disfavor with him, and there is every reason to believe that it will become more markedly so. At the same time it is doubtful whether he is going to tolerate much longer those authors of the so-called "wacky" school, imitators of the *Thin Man* cycle, whose entertainment value lies almost wholly in the wisecracks of their characters.

In this active world the call is certainly going to be for more smartly paced action in fiction. With novels of crime becoming shorter, this would seem to necessitate a curtailing of the element of ratiocination, whence a trend away from the bona fide detective story toward the mystery and the thriller.

In any event, the writer contemplating an entry into this field at the present time has more cause than ever to study his market and painstakingly comply with its demands. It's a crowded field, one in which the financial rewards for the average writer aren't anywhere near so great as popularly supposed. But it is one that may be counted upon to endure until we reach some Utopia wherein we feel no urge to escape, even for a few hours, from our everyday lives. For, the author should bear always in mind, this is nothing else than the literature of escape.

Author's Note:

"Murder is a Rather Serious Business" originally appeared in 1943 in volume fifty-six of *The Writer* and was reprinted in A. S. Burack, ed., *Writing Detective and Mystery Fiction* (1945). This essay of just under 2000 words is Todd Downing's longest single piece on the art of crime fiction.

Downing opens his essay by pointing out the art of crime writing lies in making it *look* easy—even though it assuredly is not. Downing mocks highbrow or would-be writers with no true love for the mystery who blunder into the field, mistakenly thinking it easy to write one. Not only is an "addiction to murder stories" required of a prospective mystery writer, Downing declares, but also the ability to plot with ingenuity. This is true especially in the modern era, Downing argues, when mystery writing "has become a highly specialized field, marshaled by the most critical and exacting group of readers in the literary world." These readers "may pay only two or three nickels to the rental library for a book," declares Downing in a memorable line, "but their attitude toward it is that of gem-buyers."

Downing distinguishes among three forms of crime novels: the detective story proper, "devoted more or less exclusively to the presentation of the problem and an account of the process by which the detective reaches a solution of it" (typified by R. Austin Freeman); the thriller or shocker (Edgar Wallace); and the mystery story, which combines the "essential elements" of the two previously listed categories (John Dickson Carr). Downing indicates that potential crime writers who "yawn over Mr. Freeman's stories" but find "those of Mr. Wallace too sensational" will find a "happy medium" in John Dickson Carr.

Though Downing praises Carr for combining atmosphere and thrills with detection, he notes there is a growing interest on the part of readers in strong character delineation. "[I]n the hands of many widely read authors," asserts Downing, "the detective story is approaching the psychological novel." Despite his admiration for Carr, the master of the locked room mystery, Downing argues that characterization is "a more fertile field for creativeness than" the devising of "contraptions whereby a door may be unlocked from inside."

Downing observes that there also has been a movement in crime fiction towards "conciseness, sprightliness and action." Publishers, he notes, now frown on crime novels of over 80,000 words, with 60,000 words being the favored length. He expects the trend in favor of "smartly paced action" to increase. This increasing trend, he adds, will "necessitate a curtailment of the element of ratiocination," leading crime writers away from "the bona fide detective story toward the mystery and thriller." This was an accurate forecast of the modern tendency in mystery fiction, except that crime fiction readers of the last twenty years or so have again embraced verbiage in crime novels—Steig Larsson's *Millennium Trilogy* runs to nearly 2100 pages in the current American mass market paperback editions—while tending to keep detailed ratiocination decidedly at arm's length.

Downing also predicts that readers will not be able "to tolerate much longer" what he calls the "wacky" school of mystery, "whose entertainment value lies almost wholly in the wisecracks of their characters." Yet Downing believes that in general crime literature—which he deems "nothing else than the literature of escape"—will last until finally we much put-upon humans "reach some Utopia wherein we feel no urge to escape, even for a few hours, from our everyday lives."

APPENDIX FIVE

An Oklahoma Angle on Things Literary: *Daily Oklahoman* Articles about Todd Downing, 1933-1935

"TODD DOWNING IS LATEST TO ARRIVE"
May 28, 1933, p. 42

Add one to the already imposing list of Oklahoma literati who have arrived. Todd Downing, Oklahoma university instructor in modern languages, who is probably Oklahoma's foremost authority on Mexico and things Mexican, and who passes stern if slightly sardonic judgment on current mystery fiction from the Olympian seat of "Clues and Corpses" on this page, has just sold to G. P. Putnam's Sons a detective story of his own, *Murder on Tour*. Moreover, the publishers wish to take an option on two novels a year from his facile typewriter. Readers of "Clues and Corpses" are familiar with the trenchant, economical style and the unassailable logic of Mr. Downing's criticisms.

"THE WAY I SEE IT," by Kenneth C. Kaufman
August 20, 1933, p. 36

All my life I had read detective stories; not for intellectual stimulus, not for relaxation, after a hard day, not to tease my brain (if any) by trying to guess the murderer, but simply and solely because I like them. And furthermore, because taken by and large, they are, nowadays, written with a finish and technique which places them on the average far above the general run of popular literature.

I had never realized how complex and rigid this technique is until I heard Todd Downing lecture this June in the Oklahoma Writers' Forum at the University of Oklahoma on "That Blunt Instrument."

I had always supposed that the detective story writer sat down at his typewriter, inserted a clean white sheet of paper, started out with the discovery of Sir Wilfred Willingham of Willingham-on-the-Rye stretched out on the library floor, and then proceeded to pin the crime on someone who couldn't possibly have committed it.

But as I heard Mr. Downing lecture, I realized that the construction of a murder story is part of a science; it began away back with Poe and William Wilkie Collins and developed through Arthur Conan Doyle into the art of the present day through slow and inevitable processes. And I also realized that this quiet young Oklahoma Spanish teacher had read practically all of the detective stories ever printed and all of the technical literature on the subject; that he had laid the ground work for his own writing with all the care and hard training which an engineer devotes to the preparation of his life work.

And this week when I received from his publishers, G. P. Putnam's Sons, the editorial copy of his first book, *Murder on Tour*, I realized that he had mastered the technique of a difficult art. *Murder on Tour* has everything: suspense; complication of plot; false values, but with all of the true ones prominently displayed; a careful avoidance of any love element.

The plot concerns a wholesale theft of antiquities rifled from the old tombs in Mexico and smuggled across the border by someone who poses as a member of the tourist party. Two governments are interested, the Mexican because of the theft, the American because of the smuggling. A department of justice operative who has joined an "Inter-America" tour is murdered in a San Antonio hotel, presumably because he knows too much, and another takes his place. The game of hide and seek is played out on the Pullman from Laredo to Mexico City and back to the border, with suspicion flitting from the tour manager, the gambler, the honeymooners, the artist, the schoolteacher, with tension ever increasing until the snap of handcuffs as the train crosses the Rio Grande onto American soil. And along with the plot technique goes a wonderfully incisive, economical style and a wonderfully impressive atmosphere of the Mexican setting, where death is an ever present preoccupation.

Mr. Downing is under contract to write two detective stories a year for Putnam's. In a letter to me a few weeks ago, the president of the publishing house asserted that he intends to make Todd Downing's name a household word. If his subsequent output is up to the standard set by his first book I have no doubt that his name will someday rank with that of S. S. Van Dine, Mary Roberts Rinehart and Agatha Christie.

"OKLAHOMA BIOGRAPHS: TODD DOWNING"

August 25, 1935, p. 49

George Todd Downing was born in Atoka March 29, 1902. He is of Choctaw descent, his paternal grandmother having been one of the migrants to Indian Territory in 1832. He attended Atoka high school and the University of Oklahoma, graduating from the latter institution in 1924. From 1925 to 1935 he was instructor in Spanish at the University of Oklahoma, receiving his M. A. degree in 1928. He resigned his position this spring to devote his time to writing.

Four summers spent as conductor of tours in Mexico and in study at the National University of Mexico provide a background for his first novel, *Murder on Tour*, published by G. P. Putnam's Sons in 1933. Somewhat to his regret he cannot claim to have had the irresistible urge to write which is supposed to spur on embryo authors. On the contrary, it took the disruption of a tourist party with consequent enforced stay in the proximity of a typewriter, combined with the counsel of the editor of this page, to turn his thoughts in the direction of fiction.

The Cat Screams (Doubleday, Doran 1934) and *Vultures in the Sky* (Doubleday, Doran 1935) followed. Both were Crime Club selections and the former has been brought out in Swedish and German translations as well as in an English edition by Methuen of London. Doubleday, Doran will publish his *Murder on the Tropic* in 1936. *Mystery Magazine* is running a series of his short mystery stories. The first, "My Blood That You See Flowing," will appear in an early issue, followed by "Garotte."[1]

All his work so far has had a Mexican setting and he intends to continue in this field. *Murder on the Tropic* will be followed by a non-mystery novel, not yet titled, in which he will try to make the spirit of Mexico comprehensible to machine-age readers. He believes that Mexico is of particular interest to Oklahomans, since there the Indian element is absorbing the white, reversing the process that has taken place in this state.

His only hobby is indulgence in a busman's holiday reading other people's books, particularly mystery stories. In common probably with most other mystery writers, he has never witnessed a murder and has no desire to, he is completely hopeless at any games that require deductive analysis and he is never able to identify the perpetrator of a crime of fiction.

He leaves this month for an indefinite stay in New York but intends to return eventually to Oklahoma. Save for the business side of the profession he believes that an Oklahoma town is as good a place as any in the world for writing.

1 The Todd Downing stories "My Blood That You See Flowing" and "Garotte" have not been located.

APPENDIX SIX

Crime and Mystery Authors Reviewed by Todd Downing in the *Daily Oklahoman*

Anthony Abbot

About the Murder of Geraldine Foster (March 1, 1931)

About the Murder of the Clergyman's Mistress (May 31, 1931)

About the Murder of the Circus Queen (November 27, 1932)

Herbert Adams

The Woman in Black (December 25, 1932)

The Golf House Murder (May 21, 1933)

The Strange Murder of Hatton, K. C. (November 12, 1933)

Mystery and Minette (August 19, 1934)

The Body in the Bunker (March 1, 1935)

R. C. Ashby

He Arrived at Dusk (August 20, 1933)

Out Went the Taper (August 12, 1934) (not included, original source is fragmentary)

Mary M. Atwater

Crime in Corn Weather (June 2, 1935)

Hugh Austin

It Couldn't Be Murder (July 21, 1935)

Murder of a Matriarch (August 9, 1936)

The Upside Down Murders (June 10, 1937)

H. C. Bailey

Mr. Fortune Speaking (November 8, 1931)

Mr. Fortune Wonders (January 21, 1934)

Mr. Fortune Objects (May 5, 1935)

The Sullen Sky Mystery (January 12, 1936)

A Clue for Mr. Fortune (October 11, 1936)
Black Land, White Land (May 23, 1937)

Hugh Baker
Cartwright is Dead, Sir! (July 15, 1934)

Richard M. Baker
Death Stops the Manuscript (September 6, 1936)

Edwin Balmer and Philip Wyle
The Golden Hoard (December 2, 1934)

Peter Baron
The Round Table Murders (March 8, 1931)

Francis Beeding
Death in Four Letters (June 9, 1935)
The Norwich Victims (November 3, 1935)

Dorothy Bennett
How Strange a Thing (March 17, 1935)

Earl Derr Biggers
The Keeper of the Keys (December 4, 1932)

George A. Birmingham
The Hymn Tune Mystery (April 12, 1931)

R. Jere Black
The Killing of the Golden Goose (March 11, 1934)

Nicholas Blake
A Question of Proof (August 25, 1935)

Charles G. Booth
The Cat and the Clock (January 12, 1936)

Dorothea Brande
Most Beautiful Lady (May 26, 1935)

Gelett Burgess
Two O'Clock Courage (February 4, 1934)

Anna Robeson Burr
Wind of the East (May 21, 1933)

Christopher Bush
The Case of the April Fools (July 16, 1933)

James M. Cain
The Postman Always Rings Twice (June 17, 1934)

Alfred Betts Caldwell
Turquoise Hazard (August 16, 1936)

John Dickson Carr / Carter Dickson

The Eight of Swords (February 25, 1934)

The Blind Barber (November 4, 1934)

The Three Coffins (October 13, 1935)

The Unicorn Murders (December 22, 1935)

The Arabian Nights Murder (April 12, 1936)

The Murder of Sir Edmund Godfrey (January 10, 1937)

Whitman Chambers

Thirteen Steps (January 12, 1936)

Leslie Charteris

Saint Overboard (February 9, 1936)

G. K. Chesterton

The Scandal of Father Brown (October 20, 1935)

Agatha Christie

The Secret Adversary (January 18, 1931)

The Murder at the Vicarage (March 15, 1931)

The Tuesday Club Murders (March 26, 1933)

Thirteen at Dinner (November 12, 1933)

Murder in the Calais Coach (March 4, 1934)

Death in the Air (May 19, 1935)

The A. B. C. Murders (March 1, 1936)

Clyde B. Clason

The Fifth Tumbler (March 29, 1936)

The Death Angel (August 9, 1936)

Irvin S. Cobb

Murder Day by Day (February 18, 1934)

Charles Francis Coe

Ransom (August 12, 1934)

G-Man (August 25, 1935)

Octavus Roy Cohen

The Townshend Murder Mystery (September 17, 1933)

G. D. H. and Margaret Cole

Death of a Star (June 25, 1933)

Big Business Murder (April 7, 1935)

The Sleeping Death (April 5, 1936)

George Harmon Coxe

Murder with Pictures (December 22, 1936)

Freeman Wills Crofts

The Crime at Nornes (September 15, 1935)

Richard Curle

Corruption (March 12, 1933)

Means Davis

Murder without Weapon (January 13, 1935)

Tech Davis

Terror at Compass Lake (December 1, 1935)

Reginald Davis

The Crowing Hen (September 6, 1936)

Gregory Dean

The Case of Marie Corwin (September 17, 1933)

Simone d'Erigny

The Mysteries Madames (February 18, 1934)

August Derleth

Murder Stalks the Wakely Family (March 11, 1934)

Roger Francis Didelot

Murder in the Bath (September 24, 1933)

Death of the Deputy (August 18, 1935)

Charles J. Dutton

Murder in the Library (May 17, 1931)

The Circle of Death (March 12, 1933)

Frederick G. Eberhard

The 13th Murder (March 1, 1931)

Mignon G. Eberhart

The White Cockatoo (May 28, 1933)

The Dark Garden (January 21, 1934)

The House on the Roof (May 19, 1935)

Fair Warning (May 10, 1936)

James G. Edwards

Murder in the Surgery (July 21, 1935)

Guy Endore

The Werewolf of Paris (June 4, 1933)

John Estevan

By Night at Dinsmore (July 7, 1935)

Sidney Fairway

The Long Tunnel (April 19, 1935)

Jefferson Farjeon

The Mystery of Dead Man's Heath (March 4, 1934)

Rudolph Fisher

The Conjure Man Dies (November 27, 1932)

Cortland Fitzsimmons

Red Rhapsody (November 12, 1933)

Crimson Ice (January 27, 1935)

J. S. Fletcher

Murder in Four Degrees (November 22, 1931)

Murder of the Lawyer's Clerk (January 1, 1933)

The Eleventh Hour (July 7, 1935)

Hulbert Footner

The Whip-Poor-Will Mystery (March 1, 1935)

R. Francis Foster

Murder from Beyond (April 26, 1931)

R. Austin Freeman

Dr. Thorndyke Intervenes (November 26, 1933)

David Frome

Mr. Pinkerton Goes to Scotland Yard (June 24, 1934)

Arthur Gask

The Lonely House (July 19, 1931)

H. L. Gates

The Laughing Peril (April 23, 1933)

Newton Gayle

Death Follows a Formula (April 7, 1935)

Bruce Graeme

The Imperfect Crime (February 26, 1933)

Epilogue (March 25, 1934)

Ward Greene

Death in the Deep South (January 3, 1937)

Edwin Greenwood

The Deadly Dowager (May 19, 1935)

F. L. Gregory

The Cipher of Death (May 20, 1934)

Jackson Gregory

A Case for Mr. Paul Savoy (June 4, 1933)

The Emerald Murder Trap (July 8, 1934)

Jason Griffith

The Monkey Wrench (November 26, 1933)

Christopher Hale

Smoke Screen (December 1, 1935)

Dashiell Hammett

The Thin Man (February 18, 1934)

Georgette Heyer

Why Shoot a Butler? (February 23, 1936)

Behold, Here's Poison! (November 29, 1936)

James Hilton

Was It Murder? (April 21, 1935)

Elisabeth Sanxay Holding

The Unfinished Crime (February 17, 1935)

Sydney Horler

The Menace (December 15, 1933)

Royce Howes

Death on the Bridge (January 12, 1936)

The Callao Clue (April 26, 1936)

Richard Hull

Murder Isn't Easy (August 9, 1936)

T. C. H. Jacobs

Documents of Murder (February 26, 1933)

Cora Jarrett

Night over Fitch's Pond (January 14, 1934)

Charles Reed Jones

The Torch Murder (December 7, 1930)

Harry Stephen Keeler

The Matilda Hunter Murder (December 6, 1931)

The Box from Japan (January 1, 1933)

The Mystery of the Fiddling Cracksman (April 8, 1934) (see addendum)

X. Jones of Scotland Yard (August 2, 1936)

Jesse Douglas Kerruish

The Undying Monster (September 20, 1936)

C. Daly King

Obelists at Sea (June 25, 1933)

Rufus King

Murder on the Yacht (November 13, 1932)

Valcour Meets Murder (December 4, 1932)

Profile of a Murder (April 21, 1935)

The Case of the Constant God (September 27, 1936)

C. H. B. Kitchin

Crime at Christmas (February 10, 1935)

Norman Klein

No! No! The Woman! (December 4, 1932)

Kathleen Moore Knight

Death Blew Out the Match (February 17, 1935)

The Clue of the Poor Man's Shilling (April 26, 1936)

K. T. Knoblock

Take up the Bodies (July 16, 1933)

Timothy Knox

Death in the State House (July 15, 1934)

Charles Koonce

The Weeping Willow Murders (February 25, 1934)

Jonathan Latimer

Headed for a Hearse (September 8, 1935)

The Lady in the Morgue (September 20, 1936)

Armstrong Livingston

The Murder Trap (February 8, 1931)

Jeremy Lord

The Bannerman Case (May 26, 1935)

Marie Belloc Lowndes

The Chianti Flask (December 9, 1934)

Philip Macdonald

Death on My Left (July 9, 1933)

Kenneth Macgowan

Sleuths (September 20, 1931)

Marcus Magill

Murder in Full Flight (January 22, 1933)

Virgil Markham

Red Warning (March 26, 1933)

Inspector Rusby's Finale (August 20, 1933)

Gabriel Marlowe

I am Your Brother (March 1, 1935)

Van Wyck Mason

The Washington Legation Murders (February 9, 1936)

Walter S. Masterman

The Nameless Crime (January 8, 1933)

The Perjured Alibi (October 20, 1935)

Death Turns Traitor (March 22, 1936)

Victor McClure

The Clue of the Dying Goldfish (October 21, 1934)

Paul McGuire

Murder at High Noon (December 1, 1935)

H. C. McNeile ("Sapper")

Bulldog Drummond at Bay (March 1, 1935)

Kirke Mechem

A Frame for Murder (August 16, 1936)

A. Merritt

Burn, Witch, Burn! (February 26, 1933)

M. N. A. Messer

Mousetrap (September 20, 1931)

Lebbeus Mitchell

The Parachute Murder (October 8, 1933)

Talbot Mundy

Jimgrim (June 28, 1931)

Dorothy Ogburn

The Will and the Deed (June 9, 1935)

E. Phillips Oppenheim

The Lion and the Lamb (April 12, 1931)

The Ex-Detective (December 15, 1933)

Frank L. Packard

Jimmie Dale and the Missing Minutes (June 9, 1935)

Stuart Palmer

The Puzzle of the Red Stallion (March 22, 1936)

Viola Paradise

A Girl Died Laughing (November 4, 1934)

Q. Patrick

Cottage Sinister (July 2, 1933)

Winifred Peck

The Warrielaw Jewel (September 24, 1933)

Eden Phillpotts

Found Drowned (July 5, 1931)

Bred in the Bone (January 15, 1933)

The Captain's Curio (September 17, 1933)

A Shadow Passes (February 4, 1934)

Mr. Digwood and Mr. Lumb (March 11, 1934)

The Grey Room (January 12, 1936)

A Close Call (August 23, 1936)

Mary Plum

Murder at the World's Fair (May 28, 1933)

Wesley Price

Death is a Stowaway (July 9, 1933)

J. B. Priestley and Gerald Bullett

I'll Tell You Everything (January 22, 1933)

Milton M. Propper

The Student Fraternity Murder (November 27, 1932)

The Divorce Court Murder (May 20, 1934)

The Family Burial Murders (December 2, 1934)

One Murdered, Two Dead (January 10, 1937)

Ellery Queen / Barnaby Ross

The Dutch Shoe Mystery (June 26, 1932)

The Greek Coffin Mystery (August 14, 1932)

The Egyptian Cross Mystery (November 6, 1932)

The Tragedy of X (December 18, 1932)

The American Gun Mystery (May 7, 1933)

Drury Lane's Last Case (November 12, 1933)

The Siamese Twin Mystery (December 15, 1933)

The Spanish Cape Mystery (May 19, 1935)

Virginia Rath

Murder on the Day of Judgment (May 10, 1936)

Arthur B. Reeve

The Clutching Hand (May 20, 1934)

The Stars Scream Murder (April 26, 1936)

Helen Reilly

Mr. Smith's Hat (April 26, 1936)

Mrs. Baillie Reynolds

Tragedy at Glaye (October 4, 1936)

John Rhode / Miles Burton

Dr. Priestley Investigates (January 4, 1931)

The Fire at Greycombe Farm (November 13, 1932)

Dead Men at the Folly (February 5, 1933)

Dr. Priestley Lays a Trap (March 26, 1933)

Dark is the Tunnel (February 21, 1937)

Mary Roberts Rinehart

The Mary Roberts Rinehart Crime Book (February 12, 1933)

The Album (June 18, 1933)

Raymond Robins

Murder at Bayside (November 12, 1933)

Sax Rohmer

The Bat Flies Low (December 8, 1935)

Charlotte Murray Russell

Death of an Eloquent Man (February 23, 1936)

Ruth Burr Sanborn

Murder on the Aphrodite (October 13, 1935)

Dorothy L. Sayers

Hangman's Holiday (October 8, 1933)

The Nine Tailors (March 25, 1934)

The Dorothy L. Sayers Omnibus (September 30, 1934)

Gaudy Night (February 9, 1936)

Marion Scott

Dead Hands Reaching (December 25, 1932)

R. T. M. Scott

Murders Stalks the Mayor (February 9, 1936)

Willoughby Sharp

Murder in Bermuda (September 24, 1933)

Murder of the Honest Broker (August 26, 1934)

Madeleine Sharps

The Black Pearl Murders (July 5, 1931)

Frank Shay

The Charming Murder (October 12, 1930)

George Simenon

The Crossroad Murders (February 19, 1933)

The Strange Case of Peter the Lett (July 2, 1933)

Andrew Soutar

Secret Ways (September 23, 1934)

Christopher St. John Sprigg

Death of an Airman (June 16, 1935)

Kathleen Sproul

The Birthday Murder (December 18, 1932)

O'Connor Stacey

Murder at Cypress Hall (February 19, 1933)

Vincent Starrett

The Great Hotel Murder (June 16, 1935)

André Steeman

The Night of the 12th-13th (April 23, 1933)

John Stephen Strange

For the Hangman (December 16, 1934)

The Bell in the Fog (December 27, 1936)

William Sutherland

Death Rides the Air Line (December 23, 1934)

W. Stanley Sykes

The Harness of Death (November 20, 1932)

Darwin Teilhet

The Ticking Terrors Murders (April 12, 1936)

Darwin and Hildegarde Teilhet

The Feather Clock Murders (May 3, 1936)

The Crimson Hair Murders (February 14, 1937)

Lee Thayer

Sudden Death (September 8, 1935)

Dead End Street (March 29, 1936)

Eugene Thomas

Death Rides the Dragon (January 8, 1933)

Basil Thomson

The Case of the Dead Diplomat (December 8, 1935)

The Dartmoor Enigma (March 1, 1936)

Who Killed Stella Pomeroy? (September 6, 1936)

John Touissant-Samat

Shoes That Had Walked Twice (July 2, 1933)

The Dead Man at the Window (September 16, 1934)

John V. Turner / Nicholas Brady / David Hume

Who Spoke Last? (June 18, 1933)

The Carnival Murder (January 21, 1934)

Dangerous Mr. Dell (October 20, 1935)

S. S. Van Dine

The Kennel Murder Case (January 15, 1933)

The Dragon Murder Case (October 29, 1933)

The Garden Murder Case (November 17, 1935)

John W. Vandercook

Murder in Fiji (August 2, 1936)

C. C. Waddell

Juror No. 17 (May 10, 1931)

Henry Wade

No Friendly Drop (November 20, 1932)

The Hanging Captain (March 26, 1933)

Edgar Wallace

The Case of the Frightened Lady (May 28, 1933)

J. H. Wallis

Servant of Death (October 22, 1932)

J. M. Walsh

The Black Ghost (March 22, 1931)

Carolyn Wells

The Umbrella Murder (November 29, 1931)

The Clue of the Eyelash (March 12, 1933)

The Master Murderer (November 26, 1933)

In the Tiger's Cage (February 25, 1934)

Eyes in the Wall (July 1, 1934)

The Visiting Villain (November 4, 1934)

Patricia Wentworth

Danger Calling (August 16, 1931)

Red Shadow (November 6, 1932)

Outrageous Fortune (June 11, 1933)

Fear by Night (March 4, 1934)

Hole and Corner (November 8, 1936)

Garnett Weston

Murder on Shadow Island (May 7, 1933)

Ethel Lina White

The Wheel Spins (September 27, 1936)

David Whitelaw

Murder Calling (December 9, 1934)

Valentine Williams

The Clock Ticks On (November 12, 1933)

The Portcullis Room (April 15, 1934)

Valentine Williams and Dorothy Rice Sims

Fog (May 28, 1933)

J. R. Wilmot

Death in the Theater (October 21, 1934)

William Almon Wolff

Murder at Endor (June 11, 1933)

Katherine Wolffe

Tall Man Walking (January 17, 1937)

Samuel Andrew Wood

Red Square (April 15, 1934)

Jack Woodford

Find the Motive (November 6, 1932)

Mrs. Wilson Woodrow

The Moonhill Mystery (December 14, 1930)

R. C. Woodthorpe

Death in a Little Town (June 23, 1935)

The Shadow on the Downs (February 9, 1936)

Richard Wormser

The Man with the Wax Face (September 16, 1934)

Lassiter Wren and Randall McKay

The Mystery Puzzle Book (April 23, 1936)

S. Fowler Wright

The Bell Street Murders (July 5, 1931)

Anthony Wynne

The Silver Scale Mystery (October 4, 1931)

The White Arrow (December 18, 1932)

The Cotswold Case (February 5, 1933)

The Case of the Gold Coins (January 21, 1934)

Death of a Banker (August 26, 1934)

Dornford Yates

Adele and Co. (August 23, 1931)

ADDENDUM: ONE ADDITIONAL REVIEW

"CLUES AND CORPSES" (REVIEWED BY TODD DOWNING)

8 April 1934, p. 52

THE MYSTERY OF THE FIDDLING CRACKSMAN, BY HARRY STEPHEN KEELER

A NEW Keeler yarn is always greeted with enthusiasm by a large number of fans who know that the author can be depended on for a veritable fusion of fact and fancy that keeps the bed lamp burning until the wee small hours. In his latest he projects the reader into the Chicago of the future (a favorite trick of his) and lands him in the midst of as intricate a webwork of mysteries as the fertile Keeler brain ever concocted.

A hooded cracksman who uses, not dynamite, but a violin and seems to have a predilection for the name John Craig; a second-hand safe bearing the name Hong Hok [?] and containing who knows what Oriental secrets; the dope on the next world (the volcanic island of Ui [?] isn't on our maps yet, but it will be some-day, pushed up out of the Pacific and ready to be occupied [?] by the Japs); a demented Oriental; a girl with a psychic trauma that can't be cured until she sells a vaudeville playlet; and young Billy Hemple, author of the bestseller *Mr. Monte Zenda of Graustark*.—Todd Downing.

BIBLIOGRAPHY

Books

Austen, Roger. *Playing the Game: The Homosexual Novel in America.* Indianapolis, IN, and New York: Bobbs Merrill, 1977.

Barzun, Jacques, and Wendell Hertig Taylor, *A Catalogue of Crime.* 1971. Revised Edition. New York: Harper & Row, 1989.

Bauer, Paul J., and Mark Dawidziak. *Jim Tully: American Writer, Irish Rover, Hollywood Brawler.* Kent, OH: Kent State University Press, 2011.

O'Beirne, H. F. *Leaders and Leading Men of the Indian Territory, with Interesting Biographical Sketches.* Volume I. *Choctaws and Chickasaws: With a Brief History of Each Tribe: Its Laws, Customs, Superstitions and Religious Beliefs.* Chicago, IL: American Publishers' Association, 1891.

Bergman, David. *The Violet Hour: The Violet Quill and the Making of Gay Culture.* New York: Columbia University Press, 2004.

Berrong, Richard M. *In Love with a Handsome Sailor: The Emergence of Gay Identity and the Novels of Pierre Loti.* Toronto: University of Toronto Press, 2003.

Black, Gregory D. *Hollywood Censored: Morality Codes, Catholics, and the Movies.* Cambridge University Press, 1996.

Bronski, Michael, ed. *Pulp Friction: Uncovering the Golden Age of Gay Male Pulps.* New York: St. Martin's Griffin, 2003.

Bryant, Jr., Keith L. *Alfalfa Bill Murray.* Norman, OK: University of Oklahoma Press, 1968.

Cox, James H. *The Red Land to the South: American Indian Writers and Indigenous Mexico.* Minneapolis, MN, and London: University of Minnesota Press, 2012.

Cypert, Rick. *America's Agatha Christie: Mignon Good Eberhart, Her Life and Works*. Selinsgrove, PA: Susquehanna University Press, 2005.

Dirda, Michael. *On Conan Doyle: Or The Whole Art of Storytelling*. Princeton and Oxford: Princeton University Press, 2011.

Evans, Curtis. *Masters of the Humdrum Mystery: Cecil John Charles Street, Freeman Wills Crofts, Alfred Walter Stewart and the British Detective Novel, 1920-1961*. Jefferson, NC, and London: McFarland, 2012.

Gibson, Arrell Moran. *Oklahoma: A History of Five Centuries*. Norman, OK: University of Oklahoma Press, 1981.

Glarens, Carlos. *Crime Movies*. Boston, MA: Da Capo, 1997.

Greene, Douglas G. *John Dickson Carr: the Man Who Explained Miracles*. New York: Otto Penzler Books, 1995.

Gregory, James N. *American Exodus: The Dust Bowl Migration and Okie Culture in California*. Oxford and New York: Oxford University Press, 1989.

Hamm, Thomas D. *Earlham College: A History*, 1847-1997. Bloomington and Indianapolis: Indiana University Press, 1997.

Hayes, Basil A. *Leroy Long: Teacher of Medicine*. Oklahoma City: by the author, 1943.

Hickenlooper, Frank. *An Illustrated History of Monroe County, Iowa*. Albia, IA: by the author, 1896.

Hillerman, Tony. *Seldom Disappointed: A Memoir*. New York: HarperCollins, 2001.

Hodge, Joan Aiken. *The Private World of Georgette Heyer*. 1984. Reprint. Naperville, IL: Sourcebooks, 2011.

The History of Monroe County, Iowa. Chicago: Western Historical Co., 1878.

Huang, Yunte. *Charlie Chan: The Untold Story of the Honorable Detective and His Rendezvous with American History*. New York and London: W. W. Norton, 2010.

Kabatchnik, Amnon. *Blood on the Stage: Milestone Plays of Crime, Mystery and Detection* Lanham, MD, and Toronto: Scarecrow Press, 2008.

Kaler, Samuel P., and R. H. Maring. *History of Whitley County, Indiana*. Indianapolis, IN: B. F. Bowe & Co., 1907.

Katz, Wendy Roberta. *Rider Haggard and the Fiction of Empire: A Critical Study of British Imperial Fiction*. Cambridge and New York: Cambridge University Press, 1987.

Kennedy, Hubert. *A Touch of Royalty: Gay Author James Barr*. San Francisco: Peremptory Publications, 2002.

Kidwell, Clara Sue. *The Choctaws in Oklahoma: From Tribe to Nation, 1855-1970*. Norman, OK: University of Oklahoma Press, 2007.

Kloester, Jennifer. Georgette Heyer: Biography of a Bestseller. London: Heinemann, 2011.

Lane, Margaret. *Edgar Wallace: The Biography of a Phenomenon*. New York: Doubleday, Doran, 1939.

Leinwand, Gerald. *1927: High Tide of the Twenties*. New York: Basic Books, 2001.

Liebovich, Louis W. *Bylines in Despair: Herbert Hoover, the Great Depression and the U. S. News Media*. Westport, CT: Prager, 1994.

Lobdell, Jared. *The Detective Fiction Reviews of Charles Williams, 1930-1935*. Jefferson, NC, and London: McFarland, 2003.

Locke, John, ed., *From Ghouls to Gangsters: The Career of Arthur B. Reeve*. Volumes I and II. Castroville, CA: Off-Trail Publications, 2007.

Loughery, John. *Alias S. S. Van Dine: The Man Who Created Philo Vance*. New York: Scribner, 1992.

Luthin, Richard A. *American Demagogues: Twentieth Century*. Boston: Beacon Press, 1954.

MacElyea, Mrs. Annabelle Bunting. *The McQueens of Queensdale: A Biography of Col. James McQueen and His Descendants*. Charlotte, NC: Observer Printing House, 1916.

Marks, Jeffrey. *Who Was That Lady? Craig Rice: The Queen of Screwball Mystery*. Lee's Summit, MO: Delphi Books, 2001.

McGilligan, Patrick. *Alfred Hitchcock: A Life in Darkness and Light*. New York: Regan Books, 2003.

Mihesuah, Devon Abbott. *Choctaw Crime and Punishment, 1884-1907*. Norman, OK: University of Oklahoma Press, 2009.

Nehr, Ellen. *Doubleday Crime Club Compendium, 1928-1991*. Duluth, GA: Offspring Press, 1992.

Nevins, Francis M. *The Anthony Boucher Chronicles: Reviews and Commentary, 1942-1947*. Vancleave, MS: Ramble House, 2002.

Nevins, Francis M. *Royal Bloodline: Ellery Queen, Author and Detective*. Bowling Green, OH: Popular Press, 1974.

Newton, Michael. *The FBI Encyclopedia*. Jefferson, NC, and London: McFarland, 2012.

Nickerson, Catherine Ross. *The Web of Iniquity: Early Detective Fiction by American Women* Chapel Hill, NC: Duke University Press, 1999.

Oney, Steve. *And the Dead Shall Rise: The Murder of Mary Phagan and the Lynching of Leo Frank*. New York: Pantheon, 2003.

Pomerantz, Gary M. *The Devil's Ticket: A Vengeful Wife, A Fatal Hand and a New American Age*. New York: Crown, 2009.

Pronzini, Bill. *Gun in Cheek: A Study of Alternative Crime Fiction*. 1982. Reprint. New York: Mysterious Press, 1987.

Pronzini, Bill. *Son of Gun in Cheek*. New York and London: Mysterious Press, 1987.

Pronzini, Bill, and Marcia Muller, eds. *1001 Midnights: The Aficionado's Guide to Mystery and Detective Fiction*. New York: Arbor House, 1986.

Reed, John Shelton. *Dixie Bohemia: A French Quarter Circle in the 1920s*. Baton Rouge, LA: LSU Press, 2012.

Rideout, Walter S. "The most civilized spot in America: Sherwood Anderson in New Orleans," in Richard S. Kennedy, ed., *Literary New Orleans in the Modern World*. Baton Rouge, LA: LSU Press, 1998.

Ruiz, James. *The Black Hood of the Ku Klux Klan*. San Francisco, CA: Austin & Winfield, 1997.

Rodell, Marie F. *Mystery Fiction: Theory and Technique*. New York: Duell, Sloan and Pearce, 1943.

Smith, Erin A. *Hard-Boiled: Working-Class Readers and Pulp Magazines*. Philadelphia: Temple University Press, 2000.

Standish, Robert. *The Prince of the Storytellers: The Life of E. Phillips Oppenheim*. London: Peter Davies, 1957.

Symons, Julian. *Bloody Murder: From the Detective Story to the Crime Novel*. 1993. Revised Edition. New York and Tokyo: Mysterious Press, 1992.

Thoburn, Joseph B. *A Standard History of Oklahoma*. Volume 6. Chicago and New York: The American Historical Society, 1916.

Thoburn, Joseph B. and Muriel Wright. *Oklahoma: A History of the State and Its People*. Volume III. New York: Lewis Historical Publishing Company, 1929.

Tuttle, Charles R. and Daniel Durrie. *An Illustrated History of the State of Iowa*. Chicago, IL: Richard S. Peale, 1876.

Usborne, Richard. *Clubland Heroes: A Nostalgic Study of the Recurrent Characters in the Romantic Fiction of Dornford Yates, John Buchan and "Sapper."* 1954. Revised Edition. London: Hutchinson, 1983.

Van Ash, Cay and Elizabeth. *Sax Rohmer, Master of Villainy: A Biography of Sax Rohmer*. Bowling Green, OH: Popular Press, 1972.

Watkins, Julian Lewis. *The 100 Greatest Advertisements: Who Wrote Them and What They Did*. 1949. Revised Edition. New York: Dover, 1959.

Articles and Essays

Abbott, Megan. "Soft-Voiced Big Men" (review of Robert Crais, *The Sentry: A Joe Pike Novel*). *Los Angeles Review of Books* (28 April 2011). At http://blog.lareviewofbooks.org/post/5011247663/soft-voiced-big-men

Altobello, Stephen. "The Thin Man and the Little Erection, or How to Imagine Myrna Loy Talkin' Dirty." *Peel Slowly* (14 October 2010). At http://peelslowlynsee.wordpress.com/2010/10/14/the-thin-man-and-the-little-erection/

Berrong, Richard M. "Pierre Loti (Julien Viaud)." *glbtq : An Encyclopedia of Gay, Lesbian, Bisexual, Transgender, and Queer Culture*. At http://www.glbtq.com/literature/loti_p.html

Breen, Jon L. "Cherchez les Femmes: The American Tradition of Mystery Novels by Women." *American Spectator* 9 (July 2004). At http://www.weeklystandard.com/Content/Public/Articles/000/000/004/272hwrue.asp

Breen, Jon L. "The Ellery Queen Mystery: Why is the Corpus No Longer Alive?" *American Spectator* 10 (October 2005). At http://www.weeklystandard.com/Content/Public/Articles/000/000/006/140ioyto.asp. Reprinted in the author's *A Shot Rang Out: Selected Mystery Criticism by Jon L. Breen* (Vancleave, MS: Ramble House, 2008)

Breen, John L. A Note on Octavus Roy Cohen. *Mystery*File*. At http://www.mysteryfile.com/cohen/Breen.html.

Chen, Anna. "BBC jumps the Orientalist shark: Fu Manchu in Edinburgh." *Madame Miaow Says* (8 August 2010). At http://madammiaow.blogspot.com/2010/08/bbc-jumps-racist-shark-fu-manchu-in.html.

"Directory Earlham College," *The Earlham College Bulletin* 13 (August 1916): 50.

Deeck, William F. Review of *Murder without Weapon* (1934), by Means Davis. In "The Backward Reviewer." *The MYSTERY FANcier* 10 (Sping 1988). Reprinted at *Mystery*File* at http://mysteryfile.com/blog/?p=2119.

Deeck, William F. Review of *Terror at Compass Lake* (1935), by Tech Davis. In "The Backward Reviewer." *The MYSTERY FANcier* 12 (Fall 1990). Reprinted at Mystery*File at http://mysteryfile.com/blog/?p=14291.

Downing, Ruth. "The Downing Family." In *Tales of Atoka County Heritage*. Atoka, OK: Atoka County Historical Society, 1983.

Downing, Todd. "A Choctaw's Autobiography" [1926]. In J. M. Carroll and Lee F. Hawkins, eds., *The American Indian, 1926-1931*. New York: Liveright, 1970.

Duncan, Dennis. "The Mystery of *The Mystery of the Ashes*." In *Bulletin of the Harry Stephen Keeler Society* 59 (October 2006): 7-10.

Evans, Curtis. "The Amateur Detective Just Won't Do" (in three parts). *The Passing Tramp* (15, 18, 19 December 2011). At http://thepassingtramp.blogspot.com/2011/12/amateur-detective-just-wont-do-ramond.html.

Evans, Curtis. "Murder in the Family: *The Warrielaw Jewel* (1933), by Winifred Peck." *The Passing Tramp* (15 January 2012). At http://thepassingtramp.blogspot.com/2012/01/murder-in-family-warrielaw-jewel-1933.html.

Evans, Curtis. Review of *Death of a Banker* (Anthony Wynne). *The Passing Tramp* (20 July 2012). At http://thepassingtramp.blogspot.com/2012/07/death-of-banker-1934-by-anthony-wynne.html.

Evans, Curtis. "H. C. Bailey—Two Mr. Fortune Collections." Review of *Mr. Fortune Objects* (1935) and *Clue for Mr. Fortune*, 1936. *Mystery*File* (10 November 2010). At http://mysteryfile.com/blog/?p=5762.

Evans, Curtis. Review of *The Scrimshaw Millions* (Lee Thayer). Mystery*File (9 February 2011). At http://mysteryfile.com/blog/?p=7839.

Hanley, Terence E. "R. Jere Black, Jr. (1892-1953)." In *Tellers of Weird Tales: Artists & Writers in The Unique Magazine* (19 August 2011). At http://tellersofweirdtales.blogspot.com/2011/08/r-jere-black-jr-1892-1953.html.

Hill, Brian. "Salonika in November." In Kyle Galloway, ed., *More Songs of the Fighting Men: Soldier Poets* (Second Series). London: Erskine Macdonald, 1917.

Hochbruck, Wolfgang H. "Mystery Novels to Choctaw Pageant: Todd Downing and Native American Literature(s). In Arnold Krupat., ed. *New Voices in Native American Literary Criticism* (Washington, D. C.: Smithsonian Institution Press, 1993): 205-221.

"James Harold Wallis." In Encyclopedia Dubuque. At http://www.encyclopediadubuque.org/index.php?title=WALLIS%2C_James_Harold.

"James William McQueen," *Alabama Authors*. At http://www.lib.ua.edu/Alabama_Authors/?p=1746.

"Kansas Historical Markers." *Kansas Historical Quarterly* 10 (November 1941): 339-368. Reprinted at the t Kansas Historical Society website at http://www.kshs.org/p/kansas-historical-quarterly-kansas-historical-markers/12884.

Keach, Mrs. O. A. "John Downing of Fairfields, Northumberland County, Virginia, and His Descendants." *William and Mary Quarterly* 25 (July 1916): 41-51, 96-106.

Lachman, Gary. "The Yellow Peril of Fu Manchu." *Gary Lachman* (6 July 2012). At http://garylachman.co.uk/2012/07/06/the-yellow-peril-of-dr-fu-manchu.

Lechard, Xavier. "Lost in Translation: Stanslas-André Steeman." *At the Villa Rose (date?)*. At http://atthevillarose.blogspot.com/2010/10/lost-in-translation- stanislas-andre.html.

Lerner, Jesse. "Edward H. Thompson at Chichen Itza's Sacred Cenote." *The American Egypt* (17 March 2008). At http://theamericanegypt.blogspot.com/2008/03/edward-h-thompson-at-chichen-itzas.html

Lewis, Steve. "Once Again with J. V. Turner a/k/a David Hume." *Mystery*File* (7 March 2007). At http://mysteryfile.com/blog/?p=107.

Massam, Katharine. "Dominic Mary Paul Mcguire (1903-1978)." In Australian Dictionary of National Biography. At http://adb.anu.edu.au/biography/mcguire-dominic-mary-paul-10965.

Maynard, William Patrick. "Blogging *The Insidious Dr. Fu-Manchu* by Sax Rohmer, Part Five—'The Green Mist." *Seti Says* (25 April 2010). *At* http://setisays.blogspot.com/2010/04/blogging-insidious-dr-fu-manchu-by-sax_25.html.

McCarthy, Daniel. "Show Me a Statesman." Review of Lee Meriwether, *Jim Reed, Senatorial Immortal: A Biography*. *The University Bookman* (20 November 2008). At http://www.kirkcenter.org/index.php/bookman

Nash, Ogden. "You Cad, Why Don't You Cringe?" In Ogden Nash, *The Face Is Familiar: The Selected Verse of Ogden Nash*. Garden City, New York: Garden City Publishing, 1947.

Nevins, Francis M. "The World of Milton Propper." *The Armchair Detective* 10 (July 1977): 196-203.

Noriss, John. Review of *He Arrived at Dusk* (R. C. Ashby). At *Mystery*File* (27 November 2010). At http://mysteryfile.com/blog/?p=6225.

Norris, John. Review of *The Man on All Fours* (August Derleth). *Pretty Sinister Books* (13 February 2011). At http://prettysinister.blogspot.com/2011/02/man-on-all-fours-1929-august-derleth.html.

Ohl, Patrick. "Mr. Smith = ?" *At the Scene of the Crime* (27 April 2012). At http://at-scene-of-crime.blogspot.ca/2012/04/mr-smith.html.

"The P. J. Wolfson Story." *wdors* (19 June 2010). At http://www.wdors.com/the-p-j-wolfson-story-bodies-are-dust/.

Parman, Frank. "George Todd Downing (1902-1974)." *Encyclopedia of Oklahoma History and Culture* (Oklahoma Historical Society). At http://digital.library.okstate.edu/encyclopedia/entries/D/DO013.html.

Pronzini, Bill. Review of *The Hangover Murders*, by Adam Hobhouse. *Mystery*File* (4 October 2009). At http://mysteryfile.com/blog/?p=1523.

Pronzini, Bill. "William Godwin, Inc." In William F. Deeck, *Murder at 3 Cents a Day: An Annotated Crime Fiction Bibliography of the Lending Library Publishers: 1936-1967*. At http://www.lendinglibmystery.com/Godwin/Covers.html.

Rummel, Rev. Merle C. *The Virginia Settlement or the Four Mile Church of the Brethren*. At http://www.union-county.lib.in.us/GenwebVA4mile/Table%20of%20Contents%204M.htm

Saylor, Steven. "Stuart Palmer & Hildegarde Withers: An Appreciation." In *Firsts: The Book Collectors Magazine* 6 (November 1996). Reprinted at http://www.stevensaylor.com/Stuart%20Palmer/StuartPalmerHildegardeWithers.html.

Schantz, Tom and Enid Schantz. "Charlotte Murray Russell." *Rue Morgue Press: Mysteries from the Golden Age of Detective Fiction*. At http://www.ruemorguepress.com/authors/russell.html.

Schantz, Tom and Enid Schantz. "Clyde B. Clason." *Rue Morgue Press: Mysteries from the Golden Age of Detective Fiction*. At http://www.ruemorguepress.com/authors/clason.html.

Smith, Charlene W. "Todd Downing." In *Tales of Atoka County Heritage*. Atoka, OK: Atoka County Historical Society, 1983.

Summers, Claude J. Summers. "Edward Sagarin (Donald Webster Cory)." In *glbtq: An Encyclopedia of Gay, Lesbian, Bisexual, Transgender, and Queer Culture*. At http://www.glbtq.com/social-sciences/sagarin_e.html

Tindall, Lora B. "The Families of George T. Downing." *Fannin County—Family Pages*. At http://www.txfannin.org/familypages.php?fam_ID=11

Vidal, Gore. "The Top Ten Best-Sellers According to the New York Times as of January 7, 1973." In Jay Parini, ed., *The Selected Essays of Gore Vidal*. New York and London: Doubleday, 2008.

Vineyard, David. "Jimmie Dale, the Gray Seal, by Frank L. Packard." *Mystery*File* (14 December 2009). At http://mydtseryfile.com/blog/?p=1715.

Vineyard, David L. "John W. Vandercook and the Bertram Lynch Mysteries." *Mystery*File* (3 April 2009). At http://mysteryfile.com/blog/?p=1078.

Waits, Wally. "Andrew W. Robb and Family." *Muskogee History and Genealogy* (13 February 2008). At http://www.muskogeehistorian.com/2008/02/andrew-w-robb-and-family.html

Wald, Alan. "American Writers on the Left." In *glbtq: An Encyclopedia of Gay, Lesbian, Bisexual, Transgender and Queer Culture*. At http://www.glbtq.com/literature/am_mawriters_left.html.

Correspondence and Interviews

Downing Family Correspondence, Confederate Memorial Museum and Cemetery, Atoka, Oklahoma.

Thomas Hamm to Curtis Evans. 28 September 2012.

Lisa Hatchell to Curtis Evans. 23 July 2012.

E. H. Rishel interview (22 June 1937). Indian Pioneer Papers, Indian Pioneer History Project for Oklahoma. At http://www.okgenweb.org/pioneer/ohs/risheleh.htm

James Mechem interview (29 October 2003). *Beats in Kansas: The Beat Generation in the Heartland*. At http://www.vlib.us/beats/mechemlow.html.

Essays, Novels, Novellas, Short Stories by Todd Downing and Contemporaries

Willa Cather. "The Sculptor's Funeral." 1905. Reprinted in Robert K. Miller, ed., *Great Short Works of Willa Cather*. New York: HarperCollins, 1993.

Christie, Agatha. *And Then There Were None*. New York: Dodd, Mead, 1940.

Christie, Agatha. *Murder on the Orient Express*. London: Collins, 1934.

Downing, Todd. *The Case of the Unconquered Sisters*. New York: Doubleday, Doran, 1936.

Downing, Todd. *The Cat Screams*. New York: Doubleday, Doran, 1934.

Downing, Todd. *Death under the Moonflower*. New York: Doubleday, Doran, 1938.

Downing, Todd. *The Last Trumpet*. New York: Doubleday, Doran, 1937.

Downing, Todd. *The Lazy Lawrence Murders*. New York: Doubleday, Doran, 1941.

Downing, Todd. *The Mexican Earth*. New York: Double, Doran, 1940.

Downing, Todd. "Murder Is a Rather Serious Business." In *The Writer* 56 (1943). Reprinted in A. S. Burack, ed., *Writing Detective Fiction* (Boston: *The Writer*, 1945).

Downing, Todd. *Murder on Tour*. New York: Putnam's: 1933.

Downing, Todd. *Murder on the Tropic*. New York: Doubleday, Doran, 1935.

Downing, Todd. *Night over Mexico*. New York: Doubleday, Doran, 1937.

Downing, Todd. "The Shadowless Hour." *Mystery Book Magazine* 2 (November 1945).

Downing, Todd. *Vultures in the Sky*. New York: Doubleday, Doran, 1935.

Hammett, Dashiell. *The Thin Man*. New York: Alfred A. Knopf: 1934.

Lewis, Sinclair. *Main Street*. New York: Harcourt, Brace & Howe.

Sayers, Dorothy L. *Gaudy Night*. London: Gollancz, 1935.

Smith, Susan. *The Glories of Venus*. New York and London: Harpers, 1931.

Government Documents

National Park Service, The Civil War, Regiment Details, Union Iowa Volunteers, 46th Regiment, Iowa Infantry. At http://www.nps.gov/civilwar/search-regiments-detail.htm?regiment_id=UIA0046RI.

Record in the matter of the application for enrollment as a citizen by intermarriage of the Choctaw Nation of Maud Downing. Department of the Interior, Commission of the Five Civilized Tribes.

Survey of the Conditions of the Indians of the United States: Hearing before a Subcommittee of the Committee on Indian Affairs. U. S. Senate, 71st Congress, Second Session (1929), 5317-5321.

1930 United States Census, Oklahoma, Atoka County.

Newspapers and Periodicals

Advertising & Selling 1944

Berkeley Daily Gazette 1929

Books Abroad 1952

Caddo Herald 1924

Chronicles of Oklahoma 1927, 1932

(Stillwater) *Daily O'Collegian* 1937

(Oklahoma City) *Daily Oklahoman* 1907, 1913, 1930-1937, 1939, 1942, 1960

Kirkus Reviews 1934

New York Herald Book Review 1957

New York Times 1912

New York Times Book Review 1932, 1934, 1935, 1937

(London) *Observer* 1936

Publisher's Weekly 1942

Saturday Review 1925, 1933-1937, 1940

The Sunday School World 1882

(London) *Sunday Times* 1933

INDEX

ABOUT THE AUTHOR

CURTIS EVANS, PH.D. is the author of *The Conquest of Labor: Daniel Pratt and Southern Industrialization* (LSU Press, 2001), winner of the Bennett H. Wall Award from the Southern Historical Association, and *Masters of the "Humdrum" Mystery: Cecil John Charles Street, Freeman Wills Crofts, Alfred Walter Stewart and the British Detective Novel, 1920-1961* (McFarland Press, 2012). He has written extensively about crime and mystery fiction for *CADS: Crime and Detective Stories* and *Mystery*File* and also at his own blog, *The Passing Tramp* (thepassingtramp.blogspot.com).

Also Available

CoachwhipBooks.com

Vultures in the Sky

ISBN 1-61646-149-7

ALSO AVAILABLE

COACHWHIPBOOKS.COM

Murder on the Tropic

ISBN 1-61646-150-0

Also Available

CoachwhipBooks.com

Also Available

CoachwhipBooks.com

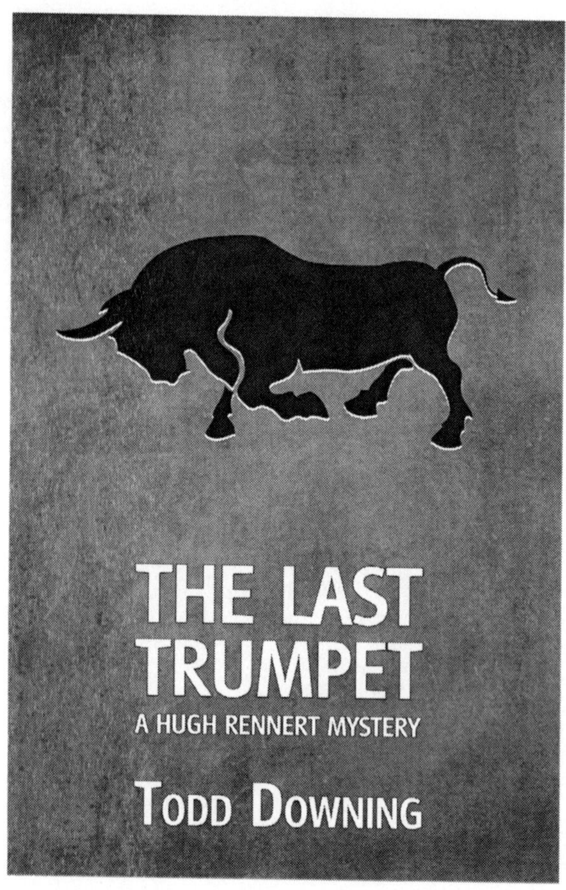

The Last Trumpet

ISBN 1-61646-152-7

Also Available

CoachwhipBooks.com

Night Over Mexico

ISBN 1-61646-153-5

DEATH
UNDER THE
MOONFLOWER
A PETER BOUNTY MYSTERY
TODD DOWNING

Also Available

CoachwhipBooks.com

The Lazy Lawrence Murders

ISBN 1-61646-158-6

CPSIA information can be obtained at www.ICGtesting.com
Printed in the USA
BVOW071238220513

321371BV00002B/165/P